Art and Culture of Italy

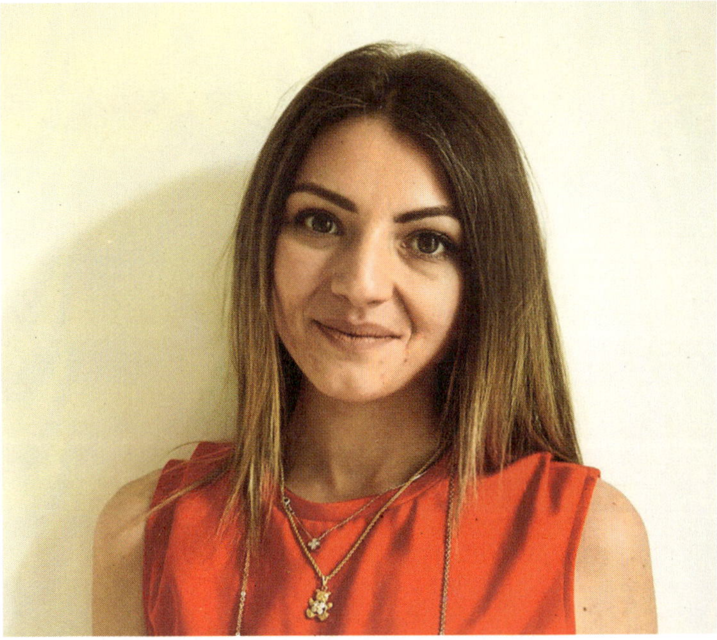

Paola Martani holds the academic title of 'dottore in philosophy' from Università degli Studi di Milano, as well as an Mphil in Linguistics. Since 2014, she has been the course coordinator and lecturer at the Italian Embassy Cultural Centre at New Delhi. She is a lecturer in many universities, and additionally teaches at Jamia Millia Islamia since 2018. She has three books to her credit; *A Student Handbook of Italian – Learning Italian through Design A1*, *A Student Handbook of Italian – Learning Italian through Design A2*, and *Travelling between Fables*, which has also been translated into Italian. In April 2018, she was awarded for her work by the Women Economic Forum. She also writes a bi-monthly column, Culture and Influence, in *AsiaOne*.

ART *and* CULTURE *of* ITALY

From the Roman Empire to Present Day

Paola Martani

HarperCollins*Publishers*India

First published in India in 2019 by
HarperCollins *Publishers*
A-75, Sector 57, Noida, Uttar Pradesh 201301, India
www.harpercollins.co.in

2 4 6 8 10 9 7 5 3 1

P-ISBN: 978-93-5357-000-2

The views and opinions expressed in this book are the author's own and the facts are as reported by her, and the publishers are not in any way liable for the same.

Typeset in 10.5/12.6 Garamond
Design by Amina Razzack

Printed and bound at
Replika Press Pvt. Ltd

CONTENTS

Foreword

In August 2018, the AJ Kidwai Mass Communication Research Centre (AJK MCRC), Jamia Millia Islamia, introduced the 'Art and Culture of Italy' course as a part of their Master's programme. Based on their studies and experiences, the students created an academic book along with guest professor, Dr Paola Martani.

Art and Culture of Italy is a celebration of many interacting art forms, from sculpture and painting to architecture, literature, and music. Spanning across centuries of Italian history, it is a tribute to the beauty and culture of the country. The pages of the book are rich with beautiful images and illustrations, as well as fascinating historical details, which provide context for the discussion of each era's artistic production. Through this book, readers will gain a wide and interesting understanding of the history and characteristics of the Italian arts.

(Prof. Iftekhar Ahmed)

The Roman Period

I

Edited by
Amina Razzack, Aymun Kaleem Naqvi,
Saniya Arshad, Aditya Gautam, Yumna Ahmad,
Fateh Veer Singh Guram, Ayushi Malik, Ameen Fatima

Designed By
Amina Razzack, Aymun Kaleem Naqvi

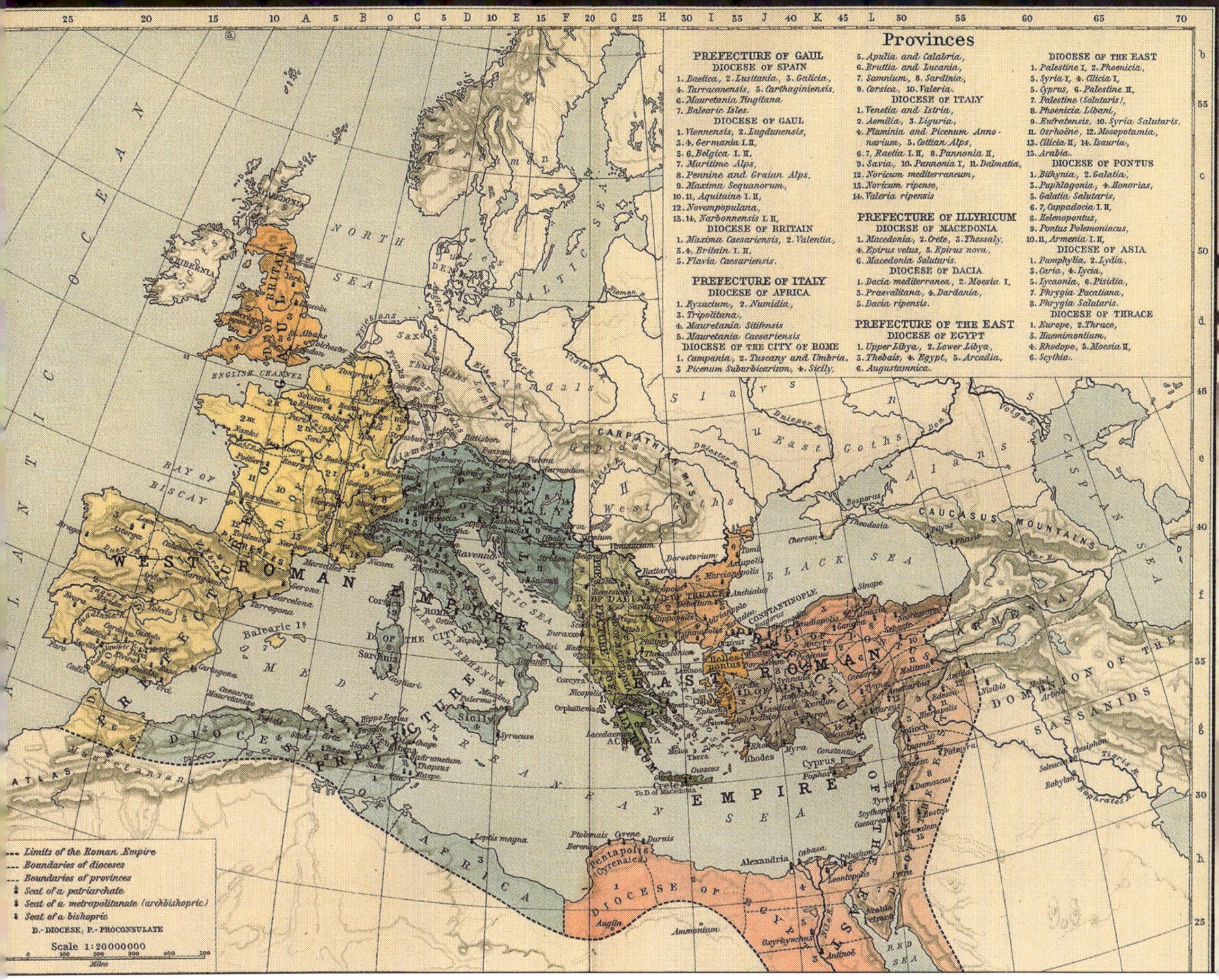

Map of the Roman Empire about 395 CE

The Roman Period

Roman society started to spread in the eighht century BCE, and by the Year 0 (The year of the birth of Jesus), Romans had already conquered all the areas surrounding the Mediterranean Sea. However, the birth of Jesus Christ marked the beginning of a religion that opposed all that Roman civilization stood for, shaking it to its very foundations.

During the Roman civilization, the city of Rome was considered to be the centre of the world. Based on a pyramid hierarchy, Roman society did not consider all men equal. Strength, order and discipline were valued, so men with these characteristics had higher status in society. People who were a part of the Roman empire, but not from Rome itself, were considered to be from the provinces. They were not held at the same level as people from the capital and were considered 'provincial'. People from beyond the provinces were simply considered barbarians. Romans were a military-based society and aimed to conquer much of the world around them. Glory lay not in death, but in the immortality of the empire.

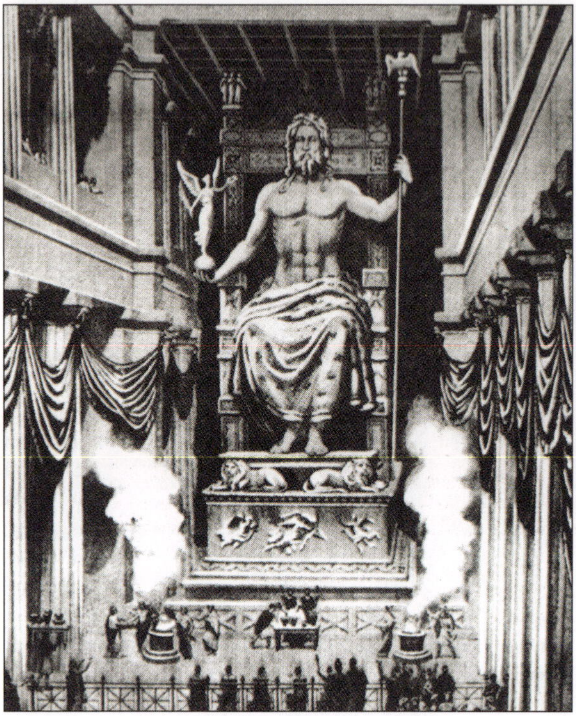

The Roman God, Zeus

The first step in analysing any society is to observe its religion. In Roman society, Gods were depicted as men and women, and considered to have human behaviours and emotions. They weren't perfect; they were a representation of human feelings, of a period of the life of a person. One might represent love, another Spring, another war, (Venus, Mars...) etc. This transformation of the divine into the mundane led the Romans to understand that the focal point of their society was the human being itself, to the extent that the gods became a mere extension or expression of human passion, quality, ability and propensities.

Christianity was completely different from the religion of the Ancient Romans. Roman religion, like its society, was anthropomorphic, centring on man and his passions. The gods of the Roman pantheon were depicted as men and women. The monotheistic religion of Christianity was founded on the principle that all people were equal, that God was an omnipresent deity without a human form and the centre of Christian culture. Biblical phrases: 'with more ease an elephant will enter the crack of a door compared to the rich who will try to enter the kingdom of heaven' and 'the last will be the first' emphasized the position of men in the eyes of God. Jesus Christ, the son of God, was the closest direct link to humanity. Such a religion upset the existing pyramid of Roman society which placed heavy distinction between men as 'Romans' versus 'the conquered people'.

With the force of Christianity pushing up from the south and the barbaric invasion pushing down from the north, the Roman Empire fell in in 476 CE.

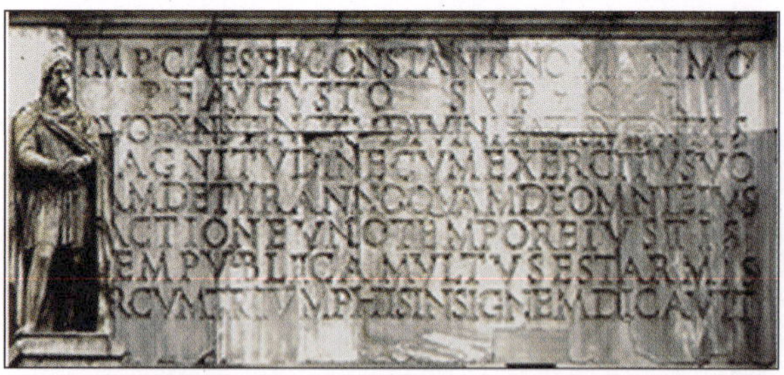

Costantino's Arch on the Roman forum

Language

The official language of the empire was Latin, commonly spoken around the Mediterranean. However, as the empire began to fall, the provinces began to speak their own dialects, creating a substratum (sostrato), resulting in overlapping languages: Latin and its dialects. The substratum created what are called Roman languages which we know today as Spanish, French, Italian, etc.

Art, Architecture and Society

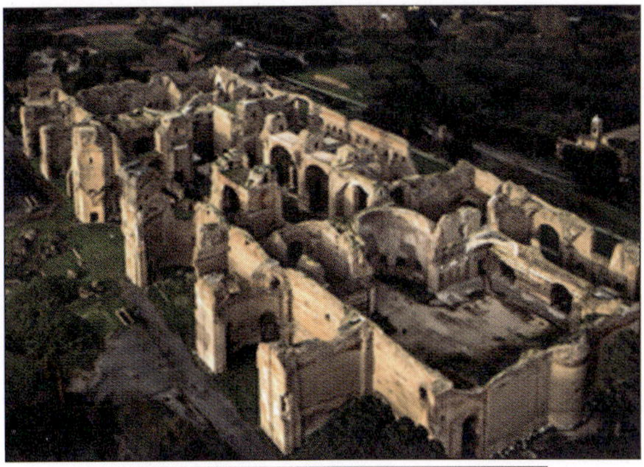

Carcalla's bath

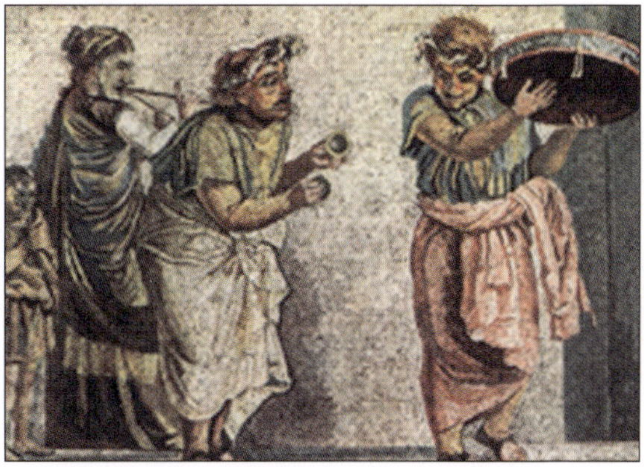

Mosaic, found in Pompei –Ercolano's villa

Art, painting, architecture and literature were used to express the civilization of the Ancient Romans. In their artwork, the Romans aspired to realism and perfection. The focus of their interests was gods and goddesses, as a representation of human beings in general. The importance and the appreciation of the human body can be seen from the clothes worn by figures in paintings and sculptures. Clothes were very simple, usually a tunic and draping cloth that was slipped on over the body, showing the lines and emphasizing its curves.

Roman society was very social and everything was done for the benefit of the Roman public; man was always at the centre. We can see this by paying attention to the importance public space held for the Romans. They innovated greatly when it came to public buildings: public baths, theatres, arenas and forums. They were also pioneers in the creation of sophisticated sewage and drainage systems, as well as waterways. The Pantheon, the Caracalla baths and the Colloseum are all incredible examples of Roman public architecture.

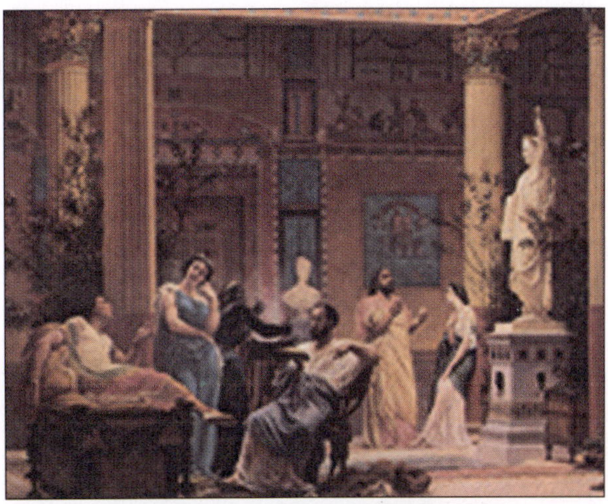

Boulanger, atrium of a roman villa

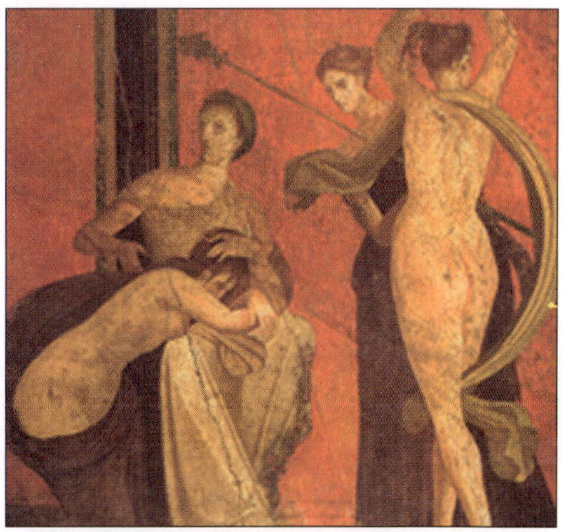

Roman fresco found in misteri's villa in Pompei

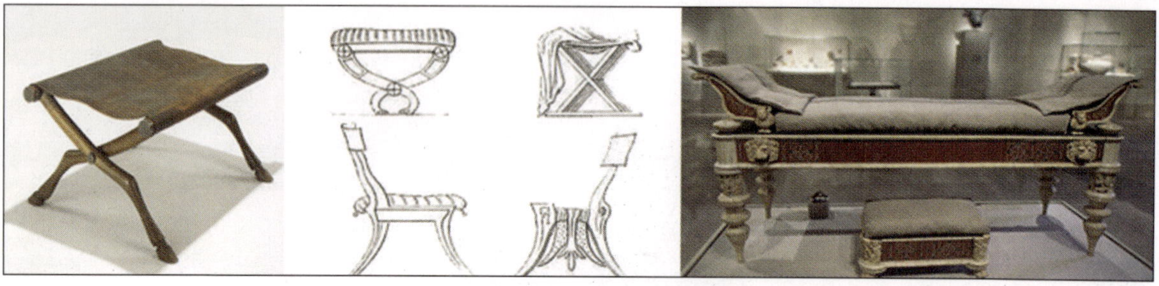

Examples of Roman Furniture

Furniture during this time was very simple and limited: beds, low tables and reclining chairs. Interiors, where people would congregate and converse, usually featured water fixtures, a good deal of natural light, frescoes and statues.

The map of the Roman city is built on a cross, from which, in straight parallel lines, a perfect grid is formed. The cities were literally built on the idea of order, rigour, and an absolutely indisputable linearity. Within the city we see impressive monuments, also with very regular forms. The choice of materials requires little interpretation: marble and stone have an incredible power to display desire for permanence and endlessness. We can also see that they mirrored the qualities of the ideal Roman man. Just by observing religion, paintings, cities and architecture, we are able to outline the basic points of an entire community: the human being at the centre with a desire to never see his sun set.

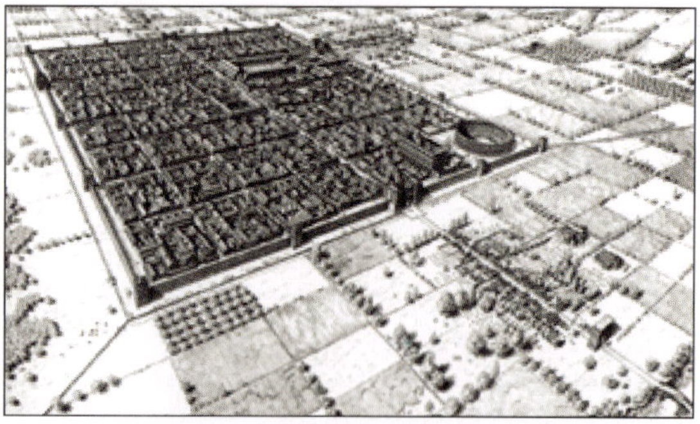

An example of a map of Roman city Aosta

Music

The transmission of Italian musical heritage since ancient times has posed a big problem. The oral tradition could not guarantee that the original sounds were handed down in their perfect, authentic form. As a result, in ancient times some Eastern, Chinese, Indian and Babylonian peoples created precise systems of notation. In Western civilization, the first example of annotated music dates back to ancient Greece, and consists of a fragment of a chorus of the 'Oreste' by Euripides dating back to the fifth century BCE. The Greeks had two systems of musical notation: Cruz and Alexis. The first was used for instrumental music, and consisted of letters of the phonetic alphabet, differently inclined according to whether they indicated a natural note, a quarter, a half or a higher tone. The second one, suitable for choral music, adopted the capital letters of the Greek alphabet. In Roman times, the Latin letters were substituted for the Greek letters and the system survived, becoming more and more complex, until the Middle Ages.

Philosophy

For more than a millennium, the centre of attention in the world was man himself. Behind the Roman empire there was stability, structure, planning, power, and many media were used to express the same common idea. Roman society was a military society based on the idea of Man: a man who must be strong, disciplined and ruled. However, with the fall of the Roman Empire, a period of history began that saw a new and completely opposite philosophy govern: Christianity. In this new mindset, the centre of attention was no longer the human being, but a God who is omnipotent, perfection, infinite and omniscient. But how is it possible to introduce this new idea into a world that has, for so long been centred on human beings?

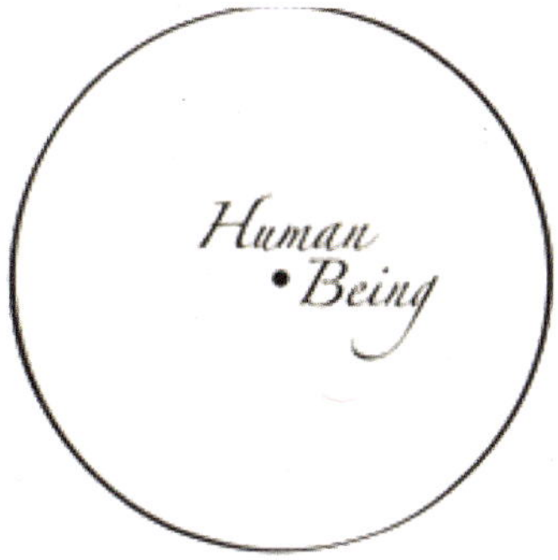

Man at the centre of society

Taking it to be true that history leads back to the principle that a macrocosm is represented by a microcosm, and vice versa, we can compare this knot of history to a sheet. If I apply a force for a period of time by folding the sheet to my left, before returning the levelled sheet, I have to apply the same force in the opposite direction for a period of time relatively similar to the previous one, bending it to the left. I have, therefore, to go from one extreme to the other in order then to find a new equilibrium. Thus, to be able to insert the idea of God in the scene, the human being had to be expelled, at least for a few hundred years, giving life to the Middle Ages.

Clothing

Roman clothes, made of wool, were homespun into garments by the women of the family. Over time, garments were produced by craftspeople or slaves, and if one could afford, wool was supplemented with linen, silk, cotton, brought to Rome from other parts of the empire.

Just as it is today, there were different clothes for men and for women. Men usually wore a tunic or a toga while women wore a stola, tunica and palla, different types of dresses for women. Clothes, at that time, were simply draped around the body or fastened with clasps and brooches because needles at the time were coarse and unwieldy, and so sewing was something done only when strictly necessary. Articles of apparel were for more than just keeping warm in the Mediterranean climate. They identified social status. For example, plebeians wore a tunic that was often dark and made of an inexpensive material or thin wool felt. In contrast, patricians wore white tunics made of expensive linen or fine wool, or even silk which was very rare at the time. Shoes also indicated social status. Patricians wore expensive red sandals with an ornament at the back or red shoes called the calcei mullei. Plebeians wore (worn out) leather sandals.

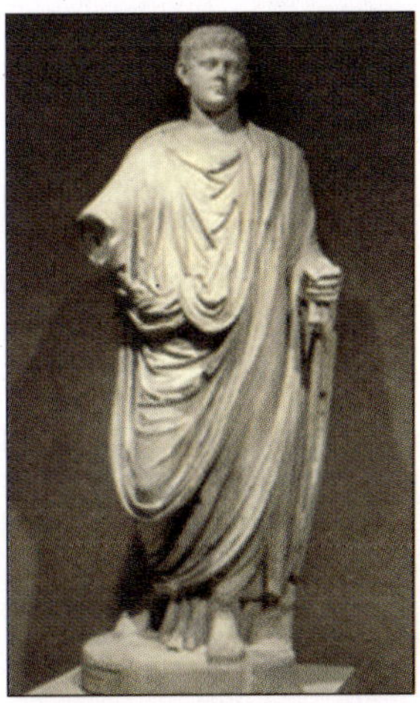

The Toga

These are clothes that Roman men wore:

Togas made out of wool were large in size and expensive.The material was not sewn or pinned but was draped around the body and over one arm. All togas were not the same and each distinctive type could mark a Roman's societal status or title. It was the law that all citizens wore togas for public events.

The tunic was standard dress for all men, from slaves to the nobles. It could be worn plain, belted at the waist, or under a cloak. Citizens of Rome would wear a tunic under their toga. The simplest and cheapest tunics were made by sewing two pieces of wool together to make a tube with holes

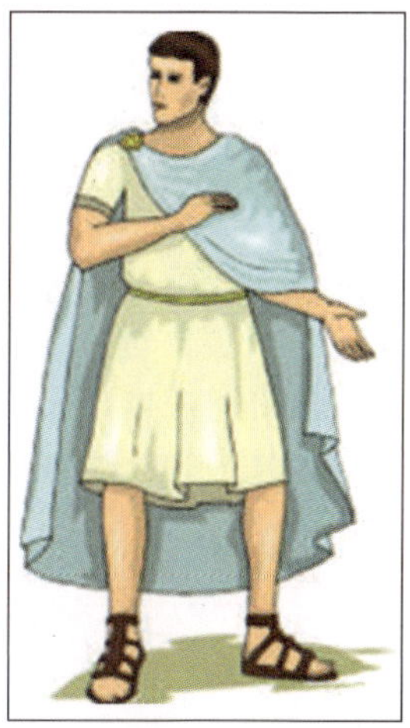

The Tunic

for the arms. For those that could afford it, tunics could be made of linen or even silk. The tunic would be worn belted at the waist and just covering the knees.

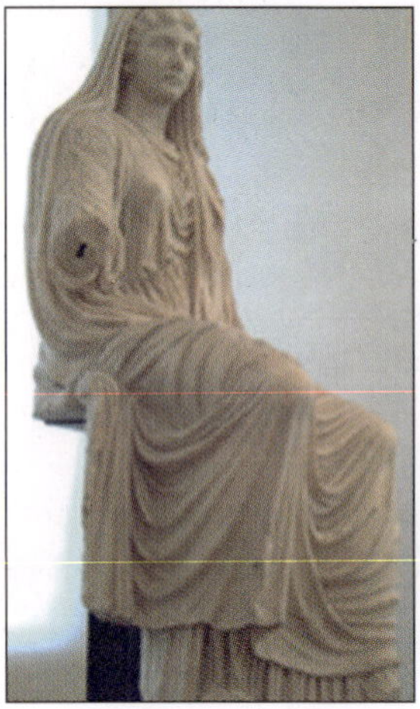

The Palla

These are clothes that Roman women wore:

The palla was a woven rectangle made of wool that the Roman matron put on top of her stola when she went outside. She could use the palla in many ways, like a modern scarf, but palla is often translated as a cloak. A palla was like the toga.

The stola was a garment for women worn under the palla and over the undertunic. It was usually made of wool. The stola could be pinned at the shoulders, using the undertunic for sleeves, or the stola itself could have sleeves.

A well known image of the stola is the one worn by the Statue of Liberty in New York City.

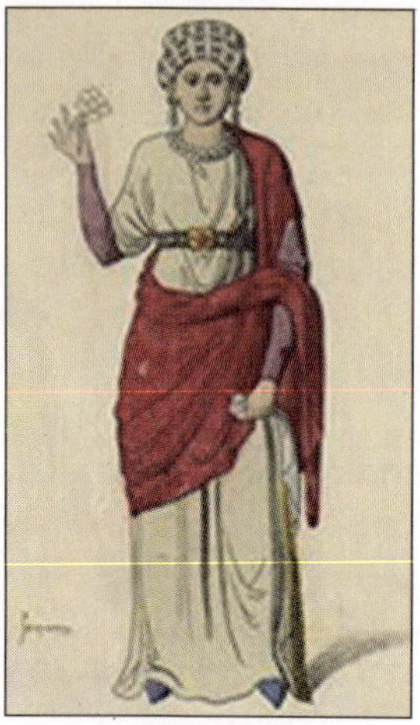

The Stola

Although not reserved for women, the tunica was part of the Roman costume for women. It was a simple rectangular piece that might have sleeves or might be sleeveless. It was the basic garment that went on under the stola, palla, or toga, or could be worn alone. While men might belt up the tunica, women were expected to have fabric extending to their feet, so if this was all she wore, a Roman woman would not belt it.

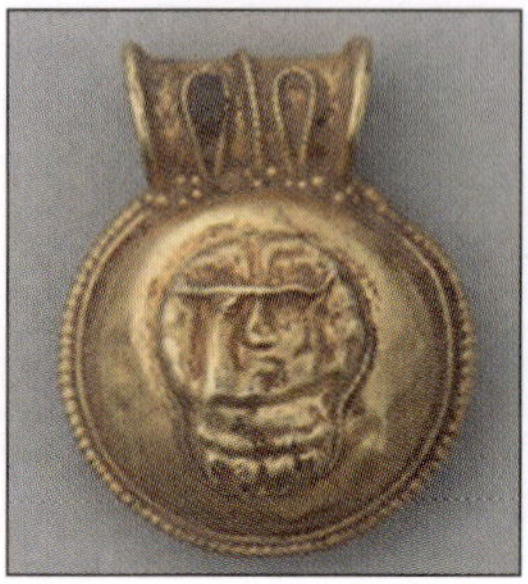

Bulla

A bulla is a type of necklace with a pouch that was worn by ancient Roman children as a type of protection from evil spirits. The pouch was made of gold, leather, or cloth depending on how wealthy the family was. The inside of a bulla contained amulets or charms. The bulla was presented to a child at birth. A Roman boy would wear the bulla until he became a man and a Roman girl wore the bulla until she got married.

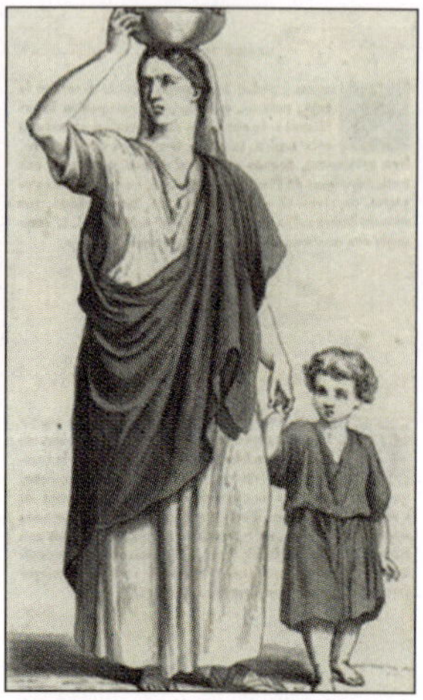

The Tunica

Ancient Roman Homes

Domus

Domus was the type of house occupied by the upper class and some wealthy freedmen during the Republican and Imperial eras, found in almost every major city throughout the Roman territories. The elite classes of Roman society constructed their residences with elaborate marble decorations, inlaid marble panelling, door jambs and columns as well as expensive paintings and frescoes. Many poor and lower middle-class Romans lived in crowded, dirty and mostly rundown rental apartments, known as insulae. These multi-level apartment blocks were built as high and tightly together as possible and held far less status and convenience than the private homes of the prosperous.

The domus included multiple rooms, indoor courtyards, gardens and beautifully painted walls that were elaborately laid out. The vestibulum (entrance hall) led into a large central hall: the atrium, which was the focal point of the domus and contained a statue of an altar to the household gods. Leading off the Atrium were cubicula (bedrooms), triclinium (dining room) where guests could recline on couches and eat dinner whilst reclining, a tablinum (living room or study) and tabernae (shops on the outside, facing the street). Surrounding the atrium were arranged the master's families' main rooms: the small cubicula or bedrooms, the tablinum or study, and the triclinium or dining room.

Given Roman society's focus on meetings with other Romans, the need to exchange thoughts, ideas, visions, it is only normal that the most important part of the house was the Atrium (plural atria), where guests and dependents (clients) were greeted. The atrium was open in the centre, surrounded at least in part by high-ceilinged porticoes that often contained only sparse furnishings to give the effect of a large space. In the centre was a square roof opening called the compluvium in which rainwater could come, draining inwards from the slanted tiled roof. Directly below the compluvium was the impluvium. The other rooms of the house where kept simple.

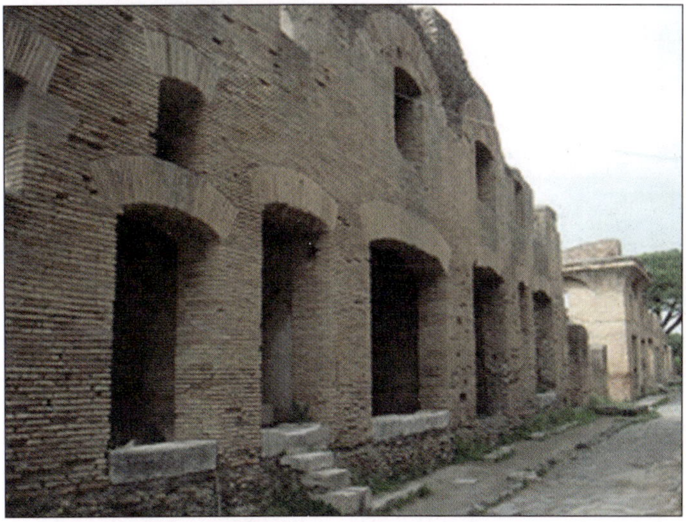

Roman insula architecture

Insula

In Roman architecture, an insula (Latin for 'island', plural insulae) was a kind of apartment building that housed most of the urban citizen population of ancient Rome, including ordinary people of lower- or middle-class status (the plebs). The ground-level floor of the insula was used for tabernae, shops and businesses, with the living space upstairs.

Insulae, like domus, had running water and sanitation. But this kind of housing was sometimes constructed at minimal expense for speculative purposes, resulting in insulae of poor construction. They were built in timber, mud, brick, and later, primitive concrete, and were prone to fire and collapse. Living quarters were typically smallest in the building's uppermost floors, with the largest and most expensive apartments being located on the bottom floors. The insulae could be up to six or seven stories high, and despite height restrictions in the Imperial era, a few reached eight or nine stories.

The lower-class Romans—plebians—lived in apartment houses, called flats, above or behind their shops. Even fairly well-to-do tradesmen might choose to live in an apartment-building compound over their store, with maybe renters on the upper stories. Their own apartments might be quite roomy, sanitary and pleasant, occasionally with running water. In the apartment houses, an entire family (grandparents, parents, children) might all be crowded into one room, without running water. They had to haul their water in from public facilities. Fire was a very real threat because people were cooking meals in crowded quarters, and many of the flats were made of wood. They did not have toilets. They had to use public latrines (toilets). Agrippa and it is believed that Hadrian left it as a gesture to his predecessor when he rebuilt the Pantheon.

The Pantheon

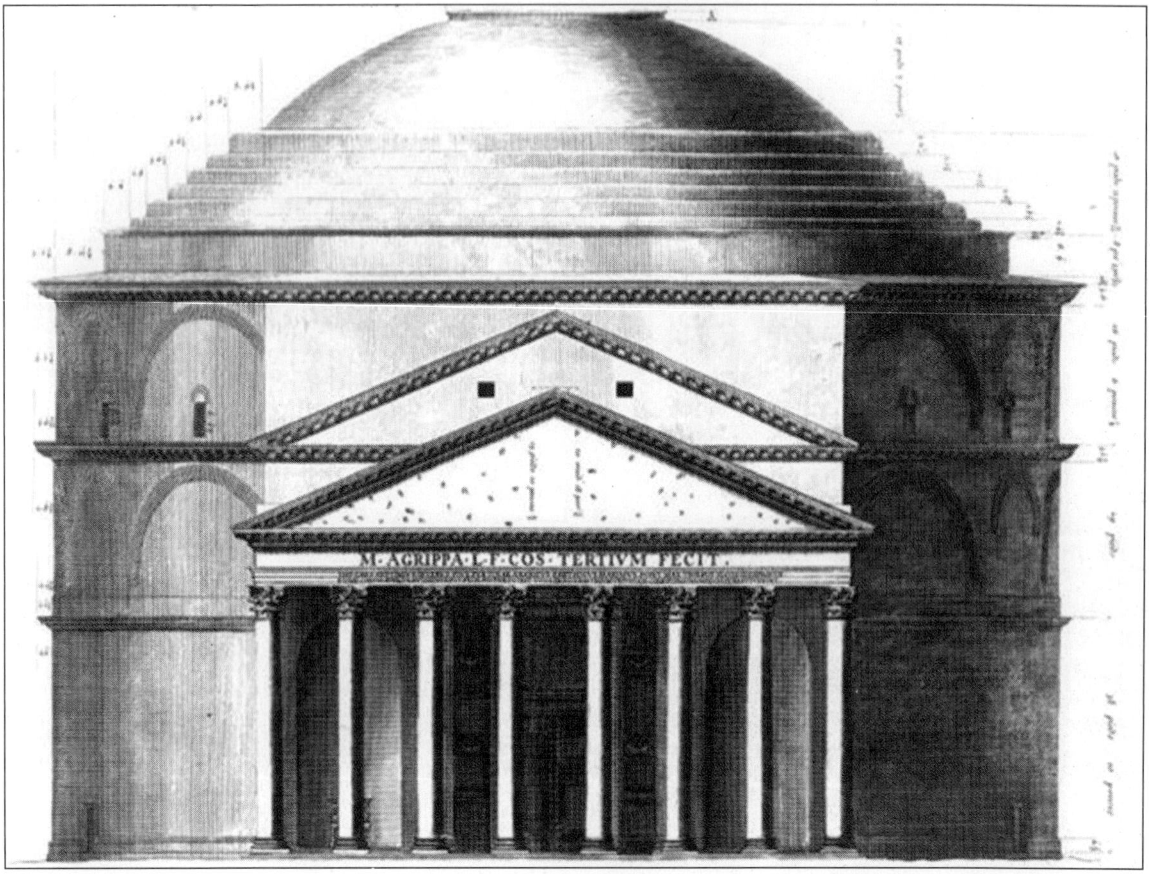

Built around 126 CE by the Roman Emperor Hadrian, the Pantheon is a temple that is one of the best preserved buildings dating to the Roman period. While originally built in honour of the seven deities of the seven planets in the Roman state religion, the Pantheon also served as a place where the emperor would make important appearances. In 609, Byzantine Emperor Phocas gave the building to Pope Boniface IV, who reconsecrated it as a Christian church. The building's rebranding as a church saved it from the neglect and ruin that, during the early medieval period, befell a majority of buildings of ancient Rome. The original Pantheon was built around 27-25 BCE by Marcus Agrippa (it was destroyed by fire in 80 CE.)

The building consists of two principal parts—the porch, which is very Classical Greek in its construction, and the circular main building, which is reminiscent of the Roman style of architecture.

At the front of the Pantheon, sixteen monolithic columns form the monument's famed portico. The shafts are made of Egyptian granite, while the decorative top of the column and bases were carved from white Greek marble. The columns support a triangle pediment with an inscription attributing the Pantheon to Marcus Agrippa. It is the only remaining part from the original temple built by The interior of the dome is intended to symbolize the heavens. The Great Eye, 27 feet across, at the dome's apex is the source of all light

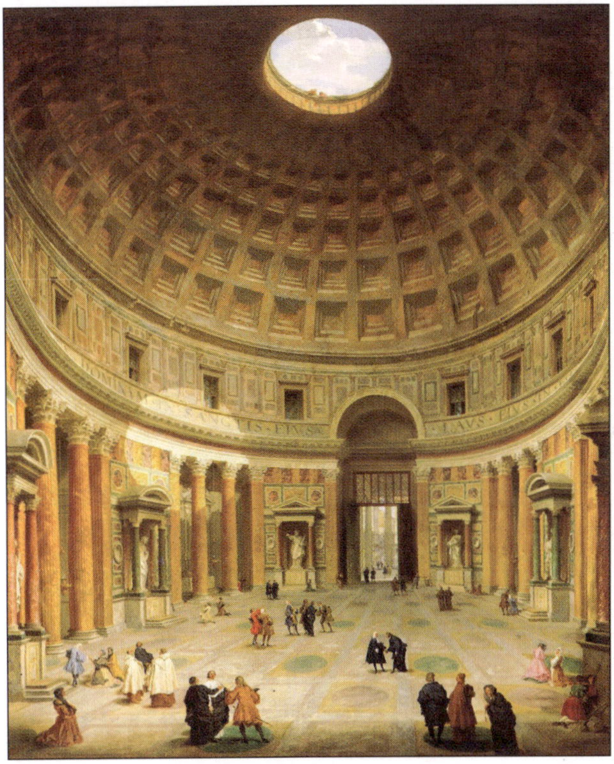

Pantheon Dome

and is symbolic of the sun. The interior features sunken panels (coffers) in 5 rings of 28, which originally contained bronze star ornaments. This coffering was not only decorative, but also a necessary engineering element, as it—along with the incorporation of the oculus as the apex—reduces the weight of the roof. The oculus at the dome's apex and the entry door are the only natural sources of light in the interior. Throughout the day, the light from the oculus moves around this space in a reverse sundial effect. The oculus also serves as a cooling and ventilation method.

The walls of the structure house seven alcoves (recesses) that surround the entire circular perimeter. These places would have been areas to place sculptures and other works of art in antiquity, but have since been converted into chapels and tombs. Triangular and rounded altars mark the perimeter of the room. Floor and walls of the interior are surfaced with fine stone sourced from across the Roman Empire, including granite and various coloured marbles.

The symbolism of the great dome adds weight to this interpretation. The coffers of the dome are divided into 28 sections, equalling the number of large columns below. 28 is a "perfect number", a whole number whose summed factors equal it (thus, 1 + 2 + 4 + 7 + 14 = 28). The sunbeam streaming through the oculus traced an ever-changing daily path across the wall and floor of the rotunda. It could be possible that the sunbeam marked solar and lunar events, or simply time.

In the Pantheon, Hadrian attempted to create a connection to the gods, as well as to Emperor Augustus. The Pantheon was constructed facing north, and prior to the construction of the city around the building, the Pantheon would have faced the mausoleum of Emperor Augustus. This position of the Pantheon was meant to honour Augustus and also associate Hadrian with the great emperor. The themes evident in the structure of the dome, meant to remind the viewer of the heavens, also gave an impression of Hadrian's connection to the gods, and thus showed the relationship between Roman government and religion.

The Pantheon stands as a testament to the ingenuity and skill of the Roman people. Its importance lies in the fact that it is the best preserved monument from ancient Rome. Throughout its history, the Pantheon's innovative combination of both Greek and Roman style has been admired by many and served as an inspiration for many buildings in Europe as well as North America. The Pantheon is an unrivalled artifact of Roman antiquity.

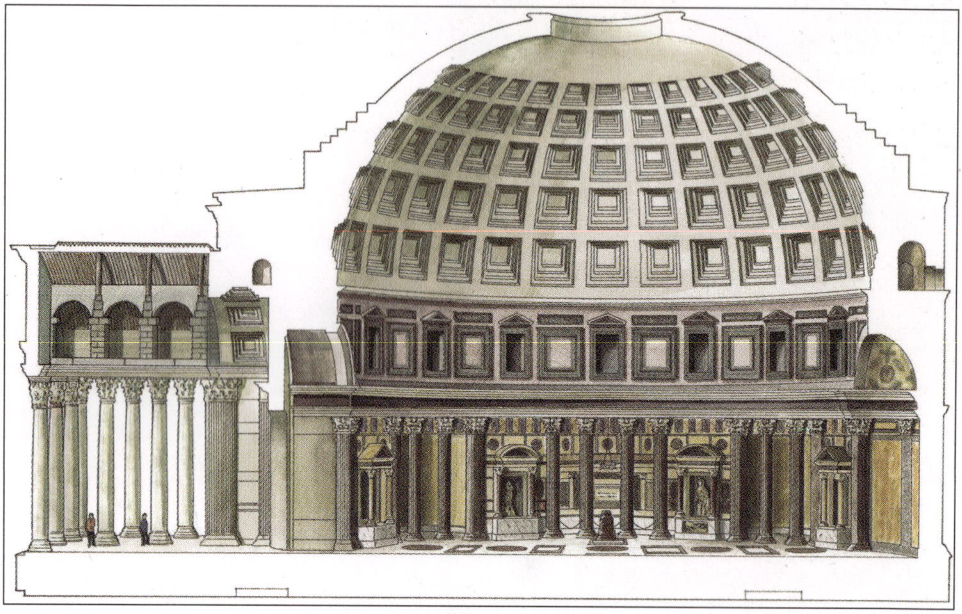

Pantheon Section

Colosseum

The Colosseum, also known as the Flavian Amphitheatre, is an oval amphitheatre in the centre of the city of Rome, Italy. Built of concrete and sand, it is the largest amphitheatre ever built. The Colosseum is situated just east of the Roman Forum. The construction of the Colosseum began in 72 CE .

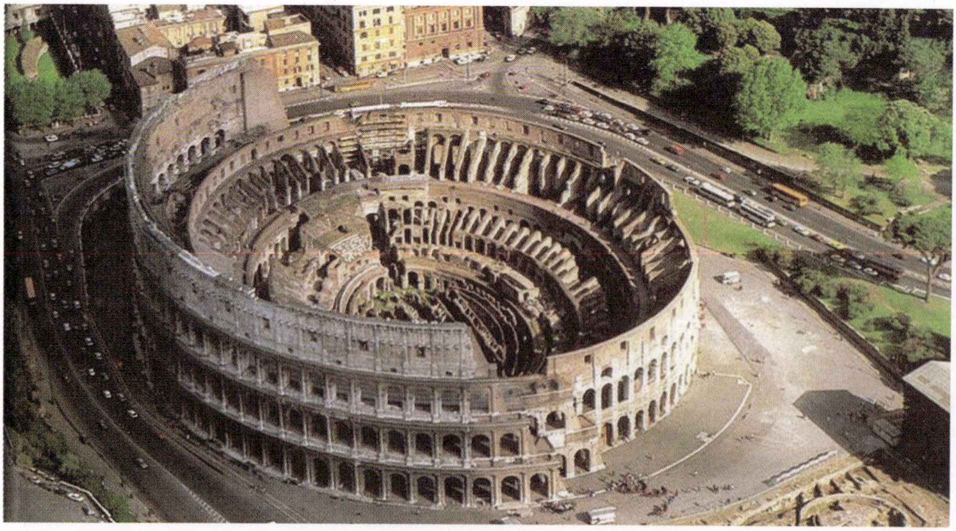

Roman Architecture of Colosseum

On the site that was once the lake and gardens of Emperor Nero's Golden House. This was drained, and as a precaution against potential earthquake damage, concrete foundations six metres deep were put down. The biggest building of its kind, it had the following features:

- four stories
- a height of 45m (150 ft)
- a width of 189m by 156m
- an oval arena measuring 87.5m by 54.8m
- a roofed awning of canvas
- capacity for 50,000 spectators

The theatre was principally built from locally quarried limestone with internally linking lateral walls of brick, concrete and volcanic stone (tufa). Vaults were built of lighter pumice stone. The theatre was spectacular even from the outside with monumental open arcades on each of the first three floors presenting statue-filled arches. The first floor carried Doric columns, the second Ionic, and the third level Corinthian.

The different levels of seats were accessed via broad staircases with each landing and seat being numbered. The total capacity for the Colosseum was approximately 45,000 seated and 5,000 standing spectators. One of the oldest depictions of the Colosseum appeared on the coins of Titus and shows three tiers, statues in the upper external arches and the large column fountains—the Meta Sudans—which stood nearby. The scene of all the action—the sanded arena floor—was also eye-catching. It was often landscaped with rocks and trees to resemble exotic locations during the staging of wild animal hunts (venatiories). There were also ingenious underground lifting mechanisms which allowed for the sudden introduction of wild animals into the proceedings. On some occasions, notably the opening series of shows, the arena was flooded in order to host mock naval battles. Under the arena floor (and visible to the modern visitor) was a maze of small compartment rooms, corridors and animal pens.

Although historically tied to earlier Etruscan games which emphasized the rites of death, the shows in the Roman arenas were designed simply to entertain. They also demonstrated the wealth and generosity of the emperor and provided an opportunity for ordinary people to actually see their ruler in person. However, blood sports and death were the real purpose of the spectacular shows and an entire profession arose to meet the massive entertainment requirements of the populace—for example under Claudius there were ninety-three games a year. Spectacles often lasted from dawn till nightfall and the gladiators usually kicked off the show with a chariot procession accompanied by trumpets and even a hydraulic organ and then dismounted and circled the arena, each saluting the emperor with the famous line: Ave, Imperator, morituri te salutant! (Hail, Emperor, those who are about to die salute you!).

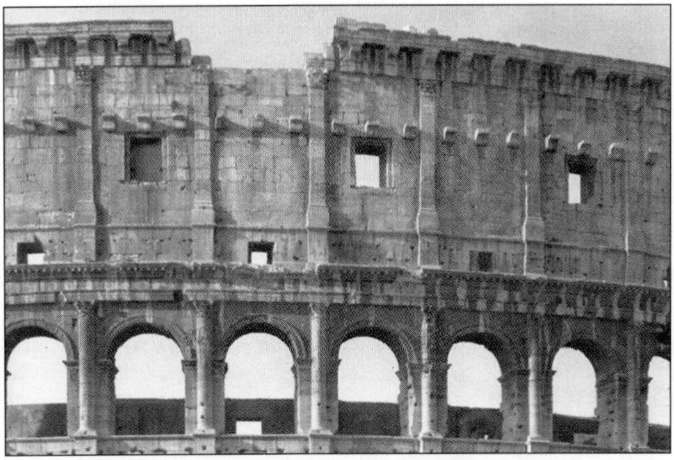

Portion of the Colosseum, Rome

In 404 CE, with changing times and tastes, the games of the Colosseum were finally abolished by Emperor Honorius, although condemned criminals were still made to fight wild animals for a further century. The great earthquake of 1231 CE caused the collapse of the southwest facade and the Colosseum became a vast source of building material - stones and columns were removed, iron clamps holding blocks together were stolen and statues were melted for lime. Indeed, Pope Alexander VI actually leased the Colosseum as a quarry. Despite this crumbling away though, the venue was still used for the occasional religious procession and play during the fifteenth century CE.

From the Renaissance period, both artists and architects, such as Michelangelo, and later tourists on their Grand Tour took a renewed interest in Roman architecture and ruins. As a consequence, in 1744 CE Pope Benedict XIV prohibited any further removal of masonry from the Colosseum and consecrated it in memory of the Christian martyrs who had lost their lives there.

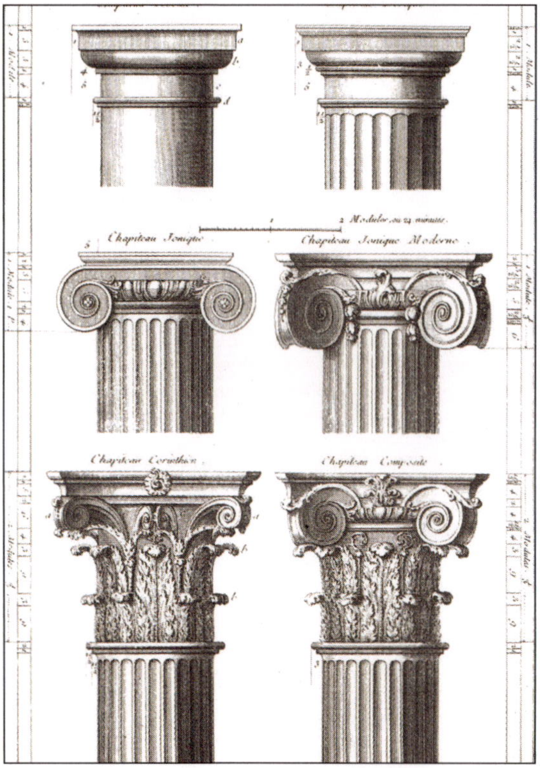

Classical order of Capitals

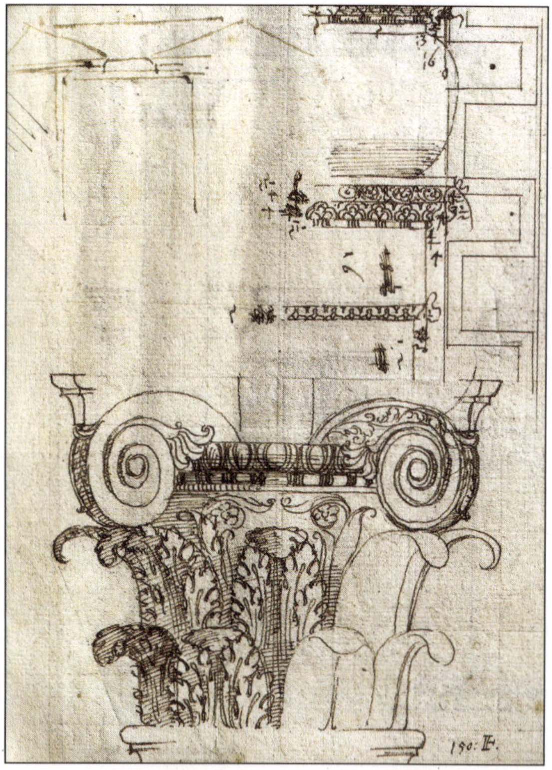

Detail of Corinthian Capital

The High Middle Ages

II

Edited by
Ameen Fatima

Designed By
Aymun Kaleem Naqvi, Aatif Nawaz

The High Middle Ages

The entire period of the Middle Ages ranges from the fifth to the fifteenth century AD.
From 476 to 1000 AD are usually referred to as the High Middle Ages.

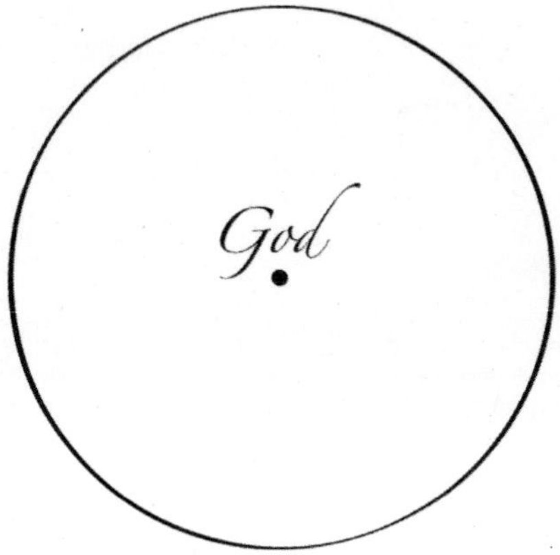

God as the centre of Society

Historical Context:

During this period, we see the definitive dissolution of the Western Roman Empire (476 AD) and the birth of the barbarian Roman kingdoms.

This resulted in the disruption of linguistic unity, initially guaranteed by the Latin language university, and the rise of vulgar latin (V-IX). There is the rise of neo-Latin languages, derived from spoken Latin (unwritten). The first document to be written in the vernacular language was the oath of Strasbourg (842)—composed by Charles the Bald and Ludwig the German. In this document we see the vernacular becoming a language of political dignity.

In 568, following the invasion of the Lombards, an era began in Italy, which remains obscure from the cultural and artistic point of view. The kingdom of the Lombards in Italy spans from 568 to 774, the year in which Longobards were defeated by Charlemagne.

The cultural civil rebirth promoted by Charlemagne, especially in the France–Germany area, resulted in the creation of a style in which Byzantine elements fused with Celtic, Lombard and Merovingian aspects. This is part of what is known as the Carolingian Renaissance.

The Influence of Religion on Art and Architecture

During the Middle Ages, Christianity was on the rise. It was a religion in which God took the central focus (a position previously held by man).

Whereas during the Roman period the architecture of religion was massive and magnificent, in this period religious architecture experienced a 'Dark Age'. This is because of one of the principles of Christianity is to make man feel guilty: there is no sense of perfection anymore; man is imperfect and the architecture embodies the culture of the period. Art was considered to come from the devil.

Creativity had to be hidden—hence the name Dark Ages—and art ceased to evolve. There was a sort of involution where creative expression went into hiding. An example of this can be seen in the power of a statue or an adorned temple compared to an unadorned church.

In the churches of this period, there are no representations of Jesus with human feelings; he is passive, his agony upon the cross is not described.

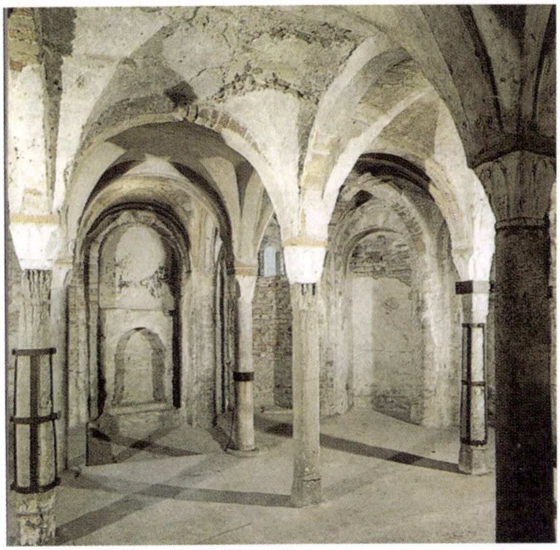

Crypt of Sant' Eusebio, Sicily, Pavia

This may sound bizarre, but it is in fact quite understandable. For thousands of years, the central focus of religion had been the concept of man. Before reaching an equilibrium of that situation, it was necessary to tip the scales to the opposite extreme—to place all the emphasis on the other end of the spectrum, namely God. Only after centuries of this new opposite extreme was it possible to find a balance between the two. This began to happen in the Early Middle Ages (fifth to tenth century CE) when man began to re-enter the picture, first by worshipping God through His own creations, and later by placing importance on the concept of man himself (as expressed through humanism and the culture of the Renaissance).

In addition to this new tendency to place God at the centre of attention, in the High Middle Ages, Europe experienced a severe geopolitical upheaval, and thus artistic production suffered a quantitative decrease. At the start of the fifth century, Roman territories in Italy, Western Europe and northern Africa fell to barbarian invasions, while the empire's central urban civilization (Rome) suffered a progressive impoverishment and depopulation, with a consequent decrease in the importance of civil institutions.

Art in the Middle Ages

The term 'early medieval art' is rather generic, and groups several currents, trends and phases.

In the Middle Ages, art was restricted to the decoration of objects of use, and the artists (or craftsmen) did not yet have that elitist aura that spread from the end of the thirteenth century. Painters, sculptors and architects were workers just like the goldsmiths, weavers and leather-makers were. The canonical distinction between the 'major arts' (painting, sculpture and architecture) and the 'minor arts' dates back to the treatises of Leon Battista Alberti, who maintained that the major disciplines had an intellectual aspect that exceeded mere dexterity.

Also during this period, the so-called barbarians settled in the West, and their art presented characteristics totally different from the Classical style. If the latter was oriented towards the study of man, the art of the barbarians was abstract, playing on the intertwining, the phytomorphic tangle. The word barbaric literally means 'stammering', and was used first by the Ellenians and then by the Romans to imply that these foreign peoples could neither behave nor live according to the customs and principles of the Greco-Roman civilization. The word came to have negative connotations: implying a person to be deprived of education, rough and uneducated.

From the middle of the third century, mass migrations pushed a series of 'barbaric' Germanic peoples to move towards the Roman territories. From the migrations, from the end of the fourth and into the fifth centuries, an escalation of violence was triggered, which led to real invasions, with looting and destruction, and accelerated the degradation of the Empire and the formation of the Roman-barbarian kingdoms.

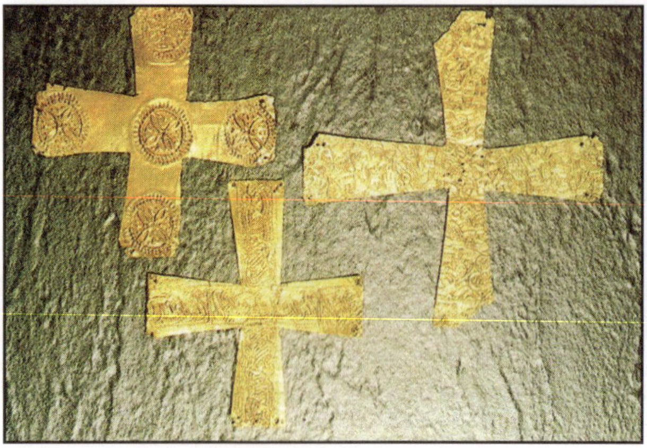

Crosses embossed in Longobard gold plate, Civic Archaeological Museum of Bergamo

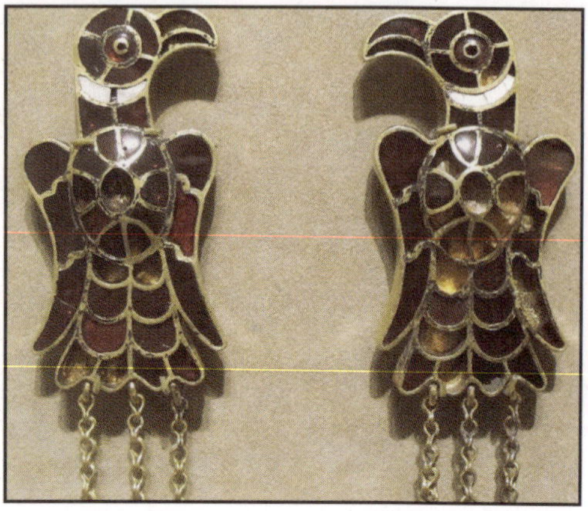

Ostrogoths earrings (gold and semi-precious stones)

These populations did not have artistic traditions related to sculpture, architecture, or painting, since their societies were nomadic and usually did not settle long enough to create monumental art forms. However, they possessed considerable knowledge of the use and decoration of light materials such as wood, metals and leather. It was in the field of jewellery that the best artistic results were achieved, with notable original contributions. The most characteristic works of the Longobard culture are characterized by the taste for chromatism and the use of precious materials, enamels, stones, and abstract decorations.

In conclusion, to define the Middle Ages as a 'dark era' is perhaps a bit misleading. Certainly compared to the previous era's art, the creative products were less exteriorized and less visible. However, although the works of painting are very scarce, numerous and splendid illuminated manuscripts have been found from the period, which bear witness to the artistic vitality of the people.

Language

Language often gives clues as to the way of thinking of the speakers themselves—thus, it is important to consider the linguistic developments at this period in time. Latin was the language that had been spreading since the eighth century BCE, and was also spoken in the lands conquered by the Romans themselves. The language had always been characterized by great diversity, and in the various regions where it was absorbed, the regional words were integrated, giving rise to ever more diverse languages. There were the Neo-Latin languages spoken by the majority of common people (these were often referred to as the 'vulgar' languages, 'vulgar' meaning 'people'), and there was the official Latin used by the learned. For most of the Middle Ages, to make it possible to somehow distinguish the holders of power from the people in general, the Latin language was the key. In this period, however, there was also a strong attempt to give value to the new nascent languages—for example, the reform of Charlemagne (which helped to differentiate between Latin and the other spoken languages), and the clerics who preached in Latin but addressed the masses in the vernacular. This period also marked the beginning of the dissemination of French Provençal texts (stories of previous heroic undertakings and legends) written in d'oc language and texts from northern France (Re Artu and Charlemagne), written in d'oil language. In Italy, the Italian vernacular thrived thanks to the flourishing of the bourgeoisie and merchant classes, and this coincided with the birth of the municipalities in the north and the reign of Federico di Svevia in the south.

An In-Depth Art History

After the fall of the Roman Empire, the formation of the Eastern Empire took place. The ancient Byzantium, a Greek colony on the banks of the bosphorus, changed its name to Constantinople because the Emperor Constantine had transferred the seat to the eastern part of the empire. For centuries, Bisanzio remained a centre of culture, faith and art. After the fall of the Western Empire, the centre of the artistic spiritual life of Italy moved from Rome to Ravenna. The flowering of Byzantine art extended from the fourth to the seventh century AD, and reached its peak under the reign of Justinian.

We, therefore, have two poles: East—Constantinople, in the West—Ravenna.
The main artistic characteristics are:

- strong symbolism
- the tendency to deify the figure of the emperor and that of Christ
- images characterized by a sense of fixity and stillness

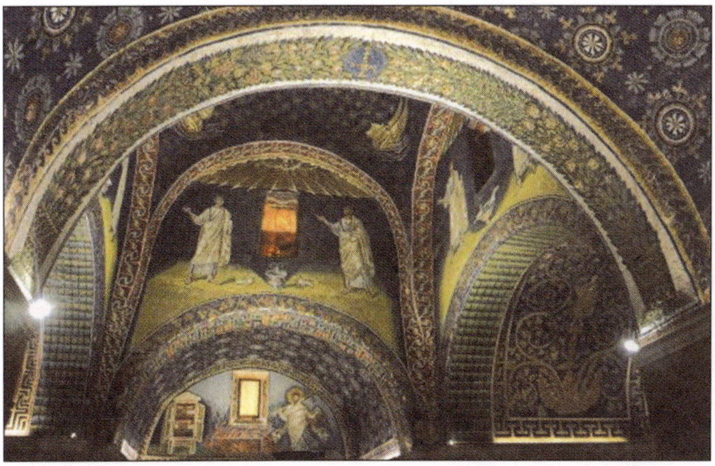

The starry vault in the Mausoleum of Galla Placidia, 425 CE Ravenna

Mosaics

The highest expression of Byzantine art is the mosaic. Mostly found in peripheral or marginal areas (such as the Balkans of Asia Minor), Byzantine mosaic production mainly featured icons painted on wood in enamel and gold, decorated with precious stones. The icon is an image, an expression of simple and popular taste, depicting the Madonna, the saints, or Christ.

Features common to both pictorial representations and Mosaics are:

- A predilection for the allegorical symbolic image
- A tendency towards abstractions and semantic images
- Flattening of the forms
- Unrealistic colour, exalted for its intrinsic value
- Frontalism of the figures and a fixity of gestures
- Little naturalistic environmental details

Frescoes in the Middle Ages

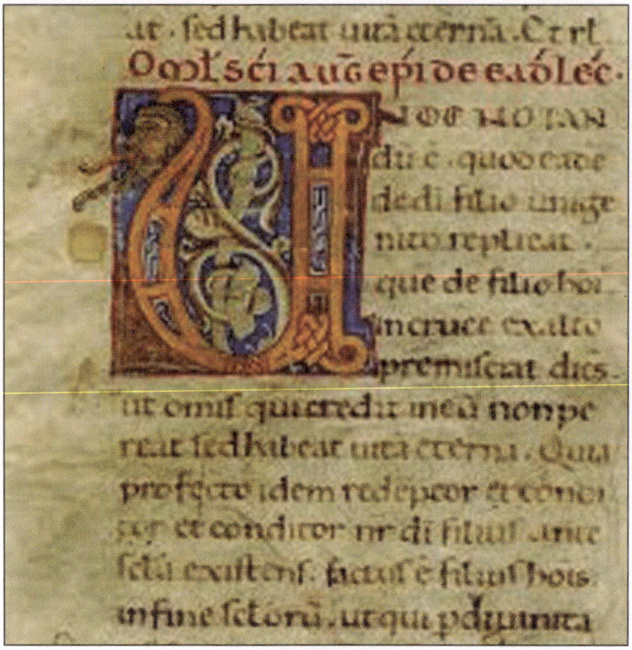

Miniati codes

In the eighth century, some cycles of frescoes began to appear in Rome as church decorations. During the ninth century and the Carolingian artistic renaissance, the fresco style of decoration was revived in the Benedictine Abbeys.

Illustration

An example of the work produced in this period is the Miniati codes. The term 'miniature' derives from the red colour used to paint the initials of the manuscript texts. The monks used to adorn the initials of the pages with small illustrations in watercolours and on parchment.

Sculpture

In the domain of sculpture, figures were represented mostly frontally, in static poses, with little sense of perspective, and as rough bodies with fixed features. There is no psychological characterization: the features appear all the same, as ecstatic stereotypes. The only sense of perspective present is in the context of the social standing of the characters: the most powerful characters are represented as the biggest, the least powerful are the smallest.

The use of ornamental relief for decoration of sacred structures prevailed. The sarcophagi (tombs) made in Ravenna from the fifth century show a different structure compared to the Roman ones: the case is decorated on all four sides, surmounted by a semi-cylindrical cover. The reliefs present single figures.

Architecture

In this period, the conversion of the Lombards to Christianity by Pope Gregorio Magno took place. Architecture was based on Byzantine early Christian aspects; however, there was also a new barbarian influence on the masonry components and abstract decorations.

San Marco Venezia

The Basilica of San Marco in Venice, begun in 1063, was built over an older church which had been destroyed by fire. It was modelled on the Basilica of the 12 Apostles of Constantinople (also called

S.Sofia a Istanbul). The Byzantine style of this church definitely distinguishes it from contemporary Italian Romanesque buildings. In fact, Venice transfers the material-spiritual heritage of Byzantium to the West. The Basilica also introduced the New Greek cross structure. The decoration of the mosaics began in 1071. The mosaics cover the walls, the vaults and the domes of the basilica for over 8000 m^2. They depict stories taken from the Bible (ancient and new testament), events of the life of Christ, of the Madonna, and of San Marco. The golden aura that is the background to the mosaics gives unity to the entire mosaic coating and also conveys a symbolic value; the images are, of God himself.

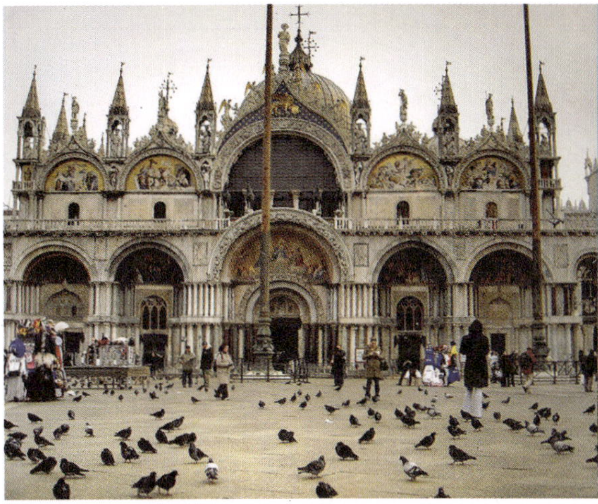

San Marco, Venezia, Italy

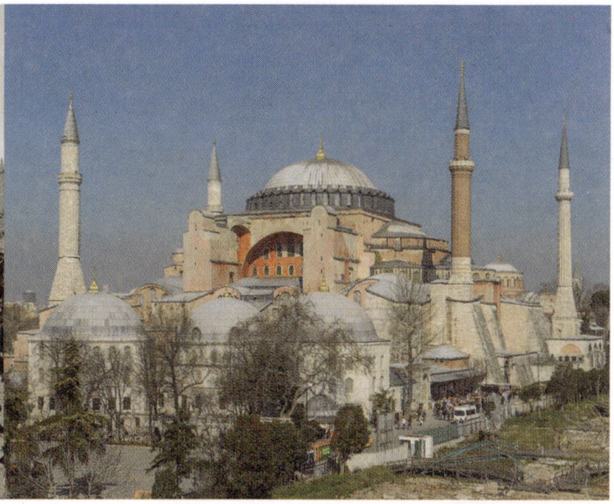

Santa Sofia, Istanbul , Turkey

Music

Between the sixth and the seventh century, when the liturgical chant was rearranged by St. Gregory the Great, alphabetic notation was established by the neuMatica, using signs called neumi. These were small lines derived from accents, and they were placed above or below the syllables of the word of the text to be sung. These signs were anything but precise, indicating only approximately the ascending downward movement of the voice without defining the intervals. They were a reminder of already-known melodies. This notation was used for vocal music, while the capital letters of the Latin alphabet continued to be traced to instrumental music. Over time, the neuMatic notation began to stabilize: the neumes assumed a distinct form and were connected by a line, and particular signs indicated the keys of C and D. In the seventh century, bar divisions were introduced.

In the eighth century, the ternary concept prevailed and was largely reworked with L'ars Nova at the time of Marchetto da Padova. Alongside the tertiary system, which was said to be 'perfect', the binary concept, called 'imperfect', was also used. In the ninth century, Guido d'Arezzo adopted a four-line system, the tetragrammaton, which could indicate the height of the sound for the neumati presentation whilst retaining the alphabetic signs as the key to reading the annotation.

Between the years 1450 and 1600, the rhythmic modes underwent a transformation. They began to delineate with particular significance the maximum, the long, the short, the semibreve, the minimum, and so on. Notes changed from a square shape to the current round shape for speed and convenience's sake.

The Lower Middle Age

III

Edited by

Rushda Anwer, Vibhushita Singh

Designed By

Aatif Nawaz, Saniya Arshad,
Vibhushita Singh, Yumna Ahmad

The Lower Middle Age

Historical Background (Ninth to Fourteenth Century)

- Disaggregation of the Holy Roman Empire (which had been founded by Charlemagne in the ninth century) and full affirmation of feudalism (ninth to twelfth century).
- Thanks to a general recovery of the economy and the rebirth of the cities, we see the rise of the bourgeoisie class. The new city centre, which is the protagonist of a political and social renewal, will find its maximum expression in the 'Municipality'—the antithesis to the feudal system.
- Although the church remains a powerful centre for the dissemination of culture, it no longer retains its monopoly. This enables the development of secular schools.
- Emperor Svevo Federico II founded the University of Naples, and between the years 1230 and 1250, scholars gathered around his court in Palermo. These exponents of European and Arab culture gave life to the Sicilian school, and were protagonists of the first attempt at poetry in the common tounge.
- Between the end of the twelfth and the beginning of the thirteenth century, the dominions begin to replace the seigniories. The sunset of the two guiding institutions of the medieval age also began: the empire, which approaches its decline after the death of Frederick II of Swabia in 1250, and the Church, weakened by the transfer of the papal seat to Avignon in 1308.
- At the beginning of the thirteenth century, we have an abrupt cultural arrest due to famine between 1310–1347which concluded with the terrible European Black Plague in 1348.
- After the sunset of the Sveva house, the primary cultural seat passed from Palermo to the Tuscan municipalities. The vulgar language triumphed while Latin lost vitality.

Religious Life Post 1000 CE

From 1000–1300 CE, the universal powers of the papacy and the Holy Roman Empire (which had just reached its apogee) began to decline inexorably in favour of the national monarchies that now asserted themselves. This enabled the creation of a Europe which was a mosaic of states and peoples, often similar, but at the same time different from each other.

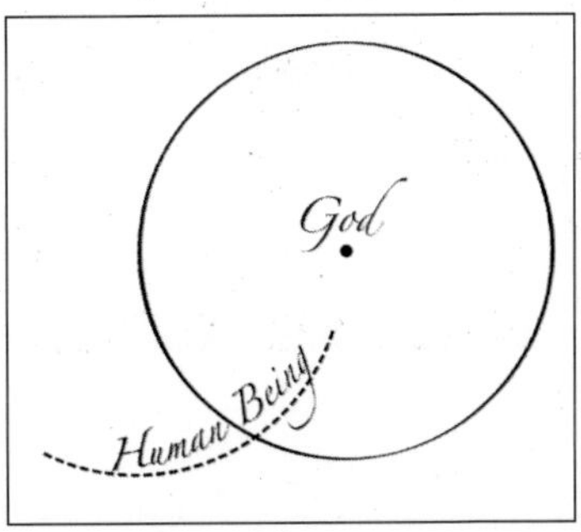

Convergence of man in a society where God was at the centre

This was an extremist period, one which saw all the attention focused on God. During this period, a new spirituality was inserted within an old mindset, one which allowed the insertion of new cultures and new peoples. Man was able to feel less guilty and thus started to express himself creatively again.

We can see a synchronism taking place—God is still in the centre, but man is slowly starting to converge on that focal point. This fact was directly reflected in the architecture of the period, an example being the Romanesque, prevalent in medieval Europe from the eleventh to the twelfth centuries.

The term is not contemporary with the art it describes, but is rather an invention of modern criticism based on the style and materials used by the Romans (who were supposedly the inspiration behind this architecture).

The style is that of thick walls, simple, austere, and not too elaborate architecture. The art is that of frescoes, mosaic or sculpture. The subject of the art is linked to the bible and the church. Examples: St. Ambrogio church in Milan (most important), San Geminiano Church in Modena, San Michele Maggiore in Pavia, San Nicola church in Bari. Artist: Cristo Triumphant by Maestro Guglielmo (strong emphasis on symbolism instead of realism).

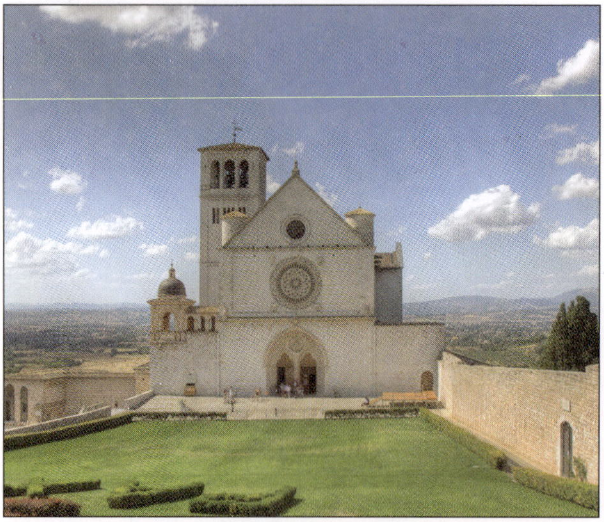

San Francesso Church, Assisi Italy

This period also saw the birth of the 'comuni' municipality (cities which achieved substantial independence), the first universities of the world (often linked to the monasteries), and the birth of religious orders. These gave life to a new movement of liveliness which was expressed in a renewed literary and artistic productivity.

This is particularly well documented in the example of Saint Francis of Assisi (chiesa san Francesco d'Assisi, half gothic and half Romanesque) who celebrated God in a new way—through the worship of His creatures. It is important to point out here that man is one of them, and this shift in thinking brought man back onto the scene.

At this stage the Latin language was not in use among the populace, as only very cultured people were using it. St. Francis started to write in what is known as 'Vulgar Latin', or 'vulgar language' (lingua volgare, volgus meaning normal people), the language of the populace, so that he could be understood by all. He wrote the first poem in Italian called Il Cantico delle Creature. This was the first document in the Italian language. Up until this point, the Italian language was only spoken, never written, because Latin was still the official language of Italy. St. Francis (represented above talking with God's creatures) abandoned the idea of humiliation. He wrote that God's creations are the reflection of the perfection of love. He illustrated this through examples of animals, the sun and the moon. When speaking about God's creatures he is speaking about the perfection of the human being.

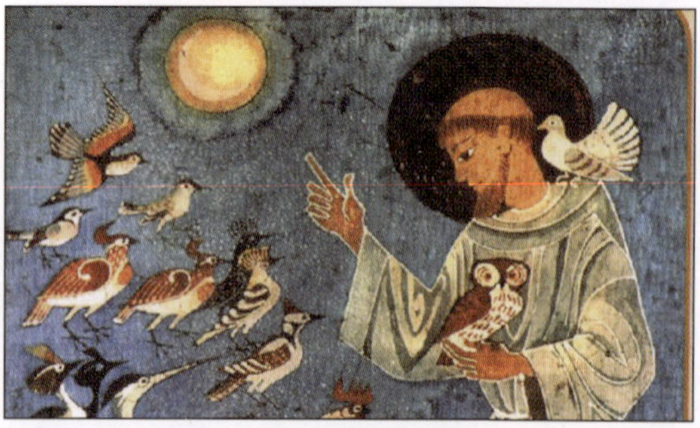

Illustation of Canticum o Laudes Creaturarum, San Francesco d'Assisi

This text is part of the so-called 'religious poetry', whose highest expression is the lauda, a composition containing praises to God. Jacopone da Todi (1236-1306) is a further example of a great religious poet who made use of the lauda.

The Sicilian and Tuscan Schools

In Italy during this period, the towns in the centre and the south of the country were once again unified under a new empire. On a cultural level, we could divide Italy in 1200 into two major groups: the Sicilian school and the Tuscan school.

The empire of Frederick II (1194–1250) was the first modern state in terms of statutes and bureaucracy. It was led by the sovereign who earned the epithet of 'Stupor Mundi' for his court formed of intellectuals, and the continuous and inventive exchange between East and West (transcription of Arabic, Latin and Greek codes).

His court was the home of the Sicilian school, and the poets of this court, in a stable and welcoming political situation, focused on themes of love, staying away from any political content. Inspired by the Provençal tradition, they all used Italian vulgar in their compositions and considered poetry only a refined instrument with which to entertain the aristocratic people of the court.

The head of the Sicilians was Giacamo De Lentini, who gave life to the sonnet (Sonet-melodia).

Io m'aggio posto in core

Io m'aggio posto in core a Dio servire,
com'io potesse gire in paradiso,
al santo loco ch'aggio audito dire,
u' si manten sollazzo, gioco e riso.

Sanza mia donna non vi voria gire,
quella c'ha blonda testa e claro viso,
ché sanza lei non poteria gaudere,
estando da la mia donna diviso.

Ma non lo dico a tale intendimento,
perch'io peccato ci volesse fare;
se non veder lo suo bel portamento

e lo bel viso e 'l morbido sguardare:
ché lo mi teria in gran consolamento,
veggendo la mia donna in ghiora stare.

I have made a promise,
A promise, to serve God,

So that I can go to Heaven.
To that holy place I've heard about, where fun, play and rice lasts endlessly.

I would not want to go without my woman, the one with the blond hair and the luminous face, the light complexion because without her I could not have joy, being divided from my woman.

But I do not say it (I'm not saying all this) in order to want to sin with her, but only because I would like to see her behaving well, her dignified conduct,

And his beautiful face and sweet look; I would consider this a great consolation, see my woman in the glory of paradise.

The Tuscan school, which spread in the area of the municipalities (societies much less stable than that of an empire) stopped not only with 'laudi', sonnets and love songs, but expanded to political and religious themes. Guittone d'Arezzo (1230–1293) was undoubtedly the leader, paving the way for a great artistic flowering which made Florence the centre, for many centuries, of the rebirth of creativity and art.

Romanesque Art

Around the year 1000, the cultural social panorama in all of Europe changed profoundly in comparison to previous centuries with the development of Romanesque art. The definition of Romanesque is attributed to the French archaeologist Clemoun in 1824. He created a parallel between the figurative arts and the creation of Romance languages originating from Latin. The characteristics of Romanesque art include:

- It is unitary, in the sense that it presents a unitary vision of reality
  It is symbolic, as god's vision of the world is expressed in a symbolic language
- It is universal, which becomes the style common to all European architecture
- It is popular, because in the different regions the Romanesque finds its own particular and spontaneous interpretation

The buildings of Romanesque art are simply religious buildings that are made of not necessarily precious material. The use of the cross vault is typical, and the Romanesque church plan is a Latin cross.

Basilica Sant'Ambrogio a Milano

Considered the prototype of Romanesque architecture, this basilica is built in brick on the earlier Paleo-christian basilica. Preceded by a deep quadriportico, it has a gabled façade and a plan with three naves. The central nave is covered by vast cross vaults. Before the presbytery, covered by a barrel vault, there is an octagonal dome.

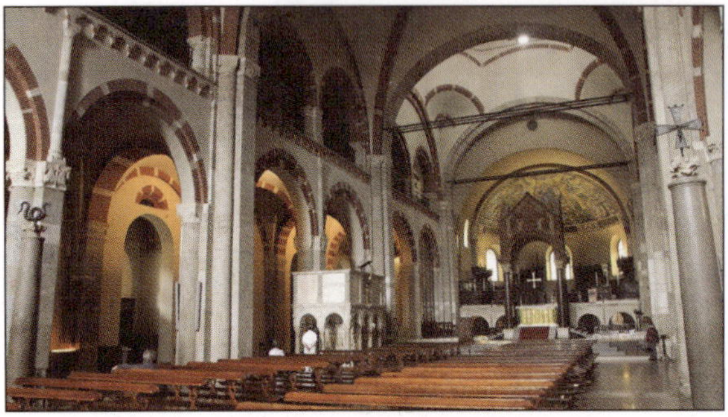

Interiors of the Basilica Sant'Ambrogio

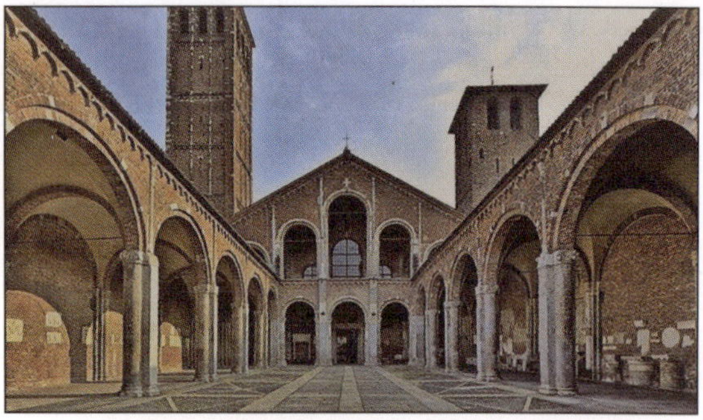

Atrium of the Basilica of Sant'Ambrogio

The Tower of Pisa and the Bell Tower of the Cathedral of Pisa (1173)

The architects involved in these constructions included Bonanno Pisano (who started the works), Giovanni di Simone (who continued the project), and Tommaso Pisano. The projected straight tower began to bow during construction due to the subsidence of the land where it is built. Today, the tower increases its slope by 1mm each year. Its height is 56m. Here Galileo performed his first experiments conceiving the theory of gravity. The Romanesque style is a red thread which characterizes the four monuments of the Pisan square: the tower, the cathedral, the Camposanto and the baptistery—together giving the perfect representation of Romanesque art. The cathedral church stands in the centre of the city, dominating with its the size the houses that are nearby, with the cathedral as the centre of community life.

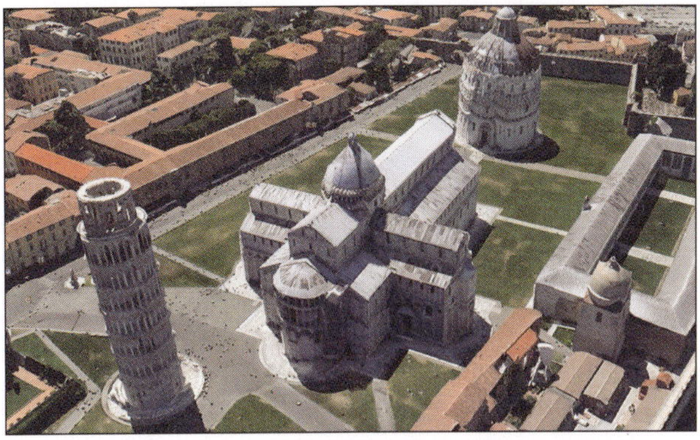

Aerial view of the tower of Pisa and the Piazza dei Miracoli

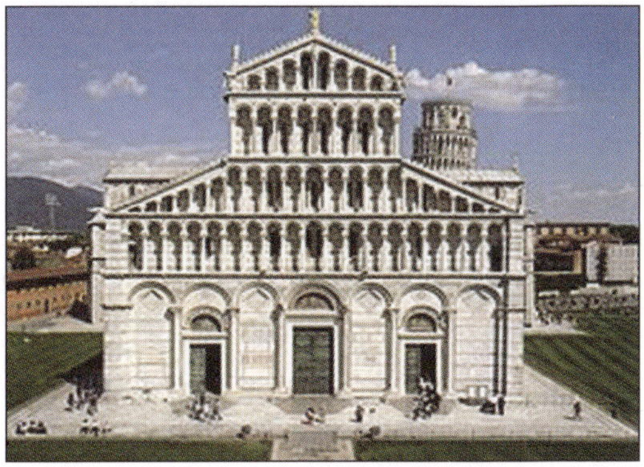

Pisa Cathedral was completed in the year 1092

Sculpture

In Romanesque art, sculpture was considered a necessary integration of the architectural whole of the sacred building, with both a decorative and a structural function. The two key characters were:

- Wiligelmo, who worked in Modena. His work was characterized by a strong expressiveness and archaic plastic conception of the large and heavy sculptural masses that seem to emerge with difficulty from the smooth background.
- Benedetto Antelami was the sculptor who began the history of Italian figurative art of the thirteenth century. This work represents the point of greatest maturity reached by the Lombard Romanesque, and points to the turning of sculpture in the direction of the classical forms of the Italian Gothic.

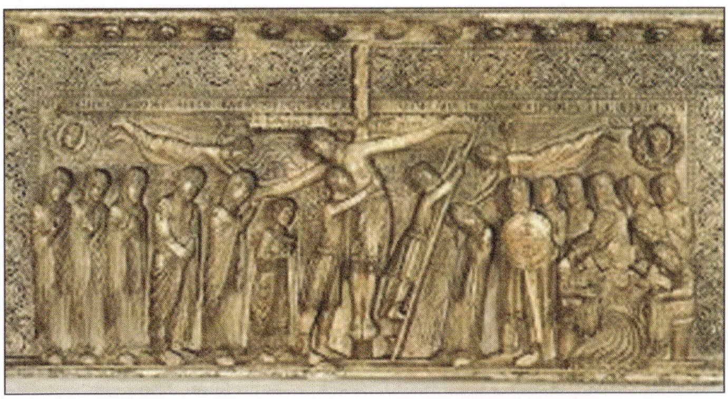

Benedetto Antelami—'Deposition' of Christ, 1178

Painting

Painting and fresco, inspired by naturalism and grandiose classical realism with a mystical imprint, tended towards to a freer and more lively style during this period (see Cimabue). The stylistic features of Romanesque painting are as varied as ever, with Byzantine and Ottonian influences.

Typical characteristics of Romanesque aesthetics:

- Drawing of sharp outlines and use of strong colours
- Plastic sense of the figures
- Expressive, vivacious forms

The main artistic currents:

- The first, inspired by Byzantine art, finds its expression in the Sicilian Venetian mosaics
- The second, which includes the frescoes, is a return to the figurative culture promoted by the Benedictines

1300 CE
Love links man to God

The attempt to bring the human being to the centre of attention is re-emphasized in 1300 CE, with excellent results in the Italian Tuscan area. The city of Florence is key to this. In Italy, a mosaic of municipalities, cities and independent Seigneuries, in their rediscovered freedom, begin to interpose, in their art, subjects that are no longer just religious. Human feelings, through the intercession of God, take shape again. The focus is on love and especially on woman—not intended as a human subject but a creature of God, similar to an angel. This is still far from a dimension in which man, alone, regains all the dignity possessed during the Roman Empire: the woman is not the wife but an idealized Madonna who gives rise to a 'disease', a disease of love, which it is transmitted through sight—the eyes. The ability to overcome this disease, to overcome the crisis, raises the poet spiritually.

This current of thought takes the name of 'stilnovo' (a name coined by Dante Alighieri, in his book *Purgatory*), and was founded by Guido Cavalcanti in 1260. This literary current drives the philosophy underlying all the arts of the age: love. Love is experienced as a deep disturbance, a great passion that, if experienced in the teachings of God, can lead to the rise of the human being. All the characters involved are personifications of feelings and powers of the soul which, through divine breath, can give rise to growth and works of art. To understand this concept, we can look to the manifesto of the movement: 'Al cor gentile remparia semper amore' written by the father of the stilnovo, Guido Guinizzelli. The combination of salute-health (salvation) and love-kindness is explained as two indivisible conditions. Nobility is of the heart, and one who does not possess courage (heart, value) cannot enjoy love.

Women

- Angel or Madonna
- Divine creature who enables the improvement of man

Love

- platonic
- a disturbance that rises
- a quality of noble hearts
- contagion through the eyes

Giotto di Bondone

Giotto provides an example of an artist who was considered a professional, and one who did not hide his talents. He believed in using human abilities to glorify God.

While Cimabue (another artist of the period) painted in a manner that is clearly medieval, Giotto's figures are not stylized or elongated. They are solidly three-dimensional, have faces and gestures that are based on close observation, and are clothed not in swirling formalized drapery, but in garments that hang naturally and have form and weight. He also took bold steps in foreshortening and with having characters face inward with their backs towards the observer—creating the illusion of space.

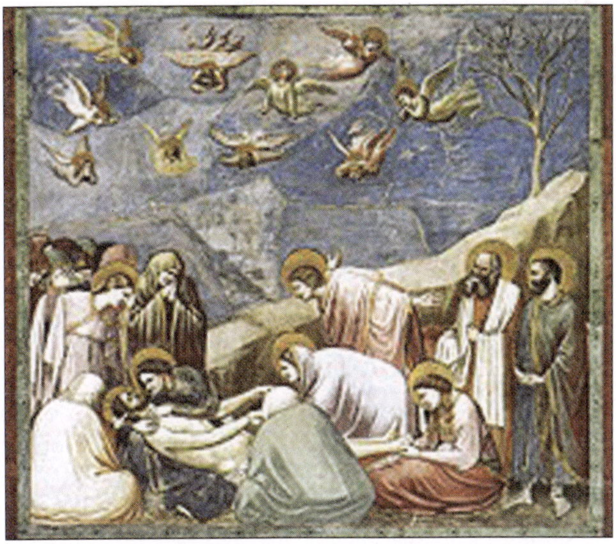

Lamentation (The Mourning of Christ)– Giotto di Bondone

The figures occupied compressed settings with naturalistic elements. Forced perspective techniques were often used so that the settings resembled stage sets. This similarity is increased by Giotto's careful arrangement of the figures in such a way that the viewer appears to have a particular place and even an involvement in many of the scenes. That can be seen most markedly in the arrangement of the figures in the Mocking of Christ and Lamentation, in which the viewer is bidden by the composition that Giotto has created to become mocker in one and mourner in the other.

Giotto's depiction of the human face and emotion sets his work apart from that of his contemporaries.

Of Giotto's realism, the nineteenth-century English critic John Ruskin said, 'He painted the Madonna and St. Joseph and the Christ, yes, by all means... but essentially Mamma, Papa and Baby'.

Besides his pivotal contribution to the development of a new realistic visual language, Giotto might have also been responsible for the reintroduction of true fresco technique to Western art. Technological development allowed for the creation of more durable murals with unprecedented colours and brilliance.

From this period onward in architecture, a mix of Romanesque and gothic styles began to appear. The Duomo di Milano was built—representing the perfection of man in reaching God.

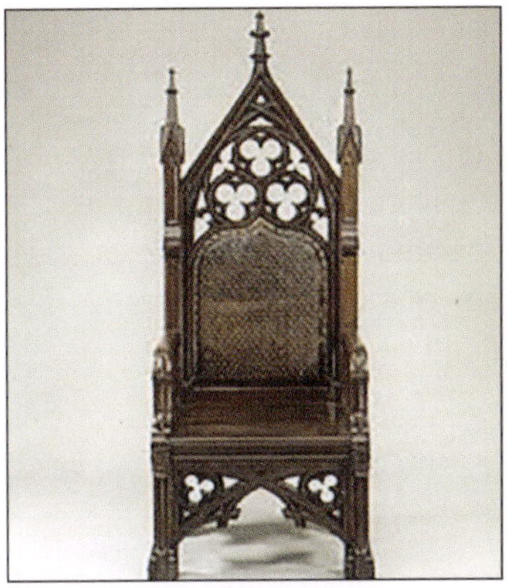

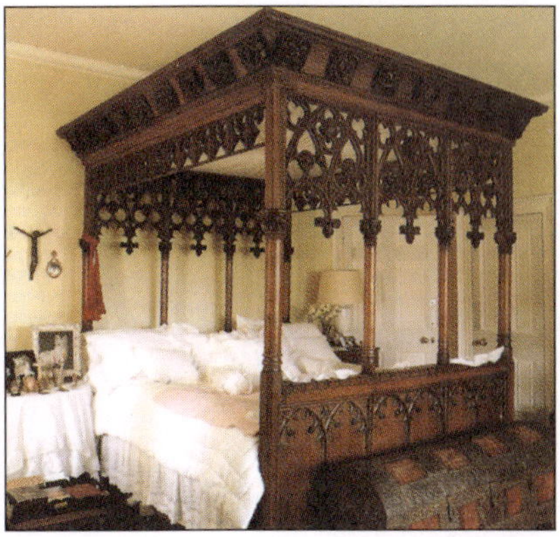

Depiction of the furniture in this era

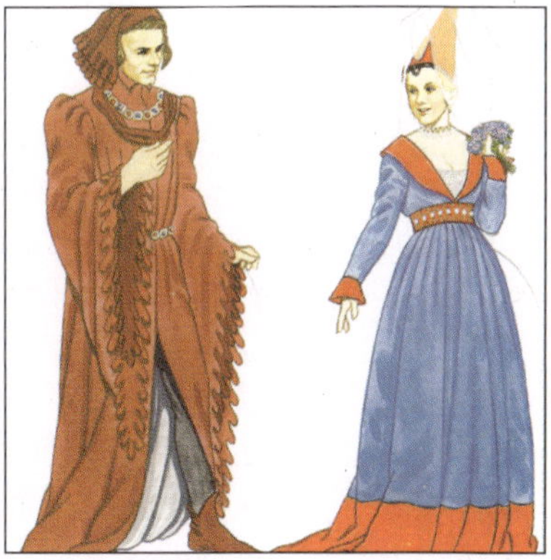

Depiction of the fashion in this era

The new design and aesthetic featured many windows and light, thin walls, an architecture pointing to the sky (symbolically trying to go closer to God), flying buttresses, pointing arches, perforated and aerial structure, accentuated verticalism, and pinnacles. Structure and ornament worked together. There was also a close link between art and architecture: such as new techniques of glass art and paintings on the windows of the churches. Notable artists include Cimabue and Duccio di Buoninsegna (who specialized in the use of gold). Architectural trends correlated closely with the fashion and furnishings of the period. Books were predominantly produced by hand during this period, slowing production and distribution.

Politics

Even in politics, the attempt to return man to the centre of attention is quite visible. In the thirteenth century there is a very strong political and social transformation, the stabilization of the municipal society. This is a break from the Middle Ages, during which the major authority was the papacy (with both spiritual and material power). In 1075, Pope Gregory VII had proclaimed the supremacy of the church over the empire: as far as the power of the church is concerned, however, now, with the attention moving again to man in an attempt to equate interest between human beings and God, the need is begging to be felt to defend spiritual power over material power. Emperor Frederick of Swabia, called 'Barbarossa', wanted to reacquire material power for the empire, leaving the pope with only spiritual power. This struggle is also reflected in the municipalities, which divided internally into two groups: one pro-imperial—defenders of municipal freedom against the papal aims, the other pro papacy.

Dante Alighieri (Florence 1265–1321)

Dante is known as the father of the Italian language. This is because he was the first true theorist of the language, providing rules for the different styles and creating fixed models for prose. In an era in which the themes of high culture were all Latin, he used Italian, enriching it with dialect themes and spoken language. One cannot forget his work, the 'de vulgari eloquentia', which, despite being written in Latin, reaffirms the equal dignity of the Italian language. His two main topics were love and politics. On the one hand, we have in fact the perfect representative of the current of time (the 'Stilnovo') with the themes of love and its unity to nobility of the heart, the woman understood as an angel that elevates to God, a refined language, and a sweet atmosphere. On the other hand, we have the forerunner of political themes such as the belief that philosophy leads to truth and allows us to improve ourselves.

Important landmarks in Dante's life include his meeting with Beatrice (Bice Portinari), a woman whom he did not marry, but who was the personification of this love that allows this elevation. We will now approach the text taken from 'la vita nova', a collection of poems and prose inspired by love for Beatrice. (This work can be divided into two sections, the first part when Beatrice is alive, the second after Beatrice's death.)

Tanto gentile e tanto onesta pare
la donna mia, quand'ella altrui saluta,
ch'ogne lingua devèn, tremando, muta,
e li occhi no l'ardiscon di guardare.

Ella si va, sentendosi laudare,
benignamente e d'umiltà vestuta,
e par che sia una cosa venuta
da cielo in terra a miracol mostrare.

So noble of soul and so full of decorum is my woman, when she greets to others, that every tongue becomes, trembling, mute, and the eyes do not have the courage to look at it.

So she goes, feeling herself praised, benevolent and mild in acting, and appears to be a creature descendant to earth to perform a miracle.

Mostrasi sì piacente a chi la mira
che dà per li occhi una dolcezza al core,
che 'ntender no la può chi no la prova;

e par che de la sua labbia si mova
un spirito soave pien d'amore,
che va dicendo a l'anima: Sospira.

It proves so fascinating to those who look at it that transmits, through the eyes, a sweetness to the heart, such that one who has not felt it cannot understand it;

And it seems that from its physiognomy comes out a sweet spirit filled with love that goes saying to the soul: Sighs.

Dante's most famous work is the *Divine Comedy*. Comedy is a style characterized by a tragic beginning and a happy ending, and this work is written in a medium style which unfolds on the number 3: 3 cantiche (divided into 33 songs plus the introduction) and is written in triplets—stanzas of 3 verses each. This summarizes the structure of the world according to the Ptolemaic system, whereby the earth is in the centre and around it rotate 9 mobile celestial spheres. The northern hemisphere of the earth is inhabited, the inside is constituted of a cavity, and the southern hemisphere is formed by the ocean and purgatory. The *Divine Comedy* is a look at medieval civilization which summarizes the ideologies and knowledge of the era, as well as presenting an awareness of the need for change brought about by linguistic innovations. This work unfolds on the concept that man must strive for good, for a God who gives free will, and for sin to be understood as perverse love—compared to earthly and worldly things instead of heaven and spirituality. It is the story of a journey, intended as a vision of the afterlife, which starts with the author getting lost (concretely in a forest, metaphorically in the principles of life and worldly sin) and then being guided through the 3 kingdoms (hell, purgatory and paradise). Virgil (a representation of human reason) guides the author through the underworld, where hell is divided into 9 circles, in turn divided into 3 categories: sins of inconstancy, of beasts, of malice.

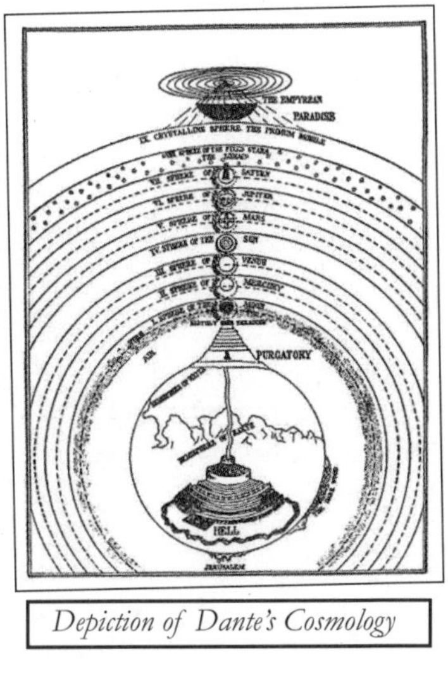

Depiction of Dante's Cosmology

Here, in a sort of law of divine retribution, the penalty varies according to the fault. Hell is characterized by darkness, which is the opposite of divine light. The conduit is eternal. Purgatory kingdom divided into 3 bands: antipurgatory, purgatory—in turn divided into 7 layers like the 7 sins, and, heaven on earth. This kingdom is characterized by punishment but with the hope of redemption and salvation. The atmosphere here is melancholic but sweet at the same time. In heaven, or Paradise, Beatrice is the guide, and having reached the Empyrean, Dante contemplates God and acquires true knowledge. Political-moral themes are dealt with, now clarified and enlightened by divine truth. This kingdom is characterized by brightness and joy. Allegorically, this is the path of the soul.

Francesco Petrarca (Arezzo, 1304)

Another precursor of humanism and of the Renaissance was Francesco Petrarca. Just as with Dante, a woman was his muse and the centre of his poetic work throughout his life. This woman was Laura (Countess De Sade); she did not return the poet's love.

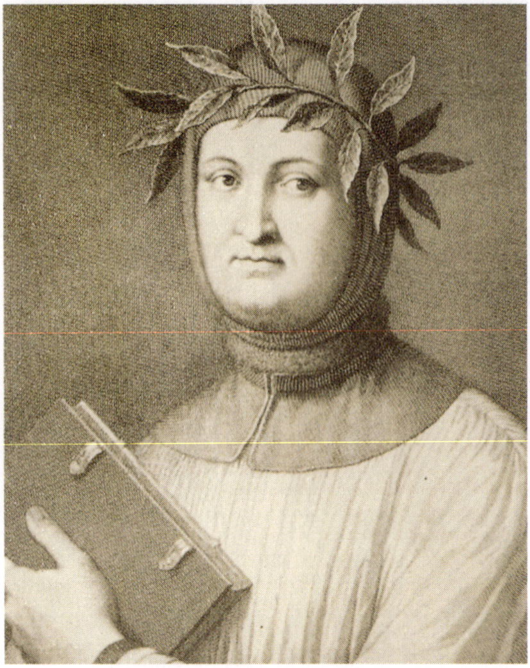

Francesco Petrarca

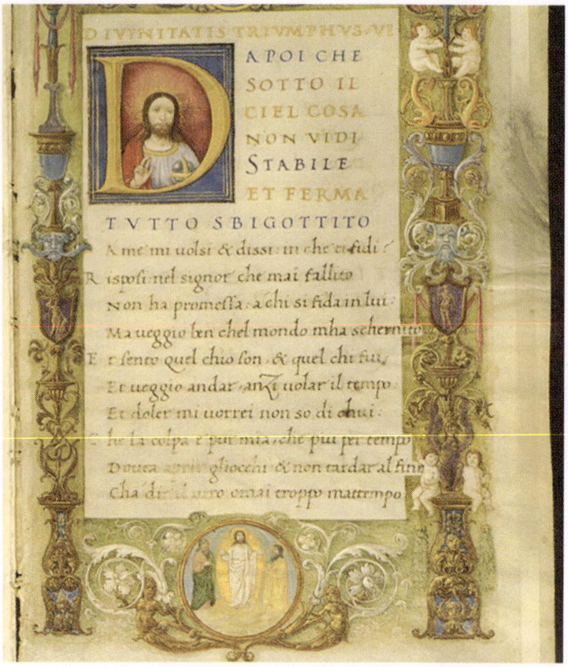

DIVINITATIS TRIVMPHVS VI

DA POI CHE SOTTO IL CIEL COSA NON VIDI STABILE ET FERMA

TVTTO SBIGOTTITO

Non ha promessa a chi si fida in lui:

Ma ueggio ben chel mondo mha schernito

Et sento quel chio son & quel chi fui,

Et ueggio andar anzi uolar il tempo

Et doler mi uorrei non so di chui:

Leaf from Petrarca's Trionfi

Petrarch represented a new type of intellectual, one far from political life, a defender of the freedom of thought. With him the idea of writing as a profession was born: honoured in the various Italian courts, he was the model of the writer who commits his life to culture. We still see the idea of earthly love as a desire for spiritual elevation: through the inner analysis of restlessness and moods the poet can rise to God.

Petrarch is often defined as 'the first humanist', and his work often featured critiques of Latin texts such as those by Cicero and Seneca. Although he did not participate in politics, he exposed his ideals by extolling 'Rome', and suggesting that feudal lords should end the internal battles to give life to 'Italy'—the 'heir to culture'. He also continued the great work of enriching the Italian language, perfecting it and making it elegant (this would give life, in 1500, to the movement called Petrarchism, a phenomenon of imitation of the poet in which the language used is particularly refined, full of metaphors and analogies). Despite this, several of his works are written in Latin. His main work is surely *The Songbook*—a collection of fragments of the soul—the story of unrequited love composed of 366 poems (before and after Laura's death). In these pages, Laura is a vision and a dream who allows the poet to hold an interview with himself, an analysis of the effects of love on his soul (expectations, hopes, anguish...) and a meditation on the fugacity of material things.

Additionally, the text that best embodies Platonic love and woman-as-divine is surely *Erano i capei d'oro a l'aura sparsi* :

Erano i capei d'oro a l'aura sparsi
che 'n mille dolci nodi gli avolgea,
e 'l vago lume oltra misura ardea
di quei begli occhi, ch'or ne son sì scarsi;

Laura's blonde hair was scattered in the wind that enveloped them in many sweet curls, and the seductive splendour of those eyes, now much less luminous, sparkled in an extraordinary way;

e 'l viso di pietosi color' farsi,
non so se vero o falso, mi parea:
i' che l'esca amorosa al petto avea,
qual meraviglia se di sùbito arsi?

Non era l'andar suo cosa mortale,
ma d'angelica forma; e le parole
sonavan altro che, pur voce umana;

uno spirto celeste, un vivo sole
fu quel ch'i' vidi: e se non fosse or tale,
piagha per allentar d'arco non sana

and it seemed to me that the face, I do not know if it really or only in my imagination, was coloured with pity; I, who had placed the loving bait in my heart, Is it any wonder if you immediately flared with love?
Her gait was not that of a mortal body, but of a heavenly angel, and her voice sounded like something different from the human voice.

A heavenly spirit, a shining sun, it was what I saw, and if even now it was not so, the wound does not heal by loosening the arch.

Giovanni Boccaccio (1313–1375)

Boccaccio is another of the great characters of the 1300s. He was the first practitioner of the novel is well as being its creator. Whilst at the court of Naples, Boccaccio was under the spiritual direction of Petrarch, who pointed him towards to humanistic studies. Also, he focused on classical Greek, and wrote several works in Latin. His masterpiece is certainly the 'Decameron' (1349–1351), a title derived from the Greek word for 10 days. It is a set of 100 novellas told in 10 days by 7 girls and 3 boys—refugees in the countryside escaping the plague (here is the frame for the entire book).

Every day these children tell 10 stories on a theme set by the 'king' or 'queen' on duty: these themes are the perfect fresco of contemporary society, and of the framework of all the social classes that make it up. The varied situations, classes and environments are represented by a different style depending on the speaker. It is a secular comedy: a comedy of man told in a relational language. It portrays a world in which man is the only one who captures the centre of attention—a reality guided by the power of love and fortune that man exploits thanks to intelligence.

The most salient themes are: intelligence in all its forms (the most astute to the simplest), love in all its variations (sexual, passionate, unhappy), luck, (understood not as destiny connected to God, but as a chance that modifies situations and gives opportunities) courtesy, nobility of sentiments, and dignity (not based on the social condition but on the soul of man). The addressees of the work are women; to distract them from the pains of love and to alleviate the suffering in their lives. However, in reality, this represents the will of the author to turn to a new public, not belonging to the narrow circle of writers, but to the new social elite: the courtly bourgeoisie.

This marks this emergence of a new literary genre, the novel, in which stories are narrated for the simple entertainment of the reader.

Other Literary Genres

Poetry in the Vernacular

In the second half of the 1200s, vulgar poetry, consisting of vulgarizations (more or less free translations of text in Latin or French), continued to spread also by the expressive medium of historiographic memorial production.

The Provençal Lyric

Since the end of the eleventh century, troubadours had been working in the courts of southern France—especially in Provence—composing verse and music. The Occitan lyric, named for the language in which it is written (the language of Oc), is transmitted orally and enjoys a musical accompaniment; it is recited in public by the jesters. Each of them prefers above all the theme of love, but also features political, satirical and moral themes.

The Epic-Chivalric Lyric

In the mid-eleventh century, in the north of France, Turoldo signed himself as the author of the chanson de Roland. This work inaugurated the epic-chivalric literary vein—addressed to the aristocratic environment of the courts. The production is divided into three cycles: Carolingian cycle, Breton cycle and Classic cycle. The knightly epic elaborates the legends from Celtic mythology and the stories of King Arthur (the king of Bretons), who lived in the fourth century. The protagonists are courageous knights such as Lancelot and Percival.

Art (continued)

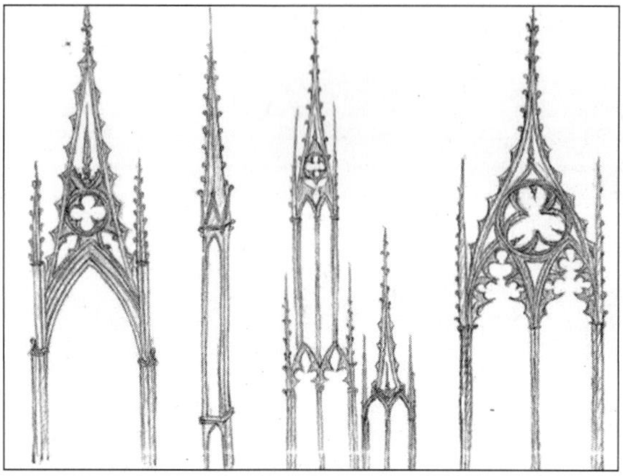

Gothic elements

In the first half of the twelfth century, Gothic art developed in the area around France, stretching out around Paris. In the thirteenth century it spread to Germany, England, the Netherlands and Italy. Originally, the term 'Gothic' was used in the Italian Renaissance with negative connotations, indicating medieval art. Considered to be of little value, it was the work of barbarian peoples.

At the base of gothic art is the idea of the 'perfect' work: the artist, through his work, must succeed in creating beauty, which means the divine moment of spiritual elevation, and a constant search for perfection. Thus, Gothic art brings to an extreme the consequences of the elements that emerged in the Romanesque period: lines are lengthened and stylized, structures are lightened, forms become more ethereal, sweet and sinuous. In architecture, sacred constructions must surprise and astonish, pushing vertiginously towards The Other spires, pinnacles, decorations and sculptures.

Religious Architecture in Europe

The highest expression of the Gothic was in the field of religious architecture. In clear contrast to the Romanesque style (characterized by the use of a round arch, robust structures and small windows), the Gothic style featured pointed arches, slender spires and stained glass windows. Usually, the façade was topped by twin spires and had a large rose window above the central door. Examples of such structures include

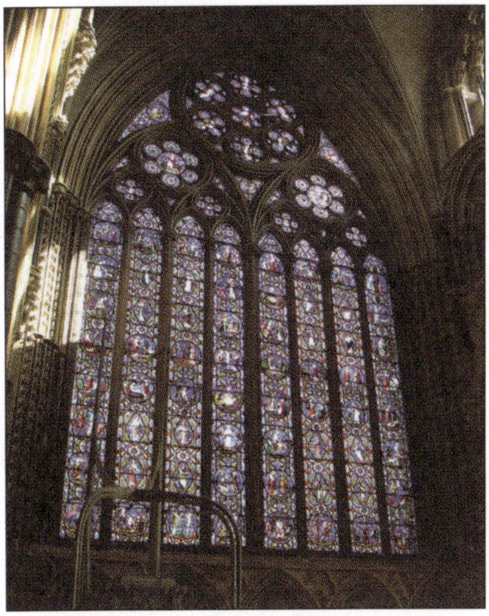

Gothic, Lincoln Cathedral, Gothic window

the Notre Dame in Paris (built 1163–1220). During the thirteenth century, the Gothic style spread in southern France (Provencal Gothic), in Germany, in England and in Spain. By the start of the fifteenth century, the Gothic style had assumed a more ornamental and lively character (flamboyant or flowery Gothic).

In Italy, the Gothic style adopted details such as acute arches within a measured system that continued the Romanic harmony. Italian Gothic cathedrals were characterized by a balance between the vertical momentum of the horizontal structures and the clear play of geometric masses and flat surfaces. An example of a Gothic cathedral is Milan Cathedral (begun in 1386).

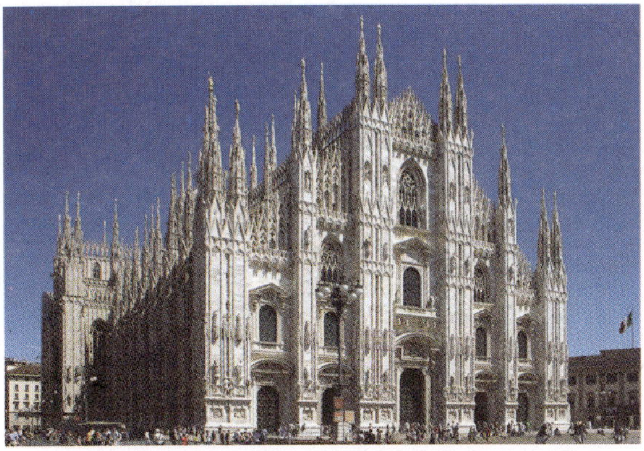

The Cathedral of Milan

The Cistercian order, founded in 1908 by San Bernardo, made a decisive contribution to the spread of the Gothic style—promoting an austere version without any superfluous ordering. In its rigorous simplicity, it differed profoundly from the style of Gothic cathedrals.

From the thirteenth century, the churches erected by Franciscans and Dominicans met a need common to the two orders—to establish an intense communicative relationship with the faithful. The churches featured a single and wide nave, 'poor' materials, a simplicity of structure and a thick roof.

Civil architecture

The importance of the city is growing during this period; their centres of gravity constituted by the cathedrals and the municipal buildings. In the thirteenth and fourteenth centuries, the cities are enriched by increasingly sumptuous public and private buildings that progressively move away from the fortress type of house and towards the representative city palace. Examples are the Palazzo della Signoria in Florence or the Palazzo Ducale Venezia.

Sculpture

Sculpted figures are no longer confined to wall murals; they assume greater dignity and a more defined volume as free-standing statues. The fundamental characters are: linearism, sinuous features, expressive naturalism in the characterization of the characters depicted, and a balanced composition of statues and reliefs. Key sculpters from the period include:

Nicola Pisano (1210—1280)

Classicism, inspired by the composition of ancient sarcophagi, is combined with a Gothic form of expression in Pisano's work. His sculpture represents a synthesis of the different conceptions of Italian sculpture reworked in a plastic language- rich in human sensitivity and characterized by the presence of a formal compositional balance.

Giovanni Pisano (Pisa, 1248–1314)

The son of Nicola, Giovanni developed the Gothic component, exaggerating the expressiveness of the characters and accentuating the dynamic aspects of his compositions. He introduced a strong chiaroscuro play in the juxtaposition of mobile and luminous surfaces, and of deeply excavated voids.

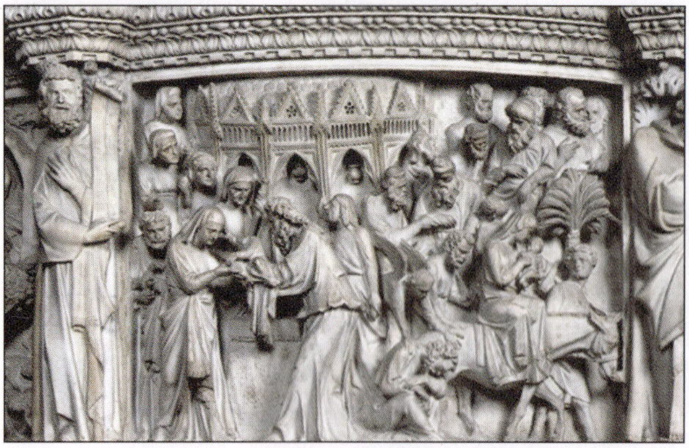

Giovanni Pisano, Pulpito del Duomo di Pisa, 1302–11

Arnolfo di Cambio (1245–1302)

Cambio was a sculptor, architect and author of the project of the Duomo of Florence. His compositions were termed 'humanistic', conceived for clear volumetric masses.

Andrea Pisano (Florence, 1290–1349)

Pisano is known for being the executor of the first bronze door for the baptistery of Florence and the panels carved for Giotto's bell tower.

Santa Maria del Fiore Cathedral

Construction of the cathedral of Santa Maria was begun at the end of the twelfth century on the site of the previous Romanesque structure. It was completed only at the end of the following century. Between 1258 and 1285, the direction of the works was entrusted to Nicola Pisano and his son Giovanni. Nicola Pisano decorated the lower part of the facade and its magnificent portals, considered one of the best representations of Italian Gothic style. The outside of the church does not have the typical buttresses of the Gothic, as the façade is entirely covered with white Carrara marble crossed by green strips of Prato marble.

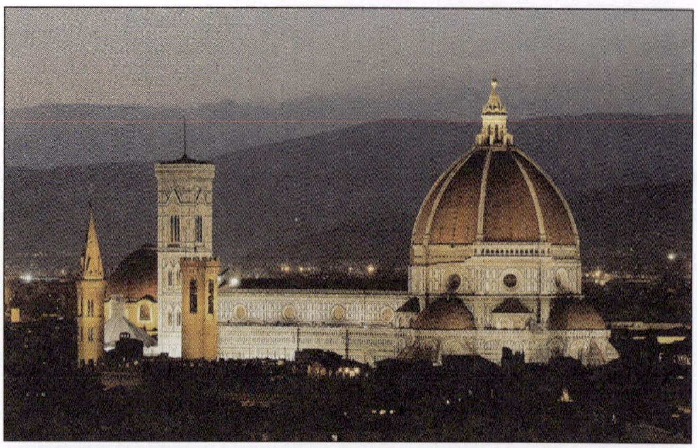

Cathedral of Santa Maria del Fiore, completed in 1434

The works stopped for some time because of the plague of 1348. The upper façade was created by Giovanni di Cecco, and the dome of the bell tower is in

Romanesque style. The interior follows the Latin-cross design. In the left transept is the octagonal pulpit by Nicola Pisano; supported by lions, the seven slabs that make up the parapet represent stories of Christ: the Nativity, the adoration of the Magi, the presentation at the temple, etc.

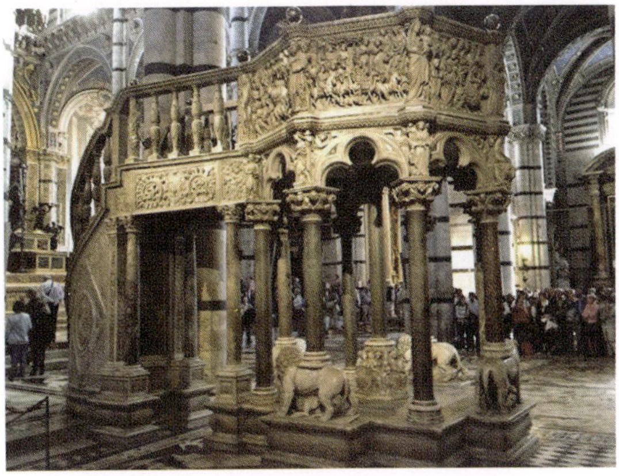

Nicola Pisano's baptistery pulpit

Painting

Up until the third century, paintings featured very stylized figures surrounded by decorative elements. The subjects were generally sacred, and greater importance was given to them, rather than the development in depth of the composition. The painters were Cimabue, Giotto and Duccio di Buoninsegna, each one central to Sienese painting of the thirteenth and fourteenth centuries.

Cimabue

Cenni of Pippo, called Cimabue, was born in Florence around 1240 and died around 1302. He was responsible for the first structural reform of painting; similar to that made in the domain of sculpture by Nicola Pisano. The reform was based on the rediscovery of the classical Latin matrix and on the Byzantine iconographic tradition, and was expressed in the plastic value given to the chiaroscuro figures.

Three of his masterpieces:

The crucifix of Santa Croce

The crucifix on the table of the church of Santa Croce in Florence is characterized by the use of chiaroscuro and a dramatic representation of the position of the body of Christ. It demonstrates the beginning of an artistic evolution which goes beyond Byzantine style.

La maestà, 1280

The image of the Madonna, created for the church of The Holy Trinità of Florence, shows the woman portrayed in the foreground surrounded by angels and prophets,
depicted with more human features than the Byzantine style.

Fresco

The frescoes of the Upper Basilica of San Francesco d'Assisi (1280). These feature a great and dramatic representation of figure and space.

Duccio 1250–1318

Perhaps the greatest exponent of Sienese painting of the thirteenth and fourteenth centuries, Duccio expressed the transition from the Byzantine forms to the new stability of the Gothic style.

In his painting he achieved an ideal beauty through the creation of images in which the profound sense of the sacred is expressed in a language of extreme formal elegance. This elegance, together

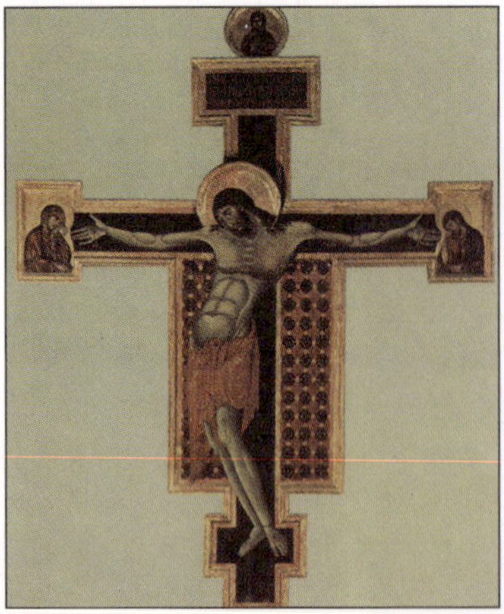

The Crucifix by Cimabue at Santa Croce

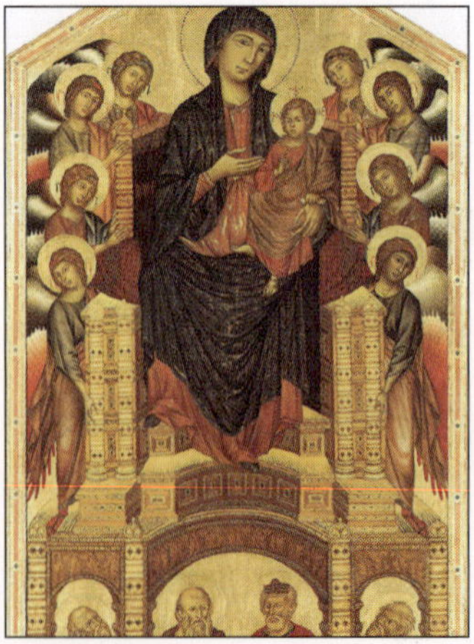

Maestá of Duccio at the Siena Cathedral, 1308

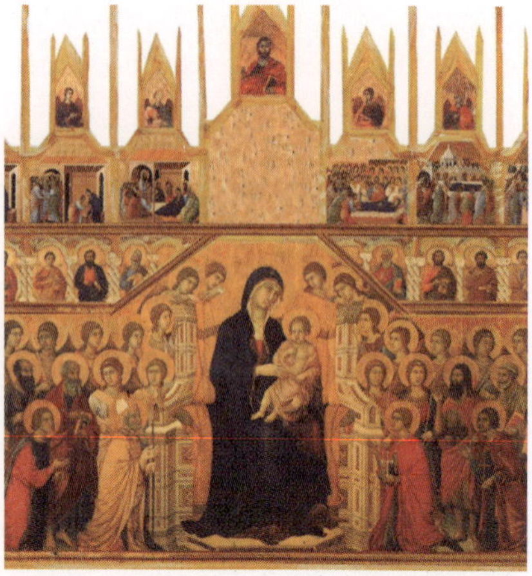

Madonna and Child, Duccio di Buoninsegna, 1300

with the line, enhances the bright and intense colouring, allowing expression of an antiplastic and strictly colouristic concentration. An example of his work is la maestà of the Duomo of Siena (created in 1311). This masterpiece of Sienese painting of the fourteenth century was called 'Majesty' on account of the position in which the Madonna is portrayed. In most medieval paintings, the main figure was represented in front, at the height of his or her power. The part depicting the Madonna enthroned with the child, surrounded by saints and kneeling angels, addressed the central nave (and therefore, the faithful). The back part, illustrated with 26 scenes of the Passion of Christ, was reserved for ecclesiastics. It focuses on the elegance of the shapes, and on the lines of colour harmony.

Giotto di Bondone

Born around 1267 in the countryside near Florence, Giotto completed his apprenticeship at Cimabue. He was the greatest painter of his time, and also the greatest innovator of the figurative language of his time, like Dante was in the poetic field. His work represents a synthesis of the different artistic visions of his time, from the Byzantine Romantic tradition to the taste of the gothic and the recovery of early Christian classical art.

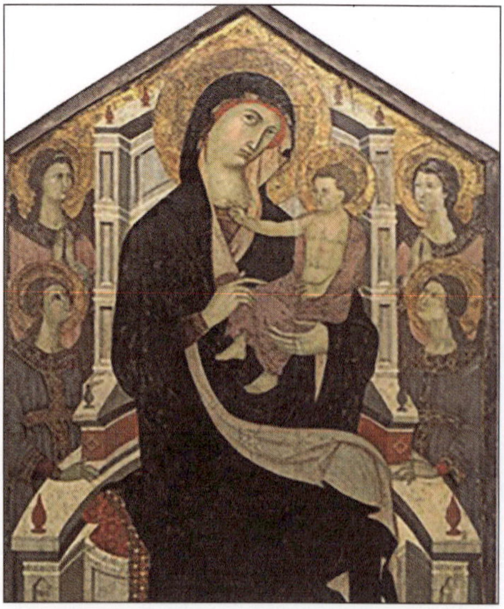

Maesta of Duccio at the Siena Cathedral, 1308

The profound transformation carried out by Giotto concerns the figure of the artist, whose inventive capacity is enhanced, art being no longer considered simply a technical/ manual skill as was the case in the past. Naturalism, with its plastic description of reality, represents the possibility of interpreting nature, history and life, as well as being a valid tool for translating emotions and feelings into images. With Giotto a new era is born.

The image of the Madonna, created for the church of The Holy Trinità of Florence, shows the woman portrayed in the foreground surrounded by angels and prophets, depicted with more human features than the Byzantine style.

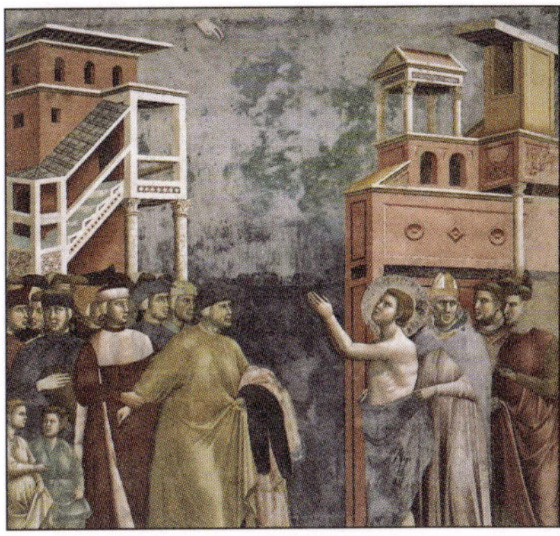

Renunciation of Worldly Goods

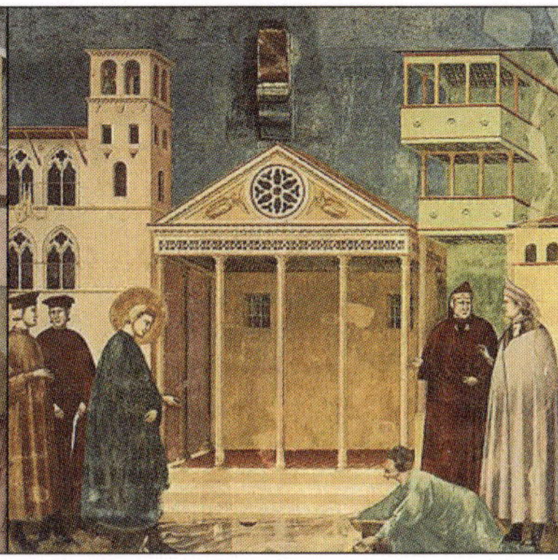

The Legend of St. Francis

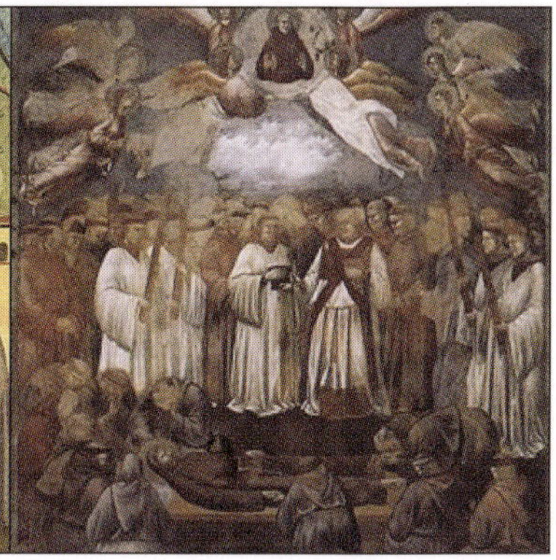

Death and Ascension of St. Francis

His main works are:

- The frescoes of the church of San Francesco d'Assisi

In 1296, the Franciscans of Assisi called on Giotto to paint in the superior church, and entrusted him with the task of painting the cycle of the stories of St. Francis (1296–1300). There are 28 squares located under the windows, where Giotto tells the most popular episodes of Francis's life. The painter paints the space and the characters, representing them in the reality of everyday life. The medieval cities are depicted with the edifice, the real characters in the clothes of the time. Each painting is a complete story, and the scene is told between the space of the painting and the architectural space of the nave.

- The frescoes of the Scrovegni Chapel in Padua

The banker Rico of the Scrovegni family, called Giotto to decorate the walls of the family chapel between 1303 and 1310. The painted figures recall gothic sculptures, because the painter creates, with colours and light, the illusion of depth on a flat surface.

Of the Sienese painters, the most significant were Simone Martini, Pietro Lorenzetti and Ambrogio Lorenzetti. They followed aulic and refined ideals, typical of the Sienese taste for an aristocratic and chivalrous vision and elegance in linear design.

Dramatic and Theatrical Style

Lauda drammatica

In Italy, a particular type of sacred drama was born: Lauda—a poetic composition of religious inspiration. Its emergencc coincided with the recurrence of the liturgical calendar, and it flourished within the lay confraternities in the middle of the thirteenth century. The most famous work is the 'Tears of the Madonna', also known as 'donna de Paradiso' by Jacopo ne da Todi (1236–1306). This work is a dramatic conversation between Jesus and the Madonna, set against the backdrop of the Passion and the blasphemous screaming croud. From the tragically sweet affection of the virgin to the violent cruelty of the crowd, from the separation of the pain of the son to sadness and the contemplation of a divinity distance, a new accent is born in which drama becomes a commissioned meditation on the human condition. The Lauda was a dialogue for multiple voices: the voice of the soloist sang to the room, and the chorus answered with the refrain.

Humanism

IV

Edited by
Kriti Kundu

Designed By
Yumna Ahmad, Fateh Veer Singh Guram,
Shazaib Ali Naik

Umanesimo (Humanism)

History

In the fifteenth century, Italy is divided into many small states. Most of these are lordships, i.e., territories in which power is in the hands of a single lord. Among the Italian lords of the fifteenth century, the lordship of Florence (the Medici family) predominates. When Lorenzo, called 'the magnificent', becomes lord, the city experiences a great cultural flowering. In Italy there are also republics, the most prestigious being the Republic of Venice, also called 'serenissima'.

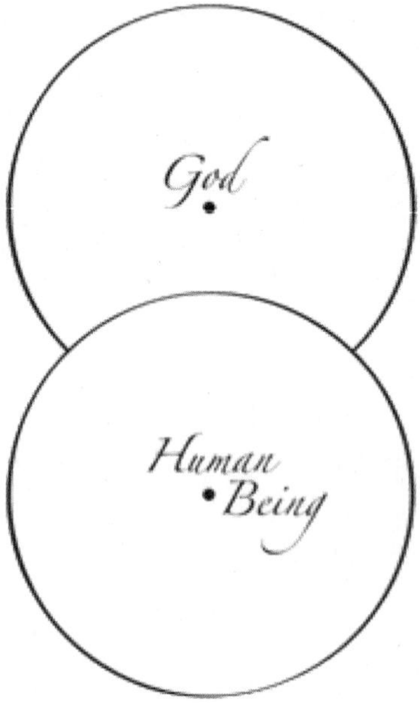

The juxtaposition of human beings and God

The year 1492 is the most important of the century owing to the discovery of America by the Genoese Cristoforo Colombo, but it is also the year of Lorenzo's death and the beginning of the decadence of the lordship of Florence. One of the most important inventions is that of movable type printing. Thanks to the press, it will be possible to produce copies of books more easily (Giovanni Guttenberg published the first printed Bible in 1455).

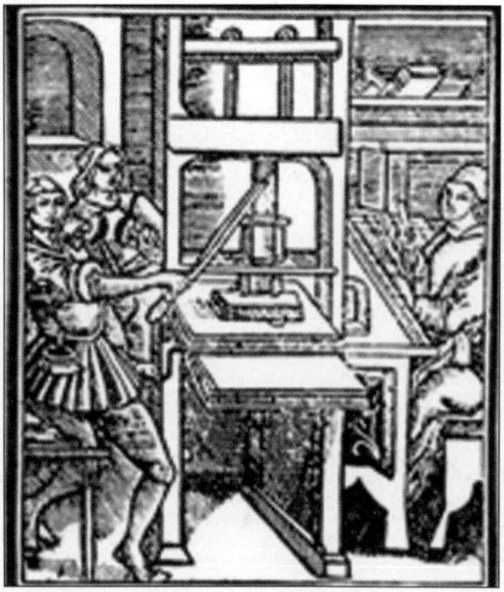

Guthenburg printing press

Until now we have seen how, after the Middle Ages, there had been an attempt to bring man back to the centre of attention, close to God. This process initially occurred in 1200 through the attempt to praise God through his creatures and therefore also through the grandeur of man (here we remember St. Francis of Assisi). The Sicilian and then Tuscan poets contributed in this direction, introducing the theme of love, a human feeling. The authors of the fourteenth century have taken up this vein and have greatly enriched it, thanks to the fact that love could raise man to God himself, endowed by the goodness of God, with woman as a means by which the poet could overcome limits until rising to the divine.

In 1400, we finally see the completion of the process that had begun in 1200: man no longer needs God to regain his dignity. Man is back at the centre in a unequivocal way and we see a return in interest in the historical period that had idealized man in all his splendour: Greek and Roman periods.

The age of humanism and the Renaissance occupies the fifteenth and the first half of the sixteenth century. Referring to this era, we speak of renewal, rebirth, humanism and the Renaissance. This period could be divided into two phases: Humanism, which characterized the entire fifteenth century, and the Renaissance, which occupies the first three decades of the 1500s.

The two moments must be considered together because, despite their differences, they are linked by a continuity of attitudes and objectives. If humanism is the age of the study of the Latin and Greek classics, of a new conception of life based on the centrality of man, we cannot forget that humanism is also preparatory to the Renaissance.

Starting from the middle of the fifteenth century, there is a noticeable political, economic and cultural recovery: this brings to light the new secular concept, which is worldly and has been conveyed by humanism. Salient aspects of humanism are:

- The rejection of the Middle Ages, seen as a dark century, an era of cultural, spiritual obscurantism
- The exaltation of anthropocentrism, man considered the absolute author of his own destiny
- The affirmation of values such as wealth, political activity and civil commitment
- The passionate attention to the classical world, to philology (the study of human letters), and to the disciplines which have as their object man in his earthly experience. The scholars, in fact, are humanists, in reference to the definition of Cicero, which is called 'umanitates', the disciplines aimed at perfecting the spirit. In the linguistic field, the humanists express themselves rigorously in Latin, even if they promote the literary model of Dante Boccaccio's Tuscan vernacular
- The affirmation of the Academy's courts

The objectives are changing in this historical period, and so, as often happens, the vernacular language changes too. The question of language we are discussing here is of fundamental importance for the expansion of spoken Italian. In 1441, Leon Battista Alberti established the 'certame coronario', a poetic vulgar competition that gives dignity to Italian intellectuals and writers. This poses the problem of setting a written norm for Italian.

This is a debate that confronts three theories: written Italian must be the language which was spoken in the courts of the entire peninsula with a certain homogeneity. The second current, with Nicolò Machiavelli, argues that we must adopt the contemporary Florentine. Finally, the third group, whose thesis will prove to be successful, maintains that the Florentine written from 1300 should be based on the models of Petrarch and Boccaccio.

This does not detract from the fact that during the first half of the fifteenth century, most work is written mainly in Latin. In this period, we have the recovery of classical antiquity. The literary genre that dominates is the treatise: the treatise appears, in fact, the ideal genre to explain the new values to the new vision of the world.

Next to the treatises, however, lyrical and narrative works are written, and it will be the narrative, with the spread of the chivalric poem, which dominates the second half of the century. Another genre is theatre, with the revival of the comedies of Plautus and Terence.

In the Middle Ages, he who practised the profession of, a scholar was generally a judge, notary, or merchant, who devoted himself to literature for fun. However, now we see the emergence of the full time scholar (such as Petrarch). The humanist scholar is a professional writer who maintains close relations with the court and the Church.

The Triumph of Bacchus

One of the most famous compositions of Lorenzo de Medici (lord of Florence) is the triumph of Bacchus and Ariadne, a ballad which is a symptomatic composition of the hopes and fears of the age: an insistent invitation to enjoy the joys of the present accompanied by the melancholy observation of the irremediable passage of time.

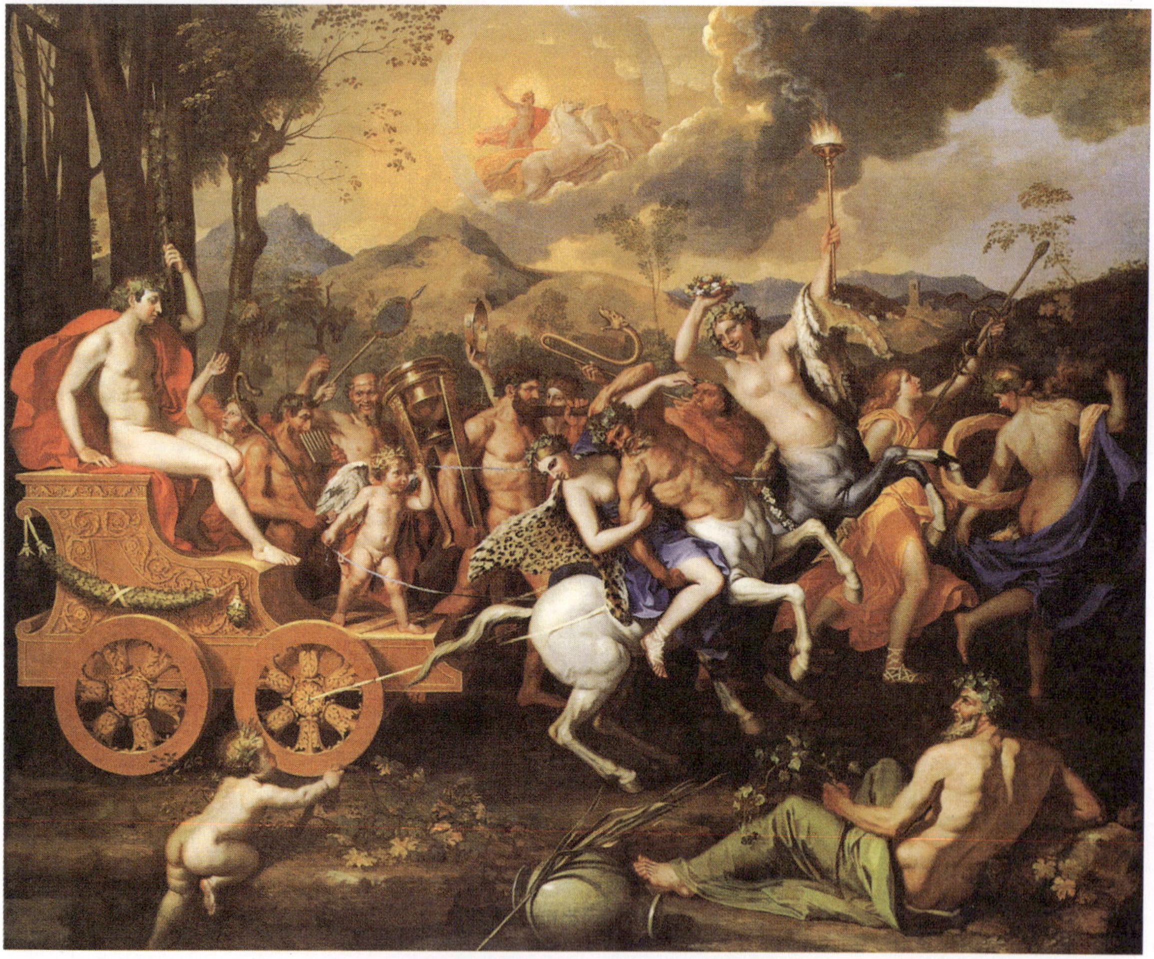

The Triumph of Bacchus and Andriane

Quant'è bella giovinezza,
che si fugge tuttavia!
Chi vuol esser lieto, sia:

The time of youth indeed is sweet,
But all too soon it slips away.
If you'd be happy—don't delay!

di doman non c'è certezza.

Quest'è Bacco e Arianna,

belli, e l'un dell'altro ardenti:
perché 'l tempo fugge e inganna,
sempre insieme stan contenti.
Queste ninfe ed altre genti

sono allegre tuttavia.

Chi vuol esser lieto, sia:
di doman non c'e certezza.
Questi lieti satiretti,
delle ninfe innamorati,
perché 'l tempo fugge e inganna,
sempre insieme stan contenti.
Queste ninfe ed altre genti

sono allegre tuttavia.

Chi vuol esser lieto, sia:
di doman non c'e certezza.
Questi lieti satiretti,
delle ninfe innamorati,
ballon, salton tuttavia.
Chi vuol esser lieto sia:
di doman non c'è certezza.

Queste ninfe anche hanno caro
da lor essere ingannate:
non puon fare a Amor riparo,
se non genti rozze e ingrate:

ora insieme mescolate.

suonon, canton tuttavia.
Chi vuol esser lieto, sia:
di doman non c'è certezza.
Questa soma, che vien drieto

sopra l'asino, è Sileno:

così vecchio è ebbro e lieto,
già di carne e d'anni pieno;
se non può star ritto, almeno
ride e gode tuttavia.

Tomorrow's ills we've yet to meet.
Welcome Bacchus, Ariadne!
An ardent couple, loving, fair.
They spend as one their days with glee,
For time flies fast and does not spare.
Thus these nymphs—and others—fare.
Happy they the livelong day!
If you'd be happy—don't delay!
Tomorrow's ills we've yet to meet.
These nymphs are tickled by the thought
To be deceived by lover's wile.
If Love's sweet remedy were naught,
Folk sure would be uncouth and vile.
Commingled now, they dance and smile
And sport and play the livelong day!
If you'd be happy—don't delay!
Tomorrow's ills we've yet to meet.
These nymphs are tickled by the thought
To be deceived by lover's wile.
If Love's sweet remedy were naught,
Folk sure would be uncouth and vile.
Commingled now, they dance and smile
And sport and play the livelong day!

Years and blubber on him lay.
He can't stand straight, he is quite bent—
Yet still he smiles the livelong day!
If you'd be happy—don't delay!
Tomorrow's ills we've yet to meet.
All ye lovers, boys, girls too—
Long live Bacchus, and Love, I say.
Play, dance, and sing, each one of you,
Let sweetness o'er your hearts hold sway.
Fatigue and weakness throw away,
For what must be you cannot beat.
If you'd be happy—don't delay!
Tomorrow's ills we've yet to meet.

The time of youth indeed is sweet,
But all too soon it slips away.
If you'd be happy—don't delay!
Tomorrow's ills we've yet to meet.
Welcome Bacchus, Ariadne!
An ardent couple, loving, fair.
They spend as one their days with glee,
For time flies fast and does not spare.
Thus these nymphs—and others—fare.

Chi vuol esser lieto, sia:
di doman non c'è certezza.
Mida vien drieto a costoro:
ciò che tocca, oro diventa.
E che giova aver tesoro,

s'altri poi non si contenta?

Che dolcezza vuoi che senta
chi ha sete tuttavia?
Chi vuol esser lieto, sia:
di doman non c'è certezza.

Ciascun apra ben gli orecchi, ?

di doman nessun si paschi;
oggi siam, giovani e vecchi,
lieti ognun, femmine e maschi;
ogni tristo pensier caschi:

facciam festa tuttavia.

Chi vuol esser lieto,
Ciascun apra ben gli orecchi, ?

di doman nessun si paschi;
oggi siam, giovani e vecchi,
lieti ognun, femmine e maschi;
ogni tristo pensier caschi:

facciam festa tuttavia.

Chi vuol esser lieto, s
di doman non c'è certezza.
Donne e giovìnetti amanti,
viva Bacco e viva Amore!

Ciascun suoni, balli e canti!

Arda di dolcezza il core!
Non fatica, non dolore!
Ciò c'ha a esser, convien sia.
Chi vuol esser lieto, sia:
di doman non c'è certezza

Happy they the livelong day!
If you'd be happy—don't delay!
Tomorrow's ills we've yet to meet.
These nymphs are tickled by the thought
To be deceived by lover's wile.
If Love's sweet remedy were naught,
Folk sure would be uncouth and vile.
Commingled now, they dance and smile
And sport and play the livelong day!
If you'd be happy—don't delay!

Tomorrow's ills we've yet to meet.
Upon a donkey, corpulent,
Silenus wends his weighty way.
Heavy, drunk and senescent,
Years and blubber on him lay.
He can't stand straight, he is quite bent—
Yet still he smiles the livelong day!
If you'd be happy—don't delay!
Tomorrow's ills we've yet to meet.
All ye lovers, boys, girls too—
Long live Bacchus, and Love, I say.
Play, dance, and sing, each one of you,
Let sweetness o'er your hearts hold sway.
He can't stand straight, he is quite bent—
If you'd be happy—don't delay!
Tomorrow's ills we've yet to meet.
All ye lovers, boys, girls too—
Long live Bacchus, and Love, I say.
Play, dance, and sing, each one of you,
Let sweetness o'er your hearts hold sway.

Fatigue and weakness throw away,
For what must be you cannot beat.
If you'd be hhappy—don't delay!
Tomorrow's ills we've yet to meet.

Angelo Ambrogini (1454)

Angelo Ambrogini was born in 1454 in a town called Poliziano, this is why he is called Angelo Poliziano, from the Latin name of the city of origin. His main work is the story of Orpheus. This is a theatrical text, written in 1494, on the occasion of a court festival, and is considered the first theatrical work in the vulgar tongue and on a non-religious topic, with characters drawn from the classic tradition of Virgil and Ovid.

The Cantari are rhymed texts composed by jesters who narrate in the squares, often accompanied by music. The topic of the Cantari is taken from the matter of the Carolingian and Breton cycles. These oral works are at the origin of the birth of the chivalric poem. The poem is part of the narrative genre, and is a composition in verse, generally in octaves that speak of Arthur or Charlemagne. Compared to the Cantari, the chivalric poem introduces some important novelties.

The authors are educated people, often courtiers, and the works are composed to be published and not disseminated orally. An important difference lies also in the intended audience: the jester sings for the public square, while poems of chivalry spread among a noble audience. Authors of chivalric poems include: Luigi Pulci, Matteo Maria Boiardo, and above all, Ludovico Ariosto.

Luigi Pulci (1432–1484, Florence)

Working in Florence at the time of Lorenzo de Medici, Pulci was the author of the knightly poem Morgante: full of episodes and with a complicated plot. The protagonist of the work is Morgante, a giant who, moving away from the court of Charlemagne, shares many and amusing adventures with those he meets on the street.

Matteo Maria Boiardo (1441–1480, Reggio Emilia)

For all his life he remains tied to the court environment: specifically, the court of Este. He composed the masterpiece of Boiardo and Orlando in love, a chivalric poem written in octaves which he began in 1476, but could not complete due to his death. Orlando is an epic hero par excellence, the strongest of the paladins of Charlemagne, burning with passion for Angelica, the beautiful daughter of the king of the Catai.

Literature

In pedagogical literature, the treatise entitled *Family Books*, written by Leon Battista Alberti, stands out. The most widespread genre of fiction is the novel: the model being Boccaccio's *Decameron*. Treatises on literary and linguistic subjects were composed by Lorenzo Valla, who preferred 'the elegance of the Latin language', and Leonardo Bruni, who instead defended the vernacular. The period is also characterized by the recovery of the philosophical doctrine of Plato by Marsilio. In 1459, commissioned by Cosimo dei Medici, he founded the Neoplatonic Academy in Florence. His disciple was Giovanni Pico della Mirandola.

Poetry and Theatre

For poetry in Latin, we remember Giovanni Politano.
Lorenzo de Medici's most famous work is the aforementioned song of Bacchus, belonging to the genre of carnival songs and written on the occasion of the carnival.

In the domain of theatrical production were the recovery of classical theatre (including the work of Plautus and Terence) and the spread of a new genre that derives from the classical culture, the texts of mythological profane topics. Angelo Poliziano (1454–1494) wrote the story of Orpheus as a theatrical text on the occasion of a court festival; it is considered the first theatrical work in the vernacular, with characters from the classical tradition of Virgil and Ovid. The plot: Euridice, bitten by a snake, dies; Orpheus is given the ability to descend into the realm of the dead to bring her back to earth, provided that he never turns to look at her; however, he fails, losing her forever. Poliziano also worked in the domain of descriptive narrative poetry, creating the magnificent Giuliano.

The Humanist Comedy

With the development of the humanist culture aimed at promoting the recovery of the ideals of classical civilization, in the theatrical field a new form arose from the study of the tragedies of the commentaries of antiquity. In the fourteenthth century, scholars began to create real traits of antiquity: the initiation of the humanistic comedy. Francesco Petrarca was the author of the Latin comedy. But there were other humanists, like Leon Battista Alberti who wrote autobiographical comedy in Latin. Towards the end of the fifteenth century, the interest in classical theatre spread widely in the princely courts, where the need to make works accessible to the public favoured the translation into Italian of the ancient texts.

The first comedy written in Italian, an imitation of classical models, was 'Carissaria' by Ludovico Ariosto. The work resumed in the plot the classic model of the vicissitudes of a couple of lovers; it was divided into five acts and then written and represented in prose. Additionally, Ariosto, from an early age, introduces himself into the theatrical environment, first as an actor and translator of the Plautotini and Terenziani texts, and then as the author of original comedies, inaugurating the comedy genre in the vernacular. Ariosto comedies, in which all five acts were in hendecasyllables verses, feature characters depicting human types, such as the astute servant, the greedy old man, and the young man in love. The dramas are full of misunderstanding, exchanges of person, and mock injections. These works, however, were not without limits and defects, due to a certain inventive poverty in the elaboration of the plots too bound to the classical models.

Art

The 1400s are a time of great transformation for Italy. The end of the Middle Ages marks the revival of the development of the cities, and with this occurs the revival of art, commerce, and the study of ancient letters in a new perspective more critical of the sources. In art, the concept of the balance and harmony of classical Greek and Roman prevails (classical naturalism), but perspective is introduced in the realms of sculpture and architecture. The key idea is to bring man back to the centre of the universe. This is clearly anthropocentrism: man defined as the measure of all things. This occurs alongside the rediscovery of the studies of humanity and the humane letter; hence, the defining of this period as 'humanism'.

The capital of this renaissance is Florence, but it spreads throughout Italy (although there is differentiation according to the different local cultural traditions). Even Rome experiences this great flowering, when, to affirm its function as capital of the Christian world of the seat of papal power, Nicholas V marks the 1450 jubilee by restoring the ancient monuments of the churches. This work of urban renewal is continued by Sisto Della Rovere, giving the city a monumental and classic taste.

Architecture

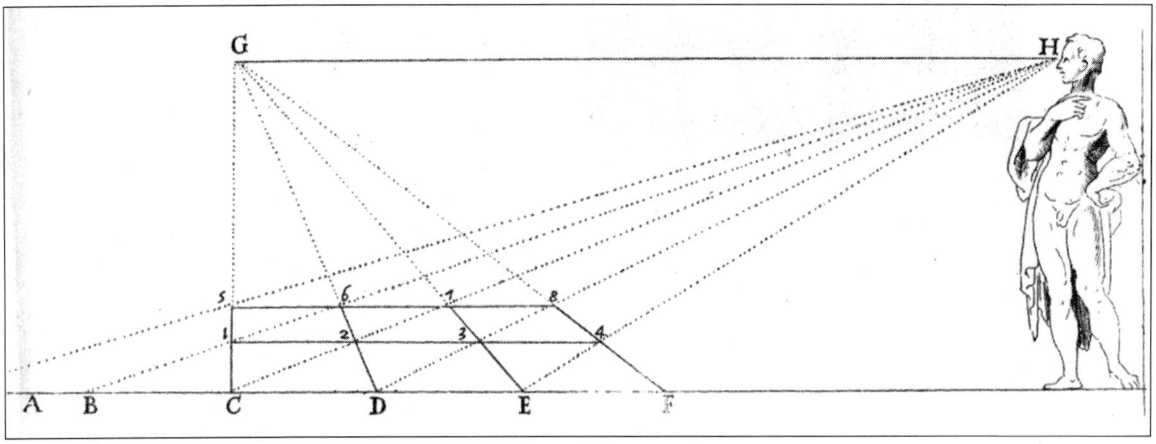

Understanding of perspective

Architecturally, a new language develops based on experimentation and on the new prospective conception of space. The basis of this new is: the perspective view (that is, the relationship to a particular point of view), the search for geometric rigour, and the theory of proportions (the application of a systematic measurement of the relationship between the elements of a construction and three different elements of the whole, this is based on the form relating the entire construction to its parts).

Vitruvio, a theoretical architect of the architecture of the first century BCE, is used as a reference point for Renaissance architecture. The greatest innovator is Filippo Brunelleschi (Florence 1377–1442), who is inspired by the models and the spirit of classical architecture and monuments which he studies on visits to Rome with his friend, the sculptor Donatello.

His artistic career is linked to the competition announced in 1402 for the execution of the second bronze door of the baptistery of Florence. His tile was judged victorious together with that of Ghiberti, to whom the execution of the work was entrusted. In 1418, he won another competition for the construction of the dome of Santa Maria del Fiore, affirming the new position of the architect as a designer responsible in person for his work, and able to face formal technical problems under both theoretical and executive point of views.

Brunelleschi is credited with the invention of perspective, understood as the application of mathematical principles and visual perception to architecture. To solve the problems posed by the large diameter of the dome of Santa Maria del Fiore (about 45m), Brunelleschi invented a new technique, based on the Roman way of measuring. He built the dome so that its structure was self-supporting, arranging the herringbone bricks so as to create a solid wall texture and adopt an ogival shape, emphasized from the outside by eight pointed ribs.

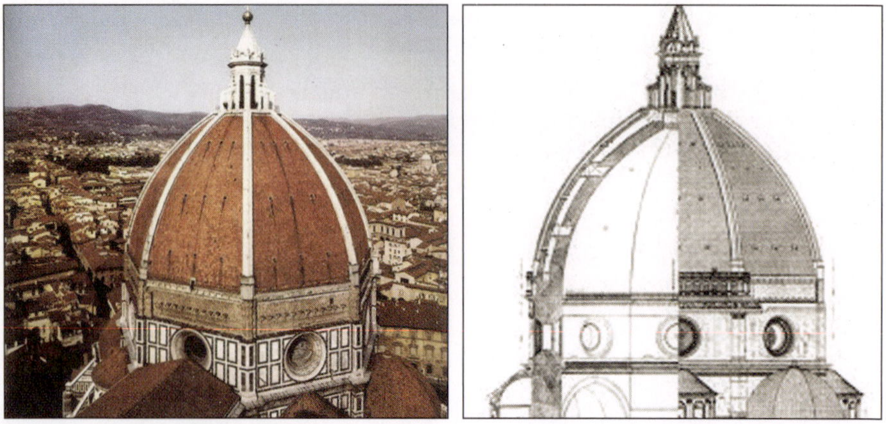

The dome of Santa Maria del Forie designed by Filippo Brunelleschi

Leon Battista Alberti (1406, Genoa)

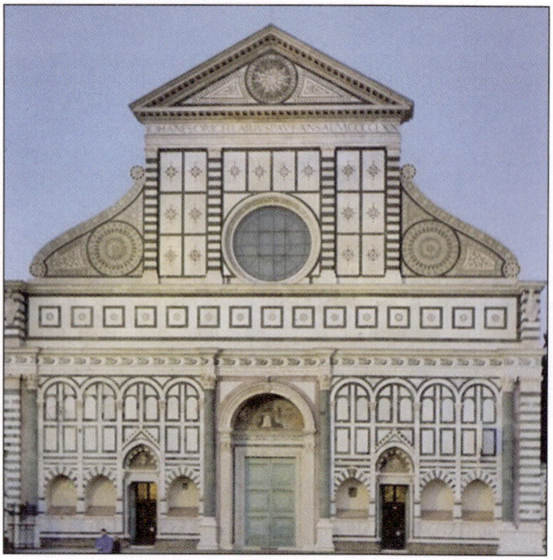

Santa Maria Novella, Florence

Alberti fully embodied the ideal of a Renaissance man of culture—versatile, a literate, a theoretician of art, and an artist whose work was based on culture and theory. Alberti's goal is to ennoble art, elevating it to the rank of 'liberal arts' and innovating it above simple crafts. Alberti was more a theorist than a technician.

Through his written works, which gave theoretical and scientific bases to artistic activity, painting, sculpture and architecture are promoted to 'liberalis', that is, on the same level as the literature of philosophy.

He designed the facade of Santa Maria Novella Florence in 1450, in which the typical motif is resumed—geometric-coloured marble according to the classical laws of harmony and modular relationships based on the square.

In 1470, Alberti added a triangular pediment between the two large scrolls of the facade. The facade of Sant'Andrea (Mantua) can be inscribed in a square. In the centre there is a large arch similar to a triumphal arch. Alberti's intention was to treat the façade not as a plan but as an autonomous plastic organism.

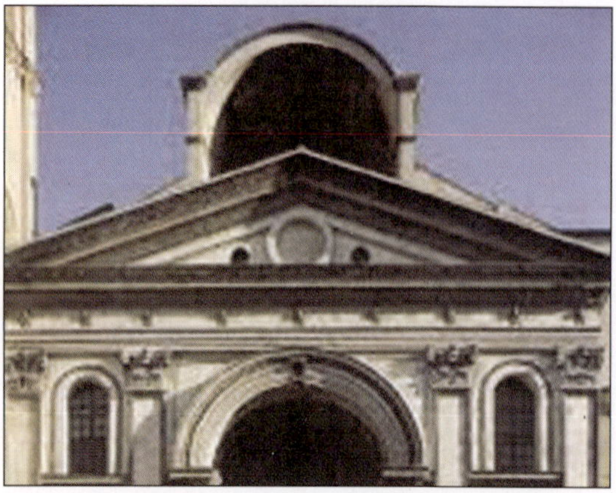

Basilica of Sant'Andrea

Sculpture

Based on the reworking of the classicism of Nicola and Giovanni Pisano, and of the naturalism of Giotto, Renaissance sculpture is founded. The main elements are: for naturalism, the careful characterization of the characters, depicted with psychological aspects as a symbolic ethical sense of action; and for classicism, the inspiration of ancient statuary, not to imitate the models but to operate following the same universal aesthetic laws.

The century begins with an extremely important artistic and cultural event: the competition for the second bronze door of the baptistery of Florence in 1401. Victory was awarded to two panels—one by Ghiberti and the other by Brunelleschi, both representing the sacrifice of Isaac. Lorenzo Ghiberti (1378–1455) was a goldsmith, Florentine sculptor, and architect. In the Ghiberti tile, the scene takes place with balanced rhythms, within a unitary space that gently slopes towards the bottom of the tile itself.

The figures appear almost in pose, and the reference to the ancient style is expressed in the elegant nude figure of Isaac. In Brunelleschi's 'Formelle', we see an innovative character. The figures in the foreground cross the borders of the frame projecting outwards, and the scene is fragmented into distinct episodes that find their dramatic centre in the gesture of the angel intervening to stop the hand of Abraham.

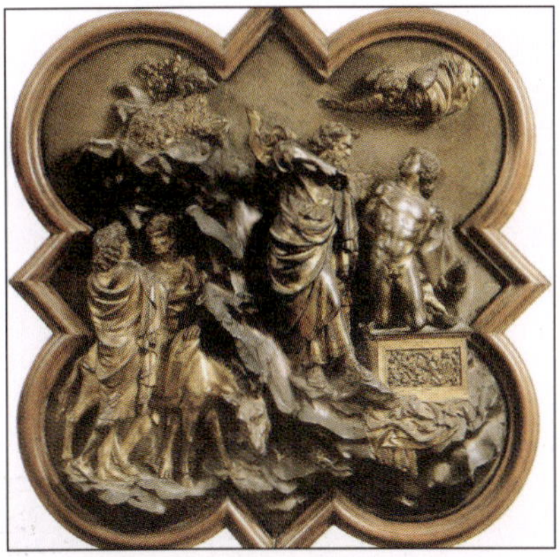

The sacrifice of Isaac by Lorenzo Ghiberti

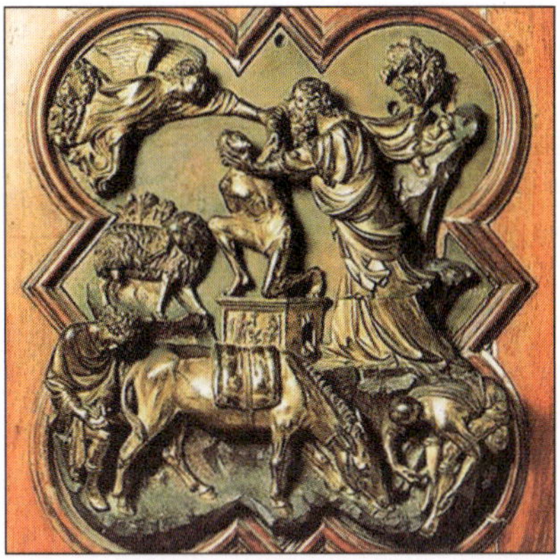

Formelle by Brunelleschi

Donato di Nicolò Tipetto Bardi

Better known as Donatello, he was born in Florence in 1386. He worked in Ghiberti's Battega, and went to Rome together with Brunelleschi to study the works of Classical Art.

He was the creator of a bronze David sculpture. Although inspired in a striking way by the classic models, Donatello confers the freedom of divine inspiration on the work. He was original in the centering instability of the composition, in the continuous modulation of light and shadow and in the deeply thoughtful attitude of his work.

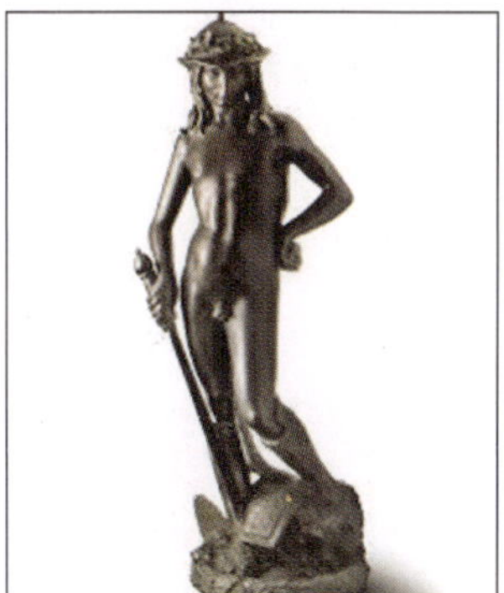

A bronze statue of David by Donatello

Verrocchio, Andrea di Riccione (1435–1488)

This goldsmith, Florentine painter, and sculptor is famous for his workshop where he trained artists like Leonardo and Perugino. His sculptural work shows a pictorial tendency that accentuates the chiaroscuro aspects and the soft play of the light of the surfaces. With his bronze David, he contrasts the thoughtful image of Donatello and his poetic sense of heroism, with the bold image of a young man with a slightly unstable pose.

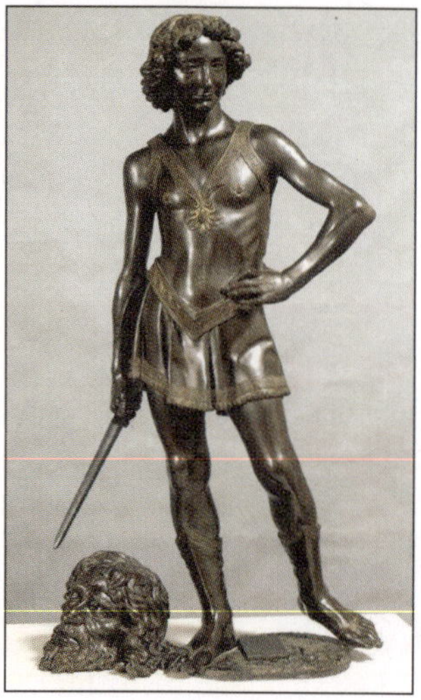

Statue of a young man, by Verrochio

Painting

Late Gothic painting

In contrast with the new pictorial tendencies that are affirmed in Florence, Europe and northern Italy, between the end of the fourteenth and the beginning of the fifteenth century, the artistic current known as International Gothic develops. A key feature is linearism, and the typical chromatic taste is ornamental of the details. Works suggest legendary and fairytale motifs, typical of the taste of feudal courts. Sassella (1390–1450) is considered the greatest representative of Sienese painting of the fifteenth century, an interpreter of the elegant Gothic figurative tradition of Siena.

Renaissance Painting

Characteristic elements of Renaissance painting are: the perspective conception of space, the placement of figures in a real space, the centrality of the human figure (represented realistically both in the anatomical structure and in the character expression), and the use of light (which highlights plastic values of shapes, often interpreted purely volumetrically).

Masaccio (1401–1428)

He was the artist who most revolutionized painting by developing a sober, severe figurative language, favouring figurative psychological realism in the rendering of the characters. A precise perspective framing characterizes his works, in which man is represented as exalted in his truth. Melodramatic episodes are concentrated in action, in the gestures and expressions of a few essential protagonists without giving anything to the decorative digressions. An example can be seen in the frescoes of the Brancacci Chapel in Santa Maria del Carmine (Florence). In the crucifixion panel of the deconstructed Pisan polyptych (1426), we see the traditional image of Christ between the Madonna and San Giovanni is charged with the drama of the desperate gesture of Mary Magdalene, who raises her arms towards Christ. The mute cry of pain from Magdalene is considered to be the highest dramatic expression in painting after Giotto.

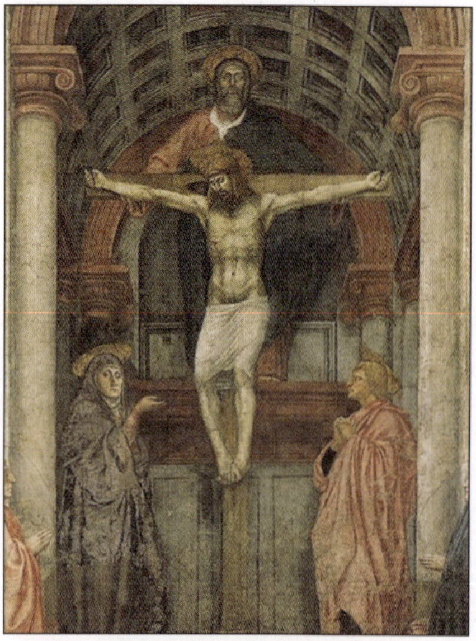

Massacio's Holy Trinity

Sandro Botticelli (1445–1510)

In art, Sandro Botticelli (Alexander of Mariano di Vanni Filipepi) combines the classic and compositional sense of the Verrocchio school with a new focus on linear design, creating restless, melancholic characters of poetry. The central figures of his paintings are human figures as testimonies to feelings and moods. His artistic production can be divided into two major phases: the first between 1470 and 1486, influenced by Neoplatonic culture, tends to an idealized vision of beauty of classical intellectual inspiration—a representation of reality veiled by the myth of allegory, which takes on the tone of the ancient fable. Ater 1490, his work is characterized by a tormented vision of restlessness, attributable to the rejection of the classical culture preached by Savonarola and the crisis of humanism.

In 'The Birth of Venus', the goddess is born from sea foam on a shell, inspired by mythology and classical poetry. The nudity of Venus, a symbol of an ideal beauty, natural and spiritual together, recalls the concept of the rebirth of the soul. Venus here is not only the representation of the beauty of love, but of the birth of humanity, that is, the virtue which, according to Neoplatonic culture, is produced by the union of spirit with matter. The nudity of the goddess is not only a representation of beauty, but an exaltation of the purity of the simplicity of the soul. The birth of Venus could also be read from a religious angle: Venus could be the soul of the believer who is reborn through the water of baptism; the shell would be the baptismal font.

It is very important to pay attention to the curved line that has a predominant role throughout the painting: in the waves, in the inlets of the coast, and in the hair of the four figures, in the clothes, in the cloaks.

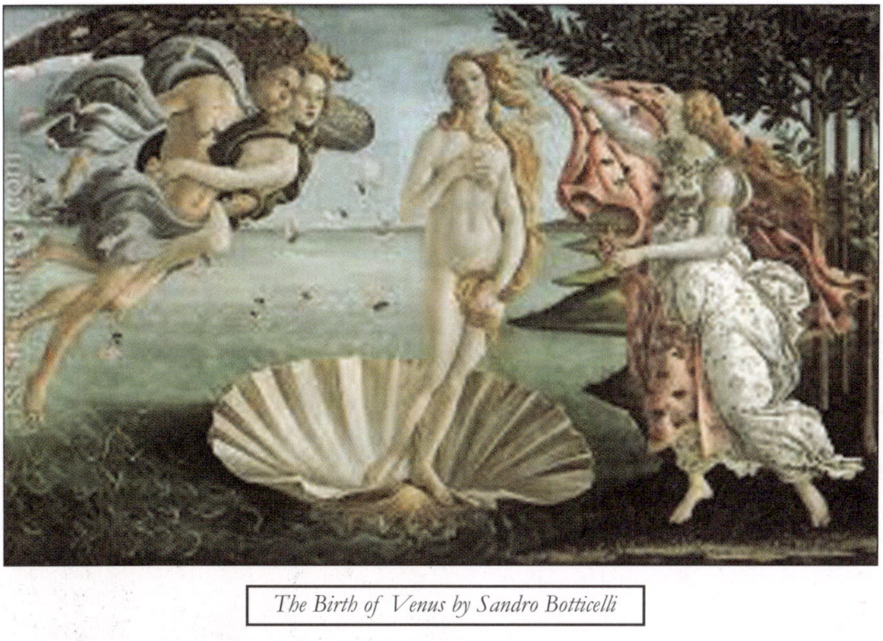

The Birth of Venus by Sandro Botticelli

Another famous work by Botticelli is 'Primavera' (Spring) in which Venus is depicted at the centre of the composition, surrounded by safilius, Flora, Mercury and the three graces. Here, one can recognize the double meaning, natural and intellectual, of the creative capacity of Venus, or love—the maximum force of the universe according to neoplatonic conceptions. The new characters stand in the shade of a grove, on a lawn covered with herbs, medicinal plants and different flowers.

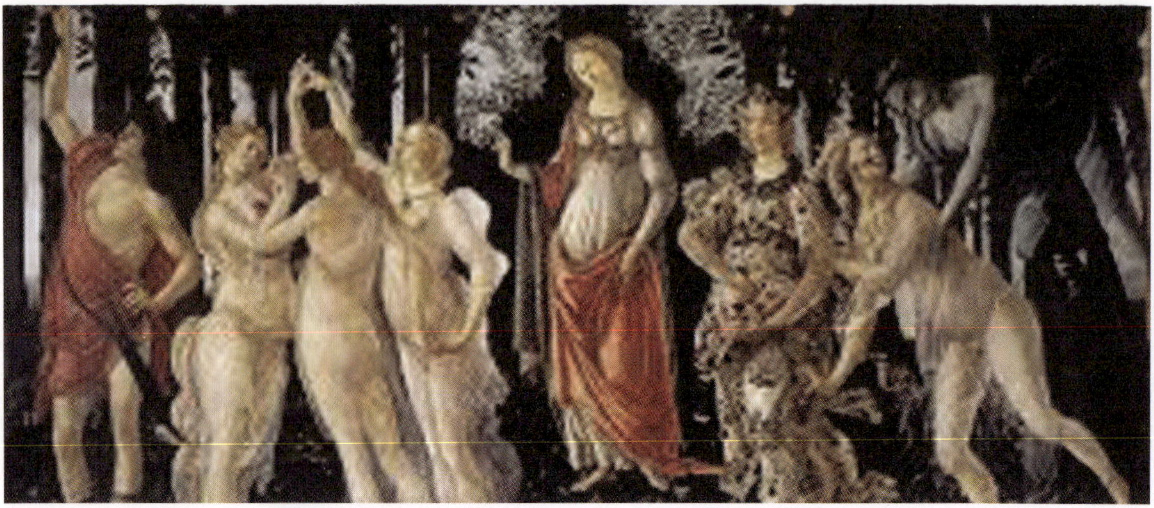

Primavera (Spring) by Botticelli

Piero della Francesca (1410–1492)

Francesca was influenced particularly by Leon Battista Alberti. He was not limited to the application of his precepts in the paintings; he deepens his theoretical study, thus succeeding in embodying the figure of a learned artist desired by Alberti. He uses geometric perspective rigour, together with a static impassibility of the characters and a limpid brightness of the colours. For him, nature and human figures are traceable to geometric shape by virtue of a conception reinforced by the impeccable perspective structure in which the figures are framed within a unitary spatial texture. This gives an abstract, impassive, and almost unrealistic fixity. Three masterpieces:

The scourging of Christ

A painting that appears divided into two parts: on the left, within an architectural perspective, the scene of the scourging; on the right, in the foreground between figures, we see the young duke Oddantonio da Montefeltro and his two bad advisors. The figures in the foreground, in their geometric mobility in the inconsistency of their presence in relation to the episode of the scourging, demonstrate the possibility of bringing together different moments, placing them outside their historical development.

The Legend of the True Cross (1452–1459)

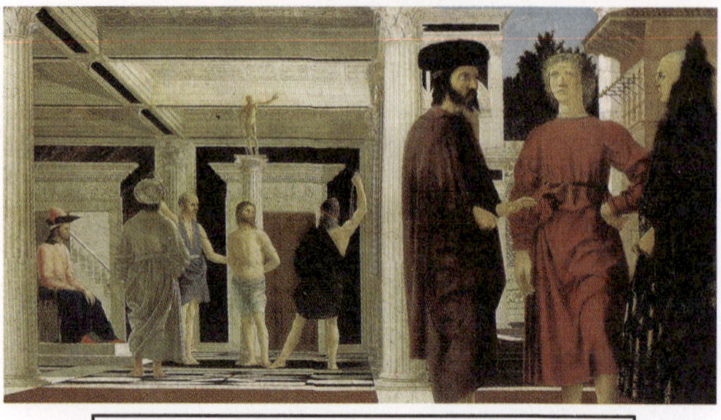

The Scourging of Christ by Piero della Francesca

This is a cycle of frescoes, executed for the choir of the church of San Francesco in Arezzo, which constitute one of the major works of Renaissance art as well as being the most complete testimony of Piero della Francesca's art. The episodes described assume a solemn ritual trend that places them outside the historical time. Adam on the verge of death asks his son Seth to go to the Archangel Michael to ask him for the oil of mercy. The archangel instead gives him the seeds of the tree of sin, and orders him to plant them in his father's mouth to save his soul after death. Seth obeys, and the tree of good and evil is born from the mouth of Adam. Many years later, King Solomon cuts the tree for use in the construction of the great temple of Jerusalem.

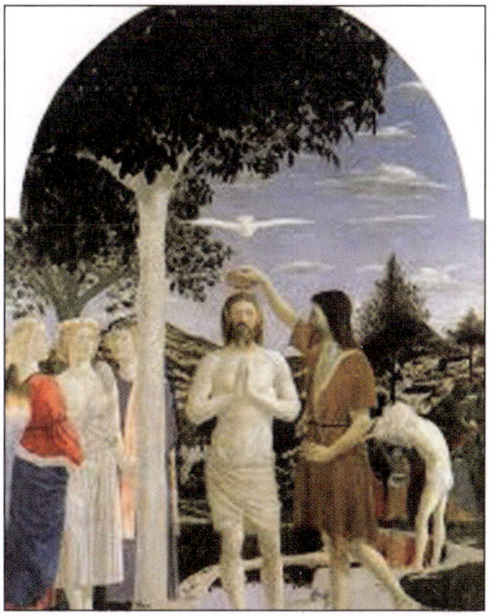

The Baptism of Christ by Piero della Francesca

Then, however, the wood is not used and ends up becoming a bridge over a small river. One day, the Queen of Sheba arrives in Jerusalem and wants to visit King Solomon. While the Queen is crossing the bridge she has a vision: she understands that the wood of the bridge will be used to build the cross of Jesus. Upon learning of the fact, King Solomon orders the burial of the wood underground to prevent the vision of the queen from foretelling the end of the kingdom of Israel. In reality, the wood is found and will be used for the construction of the cross. Later, the cross was hidden and then found again by Constantine in 313.

After the victory over Maxentius, Constantine converted to Christianity and he went to Jerusalem to reveal the hiding place of the cross to a Jew. The cross of Jesus is immediately recognized because it miraculously resurrects a dead young man. In 614, the king of the Persians stole the cross but, after a battle, the Byzantine emperor Heraclitus managed to bring the cross back to Jerusalem.

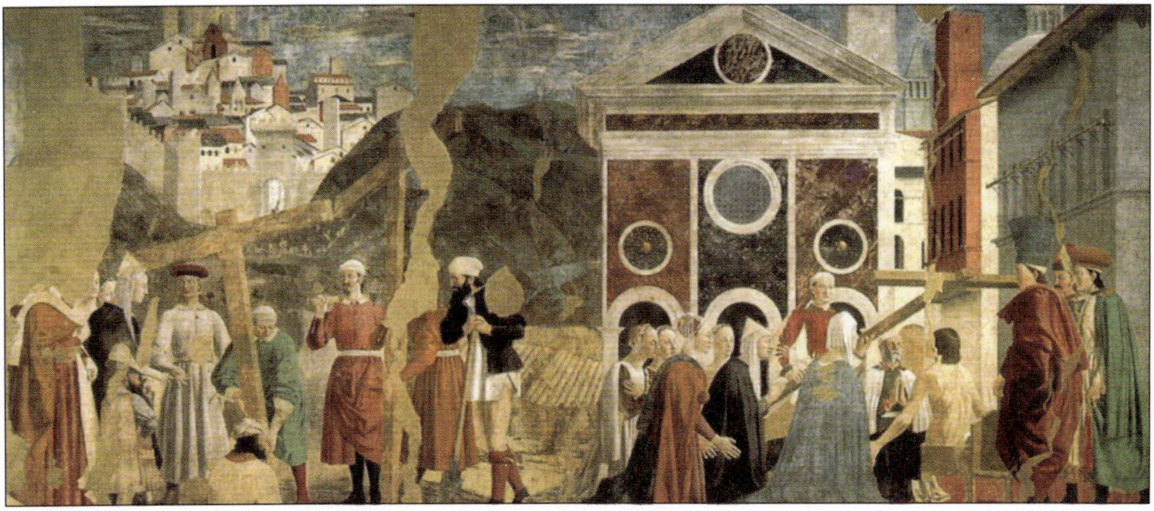

Proof of the True Cross

The Renaissance in Italy

V

Edited by
Saniya Arshad, Aymun Kaleem Naqvi

Designed By
Shahzaib Ali Naik, Ayushi Malik,
Rushda Anwer

The Renaissance in Italy

The Renaissance or rebirth began in Italy at the end of the fourteenth century and became an era of many cultural and architectural achievements in Europe. The peak of the Renaissance occurred towards the end of the fifteenth century, a time when numerous foreign invasions began in Italy. This was the beginning of the famous Italian Wars, which saw Renaissance advancements in science applied to warfare. It was also during this time, the beginning of the fifteenth century, that elements of the Italian Renaissance spread to other countries in Europe which led to a pan-European rediscovery of art and science.

The Renaissance period in European civilization immediately following the Middle Ages is conventionally held to have been characterized by a surge of interest in Classical scholarship and values. The Renaissance also witnessed the discovery and exploration of new continents, the substitution of the Copernican for the Ptolemaic system of astronomy, the decline of the feudal system and the growth of commerce, and the invention or application of such potentially powerful innovations as paper, printing, the mariner's compass and gunpowder. To the scholars and thinkers of the day, however, it was primarily a time of the revival of Classical learning and wisdom after a long period of cultural decline and stagnation.

In the sixteenth century, there are numerous wars that are fought on Italian soil. 1527 is one of the most difficult years: Rome is destroyed by French, Spanish and mercenary soldiers: 'Il sacco di Roma'. The sixteenth century is also the century of the Protestant reform of Martin Luther and the Council of Trent.

The second half of the sixteenth century is often called the 'era of mannerism' by historians. The Catholic Church, urged by the events of religious struggles, is forced to intervene to stop the expansion of Protestant ideas. To speak of the age of the Counter-Reformation means to refer to that time when the church tried to assert itself in the struggle against Protestantism.

The beginning of this age can be fixed with the opening date of the Council of Trent, 1545. In this council, key events included the enlargement of papal power, the desire for absolute orthodoxy, the creation of the index of prohibited books, and the Inquisition Court. This marked an age of crisis of Renaissance values, uncertainties and doubts. This historical period leaves a clear mark on literature and architecture.

Cultural and Political Evolution during the Renaissance

In 1492, Italy lost the fragile political balance achieved with the peace of Lodi, and became subject to the expansionist ambitions of the king of France, Charles VIII. The Church stiffened controls on the works of artists, intellectuals and the press: through the Inquisition Court. In the meantime, the diffusion of the printed book confirmed the prevalence of the use of the vernacular over Latin.

The new geographical discoveries (in 1492, Colombus discovered America) offered the opportunity to some countries to increase their wealth through overseas colonies. The Mediterranean is no longer the most popular commercial route.

The liveliness of cultural artistic life is guaranteed by the courts and also by the papacy, which gives prestigious commissions to numerous artists. In 1516, the first printed grammar of Italian is produced: the rules of the vernacular language of Giovanni Francesco Fortunio. In the city courts, modern theatre is born, with structures designed for representation and the formation of actors' companies.

Religious drama developed in Spain during the Middle Ages only in the northeast because the Moors occupied the remainder of the peninsula. During the sixteenth century, as Spain became the most powerful country in Europe, it started to develop a sophisticated theatre. Following a period of interest in classical drama and the introduction of printing, in the late fifteenth century there appeared Juan del Encina, the founder of modern Spanish drama.

During the Renaissance period, great changes occurred in the field of literature. One of the major changes was the break from Latin languages; people started writing in other languages. Propelled by humanism, Renaissance scholars sought to revive the study of classical literature, as well as to create new literature in the spirit of the classics. Renaissance authors embraced humanism by injecting a measure of realism (physical, social, emotional) into the characters, plots and settings of this new literature, distinguishing it from medieval work (which lacked such realism).

Spanish literature culminated during the Spanish Golden Age (1500–1650), the literary pinnacle of which is occupied by Miguel de Cervantes, foremost author in the Spanish language. As noted earlier, the 'formative age' of the novel spanned 1500–1800; Cervantes' masterpiece, *Don Quixote* (published in the early seventeenth century), is considered the greatest and most influential novel of this period. *Don Quixote* follows the comical adventures of a retired gentlemen who, in a state of idealistic madness fuelled by medieval romances, embarks on a series of delusional chivalric quests.

The late sixteenth and early seventeenth centuries also witnessed the most renowned figure in all of literature: William Shakespeare, the greatest dramatist of all time. Shakespeare's repertoire consists of some three dozen plays, conventionally divided into comedies, tragedies and histories (tragedies drawn from English history); the tragedy *Hamlet* is often singled out as his masterpiece.

The Liberated Jerusalem (Torquato Tasso)

The first draft of this significant epic poem, entitled Jerusalem, was published without the author's consent. Deeply disappointed by the circulation of a work that he did not consider definitive, Tasso put his hand to the poem the moment he was released from prison. The work was re-published in 1593, (titled *Jerusalem Conquered*) after many modifications and suppressions of entire episodes.

Ludovico Ariosto

He was born in Reggio Emilia in 1474. The most famous chivalric poem in his work, which more than any other characterizes the Renaissance, is the furious *Orlando*. Dedicated to the Poliziano, Ariosto's poem continues the story of Orlando in love, starting from the exact moment when Boiardo's poem is interrupted. With Ariosto, the chivalric poem becomes a contemporary novel of the passion and the aspirations of the men of that time. Orlando, first in love, is then furious. The plot of the two poems is very complicated and difficult to summarize because often the events narrated are abandoned, returned to only later; moreover, there are frequent episodes independent of the main plot.

Political Writings

The works of political argument can be divided into two groups: the texts that start from the real political situation, and those that are not based on reality but that describe an ideal non-existent society, on the model of utopia by 'di Moro Tommaso. The main features of these treatises are: the use of the Latin language, the models of classical texts (such as the politics of Aristotle), and the predominantly moral content. *Il de Principe* stands out amongst these works.

Nicolo Machiavelli

He was born in Florence in 1479, which was ruled by Lorenzo the Magnificent. His first works were reports of political-concrete situations. With the fall of the Republic and the return to power of the doctors in 1512, he was expelled from office, tortured and forced to leave Florence for a certain time. In the second part of his life, he devoted himself mainly to his works. *The Prince* and *The Speeches on the First Deco of Tito Livio* are his main historical political works.

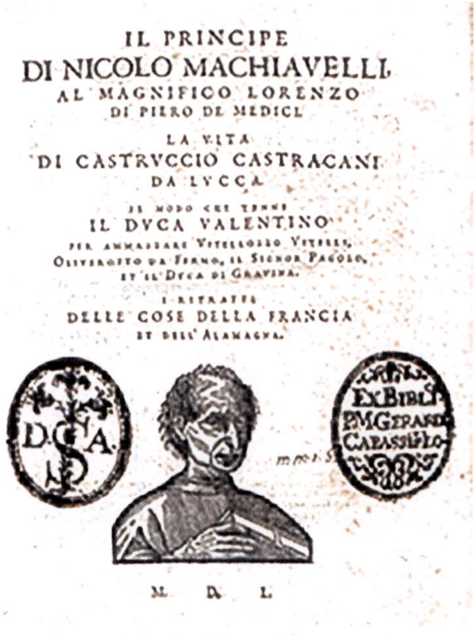

Cover page of Machiavelli's 'Principe'

In these texts Machiavelli elaborates a real political science. At the centre is his conviction of the wickedness of man, who never does anything good except by necessity. The second point is the certainty that history seems to be dominated by chance and that therefore man, in order to intervene in the course of things, must know how to exploit virtue and fortune. It is not enough for man to know how to survive because he is associated with luck anyway, and therefore he must know how to choose and act in the right way at the right time. Macchiavelli also believed that fixed immutable laws govern the history of men.

Francesco Guicciardini (1483–1540, Florence)

Faithful to the doctors, he began his career as an ambassador in 1527, the year of the famous check of Rome, during which the city was destroyed by mercenary troops. The government of the doctors collapsed again, Guicciardini is accused, tries to seize the money for the payment of the soldiers, and withdraws to private life.

Returning to power, the doctors are recalled, but due to misunderstandings with Cosimo Dei Medici, who intended an absolutist policy, he withdrew again to private life. He embodies the classic figure of the intellectual official, one whose main interest is turned to the technical aspect of the state, of which he examines the constitution exactly. In his works, he tries to design a good government of the state and defines with great precision the task of the various magistrates.

Renaissance Art

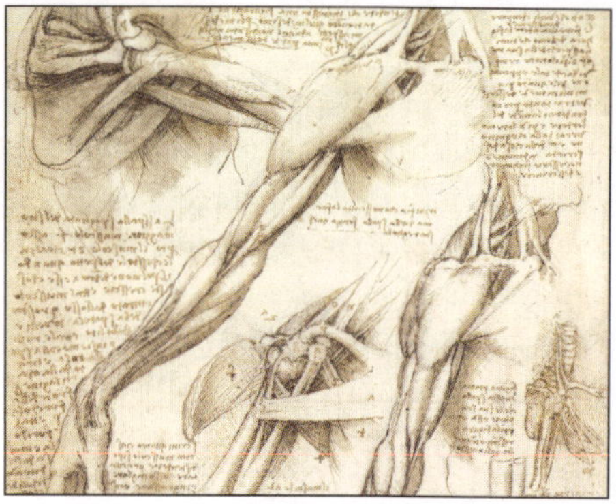

Sketch by Leonardo Da Vinci

It was in art that the spirit of the Renaissance achieved its sharpest formulation. Art came to be seen as a branch of knowledge, valuable in its own right and capable of insights into man's position in the universe. In the hands of men such as Leonardo da Vinci it was even a science, a means for exploring nature and a record of discoveries. Art was to be based on the observation of the visible world and practised according to mathematical principles of balance, harmony, and perspective, which were developed at this time.

Donato Bramante (1444) worked in Lombardy and Rome. Bramante expresses himself more fully in architectural language, of which he was a great innovator in the classical sense, synthesizing the laws of configuration (founded on the relationship between the historical situation in use of classical orders and their combinations) within structures carefully calibrated from the point of view of spatial relationships. The study of ancient classical building led him to use classical architectural forms to create balance and harmony. Among his most important works are: the Santa Maria Delle Grazie in Milan, and San Pietro in Montorio, in which Bramante is inspired by the classic round system.

Leonardo da Vinci (1452–1519)

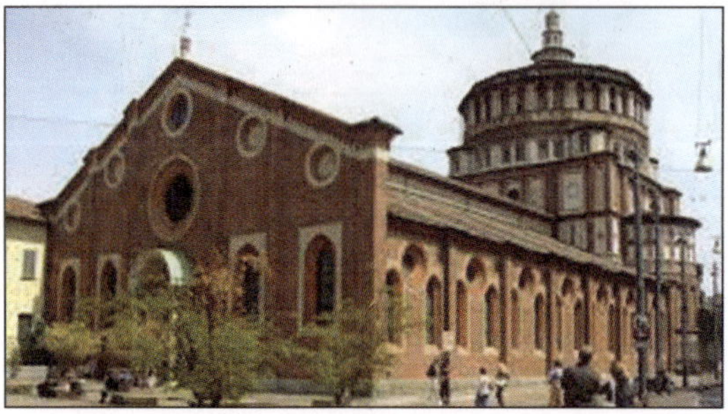

The Santa Maria Delle Grazie, Milan

Leonardo da Vinci (1452–1519) began his apprenticeship in the Verrocchio workshop, one of the most famous in the city of Florence. To define him as a painter alone is reductive, as he embodies in full sense the ideal of the artist at 360 degrees: an inventor, sculptor, architect, and engineer in Florence, Milan, and France. He left, in testimony to his universal genius, a large number of manuscripts and drawings relating to his studies of anatomy, botany, mechanics, geometry, engineering.

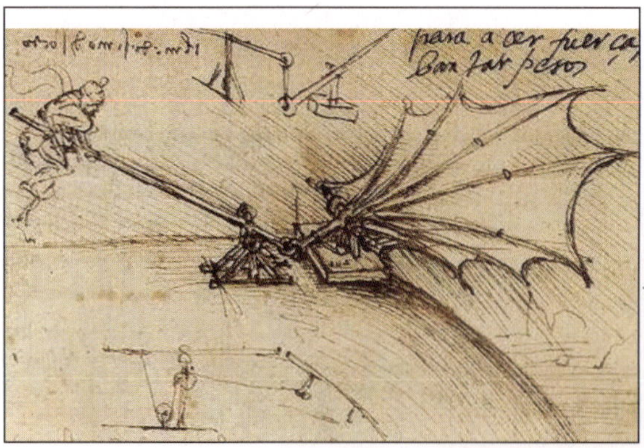

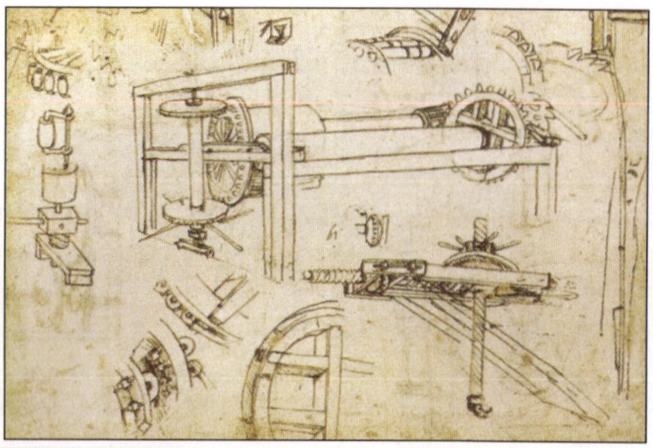

Leonardo da Vinci's Sketches

The Cenacle (1495–1497)

The Cenacle (1495–1497) is a fresco located in the refectory of the convent of Santa Maria Delle Grazie in Milan. Also called 'The Last Supper', it is a work in tempera and oil, patronized by the Duke of Milan. Leonardo rejects the traditional procedure of fresh painting that does not allow for second thoughts. Experimenting with his technique, he works on dry plaster with colours similar to those he uses for the boards. The result is that the colour already begins to fade while he is working on it. The scene is taken from the gospel of John, in which Jesus announces that he will be betrayed by one of his disciples. The moment that Leonardo chooses is when Jesus says the phrase: 'One of you will betray me.'

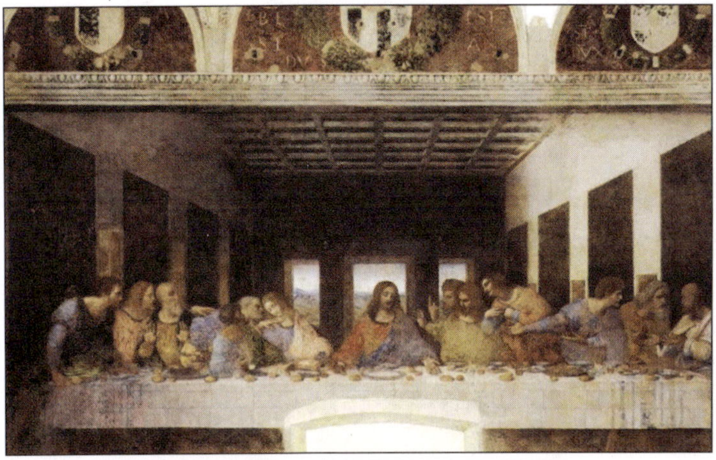

The Last Supper, Tempera and Oil, Louvre

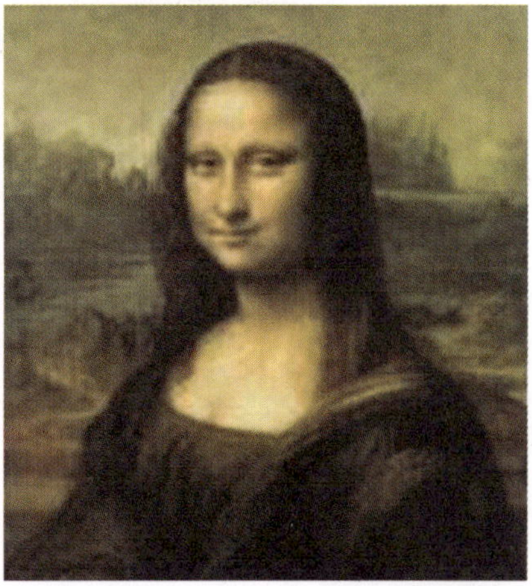

Leonardo da Vinci's Mona Lisa

The Mona Lisa (1503–1506)

This famous portrait is a key example of Leonardesque naturalism, found in the fading of colours and tones and in the calibrated chiaroscuro game of composition. The painting that shows a woman with a pensive expression and a slight smile. The expression of the face is due to the use of the gradient and the corners of the eyes and the mouth, giving the painting an air of mystery. The enigmatic smile is central to the painting. The subtle and elusive psychological definition of Mona Lisa provides a strong expression of the intimate essence of the human person, a mirror of the soul.

Raffaello Sanzio (1483–1520)

Raffaello Sanzio (1483–1520) Raphael's drawing is expressed above all in painting, where he manages to achieve his ideal of formal perfection: chromatic balance and an expressive sweetness of faces and limbs. For Raphael, architecture and decoration come together in the classic beauty of the imperial monuments: the architectural structures are embellished by dense decoration in stucco fresco, inspired by the style of the Roman caves from the Domus area. Works to remember are the 'The Marriage of the Virgin': composed in 1504, the last among the altarpieces made for the church of the city of Castello, and the first work dated and signed by the artist. At the centre of the composition is the figure of the priest who holds the wrists of Joseph and Mary. Raphael constitutes the scene on the prevalence of the curved line.

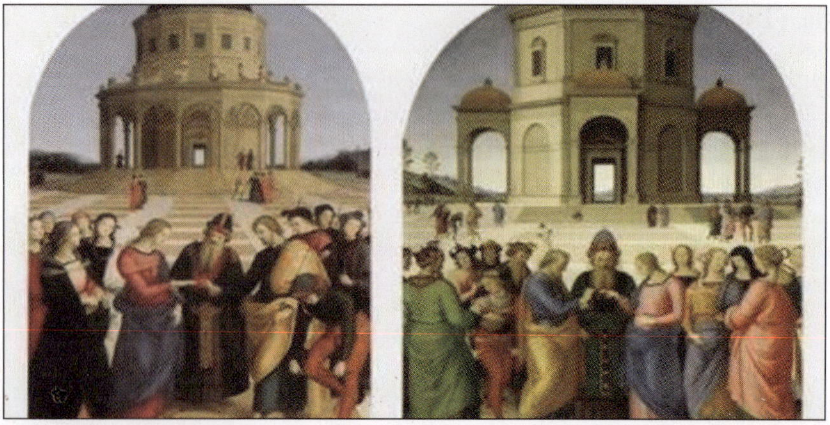

The Marriage of the Virgin by Raffaello Sanzio 1504 and Perugino

The School of Athens (1509–1511)

This fresco was painted between 1509 and 1511, and is preserved in a room in the Vatican. The painting is one of the greatest masterpieces of the Renaissance. In an imaginary classical building, the philosophers of antiquity are presented as they discuss their thoughts. To the left of the scene is the statue of Apollo, while on the right is the statue of Minerva. In the centre, illuminated by an open arc of sky, are the two main philosophers of antiquity: Plato and Aristotle.

Plato, painted with the face of Leonardo da Vinci, holds his book *Timaeus* in his hand and indicates the sky with a finger, while Aristotle holds his *Ethics* and indicates the earth with the palm of his hand. Among the various philosophers, we find Heraclitus (with the face of Michelangelo) and Euclid (with the face of Bramante). There are two figures in contemporary clothes: these are self-portraits of Raphael and his friend.

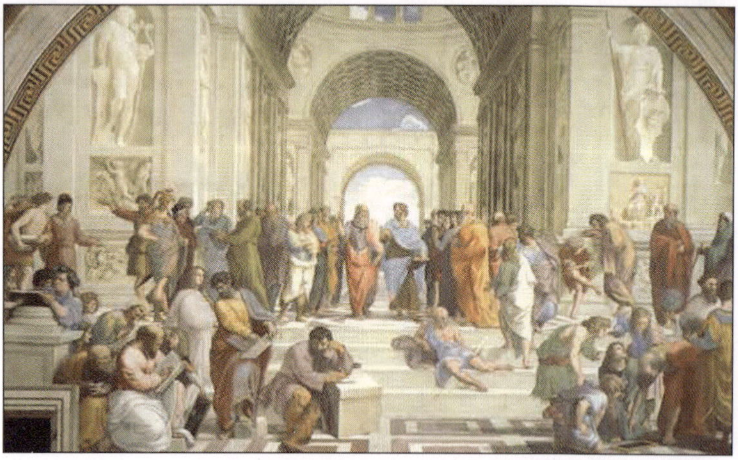

The School of Athens, 1509–1511by Raphael

Michelangelo

Michelangelo expressed all his genius in the constant search for a beautiful ideal. He was under the clear influence of Neoplatonic philosophy, and produced much work for Pop Julius II. Michelangelo's favourite medium was sculpture, which he premised upon a removal rather than a layering of material. His forms were enclosed, almost imprisoned, in gigantic blocks of marble, and he struggled to bring them to light, to bring out the movement and the tension of the life from the static nature of the matter. The conflict between the inert matter and the creative will of the artist who animates it becomes evident in the 'unfinished' sculptures.

St. Peter (1497–1499)

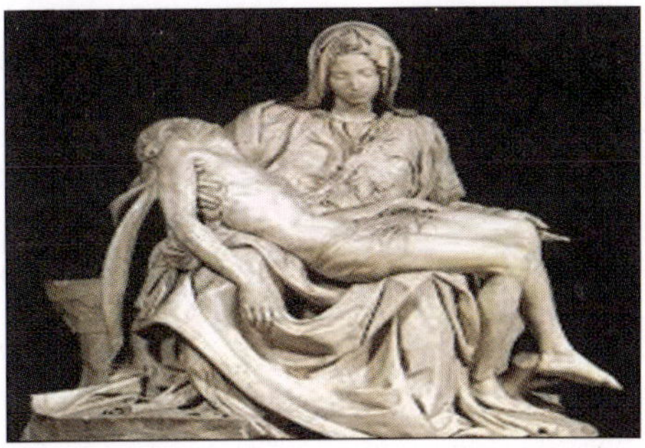

Figure Piety of St. Peter 1497–1499 by Micheangelo

His sculptural works include the Piety of St. Peter (1497–1499), which was composition in pyramidal form on a block of Carrara marble and shows the Virgin (depicted as a young woman) supporting the dead Christ on her knees. One of the things that is most surprising in this sculpture is the extremely youthful aspect that the artist wanted to give to Mary's face. It is likely that according to the intentions of the sculptor, the Madonna represents the whole of humanity. Michelangelo does not want to objectively represent death, but to show the communion between God and man.

The Rodanine Piety (1564)

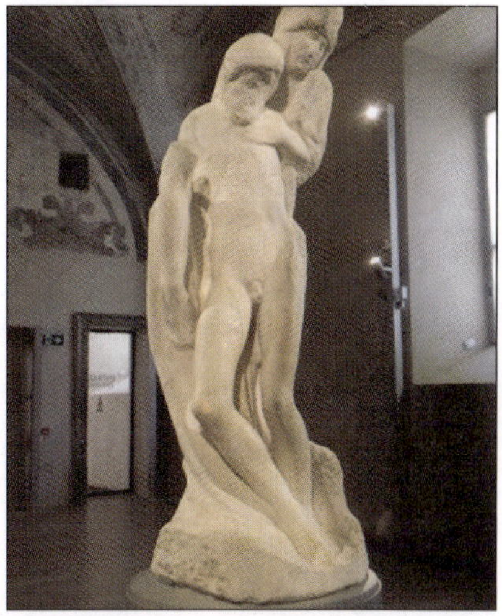

Tondo Doni, Panel Painting by Michelangelo

This 'unfinished' dramatic masterpiece reflects the spiritual tension which animated the last years of Michelangelo's life: the dilution of his heroic vision of man and the awareness of the presence of cosmic pain.

Tondo Doni

Amongst Michelangelo's paintings, it is worth considering 'Tondo Doni'. This image of the holy family expresses the Neoplatonic concept of the succession of generations in the powerful energy of a spiral motion within a pyramidal structure. The painting depicts a group of people: the child Jesus, Joseph and Mary. In the background we see young nudes seated and lying on rocks. You can interpret this painting as a representation of the passage of different eras in the history of man: the nude figures represent the pagan civilization, St. John and Joseph represent the era of Moses, and the virgin with the child represent the era of Christ.

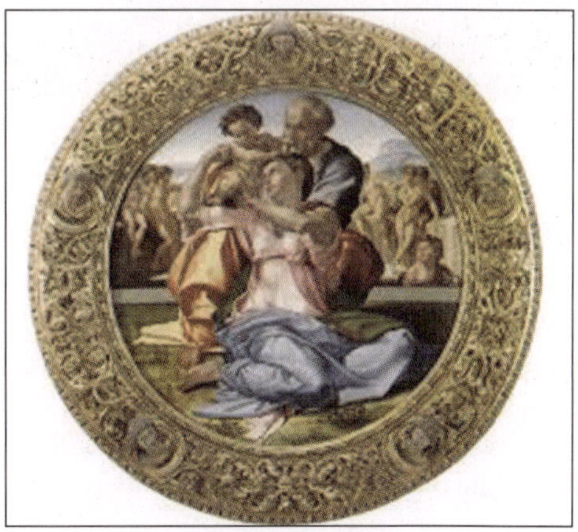

Tondo Doni

This interpretation is also confirmed by the heads carved on the original frame: the sibyls are the pagan age, the two prophets are the life of Moses, and the head of Christ represents the era of man's salvation. Between the sculpted heads there is a frieze with the animal. The design appears clear and aims towards a volumetric construction of the figures, almost like they are sculpted, unlike the nuanced images of Leonardo.

The colours, cold and pure, are not fused together with chiaroscuro; the plastic sense of the volumetric forms is determined by the contrast between the lighter and darker circles. This round (it is not perfectly circular) takes its name from the fabric manufacturer who commissioned the work: Agnolo Doni. Already the circular shape of the painting is a symbol, because the artist wants to represent the earth.

David (1501–1504)

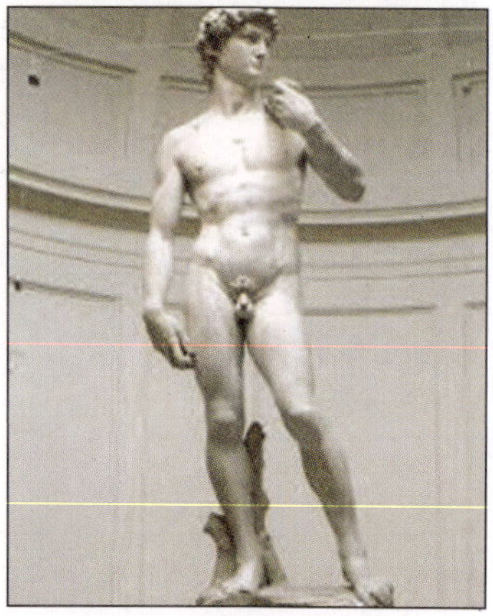

David (1501–1504) by Michelangelo

The figure is the hero killer of Goliath. The twist of his wrist, the agility of the joints, the angle of the head, and the concentration of the gaze, each enhance the movement of this sculpture. David is sculpted from a 16-foot white marble block. It is the first nude sculpture of the Renaissance period, and it represents human power.

Moses (1506)

The Biblical character is represented during the moment when, having come down from Mount Sinai with the tables of the law, he looks at the Jews who are worshipping a golden calf. In the Bible, Moses is said to have been struck by a fit of rage, but the Moses carved by Michelangelo is portrayed in an attitude of self-control, of solemn calm. The tension of the muscles, of the veins, the position of the body, and the furious gaze have made it one of the most admired sculptural masterpieces of all time. Both David and Moses are emblematic, representing imposing physical strength: one dressed, the other a naked hero because he has nothing to hide and wants to show his virtue.

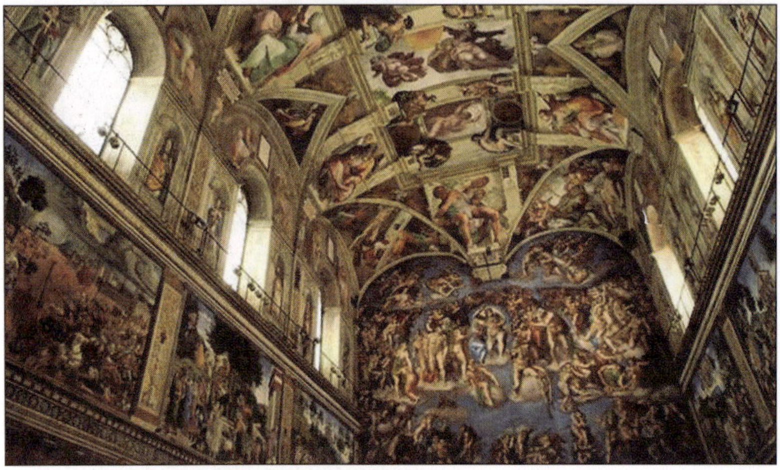

Frescoes of the Sistine Chapel

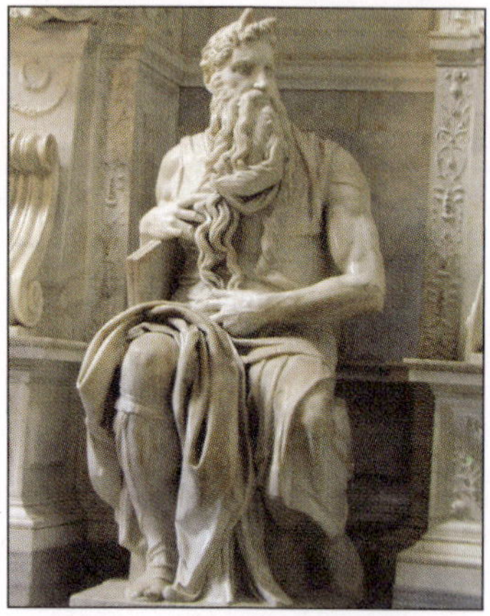

Moses (1506) by Michelangelo

Frescoes of the Sistine Chapel (1508–1512)

These are conceived by Michealangelo as a large architectural scene painted with 9 central panels showing the stories of Genesis. These are flanked by giant naked figures and surrounded by 12 other panels in which the prophets of Israel are alternated with pagan sibyls. In the lunettes and in the sails, the ancestors of Christ are depicted. Michelangelo is commissioned by Pope Julius II in 1508 to restore the ceiling, which originally depicted golden stars on a blue sky. Michelangelo paints the universal judgement over the altar. While Michelangelo paints, the first layer of plaster begins to get mouldy because it is wet. Michelangelo must remove it and start over, but he tries a new mixture, called an intonic. This preparation not only resists the mould, but also enters the Italian building tradition. He is instructed to paint only 12 figures, the apostles, but when the work is finished, there are more than 3000 characters. He also uses male models for women, as female models were more rare and expensive.

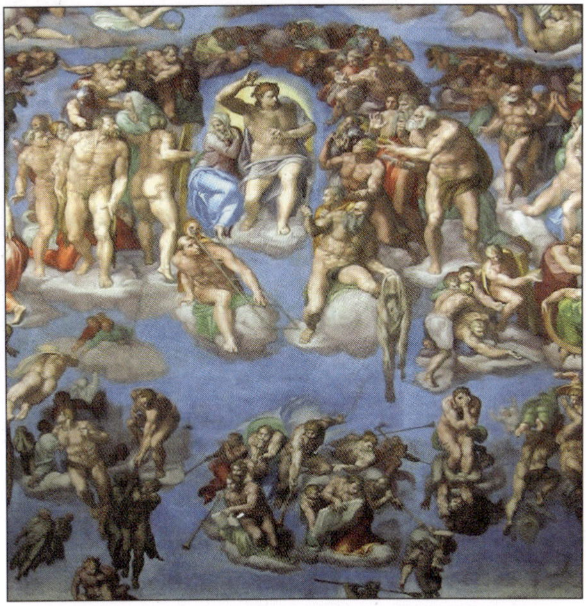

The Universal Judgement (1536–1541) by Michelangelo

The Universal Judgement (1536–1541)

This is a painting on the back wall of the Sistine Chapel which depicts a mass of figures whirling around the central figure of Christ. The dramatic and terrible character of the apocalyptic scene seems to reflect the crisis of Renaissance values. This fresco caused a serious dispute between Cardinal Carafa and Michelangelo: the artist was accused of immorality obscenity because he had painted nude figures (with the genitals in evidence) inside the most important church of Christendom.

A censorship campaign was organized to cover the intimate parts of the frescoes: Daniele da Volterra, an apprentice of Michelangelo, covered the genitals of the figures with loincloths, leaving the bodies unaltered.

The Creation of Adam

(Italian: Creazione di Adamo) is a fresco painting by Michelangelo, which forms part of the Sistine Chapel's ceiling, painted c. 1508–1512. It illustrates the Biblical creation narrative from the Book of Genesis in which God gives life to Adam, the first man. The fresco is part of a complex iconographic scheme and is chronologically the fourth in the series of panels depicting episodes from Genesis. The image of the near-touching hands of God and Adam has become iconic of humanity. The painting has been reproduced in countless imitations and parodies. Michelangelo's 'Creation of Adam' is one of the most replicated religious paintings of all time.

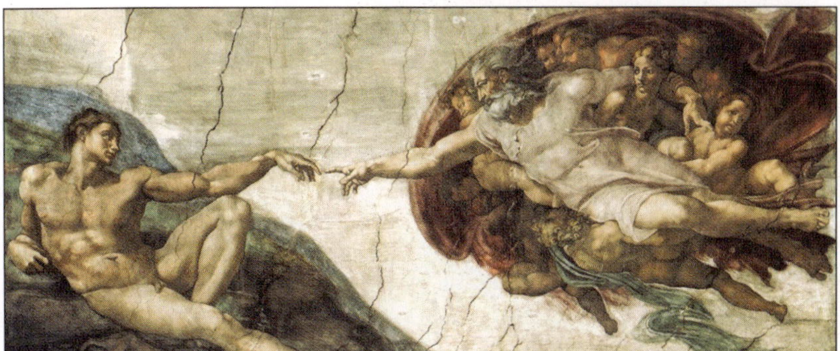

The Creation of Adam (1508–1512) by Michelangelo

Michelangelo's architectural works include the new sacristy of San Lorenzo (1520 and 1534) Here, while respecting the formal structure of Brunelleschi's old sacristy, Michelangelo radically changed it.

The simplicity of the Brunelleschi's system is disturbed by the insertion of the two monumental marble Medici tombs. Each tomb is flanked by two pairs of allegorical figures: the tomb of Giuliano di' Medici by 'Night and Day', and the tomb of Lorenzo di Piero de Medici by 'Dusk and Dawn'.

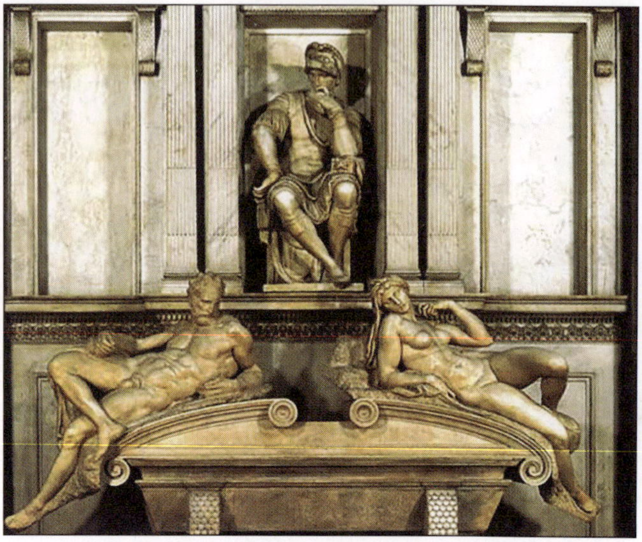

The new Sacristy of San Lorenzo (1520–1534)

Giorgione

Giorgione was born in Veneto in 1477. He provided Venice with a radical turning point: expressing a new poetic interpretation of Nature in which myth, ancient culture, symbolic language and allegory enlivened the real cognitive approach with intense suggestions. A significant work from this artist is the altarpiece of Castelfranco (1505), in which we see the Madonna enthroned with the child, positioned between the saints and Francis and in front of a large landscape background.

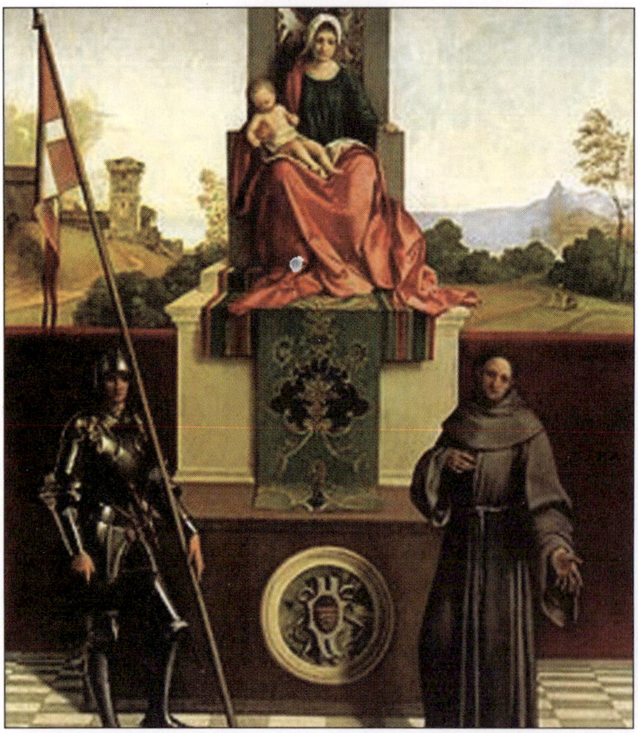

Madonna and the Child with Saints Liberale and Francis

The storm is a work in which nature is the true protagonist. The Matica figure of the naked woman who suckles the baby bestows upon the image the mysterious inner power of generative nature. It is one of the most famous images in of all history. The interpretations are numerous: ranging from the classic Biblical story to the hermetic allegory. Some see the figure as a Venus nourishing love under the gaze of the young poet shepherd. The man is actually a later addition, as originally in his place was another naked woman sitting by the water.

The fact is that the deepest sense seems to be the intimate relationship between human figures and the natural environment—perhaps the true protagonist of the story? Here the human element appears to be random, quite insignificant in the face of the power of nature. All the attention of the observer is focused on the natural event. The sudden opening from the sky is welcomed in the moment of greater brightness: a flash illuminates the scene and the sky is otherwise hidden by heavy clouds. The light delineates the distant country: the columns among the ruins, the clothes of the man, the nakedness of the woman. The suspended, mysterious atmosphere is enhanced by the charm of the colours: the soft greens from the lawn that warm up in the dark leaves of the trees, and the emerald green reflection from the sky on the earth. This dramatic scene is in poetic contrast with the apparent indifference of the protagonists.

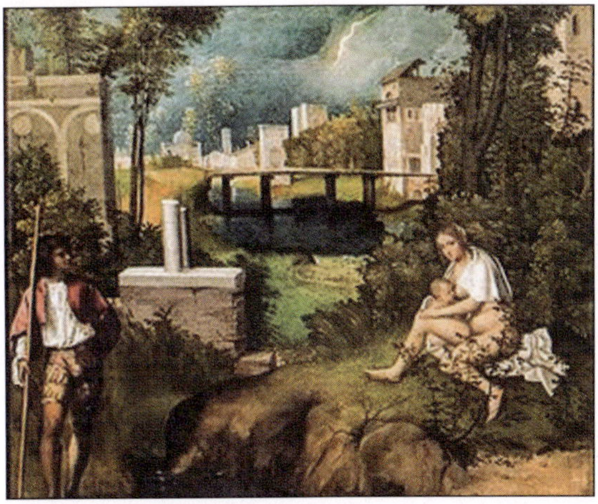

The Storm by Giorgione (1505)

Tiziano (1488–1576)

Tiziano's art stands out for its more direct approach to reality. This is experienced in the intensity of visual emotion: translated into the beauty of forms, the chromatic taste, and the capacity for psychological analysis. The use of colour becomes freer and more sensitive to the variable play of light, while in later there comes a progressive undoing of form. Among Titian's principal works is 'Sacred Love and Profane Love' (1515), an allegorical composition with a controversial interpretation, whose meaning can be traced back to the double nature of Venus as a symbol of love and procreation, but also of death. In reality, the subject of this painting is mysterious.

Probably the author intended to exalt love in both its forms. The painting features two women, one dressed and one nude, sitting at opposite ends of a carved stone fountain. Behind them lies a landscape illuminated by late afternoon sun. The two women look alike, and may be the same person. The left figure (with a nearby vase that perhaps contains jewels) symbolizes our short happiness on Earth, and the right figure (holding the sacred flame of love) represents eternal and heavenly happiness.

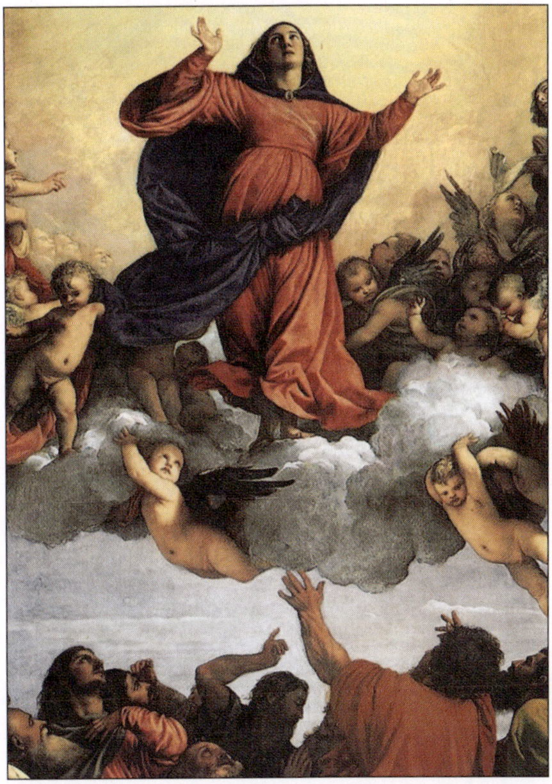

The Altarpiece of Assumption, by Tiziano (1516–1519)

The Altarpiece of the Assumption (1516–1519)

Oil painting on wood, the narrative of the painting takes place in three levels that all revolve around the figure of the Madonna. At the bottom of the painting are the apostles, who have their arms turned to the sky (except St. Peter). Their eyes are turned towards Mary, who stands between them, and God, standing on a cloud and surrounded by cherubs. Mary is facing the sky, with her hands raised high and her face in ecstasy.

We see the influence of Michelangelo and Raphael, but the use of colour and light are characteristic of the Venetian painter: it is not the drawing that defines the figure, but the colour. In the art of the sixteenth century, two trends are highlighted: one that sees the prevalence of design (favoured by the artists of the Tuscan and Roman regions), and the other based on tonal colour (favoured by the Venetians). Design is considered creative manifestation par excellence, the phase of the work in which the idea in the artist's mind is revealed. In the Veneto region, an artistic style was formed which based research essentially on colour, taken in all its variations of intensity and without contrasts.

Renaissance artists were navigators, the explorers of their time: they were driven by the spirit of adventure and the desire for knowledge. They thought about their work as an observer on the world, demanding realistic precision. Thus, in the representation of the landscape, characters are coordinated with each other via the law of perspective.

Architecture

In the sixteenth century, the innovations in the architectural field introduced by Bramante were followed by all other architects who were inspired by this model. Alongside the sacred buildings there are new types: in 1500, urban buildings and magnificent villas evidenced the wealth of the new powerful class. The growth of urban centres brought new problems: in the cities, which were becoming increasingly cramped and overcrowded, the need for enlargement was required.

Sansovino (1486–1570)

This Florentine architect and sculptor acquired a taste for the classical style of Bramante and Raphael in Rome, and he adapted it to the particular conditions of the urban character of Venice. He must be considered the main figure in the architecture of Venice in the 1500s. Of particular interest is the loggia of the Venetian bell tower.

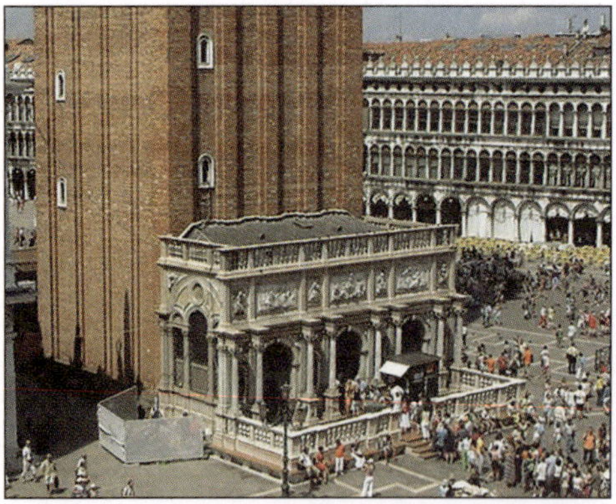

Loggetta by Jacopo Sansovino (1537–1546), Venice

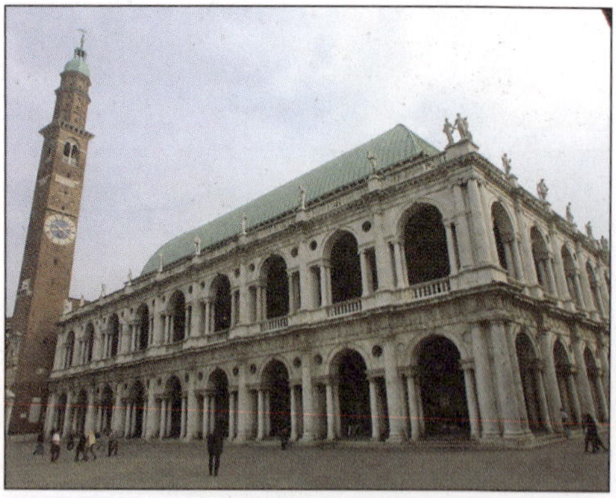

Basillca Palladiana by Andrea Palladio

Palladium (1508–1580)

This architect and architectural theorist was able to combine theoretical knowledge with classical ideals.

Mannerism

This was a style of painting which emerged during the late Renaissance period, and it refers to the work of artists who imitated the great masters such as Raphael and Michelangelo. The term was used to indicate the production of artists who limited themselves to imitating the great models, bringing formal stylistic refinement to extreme consequences.

Mannerism grew in popularity in the face of the collapse of optimistic visions of humanism: numerous artists take refuge in bizarre and surreal aesthetic, finding creative inspiration and a form of intellectual and individualistic freedom. This was a style of painting with great elegance and refinement, dominated by elongated and sinuous shapes, spiral lines, and brilliant colours. We can also consider a second phase of Mannerism starting from 1530, when it becomes less innovative and there was a new stylistic conception taking on less daring forms and becoming more systematic and prudent, in tune with the changing political conditions. Tintoretto was an early adopter of the new style in Venice.

Tintoretto

Tintoretto Giacomo Robusti (1518–1594), called Tintoretto, interpreted Mannerism with the intense enlightened sense of the Venetian tradition. A play of sudden brightness in the deep dark tones of the paintings characterizes his works, in addition to the dynamism of the forms.

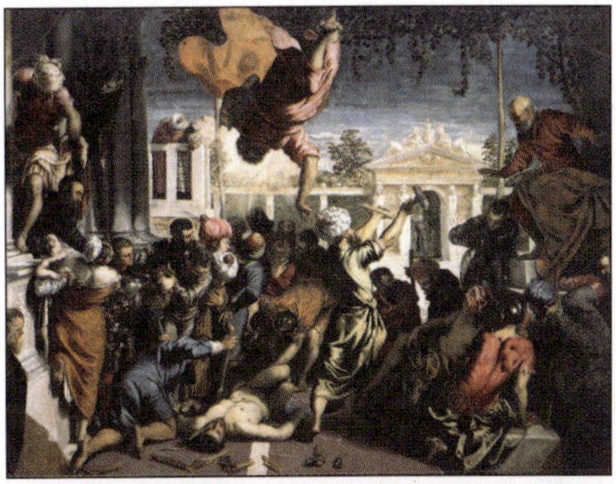

The Miracle of San Marco, 1548, by Tintoretto

The Miracle of San Marco (1548), the first affirmation of the artistic revolution of the young Tintoretto, aroused a controversy. Following the Titianesque conception of art as a source of visual motions, Tintoretto added a strong sense of emotional identity in perception. His drawings had a boldness and freedom of effort, and his painting style was quick, concise and immediate, creating images of energetic dynamism.

The Last Supper (1592–1594)

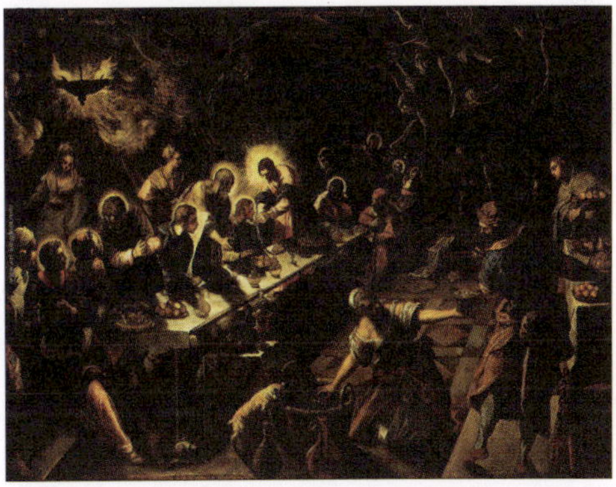

The Last Supper by Tintoretto, (1592–1594)

Here we see the representation of perspective in the crowd of figures illuminated by sudden flashes of haloes. The boundaries between the real and the fantastic cease to exist, and a spectral flight of phosphorescent entities is superimposed on to the real scene. Set in a popular tavern, the light comes from an oil lamp hanging from the ceiling, which illuminates details of objects and people in the background. Then there are the lights of the haloes and those of the angels that are in the upper right-hand corner.

The painting is divided in two by the diagonals of the table: on the left side the spiritual world, and on the right side the earthly one. Jesus spreads his arms to give bread to his disciples. His face is turned to an elder who, first, will receive bread. A kneeling apostle is approaching the table in a symbolic wedding dress. The tunic, on which the light shines, is made precious by a veil. On the sides of the canvas, a servant, seen from behind with his gaze lowered, seems to remind us of the words of the evangelists Luke and John: a servant is no more than his master. An apostle, in an act of love, hands an apple to a poorly dressed girl. Another extends bread to a sick beggar. His does not seem a sincere gesture, but one dictated by charity. This is Jude, recognizable by his bag of money tied to a wide orange band.

During the Renaissance period, both in Flanders and in the Netherlands, Flemish painting developed an original artistic flowering, above all thanks to the affirmation of a lively urban bourgeoisie.

Fashion and Style

By 'fashion' we mean those expressive modalities concerning clothing. All fashion is based on cyclical change: in modern industrial society, the expressive forms (art, languages, objects used by man in their environment) are continually renewed; this affects not only clothing but every aspect of daily life. During the Renaissance, fashion was influenced by the diffusion of silk art in Europe and the increase in international trade. The development of the fashion industry also led to the differentiation in appearance between men's and women's clothing.

Throughout the fifteenth century, the shapes of the clothes remained mainly the same as in the Middle Ages, but during the Renaissance, attention to appearance and the value of aesthetics reached the highest cultural importance. Sumptuous clothes came to be considered works of art. Clothes, like other artistic and cultural expressions, became a symbol of prestige for the richest families in the city. In this period, Italian fashion dictated the rules throughout Europe. Even the Church played a decisive role in male attire, with the sumptuousness of clergy clothing reaching such excessive levels as to provoke envy and accusations of corruption, which led to the Protestant reform.

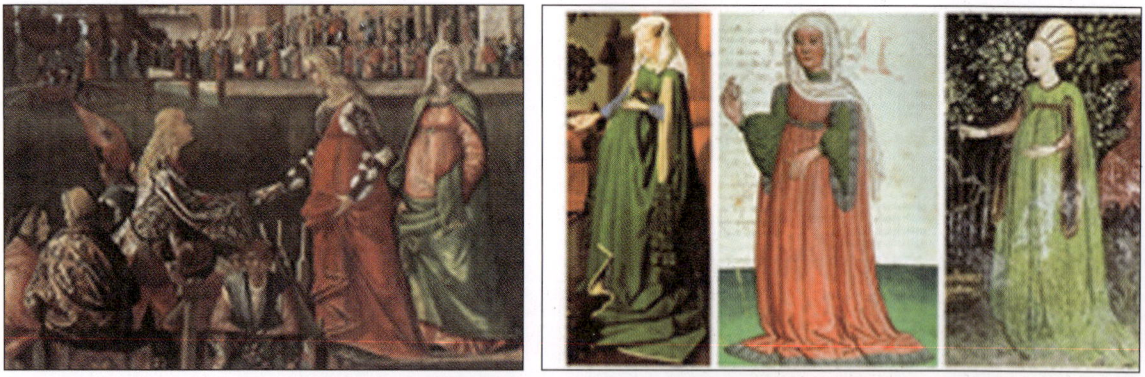

Fashion and Style during the Renaissance Period

The female dress was linear and at the same time elegant; it featured a veil held at the top of the head and under the chin, and a long dress with a tight bodice and a plunging neckline. Males wore a velvet cap and a close-fitting vest with a small velvet cape; on their legs they wore tight-fitting stockings.

The 1600s (Seventeenth Century)

VI

Edited by
Aditya Gautam

Designed By
Amina Razzack, Nikhil Prashar

The 1600s (Seventeenth Century)

Geo-Political Summary

If the Renaissance universe presented itself as ordered, stable and harmonious, the seventeenth century was one of the most violent in European history: tormented by wars, political struggles and religious division. The seventeenth century is marked by terrible famines and pestilences which cause a sharp decline in births and a significant decrease in production. The Thirty Years War (1618–1648) was fought by Spain and the German Empire against France, Sweden, Denmark, Holland.

Around the middle of the century, social revolts broke out across Europe. Some states are able to cope with the crisis thanks to a strong state organization and a solid and powerful France is ruled by Louis XVI, the sun king, whilst Peter dominates in Russia. In England, we see the first parliamentary monarchy (after a phase of civil war and the short dictatorship of Cromwell). Spain experiences a period of greatness, thanks to its domination over Portugal and Italy, but already at the beginning of the seventeenth century, it is a declining empire, badly administered by the Habsburgs. Spain and Germany are completely defeated by the Thirty Years War. The distance between Catholic and Protestant countries is widened. Productive and mercantile activity increases instead in the northern countries. The Roman Church is going through a phase of deep crisis: attacked by the Protestant reformation, the Church tries to reaffirm its power. The preaching, the sacred processions, the theatre, the baroque art, are all under the papal influence.

In the seventeenth century, Italy is governed according to the provisions of the peace treaty of Cateau Cambresis 1559, which closed the conflict between Spain and France. The country is subject to Spanish rule in Naples, Sicily, Sardinia, and the Duchy of Milan. Meanwhile, the Thirty Years' War, which upset Europe from 1618 to 1648, sees Catholic forces oppose Protestant reformers until the Treaty of Westphalia marks the definitive defeat of the Habsburg empire and the Counter-Reformation policy.

Art

The Italian baroque develops in Rome, and is something more than a simple artistic expression. This art, faithful to the norms codified by the Trento Code, involves the viewer emotionally and therefore convinces the faithful of the truths of the Catholic faith. It is spectacular, grandiose, but also ambiguous art. Alessandro Manzoni, in his Promessi Sposi, the most important Italian historical novel of the nineteenth century, will show the most evident negative aspects of the seventeenth century in Italy: the military nature of society,

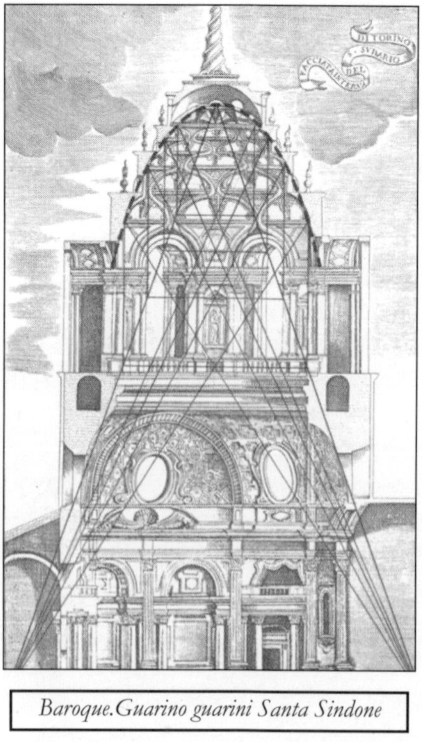

Baroque.Guarino guarini Santa Sindone

the display of the power of wealth, the arrogance of Spanish domination, the poverty and ignorance of the people, the rhetoric in language and hypocrisy in behaviour, and the ceremonious character present in all the manifestations of social life. The seventeenth century is, in fact, a century dominated by the label, by a strict respect for social and religious norms: rules in duels and human relationships, in philosophical discussions, and in art.

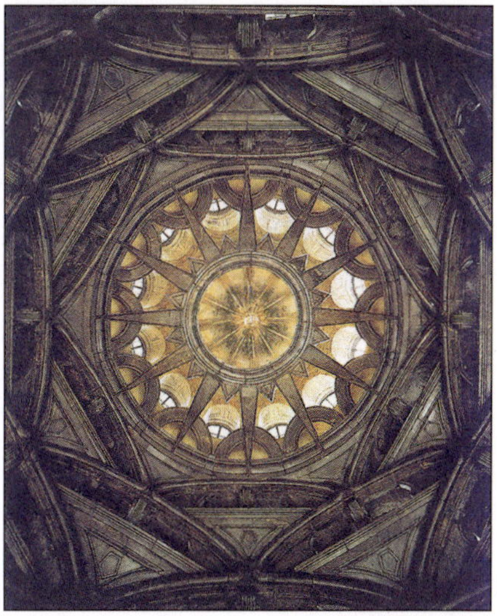

Baroque. Dome Santa Sindone in Turin

Theatre

The classicist grand theatre is affirmed, attentive to the rules of the classical formalized tragedy of Aristotle. It has its highest expression in France. On the other hand, in England, a freer type of theatre emerges: it is the season of Elizabethan theatre and of Shakespeare. In his tragedies, human reason comes into conflict with violent uncontrollable elements: love, madness, ambition and revenge; these are universal, internal themes, but linked to the unrest of 1600. At the same time, however, there is nostalgia for the irony of Cervantes, the great Spanish writer and author of *Don Quixote*. This feeling is also linked to the theme of illusion, the ability to imagine beyond real limits. In its more artificial and external manifestations, this quality often comes to life in a series of fine inventions, or in the illusionism of large decorative enterprises, when the painter fills immense spaces and skies, or, in the refinement of theatrical productions.

In its deepest aspect, this theme of illusion—the play between reality and fiction, between dreams and life—is the playground of the great authors of the time. An example is Gian Battista Marino, the most famous poet of Italy in the seventeenth century: for him, the main aim of the poet is to marvel, to amaze. Baroque poetry dominates the taste for novelty, for all that is strange, bizarre and surprising. The language used is very elaborate, rich in precious images of twisted, intellectualistic reasoning, the so-called Conceptism.

The author wants to demonstrate his skill, his wit, his cultural refinement. Metaphors are often used—the figure of speech which establishes a comparison between two words of similar meaning. Difficult metaphors are preferred. Baroque poetry thus rejects the serenity and simplicity of Renaissance art, and chooses an elaborate style to sharpen wits. The intellectual of 1600 is no longer the courtier; it is the baroque poet: salaried and called to court to entertain an ever wider audience and to increase the prestige of the lord. His main function is to entertain, to impress with effective words.

Gian Battista Marino, Naples (1569–1625), was a poet with an adventurous life, and he had great success in his time, especially in Italy and in France. His style is imitated by many poets called 'marinists'. His production was very extensive and included various types of compositions. His masterpiece is the Adonis (1623). This poem celebrates sensual love: Marino shows his inventive ability and great technical ability by paying attention to the musical value of the verses. However, in this period, no other Italian poets achieved particularly significant results. In 1600, Italy began to lose the function of cultural guidance for Europe that it had held during the course of the whole Renaissance. Alessandro Tassoni (Modena, 1565–1635), Anti-aristotelico, and also Anti-spagnolo, were the inventors of the heroic poem, where topics and epic are treated in a joking and comic tone.

Paolo Sarpi was a Venetian scientist, historian and theologian. He fought against the claims of the church, which wanted to set up a court of the Inquisition in Venice. He was consequently excommunicated by the Pope for his defence of the law of freedom of the Venetian Republic. His most important writing was a history of the Council of Trent—a historical investigation with a rigorous and modern method, attentive to facts and historical sources, (ambassadorial reports, diaries, letters of cardinals). The work expresses clearly his own criticism of the church, which is that it has organized the council for political rather than spiritual reasons.

This is a golden age of theatre in Spain, France and England. In Italy, there is choice between a simple theatrical style loyal to the Greek manner, and another theatrical style with strong colours, dominated by the taste for horror and violence, deriving from the classic tragedies of Seneca. The latter is preferred. A prominent figure is Federico Della Valle, author of tragedies on religious subjects.

The Italian melodrama was developed by a group of musicians, scientists, and writers in Florence. The term 'melodrama' refers to the tradition, both librettist and musical, that was popular from the sixteenth to the nineteenth century in Italy; opera is a more general term.

The first experiments in this field were made by the poet Ottavio Rinuccini. The Arianna, his first real opera libretto, was performed by Claudio Monteverdi. Monteverdi's own musical masterpiece, the Orpheus, was performed in 1607 in Mantua, and already contained all the most important elements of the style: recitatives, arias, refrains, inserts of dances, the choir and the orchestra. Melodrama became a form of grandiose spectacle, with singers and specialized musicians. The subjects were mostly mythological, traumatic and historical, but also religious, or comedians and popular. The musical element became more important than the literary one. The two major centres of diffusion of opera were Rome and Venice.

Science

Attention to natural phenomena had already been very much alive in the Renaissance, (astrology, alchemy), but it was fully established during the seventeenth century. There was an aspiration to a new science, no longer conditioned by morals and religion but based on the direct action of nature, and on the use of technical and adequate tools. Galileo and Newton pioneered new objective data interpretation methods.

The traditionalist scientific vision understood nature as anthropomorphic, animated by moral forces: good and evil. The scientists of the scientific revolution, on the other hand, think of a nature as governed by mathematical laws and rigorous mechanics. Many of these scholars see signs of the rationality and power of God precisely in the mathematical laws they discover.

Thus, the Renaissance myth of man at the centre of the universe collapses in science. This moment of crisis is shared by poets, philosophers and scientists, which unites them in a great desire for innovation. Astronomical studies, together with the great geographical discoveries, help to delineate the idea of a vast and boundless world without certainties.

This new attitude, however, at first had many critics. The new era in science began violently, with the burning of Jordanian Bruno in the field of flowers (in Rome, 1600). Bruno, a well-known philosopher, was judged a heretic by the court of the Inquisition; his death symbolically marks the end of the Renaissance and inaugurates the figure of the intellectual persecuted by the church.

Tommaso Campanella (1568–1639), was a Calabrian philosopher and poet, also condemned by the Inquisition for his ideas and repeatedly tortured and imprisoned. He escaped the death penalty by pretending to be crazy. His major work was 'The City of the Sun', in which he described an ideal utopian model of society.

Galileo Galilei

Galileo Galilei was born in Pisa in 1564, and according to him, the scientific method should be based on the direct observation of natural phenomena, on their translation in mathematical terms, and on the formulation of possible hypotheses (and therefore on their verification through concrete experimentation). He performed astronomical observations that contrasted many points of the Ptolemaic theory (which placed the earth at the centre of the universe), in favour of the heliocentric theory proposed by Copernicus in 1543. In some of his writings, the scientist exposes his thesis: the autonomy of scientific research with respect to the truth of the sacred scriptures. Galileo's knowledge starts from experiences based on the senses and from mathematical demonstrations, not from the Bible. Galileo does not dispute the Bible on the moral theological level, but he thinks that Biblical passages on the nature of the world are not credible from the scientific point of view.

The church refused the compromise offered by the position of Galileo, who wanted to guarantee independence and dignity both to the faith and to science. The condemnation of the church halted scientific research in Italy for over a century. Indeed, the reading of the works of Galileo, Copernico and Kepler was forbidden by the church until 1822. His 'Dialogue Concerning the Two Chief World Systems' in 1632 was a cause of particular controversy. In the writing, three characters (Aristotelian philosopher Simplicius, Copernican scientist Sagredo and impartial intellectual Salviati) are gathered in the Venetian palace of the noble Sagredo, in order to discuss philosophical and scientific problems for four days. The second day is devoted to the principle of authority: in the philosophical discussions of the time, reasoning was judged to be correct if it respected the writers and those texts considered indisputable certain authorities (for example, Aristotle and the Bible). Condemned by the Holy Office of Rome, Galileo must publicly renounce his theses in 1633.

Culture

Out of the gradual decline of the Renaissance, Mannerism and classicism, a new sensibility emerges, which seeks a more real and tangible contact with reality. This is called Baroque style. The term derives from the Spanish or Portuguese definition of an irregularly shaped pearl. The adjective, meaning bizarre, was used to define a painting in which the rules of proportions are not respected, and the composition realized according to the caprice of the artist. The innovations brought about in the field of Baroque poetry start from the decisive rejection of Renaissance classicism.

The main exponent is the Neapolitan Giambattista Marino, from whom the current of the Marinists, the architects of the poetics of wonder, originates. Marinism is aimed at capturing the most surprising aspects of reality through the sought after artificial style. Conceptualism also appears—a literary method which, through the use of great conceptual subtlety, embellishes language. A sort of reaction to the conceptism can be considered classicism, which pushes some poets to reject the refined and elaborate style of the Marinists in the name of a closer link with the classical tradition. This anti-barbaric and classical current is led by Gabriello Chiabrera, who advocated the inventive inspiration of poetic rules and pre-established schemes.

European Baroque

In France, the Baroque is not only a literary and artistic current, but also lifestyle founded on exterior, established in the cultural salons of the rich and noble, thanks to the playwright Molière. In the philosophical field, Descartes stands out as the founder of rationalism (cogito ergo sum—I think, therefore I exist). Also, Pascal is placed in the framework of moral reflection on the religious debate.
In England, the seventeenth century can be divided into three fundamental periods. The first is still under the influence of the Elizabethan age: John Donne emerges as an exponent of English conceptualism and father of metaphysical poetry. In the second period, from the ashes of the civil war comes the first example of a republic that the country has ever known. This is followed by a dictatorship headed by Oliver Cromwell. The third period sees the restoration of the Stuart monarchy, who promote the spread of French culture and the study of the sciences and philosophy. In this period, two great philosophers—Hobbes and Locke—are born. In Spain, literary production experiences an unprecedented vivacity—the so-called Siglo de Oro. In the literary field, Miguel de Cervantes creates *Don Quixote*.

The rules imposed by the council of Trento regarding the sacred and rigid images did not prevent the emergence of original and nonconformist forms of artistic expression, such as that of Caravaggio, whose luminous inventions displayed a profound realism. Realism was not the only expressive modality of the seventeenth century, which was a rich and complex century, from an artistic point of view. Italy experienced its last great season: from the eighteenth century, France assumed the leading role in the field of art. The most advanced centre of culture was Rome, where the illuminated and cultured popes gathered the greatest artists in Italy, commissioning works of the highest value; works that were able to overwhelm the faithful, to amaze them with sinuous, original, exuberant and theatrical forms. All the characteristics of baroque art tended to break every possible equilibrium, overturning the classical concept of harmonious measure.

Alongside realism and baroque, in the seventeenth century, a current inspired by classicism also emerged—the one inaugurated by Carracci—which, through didactic narrative images, placed itself at the service of the church by advocating that art should instruct the faithful. In the seventeenth century, moreover, an interest in multiple-genre painting developed: in addition to still life, we see interior scenes, objects, city views, and moments from everyday life.

Baroque Arcitecture

The baroque architectural style is characterized by the magnificence and richness of the materials used: marble gold stucco.

Masters of the style include Carlo Maderno (1556–1626), whose taste can be defined as preparatory, a connecting element between Renaissance architecture and the successive innovations in architectural language. With the completion of St. Peter's (1607–1612), Maderno transforms Michelangelo's central plan into a longitudinal basilical plan, so as to double its capacity. He also builds the façade.

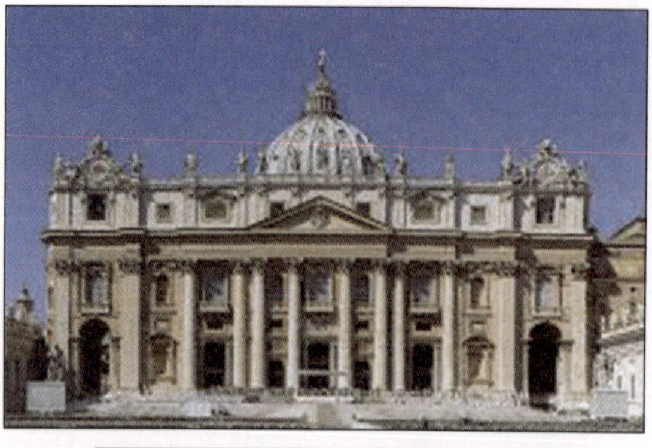

Front view of St. Peter's Basilica by Carlo Maderno (c. 1607–1612)

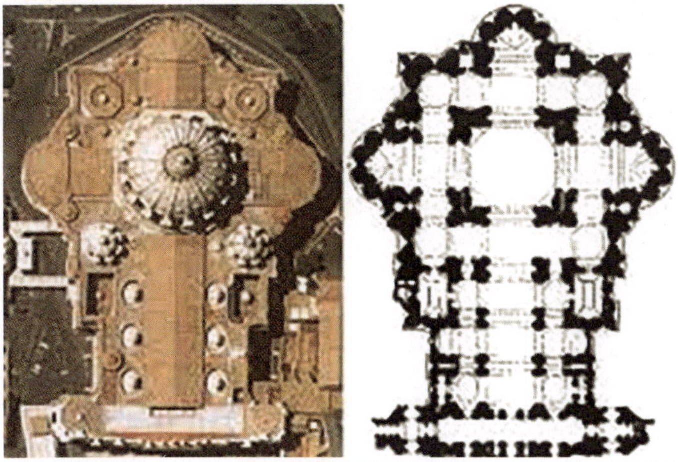

Aerial view of St. Peter's Basilica by Carlo Maderno (c. 1607–1612)

Gian Lorenzo Bernini (Naples 1598, Rome 1680)

The architect, sculptor and set designer, without denying the classic balance of the Renaissance tradition, modifies its forms with baroque sensibility and an original scenic and spectacular taste. His life is devoted to different popes, especially Pope Urban VIII. Bernini admires Classical architecture, but tries to innovate the shapes and decorative motifs with freedom and imagination. His works have a spectacular and majestic touch, in line with the baroque taste of his time and with the ideas of the Counter-Reformation. In 1624, he was entrusted with the construction of the canopy of San Pietro. For this work, he collaborated with Borromini; however, this ended after economic disappointment in 1632. The abandonment grew into a legendary rivalry.

Bernini also created the bronze canopy in San Pietro, which was supported by four huge columns. This is considered the manifesto of baroque architecture, and is the result of the brilliant inventive capacity of Bernini. The originality came from the transformation of this architectural element, usually of small dimensions, into a majestic structure. The four-strong columns, rather than appearing as supports, seem to stretch upward in a spiral motion. The cover was designed by Borromini. In this work, architecture and sculpture are merged, and the result represents the overcoming of the conception of the division of the Arts.

Pope Alexander VII charged Bernini to design a square in front of St. Peter's Basilica. In 1657, he designed the oval square delimited by an architraved portico. It featured a series of 284 columns, crowned by 140 statues of saints. The portico was inserted on two wings which connected it to the façade. With this colonnade it appears that the Church of Rome welcomes and embraces all the faithful, creating an architecture which connects the basilica to the city.

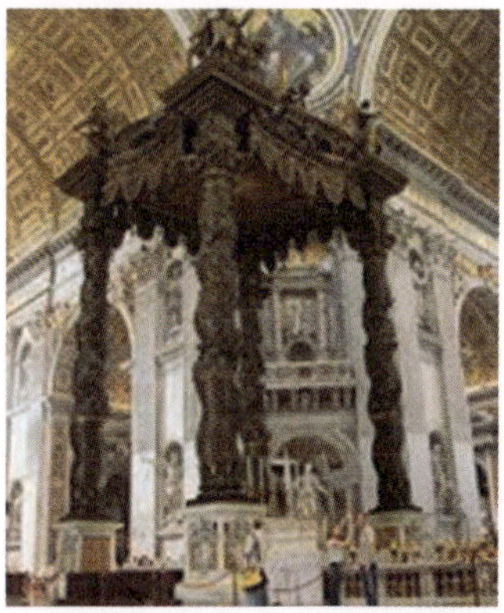

Aerial view of St. Peter's Basilica by Carlo Maderno (c. 1607–1612)

Francesco Borromini (or Castelli, 1599–1667)

Unlike Bernini, Borromini always remained outside of the courtly world. He dedicated himself exclusively to architecture, a domain in

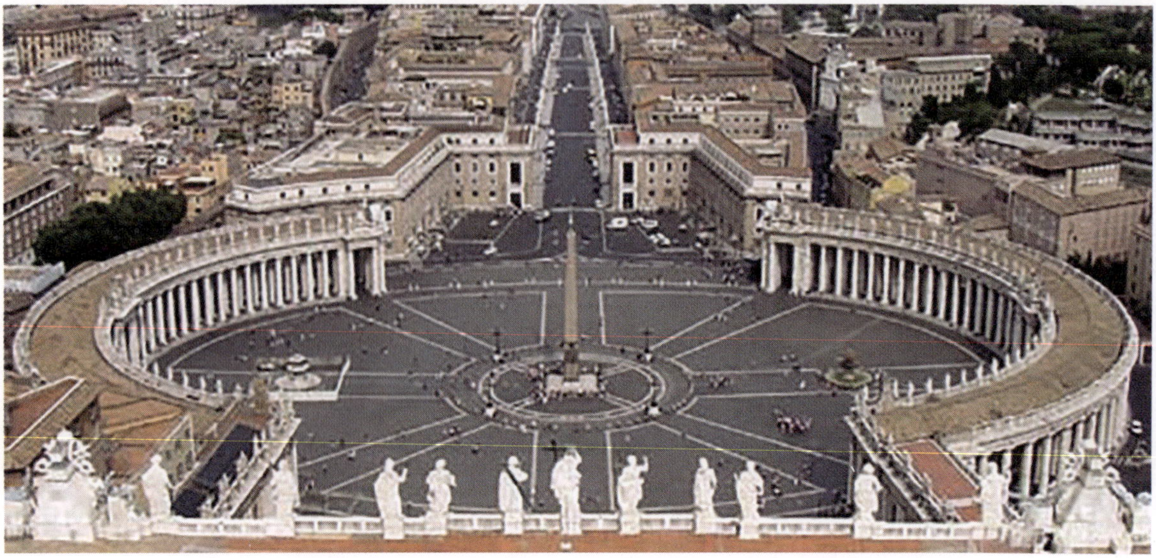

St. Peter's Square by Gian Lorenzo Bernini (c. 1656–1667)

which, through his religious fervour, he was able to combine an extraordinary technical expertise with a profound cultural education. In his work, the space is dynamically designed and poor materials are used, such as brick masonry, white plaster, and stucco decorations, rather than marble and precious materials. The surfaces assume curvatures and undulations, alternating concave and connected profiles.

Light and chiaroscuro tricks become fundamental elements. However, he was of nervous character, and in 1667, he committed suicide in a moment of depression.

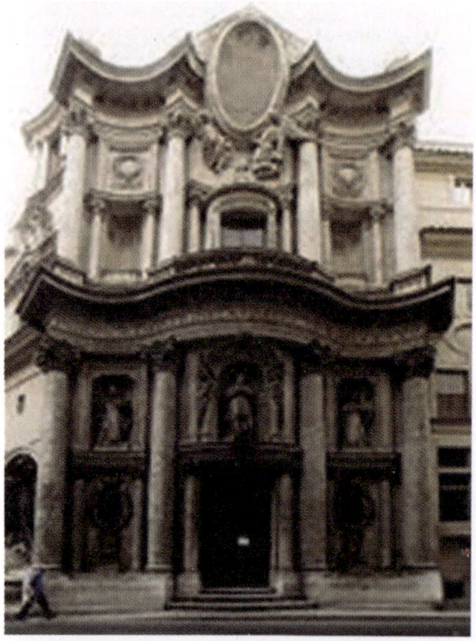

San Carlo alle Quattro Fontane by Francesco Borromini (c. 1638–1641)

Out of his work, we remember San Carlino of the four fountains. The complex of San Carlino and the house of the Trinitarians present all the elements of the Borromini style. We see the transformation of the traditional cross plant into an ellipse. The dome of the church is decorated with crosses, hexagons, and octagons, and ends with a luminous lantern. Borromini proves able to obtain a result of exceptionally formal quality. His position implies a rejection of Bernini's monumental vision: in fact, through his work, Borromini contrasts the spaces instead of extending them illusively, and his style gives the architectural forms an extraordinary sense of tension of strength.

The façade of San Carlino is founded on the alternation of connected concave surfaces, on the rough and broken contours of the profiles, and on the strong plastic value of the architectural elements: columns, cornices, niches. The facade of San Carlino seems to express, for the last time, the opposition of Borromini to the monumental equilibrium of Bernini.

Baroque Painting

The Renaissance perspective ordered and limited space, whilst the new baroque perspective opens infinite spaces and frees the energy of movement.

Pietro da Cortona (1596–1669) was a painter, decorator and architect who decisively contributed to the formation of a decorative and sumptuous taste called Cortonism. In his frescoes, the figures, posed in classical pause, are often inserted in a vibrant scenographic space. Cortona's fresco 'Triumph of Divine Providence' (1633–1639) covers the ceiling of the Barberini palace hall, and features an aerial perspective of the sky as seen from below. A bright, luminous swirl of figures and clouds seem to overflow beyond the limits of the architectural pictorial frame.

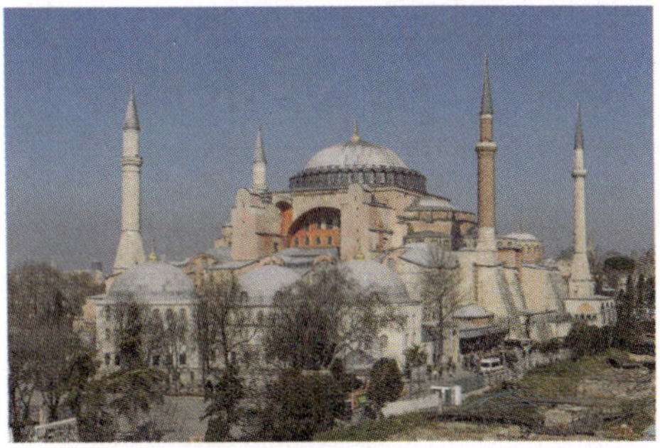

Triumph of Divine Providence

In Bologna, Ludovico Carracci (1555–1619), together with his cousins Annibale and Agostino, founded the Accademia Degli Incamminati: an artistic association whose purpose was to recover the communicative naturalness of the pictorial language. This was to be achieved through drawing from life, and from the study of the works of the great masters of the Renaissance. Carracci dominated the artistic environment in Bologna uncontested. His pictorial style was aimed at the direct, simple communication of human feelings in order to give the painting a new sense of truth. Important examples of his work include the cycles of frescoes in the palaces of Fava, Magnani and San Pieri.

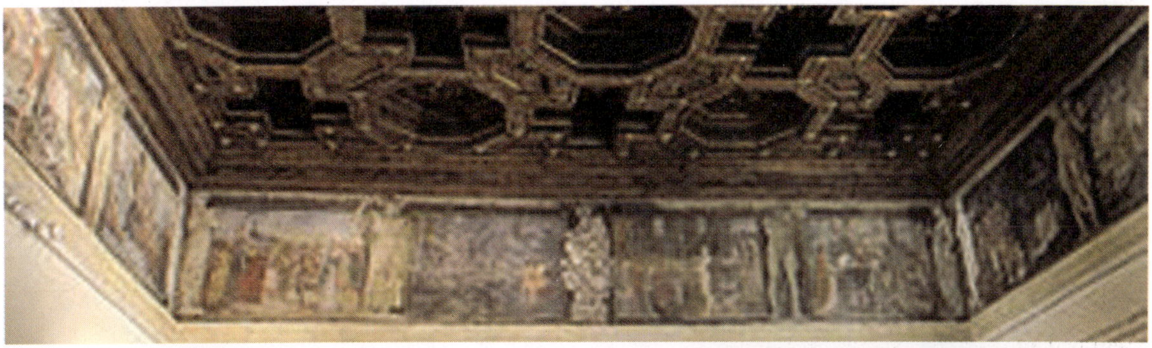

A wide view of the frescoes painted by the Caracci brothers at the Palazzio Ghisilardi Fava (c. 1583–1590)

The paintings of Michelangelo Merisi da Caravaggio (1571–1610) are in many ways antithetical to those of Carracci. While Carracci aims to portray the ideal, Caravaggio aims at the naturalistic representation of the real. The Caravaggesque raw truthfulness led to critical oppositions, to the point where numerous works were rejected by the clients. Light played a fundamental role in his work: the chiaroscuro contrasts enhanced by violent flashes of grazing light accentuated the plastic sense of the bodies and underlined their dynamic attitudes. The colours are decisive and violent, standing out clearly against the dark tones of the backgrounds.

One cannot say that Caravaggio, in his artistic existential restlessness, gave life to a school in the classic sense of the term; however, the influence of his painting on his contemporaries was profound in both Italy and with foreign artists, such as Rubens. From the art of Caravaggio, the so-called 'genre' painting (still lifes and scenes of popular environment) was also derived.

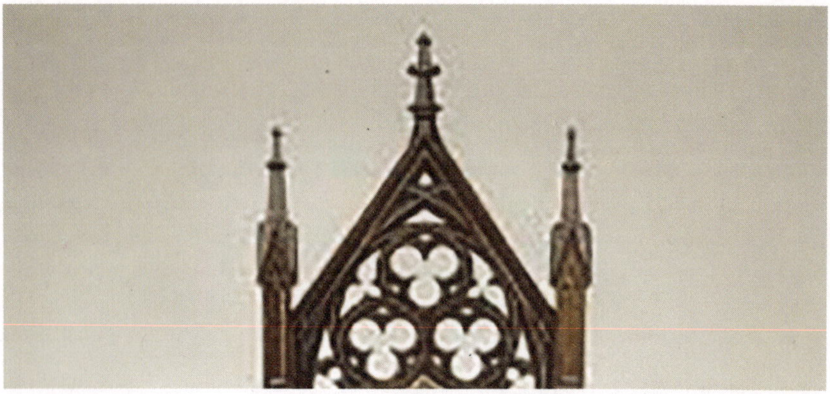

A zoomed-in view of one of the frescoes as part of the fresco cycle painted by the Caracci brothers at Palazzio Ghisilardi Fava (c. 1583–1590)

The Vocation of St. Matthew

In this Caravaggio painting is illustrated an episode from the Gospel: the calling of Matthew (who, before becoming an apostle and later an Evangelist, was a tax collector). The scene takes place in a shabby dark environment, in which, sitting around a table, some men count money greedily: it's time to collect taxes. Suddenly Jesus enters with Peter, and points to Matthew. The light brings out the face of Christ from the shadows, calling to Matthew, who is holding up his arm and hand. The light does not come from the window, but from the right, as if the door from which Christ has just entered is still open. The diagonal cut of the scene creates a very special effect, almost theatrical. In fact, even though the action happens from the right to the left, the cut of the shadow makes the observer look from the left to the right, towards the gesture and the face of Christ.

The setting is very realistic but the light of the sacred, the divine grace that descends into the darkness of sin, makes the scene real. The presence of the two figures means that spiritual salvation is obtained through the word of God (Christ), and the mediation of the church (Peter). The light of God's grace descends on all men and gives everyone a chance of salvation, but it is individual people who choose the path to follow.

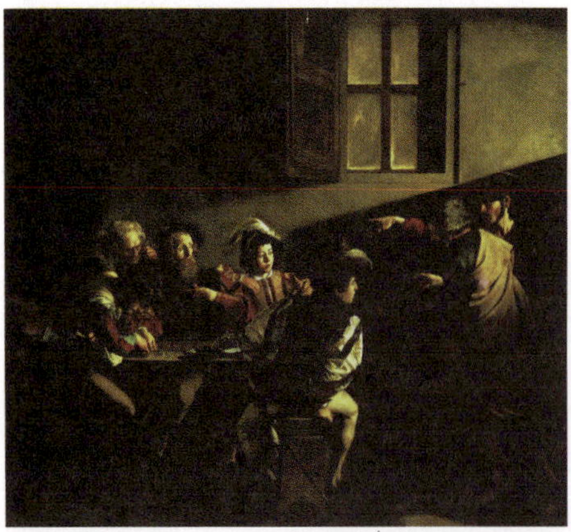

Michelangelo Merisi da Caravaggio, 'The Calling of St. Matthew' (c. 1599–1600)

Fruit Basket (Milan, 1596)

This painting is a still life without figures. The composition is seen from below, so that fruits and flowers stand out clearly on the light wall. Objects are represented as they are in reality without trying to beautify nature: the dry leaf, the blemished apple. The arrangement of the basket is based on an almost miraculous balance: the leaves are still, but there is the impression that everything could move at any moment. The light enhances the brilliance and roundness of the grapes, the apple, the peach, the lemon, and the roughness of the figs. Representations of flowers, fruit and inanimate objects was considered to be a minor genre in comparison to the representation of living and moving nature.

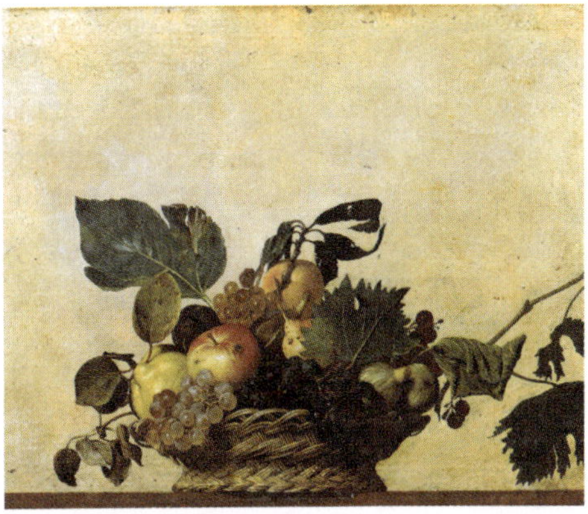

Michelangelo Merisi da Caravaggio
'Basket of fruit' (c. 1599)

The birth of the 'genre' painting and also the trend of naturalism in the late sixteenth century can be linked to the development of the natural sciences and to the new conception of nature, now considered worthy of being studied in all its aspects without religious meanings. It was above all the Flemish painters who specialized in the precise and faithful representation of the naturalistic elements.

In Italy, the genre began to become autonomous at the beginning of the seventeenth century, and the term 'still-life' began to spread with a negative connotation. In the seventeenth century, the still life genre continued to grow, and alongside the flowers and fruits, we see kitchens, tables with objects, and musical instruments.

European Seventeenth Century Painting

In Flanders, two great artists emerge. The first is Paul Rubens (1577–1640), in whose works we find the influence of Italian art, Venetian colourism, Renaissance tradition, and Caravaggio's realism, all fused with the character of northern painting. His opulent, technically expanded forms and his intense chromatism, all convey a powerful vitality and sensuality. In Holland, in the Dutch Republic, the Protestant bourgeois culture is expressed through art: through the paintings of objects inspired by daily life, permeated with sober moralism and simplicity. Van Rembrandt van Rijn (1606–1669) creates works animated by a careful ethical and religious spirit, aimed at capturing the spiritual essence of man beyond material appearances.

Music

The melodrama was based on the combination of music and poetry, like the modern opera, and was developed in Florence in the late 1500s amongst a group of musicians and poets who called themselves the camerata di bardi (the comrade of the bards) since they met in the house of the Florentine count Giovanna Bardi. As the humanists had advocated a return to the style of antiquity, this group reevaluated the monodic music of ancient Greece. They proposed to recreate a show in which, as in Greek tragedy, music, poetry and dance meet and where the text is the fundamental element. However, in polyphony, with the overlapping of the melodic parts, the text became incomprehensible, so an operation of musical renewal was needed to restore value to the word. The members of the comrade called this new style of recitation 'singing'. Thus, a new genre was born.

The first work produced by the group was the Eurydice Di Jacopo Peri (1561–1633), performed in Florence in 1600 on the occasion of Mary's wedding to Enrico Quarto. In 1602, another work was performed on the same subject, the myth of Orpheus, composed by Giulio Caccini (1545–1611).

It was the Cremonese, Claudio Monteverdi (1567–1643) who gave a sublime interpretation of this nascent musical form. Former author of madrigals, and for twenty years a composer-musician, he developed the theme of the opera on Greek music. Following the style of the Greeks, he used different ways to emphasize the various moments of dramatic action, and changed the instruments to match the characters and situations. He thus accentuated the importance of the orchestra, giving a solid structure to the instrumental pieces and designing the work as an organic and articulated whole. He changed the role of the artist: no longer a court composer who wrote music on behalf of the lord, but a man who translated reality into music, and also the feelings of his time through his experience. The highest peaks of his production are his theatrical works: the Orpheus (Mantua, 1607), and the Arianna (1623). In his seventh book of madrigals, he moved forward from the traditional concept of the madrigal, and from monody, in favour of chamber duets. In his eighth madrigal, he composed 'Il Combattimento di Tancredi e Clorinda'. The piece has the operatic text drawn from Torquatto Tasso's 'La Gerusalemme Liberata', (Jerusalem Delivered), a Romance set against the backdrop of the First Crusade, when Godfrey of Bouillon conquered Jerusalem. Between 1627 and 1641, he wrote numerous dramatic works.

In the seventeenth century, when melodrama satisfied the public fervour for theatrical performance, music was no longer the prerogative of the courts. The audiences were no longer just the cultured and refined aristocracy, but the ordinary people, who brought different cultural needs to the poetry of theatrical production. If society of the 1500s operated under the banner of grace and harmony, society in the 1600s was centred on magniloquence. The audience went to the theatre to socialize and enjoy themselves, and presented attention to the stage only in moments such as a scene change or the singing performances. The result was an impoverishment of the lyrics of the music. The recitation was neglected in favour of Ariosto, which allowed the singer to show his singing virtues, and the predominant element of the melodrama became the bel canto. In Italy, schools and conservatories were opened for the training of future singers: the cult of bel canto meant that the singers dictated the law in the field of music production; each imposed on the composer the most appropriate form for his own voice.

Dissemination of Melodrama in Europe

From Italy, melodrama spread to the other countries of Europe: firstly to France, although the performers, musicians and set designers were all Italians. French opera was differentiated from Italian melodrama because it was influenced by the development of the ballet. In the theatres of the main German cities, Italian opera was a huge success.

Baroque Theatre

The best results from the Italian theatre in the Baroque age were from the commedia dell'arte, a form of entertainment born in the second half of the sixteenth century. It was a form of theatrical representation that used professional actors, were linked to theatrical companies equipped with scenic equipment, and were directed by a coragrafo, similar to a director. In the commedia dell'arte, the acting does not take place according to a defined sample, but is based on the innovation of the actors, who had at their disposal a simple canvas. The latter offered only indications, allowing the interpreter to freely develop the character. There were also mimicry scenes, with the intent of provoking laughter. The actors tended to specialize in a distinct type of fashion, in the process popularizing the 'Colombina' and 'Pulcinella' style of masks which were a great success among the popular audience, also influencing Shakespeare's works.

Alongside the melodrama, the comedy and the tragedy are popular theatrical genres. Among the authors, we remember Michelangelo Buonarotti (1568–1646), the great-grandson of the great sculptor. He wrote *The Fair* in 1618: a comedy in 25 acts which mirrored the urban life of the time. The genre of tragedy remained faithful to the rules of Aristotle's poetics: division into five acts, presence of the choir, respect for the unity of time, place and action, and a certain predilection for the horrible element of the Senechian mould. Federico Della Valle (1560–1628) composed works on Biblical subjects and contemporary history.

Also, Carlo de Dottori (1618–1685) was inspired by Greek theatre and that of Seneca (which dealt with the theme of violence inherent in the very nature of power) to write *Aristodemo* (1655–1657). It is a quick work, accompanied by the reflections of the chorus on the precariousness of human existence. One of the fundamental themes is the contrast between hope and disappointment, which creates continuous reversals of the scenes.

The Candle-Bearer by Giordano Bruno (1548–1600) was a polemic against established knowledge. It was a comedy in prose divided into five acts, published in Paris in 1582. At the centre of the plot are the cruel jokes suffered by three different characters, against whom the author triggers an aggressive comedy. These characters embody human nonsense; a conception of culture emptied of its highest meanings and reduced to a sterile observance of rules. Bruno depicts in a grotesque way the fixations, the manias, the follies inherent in men, and their tendency to upset the value of culture. All this is done in multiple languages and varied tones, totally reversing the reality.

Fashion

The fashions of seventeenth-century Europe were turned upside down by the Thirty Years War. The benevolent attitude towards the superficial issues which had characterized the late Renaissance was noticeably weakened. The most powerful capitalist countries, Holland and England, are examples of a puritan lifestyle in which new values of comfort and moderation spread. Clothing styles are simplified. However, these trends are overturned in the second half of the seventeenth century with the restoration of the monarchy and its splendour, especially in France where the reign of Louis XIV begins.

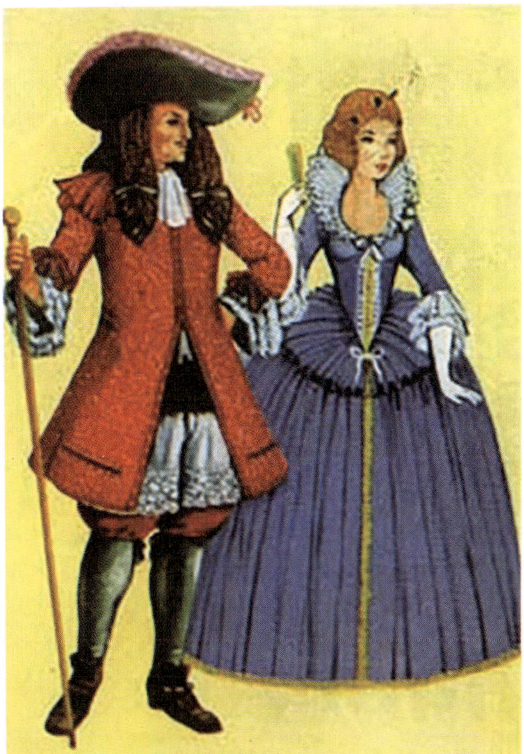

Typical aristocratic apparel during the rule of Louis XIV

The masculine suit was gaudy, it included a large feathered felt over a long hair wig, a waist-tight jacket, a shirt adorned with lace, and wide knee-length trousers. The woman's dress was full and rigid, characterized by a linen ruff with starched torches, and a wide skirt supported by inner wicker hoops. The fashionable hairstyle was short curls.

The 1700s (Eighteenth Century)

VII

Edited by
Arieb Ahmed Qureshi

Designed By
Aymun Kaleem, Aatif Nawaz,
Amina Razzack

The 1700s (The Eighteenth Century)

The eighteenth century begins with the triumph of the absolute monarchy of Louis XIV, and ends with the French revolution. It is a century of reason, of the idea of freedom, of the rise of the Bourgeois class as a new subject of rights. It is the century of the Enlightenment, an intellectual movement that spread throughout Europe. The premises of its development are born from the scientific thought of the seventeenth century, from the rationalism of Descartes, the reflections of philosophers such as Thomas Hobbes and John Locke who had challenged the concept of power and the idea that it derives from divine will (as had previously been believed). Developing these ideas, the Enlightenment philosophers analyse history and reality using a new instrument: reason. Politics, religion, literature are involved in this new vision of the world, as well as the ideas, beliefs and situations of the past. Anything that restricts the freedom of the individual is considered intolerable.

Historical Context

In Europe, the main events are the industrial revolution in England, and the French revolution that erased the absolute power of the sovereigns. In this century, Italy is still feeling the effects of the economic decline of the previous century; it is weak and a pawn of the diplomatic games of the most powerful European states. It is divided into many states and controlled by foreign powers. Austrian powers settle in the north of the country, and it is thanks to the enlightened reforms of the Austrian sovereign that the economic and social structures in Lombardy are organized. At the end of the century, Italy too was overwhelmed by the bourgeois revolution born in France. By freeing man from all forms of slavery, the Enlightenment interprets the will of the bourgeoisie, the new social class becoming increasingly important in various European countries. Above all in England, but also in Holland and France, the bourgeoisie had become rich thanks to the great expansion of trade at the beginning of the first industrial revolution. The bourgeoisie sees the social classes of nobility and clergy as the enemies that impede its strength. The struggle of the bourgeoisie against an antiquated politics becomes the struggle to assert its power.

In this century, intellectuals have a new relationship with society. The Illuminists come out of the royal courts to stay in society; they spread their ideas with new tools, such as newspapers and magazines. They think that the objective of the 'man of culture' is to improve society. For this reason, new associations of intellectuals are formed that are not limited to a single state, but which become international. Already at the beginning of the eighteenth century in England, information, political ideas are spread by newspapers and magazines, with a brilliant ironic style.

However, the spread of the Enlightenment culture had many opponents. When in France, in 1751, the first two volumes of the *Herculiteum* were published (the Pharaonic opera that wanted to organize and spread all human knowledge), the reaction of many members of the church was to accuse the Enlightenmentists of being corrupt and false, so much so that they banned the official diffusion by a decree of the French parliament. It was evident to those who held power that the project to increase culture, to propose new ideas free from any prejudice of the past, was too dangerous.

The Enlightenment critics accused Christianity of maintaining ignorance, superstition and fanaticism in the population. They argued that the clergy had conditioned society for centuries, pursuing material, economic and political interests. Some thinkers came to reject the very idea of God, and defined themselves as atheists. Others proposed a new secular religion, with the fundamental values of tolerance, justice, and humanity. The fundamental concept for the Illuminists was the right to happiness. They thought that man could reach happiness by freeing himself from prejudices and by following reason. The philosophers have the task of indicating this new path. Happiness is linked to pleasure, the elimination of pain and the achievement of desires. Every man has the right to be happy, a right that for many centuries has been denied. A free and peaceful coexistence was the new ideal- without inequality, hunger, or injustice.

The message of the philosophers is strengthened when they fight against the absolute power of the nobility and of the church. Fundamental is the work of the Frenchman Montesquieu—*The Spirit of the Laws*—which defines the new concept of the state as a body which must ensure the rights of all: guaranteeing freedom and well-being. Power cannot be in the hands of a single authority, but must be divided between legislative, executive and judicial powers. Another philosopher, Rousseau, in the work *The Social Contract* analyses the common power between men. Man must be free, but must also respect the will of others. All these ideas express a new way of life—a way that the bourgeoisie wanted to be realized. Greater democracy was expected to bring greater well-being and happiness.

In Italy, the Enlightenment intellectuals remained a minority with respect to the old-style literary ones. Enlightenment values spread slowly in a country like Italy: divided into many states, often ruled by small governments not inclined to renewal. However, even in Italy, Enlightenment ideas began to spread little by little. A good example is Pietro Verri, who revised the work of the great Galileo.

The Enlightenment marked a profound transformation in the way art was interpreted. During the Enlightenment, art moved out from the academies and the courts, and got in touch with the reality of the age. This meant that culture could no longer be a monopoly of nobility: the social class that represented the past, immobility, the preservation of old privileges. The bourgeoisie sought the total renewal of art, which became an instrument for the reform of reality. Art came to communicate pleasure—a complex pleasure able to develop the mind and communicate deep feelings. Together with the idea of pleasure, we come to the idea of good taste: that is, of balance and measure. For Illuminists, the artist must not obey prefixed rules, but create emotions, sensations and passions. So the fundamental qualities of the artist must be imagination and enthusiasm.

Despite the presence of these novelties, there was not a total change of literary genres, but there was the spread of new forms of writing. In fact, literary genres such as the Olympic tragedy seemed inadequate representations of the new world. Instead, the novel, the essay and the bourgeois comedy saw a remarkable development. In this way, social and civil problems could be represented in a new medium and discursive language.

From the mid-eighteenth century, Italian culture, after a century of removal, returned to the most advanced forefront of European culture. Until the first half of the eighteenth century, the influence of Italy on Europe was the work of small groups and isolated personalities. In the various states into which Italy was divided, the proponents of the Enlightenment collaborate actively to inspire sovereign reforms. For these reasons, the ideas of Italian intellectuals are directed to problems related to the administration of the state, and to social and civil life. The economic decadence and the strong absolutism of the powerful impede a clear affirmation of the Enlightenment in Italy, but in some cities, the new ideas begin to circulate anyway. The power of the church is criticized in Naples, and writings appear, calling for new economics, new legislation, and for the freedom of trade. In Milan, in 1764, an illuminist-oriented magazine was founded: *Coffee.* The name is referring to the usual places in which intellectuals meet—coffee houses. This magazine was founded by two brothers, Alessandro and Pietro Verri, who, with another intellectual, Cesare Beccaria, were among the most important figures working in Milan. The magazine aimed to present the truth to the public in a simple and clear way. The writings in the magazine were based on the social and economic problems of the age, and they took a stand against ignorance and against the excessive authority of the clergy. Alessandro and Pietro Verri also struggled for the renewal of Italian literature as a direct vehicle for precise ideas.

Cesare Beccaria (1738–1794)

Cesare Beccaria was the author of a fundamental work on crime and punishment which became famous throughout Europe. The book, printed in 1764, was ideally intended to enlighten rulers to do good. The main idea of Beccaria's book is the rejection of torture and condemnation of death, which were, until then, considered normal punishments. Instead, here it is said that horrible pains do not serve to improve man, but only to annul life. The treatise has a passionate tone, characterized by frequent references to different subjects.

'This useless prodigality of supplications, which has never made men better, has led me to examine whether death is truly useful and just in a well-organized government. What can be the right of men to slaughter their fellow men? Certainly not the one from which the sovereignty and the laws result. They are but a sum of minimal portions of the private freedom of each; they represent the general will, which is the aggregate of particulars. Who is the one who wanted to leave other people the will to kill him? How come in the least sacrifice of the freedom of each one there can be that of the maximum among all goods, life? And if this was done, how is such a principle agreed with the other, that man is not the master of killing himself, and should he be if he has been able to give this right to another or to the whole society? So, it is not the death penalty a right, while I have shown that this being cannot, but it is a war of the nation with a citizen, because it considers the destruction of his being necessary or useful. But if I prove not to be neither useful nor necessary death, I will have won the cause of humanity.'

After publication, the work was placed on the index of prohibited books, but despite this, it is one of the most innovative texts to come out of the Italian Enlightenment, and it has contributed to the creation of modern European civilization. In France, Robespierre was inspired by Beccaria's treaty to condemn the death penalty in a debate. In 1786, the Grand Duke of Tuscany, Pietro Leopoldo, applied the ideas of the Milanese thinker to his reform of the penal legislation. Neapolitan culture opens up to the ideas of the Enlightenment, and tries to put them into practice to solve the problems of the state (the kingdom of the Bourbons). Gaetano Filangieri writes an incomplete eight-volume treaty entitled *Science of Legislation*; in it, the European situation is analysed to reflect on the changes that are happening. Its fundamental idea is the absolute goodness of the laws.

Though Venice remains conservative in political and social fields, it still makes a significant cultural contribution thanks to the presence of numerous intellectuals and the importance of its continuous publishing activity. For example, the gazette Veneta, published in 1760, presents articles dedicated to the Venetian chronicle of a picturesque family in Venice. In the theatre, Carlo Gozzi's theatrical fairy tales invent a new, though not modern, illuminist theatre, and another Venetian, Carlo Goldoni, creates comedies.

Giuseppe Parini (1729–1799, Milan)

The work of this prose writer and poet is mystic, full of civil passion, and has a refined and elegant style. In his most famous work, *The Day* (Il Giorno), he writes a satire in verse to ridicule the idle superficial life of the nobility. This social class that the Enlightenment intellectuals regarded as an enemy to be fought is described as a group of squalid, arrogant people, who live like parasites by exploiting others. Parini's satire against the dominant, elegant aristocracy is fierce: the general feeling of contempt for intolerance is so well represented that, later on, it will explode in the French revolution.

Il Giorno is a poem in verse divided into four parts, in which Parini describes a young gentleman: a rich, young aristocrat, a lover of idleness and superficiality, one without dignity. The poet describes with irony the day of this typical arrogant nobleman, who produces nothing but exploits the hard work of others without respect. So Parini, in his works, describes the evils of his time and his dreams for a new society where there are reforms in favour of culture and science: a society without privileges, a more just tomorrow.

Vittorio Alfieri (1749–1803)

This poet and writer of tragedy and political tracts has an intense and original personality that lives on beyond the Enlightenment. The main topic of his tragedies and his political essays is the search for freedom; but the freedom of Alfieri does not have the typical historical characteristics. Instead, it is an inner freedom. In his works, he always describes a clash between a tyrant and a hero who fights for freedom. The setting, however, is not realistic, nor are the characters. On the contrary, the two protagonists, with their very strong personalities, represent not real men, but ideas: tyranny and the absolute power against freedom.

The tragedies of Saul and Mirra—two of Alfieri's romantic heroes—represent not a political struggle, but an inner struggle. The protagonists, like the writer, are tormented; they feel infinite desires that can never be satisfied. Another typical element of his tragedies is death, which is why the protagonist falls victim to murder or suicide. In Saul, Alfieri shows a king who is a desperate man; fighting against himself, full of envy for the valiant young David. The representation ends with the liberation from himself, with suicide. In the same way, Mirra is faced with a tremendous love for his father. Against this passion Mirra struggles to the end; but his freedom can only be death, suicide. Alfieri concludes the Enlightenment age of political passion and begins a new cultural era, one in which the protagonist is the romantic hero, always fighting with himself and the world. He comes from an aristocratic social class, a solitary man who seeks spiritual tranquillity but never finds it.

Late Eighteenth Century

This is an incredible moment in European history. We see the cultural revolution of Voltaire, Diderot, Beccaria, and other French Illuminists. We see the liberal revolution of Adam Smith and other savage competition theorists, after centuries of a market driven arbitrarily by a narrow list of ruling class. Also, we see the industrial revolution, the scientific revolution of Newton, and the musical revolution of Mozart. The American revolution that frees a continent from its dependency relationship with Europe, and finally we see the French revolution and the subsequent Napoleonic cyclone.

Even the lives of individuals in small cities changes radically. Goldoni is perhaps one of the acutest interpreters of this change, and still today he awaits the recognition that belongs to him—of being placed among the greatest intellectuals of his time. Goldoni is a Venetian from Paris, and alongside another great intellectual, Giacomo Casanova (also Venetian and Parisian) he is the last singer of the Serenissima Republic. When Napoleon sells it to Austria in 1797, it marks the end of the longest republic in history. Goldoni experiences a particular period in the emergence of a new social class—the bourgeoisie. On the one hand, the Enlightenment pushed bourgeois intellectuals to describe social reality, and, on the other in Venice, the mercantile bourgeoisie of trade and commerce became the most important social class (the nobles were in deep crisis).

Goldoni, through his writing, presented the culture and the ideals of the Italian bourgeoisie of the eighteenth century. His plays reveal the social transformations of his era, renewing, at the same time, the schemes of traditional theatre and the staging of modern characters and situations. The viewer he addresses is no longer the aristocrat but the bourgeois. The world staged by Goldoni comprises real situations, with characters representing socially defined human types who express themselves in the modern language, not literary, sometimes even in dialect. Goldoni adapted the bourgeois and mercantile comedies that he knew well, featuring merchant characters who had become part of the wealthy bourgeoisie through commerce, and who were now dominating the declining world of the old nobility with their cunning intelligence. Goldoni, a bourgeois intellectual, represents his world, with his dreams and his ideas.

Before Goldoni, playwrights preferred to write tragedies or sentimental melodramas characterized by unrealistic characters and formalized language. The comedy that preceded Goldoni was used only to entertain the audience, and the actors did not follow a script, but improvised continuously, because the characters did not have to be realistic, but only stereotypes which were always repeated. Goldoni renewed the genre of comedy, replacing improvisation with a written text. At first, (because both actors and audiences were used to the fixed parts and the acrobatics of the masks), Goldoni writes only the text played by the protagonist, while the other actors are given a canvas, a partial text, which they completed thanks to their improvisation skills. But starting with *The Woman of Grace* (1743), Goldoni writes the scripts of the comedies entirely, paying attention to the psychological coherence of the characters.

Goldoni elaborates his characters and describes them realistically; even if he picks up some characters from the commedia dell'arte, he gives them a new physiognomy, making them realistic individuals. The characters are contemporary, honest, clever, enterprising, and described with irony. He also pays attention also to the female characters, such as the innkeeper, Dove Mirandolina, who is able to seduce and manipulate the naive men who frequent her inn. The inn was a hotel, so Mirandolina is the owner of a hotel. She is a young, pretty, smart woman. Many customers fall in love with her. The knight is an old man, an inn customer. He is rich and is not married; he despises women but falls in love with Mirandolina, who only wants to make fun of him. Fabrizio, the inn's waiter, is in love with Pradellona, but he is shy, he does not know that she loves him too. At the end of the play, Mirandolina, a woman from the new world, will marry poor Fabrizio instead of rich noble suitors.

Politics, Economy and Culture

The first fifty years of the eighteenth century see Europe dominated by the enlightened absolutism of the King of France, Louis XIV. The period was characterized by a succession of wars: Spanish, Polish and Austrian. In the second half of the century, some European sovereigns, such as Maria Teresa of Habsburg, Catherine of Russia, and Frederick of Prussia, initiated a series of reforms which, although they are called enlightened (i.e., based on reason), aim to document the centralizing powers of the state. The end of the century, however, sees the outbreak of the French Revolution in 1789, which spreads a general desire for freedom and for the abolition of old forms of government. The eighteenth century culture of enlightenment starts in England, but finds fertile ground in France, where socio-economic-political structures need a radical renewal. The philosophical origins of the movement go back to the rationalist current, begun by Descartes, and the empiricist, interpreted by Hobbes.

The goal of the Enlightenment is to enhance the value of reason to make it the only possible instrument for human knowledge. There are attempts to pursue a systematic elimination of religion in the political, social and cultural life of the past, to have it superceded by rationality, in order to carry out a comprehensive project of global renewal. Reason is also used as a valid instrument for demonstrating the groundlessness, from a rational point of view, of any persistence of social privilege. In this way, the middle class, who oppose the nobility and the clergy, prepares to exert a hegemonic role in the new nation states. The Academy of Arcadia, where poetry is considered a means to escape from reality and withdraw into an imaginary world, dominates Italian culture in the first half of the eighteenth century.

The philosophical landscape of the time was occupied by Giambattista Vico, who, in his masterpiece *The New Science* (1744) argued that the only possible object of knowledge is history, which, analogous to the mental life of the individual, it is divided into three periods of development: the age of the gods (in which man overcomes, thanks to religion, myth, his instinctive imprisonment), the age of heroes (where imagination, strength and passion prevail), and the age of men based on the use of reason. Each civilization is destined to go through each of these historical phases, and then begin again.
In Italy, there is also the debate over language between traditionalists and innovators. The Academy of Arcadia are in favour of making fourteenth-century Tuscan the official language, whilst innovators (such as Ludovico Antonio Muratori and Gian Vincenzo Gravina) consider the language an instrument which must satisfy both the literary aspiration and the practical needs of everyday social life.

In the second half of the eighteenth century, neoclassicism also spread, which aims to be a philological recovery of the past and an affirmation of a rational aesthetic canon founded on rigour and purity of lines. At the same time, it seeks a return to the unspoiled, to the heroic, the simplicity of nature that classical art had been able to express, according to ideals propounded by numerous theoretical writings (in particular, Winckelmann's history of the art of antiquity, 1764). The dominant literary phenomenon of this period is also neoclassicism, which in Italy is affirmed with Ugo Foscolo and with Vincenzo Monti. The autobiographical genre became very widespread in the Age of Enlightenment, as private writings were published in epistolary and autobiographical form. For example, the letters of Pietro Verri to his father regarding the miseries of military life provided the reader with a personal account of participation in the seven-year war. Carlo Goldoni and Vittorio Alfieri also published autobiographies, but the most famous is that of Giacomo Casanova, the great Venetian libertine lover, who authored *Story of My Life* in French between 1791 and 1798.

In France, Father of the Enlightenment Denis Diderot collaborated with the most influential intellectuals of the time, including D'Alembert, to create, between 1751 and 1780, a famous encyclopedia of all human knowledge. This work was based on reason and rational Enlightenment thinking. Montesquieu, considered a founder of social-political sciences (and who wrote the controversial *The Spirit of Laws* in 1748) also produced *The Persian Letters*, an epistolary novel of pungent criticism of contemporary Parisian customs.

The French cultural panorama, however, was dominated by Jean Jacques Rousseau and Voltaire. The latter was the protagonist of a strong polemic against the church and the official religions.

In the United Kingdom, philosophers such as John Locke and David Hume, the proponents of empiricism, contribute to the triumph of the Enlightenment ideals throughout Europe. New periodicals such as *The Review* (founded by Daniel Defoe in 1704) and *The Spectator* (1711) were published. New literary genres come to light to meet the needs of the bourgeois public: thus the realistic novel and the modern novel are born. In poetry, the lyrical tendency prevails: intended to satisfy the basic taste of a neophyte public, the compositions are filled with everyday topics. Over the course of the century, the first pre-romantic tendencies emerge. This style promotes an inner withdrawal and the rediscovery of an intimate connection with the natural world, seen particularly in the works of Edward Young, Collins and Thomas Gray.

In Germany, the political division of the nation does not allow an agile circulation of the new revolutionary Illuminist ideals. The beginning of the century are characterized by two prevailing currents of thought: pietism and rationalism. The most incisive theorist of the neoclassical style is Winckelmann, who produces a history of art in antiquity, while in the philosophical field, Immanuel Kant stands out. Between the end of the eighteenth and the beginning of the nineteenth century, the birth of a strong national feeling occurs in Germany, contributed to greatly by the theories of the idealistic philosopher Hegel. The patriotic debate thus becomes a topic on the agenda of university intellectuals, as demonstrated by the speeches delivered to the German nation by Fichte. This ideological ferment determines the growing cultural renaissance, so much so that around 1770, Germany has its own literary revolution. During this time, works produced led to the birth of the Sturm und Drang (a term which derives from an anonymous theatrical work of 1776, translatable as 'storm and assault'), a movement destined to exert a strong ancestry on the formation of European romantic thought.

The highest expression of the Enlightenment is the triumph of science, meaning that art is forced to differentiate itself, which it does by bringing the decorative tendencies to the extreme. This leads to the birth of the 'rococo' style: the term indicating a type of decoration in shape of decorative shell. Around 1730, the term came to indicate a new ornamental style, characterized by asymmetry and curled waves. The rococo is often defined as the exasperation, in a purely decorative sense, of a baroque now emptied of its contents. Born and developed during the reign of Louis XV, the rococo is an art that has become almost a game, composed of sinuous forms, graceful, with decorations typical of a refined and fun-loving society: in short, the characteristic style of the French aristocracy and then of the various European courts in the first half of the eighteenth century. Rococo art no longer has to teach or convince like the baroque one, it does not need to communicate religious and moral messages, but it must only amuse and lighten the boredom of court life. Art also managed to adapt to fashion for scientific rigour, as happened with neoclassicism. In the sphere of the Enlightenment culture, criticism is developed into the philosophy of art, which constitutes a new artistic phenomenon.

Architecture

In eighteenth-century Italian architecture, the linguistic elements of Borromini's tradition are reflected on the one hand, while on the other, the rococo innovations lighten the heavy structures of baroque monumentality. Towards the middle of the century, a different orientation of architecture can be observed: less decorative, more functional, with a language which anticipates the subsequent affirmation of the neoclassical.

Filippo Juvarra Messina (1678–1736)

Filippo Juvarra of Madrid reconciled the freedom of baroque invention with solutions which anticipated the themes of neoclassicism. He designed the Basilica of San Superga (1716–1730), built as a temple for the 1706 victory over the French, and as a mausoleum for the Savoy, built on a hill overlooking the city where Prince Eugene of Savoy had defeated the French. It is the most important representative monument built in Turin. It was funded by the Duke Vittorio Amedeo Secondo di Savoia after the siege and the battle of Turin in 1706, and is dedicated to the Madonna Delle Grazie, whose wooden statue is kept in the chapel of the vow. Before the decisive battle with the French, Vittorio Amedeo Secondo and his cousin Eugene of Savoy climbed the hill to observe the deployment of enemy troops from above and plan the strategy to free Turin from the siege. On that occasion, the Duke vowed to the Virgin Mary that if he succeeded, a sanctuary dedicated to her would be established. The structure is 75m high, and to accommodate it, it was necessary to lower the hill of Superga to 40m. Previously, the site housed a church for local worshippers.

Filippo Juvarra did not limit himself to designing the basilica, however, but gave very detailed instructions on the materials to be used in construction and on the internal decorations: bricks, which were cooked on the hill (and had to have very precise dimensions); the iron to be used was that of Augusta di Ceres; the marbles to be used had to be the green of Susa, the black of Como, the yellow of Verona, the white of Carrara. When particularly struck by the beauty of the building, Rousseau said *'I have before me the most beautiful spectacle that can strike the human eye.'*

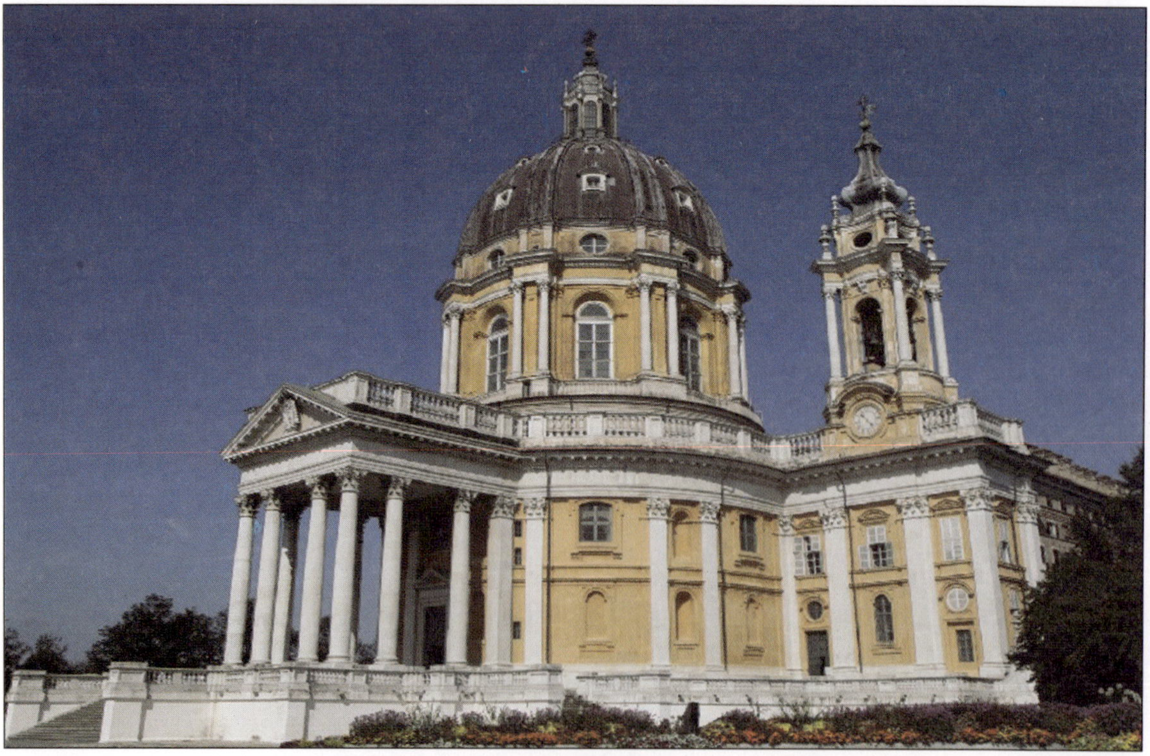

The Basilica of San Supergaby Filippo Juvarra (1716–1730)

Luigi Vanvitelli (1700–1773)

The son of a painter of Dutch origin, Vanvitelli was a classically elegant architect, a scholar of the ancient architecture of the Renaissance, and is remembered for the sobriety of his style and for his enlightenment rationalism (even if his works still have a baroque character). We remember the palace of Caserta (1751), designed on the commission of Charles III of Bourbon, which was intended to emulate two other royal residences: the Palace of Versailles and the palace of the Escorial in Madrid, in an original ideal fusion. The sumptuous palace, divided into four monumental courtyards, is crowned by a large central dome. It rises five floors and reaches a height of 36m. Inside we find 1200 rooms with festive and refined settings. An integral part of the beauty is the park, which is of the classic Italian garden model. The vast ornate lawns and square flowerbeds are accompanied by a channel of water along the central axis, pools and fountains. The water supply of the palace was supplied by the so-called Carolino aqueduct, which took the water from the slopes of the mountain and transported it along a path that ran, mostly underground, for a length of 38km.

After Neoclassicism, a great social literary movement was born in Germany at the end of the eighteenth century: Romanticism. This new culture spreads thanks to the 'Sturm und Drang' (impetus and assault), a movement born in open polemic against the French Enlightenment. This trend spread in the following decades throughout Europe, until becoming, during the first half of the nineteenth century, a common reference for European culture: from novels to poetry, music to philosophy, painting and architecture. The term Romanticism derives from the ancient French 'romaunt', meaning 'narration'. Narration indicates an adventurous, fantastic genre of literature that arouses particular emotions in the reader, although later the word becomes synonymous with sentimental. After the fall of the myth of the region at the end of the eighteenth century, with Romanticism there is a rejection of previous ideas and the search for an inner security that was lost. Romantic man lives the contrast between ideal and real, and as a consequence, his spirit is characterized by his pessimism and individualism, by the desire for freedom and affirmation of the individual with respect to the rules of society. Romantic culture enhances the spontaneity of feelings, the free creativity of each person, but at the same time discovers that man has deep ties with his society in which he lives, shares feelings, culture, and the values of the nation's tradition. In this way, the concept of the nation is born, which becomes almost a religious value for the culture of the period.

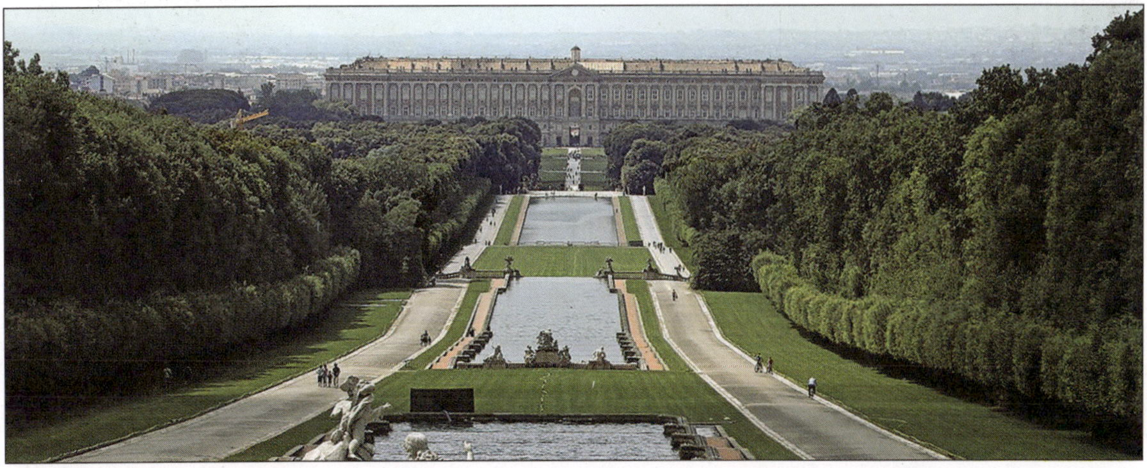

Royal Palace of Caserta by Luigi Vanvitelli (1751)

Sculpture

Eighteenth-century sculpture generally traces the baroque tradition of the previous century, in which the decorative and virtuosic character is accentuated.

Painting

In the eighteenth century, we witness the passage from baroque forms to rococo style, where the most accomplished results can be found in Venetian painting. We also see the growing success of genre painting, in which the Italian style is significantly influenced by the Flemish and Dutch styles. In the second half of the century, we witness, finally, a progressive affirmation of the neoclassical currents of inspiration. Venetian painting took on a leading role, placing itself with authority amongst the major European artistic expressions of the century, and can thus be considered the last great manifestation of the Italian artistic tradition.

Antonio Canal (1697–1768)

Antonio Canal (Canaletto, Venice) enhances the picturesque genre of the veduta, thanks to his extremely descriptive and perspective rigour, and his touches of intense and warm luminosity. An original aspect of his work is the inclusion of monuments belonging to other places; this makes his scenes look as if they have undergone photographic editing. The taste of the scenographic is evident in many of his works, owing to the contrasts of chiaroscuro and the cuts of the views. Some works are sold to the collector and merchant Smith, the future British consul in Venice, who helps to spread the canaletto's fame in England. In 1765, he was admitted to Venice Academy after the presentation of the painting 'Capriccio'—a collonaded courtyard of an imaginary palace in Venice.

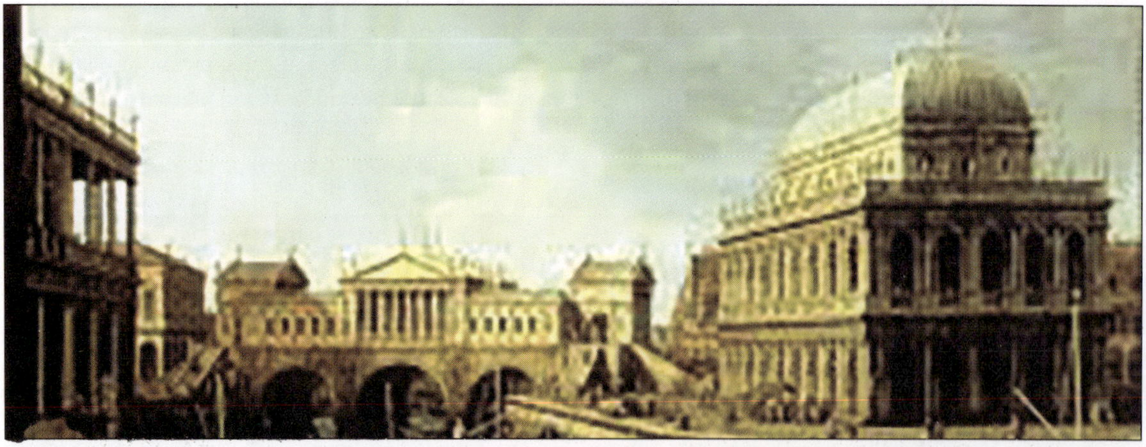

Capriccio, painting of a collonaded courtyard of an imaginary palace in Venice by Antonio Canal (c. 1765)

Francesco Guardi (1712–1793)

Francesco Guardi (Venice, 1712–1793), sensitive to the ways of contemporary painters, interprets the taste of international rococo in a personal, original version: in the romantic sense as an expression of a state of mind. For him, the choice of subject is important, as is the atmosphere, the moment in time, and the expression of a state of mind. We remember the painting 'Gondola in Laguna'.

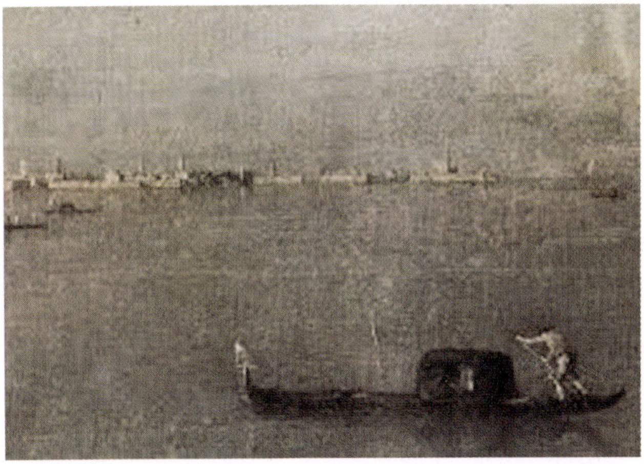

Gondola in Laguna, a painting by Francesco Guardi (c. 1780)

The genre known as Vedutismo occupies a prominent place amongst eighteenth- century Italian artists. The forerunners of this style were the great decorators of the palace of the papacy of previous centuries. These painters were in charge of representing and celebrating historical, political and religious events, and setting them against the backdrop of the urban landscape of the city where the events had taken place. Only in 1675, with the arrival in Rome of the Dutch painter Gaspar Van Wittel, was the taste for a realistic urban view full of details of everyday life, without political and religious meanings, popularized The Vedutisimo developed particularly in Venice, following the great success of the series of etchings engraved by Luca Carlevarijs in 1703. Many painters painted more or less well-known aspects of the lagoon city to meet the needs of a rather varied clientele: from those who performed the grand Italian tour to those who had never stayed in Venice, but who, sensitive to the charm of the city, wanted to decorate their residences with the San Marco and the Grand Canal.

In Europe

In the period preceding the reign of Louis XIV, France finds its most significant artistic expression in classical painting. From the beginning of the eighteenth century, a reaction developed in the transalpine country against the court and courtly art, which resulted in the rejection of monumentalism and baroque decoration. A typical exponent of this new concept was Antoine Watteau, creator of bucolic paintings showing an arcadian life, simple and carefree. During the reign of Louis XV (1723–1770) a frivolous and graceful style developed, with light, moving shapes and pastel shades. During the reign of Louis XVI, in concomitance with the developments of the Enlightenment, there was a return to more sober forms; the Louis XVI style represents the evolution of the rococo towards more classical forms. And with the progressive affirmation of neoclassical taste, the greatest French representative at the turn of the two centuries was the painter Jacques Louis David.

In Spain prevails the figure of Francisco Goya: a genial personality sensitive to Spanish traditions but also of Italian, Flemish influence. He developed a painting style with a quick touch of bright, rarefied colours. He created official portraits for the Spanish renovation and also a series of small paintings with scenes of witchcraft, madness and torture, the most famous being the representation of the shooting of 3 May 1808.

In England, from the end of the seventeenth to the beginning of the eighteenth century, a classical architectural style developed, defined as Palladianism (as it was inspired by the art of the great Venetian master). At the same time, we witness the flowering of the neo-gothic taste, thanks to the persistent Gothic traditions of the moratorium workers.

Theatre: The Comic Opera

In the seventeenth century, the trend towards decadence determines the success of the greatest musical novelty of the eighteenth century: the Opera buffa—comic opera—a genre in which some of the greatest musicians of all times such as Mozart, Rossini, Verdi and others try their hand. The opera Buffa opposes the melodrama because of the spontaneity, the coherence between thought and language, and the choice of characters and real situations against mythological and historical themes. The musical comedy, inspired by the texts of excellent authors like Goldoni, is entrusted to talented musicians and assumes its own connotation in the field of theatre production. The fashion for the comic opera begins in 1733 with the performance of Pergolesi's 'Servant Padrona', an Intermezzo inserted in the serious opera *The Superb Prisoner*. The public applauds the arias, the dances, the scenographic changes, the richness of the costumes, and the funny scenes. These features also appear in the melodrama, such as some of the buffoon episodes of the Monteverdi Poppea of Poppea in 1642, and soon crystallize in the form of comic scenes at the end of the acts (Intermezzi), performed by two characters outsie of the main story.

Initially, in such scenes, a connection with the plot is maintained; sometimes they affect the final resolution, but over time they become more autonomous. In fact, when Zeno and Metastasio try to create melodramas in which there are no digressions with respect to the main plot, these scenes are abolished. The two characters are always of humble condition: a young servant (played by a soprano), or an old nurse (a man, usually the tenor). The subject is of a kind love: for example, the old woman who tries to obtain the young man's favours and is ridiculed. Later, with more appropriate vocal realism characterized by the comic opera, the characters become a rich old man (a bass) and a poor young man (often a servant, a soprano). The topic is love and seduction.

These characters are still strongly affected by the commedia dell'arte. The most prominent author of this phase is certainly Alessandro Scarlatti (1660–1720). At the end of the seventeenth century, the comedic scenes are already presented separately, so that when carrying a work from one city to another, the funny scenes can be written by local musicians. It often happened that the same work is performed in Naples with comic scenes, and in Venice without. The Neapolitan school experiences the desire to expand these scenes that appealed so much to the public. The connection to the place of origin is seen in the setting of the language: the Neapolitan dialect. The use of dialect has been considered a sign of the popular nature of this work: in reality, from the literature of the librettos appear elements, a very complicated plot, and a series of cultured quotations. The use of dialect can probably be explained as a reaction to the Spanish style, where baroque theatre prevailed in theatres because of the greater immediacy and simplicity.

Opera buffa, however, is not always written in dialect; indeed, linguistic differences are used to emphasize the different social classes: high-calibre characters sing in Italian, while the subaltern classes express themselves in dialect. From the musical point of view, we notice a prevalence of dialogue in the monologue. This musical form, which will have so much success in opera, is developed in opera buffa. In moments of particular dramatic relief, the duets are interrupted by the dry recitative—recitatiovo secco—a sort of acting musically tuned with the accompaniment of the harpsichord. From a vocal point of view, we notice the prevalence of a syllable style, in which each syllable corresponds to a note, more suited to understanding the words so as to make the plot perfectly understandable, but involving the audience in the interstitium. The comic opera was not followed by the public with continuous attention in the eighteenth century. The lights in the hall remained bright, and the spectators followed fragmentarily, and took frequent intervals.

In Venice, we find libraries of Intermezzi as distinct publications from the serious work starting from 1706. In Naples, where the growing autonomy of comic scenes gave birth to the opera Neapolitan buffa, the first libretto Intermezzi is in 1725. Unlike the serious work, where men were often played by women in men's clothes, in the Intermezzo, the male characters are played by men, usually bass, and the females by women, in particular the sopranos. The only exception is in the papal state, where women were forbidden to sing: the female part was entrusted to a castrato. Intermezzo has reduced proportions: not only in length but also in the number of characters—only two. The events and characters are based on a search for realism. The male character is ridiculed by the cunning woman. Among the most important intermezzi is Albinoni's *Pimpione* (1708).

With the progression of the Neapolitan comic opera and its subsequent Italianization, interest in Intermezzo decreased. Intermezzo comico ends up disappearing, to be replaced by the Intermezzo di ballo, considered socially and artistically higher. The success of the opera buffa in the eighteenth century is also explained by the balance between elegance and malice that this type of theatre contains, reflecting the spirit of the time. With Mozart, the limit between comedy and seriousness is overcome: masterpieces such as *The Wedding of Figaro* and *The Bongiovanni* unite the elegance of the eighteenth-century work with a melancholy and a romance.

Instrumental Music: From the Sixteenth Century and the Baroque

Up to the 1500s, we see the diffusion of the polyphonic compositions points, replacing the deeper voices with the instruments, so as to bring out the higher voices. The substitution of the deeper voices with a harpsichord a chitarrone and an organ serves to transform them into support roles, giving rise to the basso continuo. In the writing of the work, the bass line was only noted and it was up to the interpreter to complete the harmony according to fixed patterns. Born as a form of accompaniment for singing, instrumental music gradually developed its own language. The first compositions were intended for dance: the oldest is the suite. It is in the Baroque age that we witness the birth of the orchestra, which does not yet have today's characteristics.

In the Baroque orchestra, there are two different sound groups: the first consisting of solo instruments (the concert or small concert), the second including all the instruments (the big concert). In the eighteenth century, the solo concert also spreads, achieving more interesting results with Vivaldi. Thus, the so-called 'concert style' is developed, typical of the musical baroque, that is realized in the multi-instrumental sonata. At the end of the seventeenth century, the baroque sonata assumes its decisive internal structure and is distinguished in the chamber forms and the church. One category of sonatas were performed at court, and were formed by a series of dance-times on the genre of the suite, with the basso continuo played on cello and harpsichord.

The other category were performed in religious ceremonies; they consisted of a series of sections of different trends and required the organ. Towards the end of the seventeenth century, the sonata completely diversified: the instrumental pieces were structured in three parts instead of two, and they are no longer given names of dances, but terms that indicated an expressive character. Towards the end of the seventeenth century, the continuous bass tends to run out and, while the 'big concert' evolves until it flows into the symphony, the performance is confirmed for a solo instrument. The most used instruments are the violin, the harpsichord and the organ.

In this period, instrumental virtuosity is born: the players approach the musical performance with a show of skill aimed at capturing the attention of the public. The music performed by instruments alone thus ceases to be 'background noise' for parties and ceremonial dances as it had been in previous centuries, and it acquires its autonomy on par with the musical theatre. In the eighteenth century, with the affirmation of the gallant style typical of the rococo, the contrapuntal forms are set in favour of greater harmonic tension and a more linear style.

The orchestra is also renewed by Mozart, who makes it possible to achieve a stable organization: including the strings, trumpets, hats, bassoons, horns, clarinets and flute. Vivaldi feels the need to accentuate the differences in timbres, exploiting all the possibilities of the strings through executive practices such as pizzicato. With Bach, the transition from baroque to modern music is accomplished; in the productions of the two composers there are elements of the contrapuntal tradition together with an expansion of the modulation procedures and the number of tonalities used, typical of the new music. All the linguistic elements from contemporary experience are combined in a great synthesis.

The Instrumental Forms

Since the mid-eighteenth century, the sonata form has been stated as the compositional procedure of instrumental music. The classic one is divided into four parts: exposure, development, recovery, and tail. In the expositions, two well defined and contrasting themes are presented; slow in development the two themes are elaborated and brought to distant tonalities, while in the recovery they are presented again in the initial tone, and then concluded in the tail. In the nineteenth century, the symphony will spread.

Vocal Music at the Chamber: The Lied

In German, the word 'Lied' means song, yet it serves to draw on a variety of musical forms. You can go back to the art of the troubadours and to the exponents of medieval music to see their usage. In Italian, this term is used to define a form of singing accompanied by the piano, which arose and developed in the Germanic area. The best known composers in this field are Mozart and Haydn, for whom the composition of Lied still represents a pastime compared to other musical forms. Later, the Lied is cultivated by Beethoven; we remember the titles *Adelaide* and *The Beloved Far*. Schopenhauer brings a very high level to this genre through a very strong production of more than 600 leider, fusing the legacy of tradition with the impulses of the new romantic spirituality.

Theatre: The Age of the Lights and the Reform of the Melodrama

During the seventeenth century, the melodrama featured a clear subordination of the poetic text, libretto, to the rhythmic compositional needs of the music; however, from the eighteenth century, the relationship is reversed in an attempt to give the libretto full autonomy, so as to hold up the comparison with the great tragedies of classical theatre and with the more recent ones from the French theatre. In Italy, the demand for texts for opera is particularly great. The Metastasio reform: among the most famous works of Metastasio, there are *Abandoned Dido* (1724), *Cato in Musica* (1727), and *Olimpiade* (1733). The author retained the dignity and importance of the literary part without undermining the other fundamental components of melodrama, that is, the music and the spectacle. He created a new balance between words and music, succeeding in ensuring that the text already contained the necessary melodic and scenic elements.

The melodrama is based on a system of six characters linked together by an interweaving of unhappy love affairs. These characters are presented as tormented beings, torn by conflicting feelings. The story is described through a sober, clear language, and an easy musicality, characterized by a preference for simple traditional vocabulary. It is impregnated with a rationalistic spirit.

Arcadian culture also exerts its own reformism on the comedy: already in the early eighteenth century, the genre seems to move towards the ways of the commedia dell'arte rather than focusing on the Italian Renaissance and Molière theatre. In the field of tragedy in the first half of the century, the *Merope* (1713) of Scipione Maffei (1675–1755) triumphed throughout Europe. The author worked on the reform of the tragedy, trying with this text to compete with Corneille's masterpieces. The tragedy, which had always been considered the highest literary genre, lacked representation in the Italian tradition of authentic masterpieces. The theme of jokes by the intellectuals of the eighteenth century are at the centre of the *Caio Gracco* by Vincenzo Monti (1754–1828). In this tragedy (1801), we find the story of the famous plebian tribute. The plebs, after promoting important reforms, were forced to succumb dramatically to the opposition of both senators and exponents in favour of an extremist evolution of innovative processes.

The Monti tragedy ends up eloquently expressing the ideals of the bourgeoisie of the time: predisposed to change, but strongly anchored to modern senses. Stylistically, the author does not give up the solemn tones. The tragic production of the Italian eighteenth century was dominated by the figure of Vittorio Alfieri (1749–1803), the author of six comedies and twenty-one tragedies. The tragedies reproposed the pessimistic conception that the author had of earthly life, and the sublime ideal of political and spiritual freedom in eternal conflict with any kind of tyranny. These works are written in loose hendeca syllables and in a short style that contrasted with the style of the time. They were based on a theme in which a limited number of characters acted: Alfieri conceived the tragedy as an epic lyric work, in which the hero fought against enemy forces, ending up succumbing to his destiny. In most cases, the conflict occurred in political terms: between a hero of freedom and a tyrant. He posed the problem of freedom of the individual in essentially political terms, identifying in civil servitude the greatest obstacle to the full expression of human freedom.

The condemnation of tyranny also runs through the entire work of Alfieri, which is animated by a profound need for intellectual freedom to refuse any compromise with power. This made the author a significant model for the culture of the Italian Risorgimento. From the point of view of the subject matter, the Alfieri tragedies can be divided into two groups. The first concerns classical historical matter, with a vast repertoire of heroic situations that transcend temporal circumstances: the civil and political theme prevails, and the role of the protagonist is usually Spetta libertario. The second group concerns the mythological subject.

Saul and *Mirra* are considered the author's masterpieces.
Like all tragedies, the composition of these also went through three phases: the conception of the subject, a first version in prose, and finally the writing in verse. Particular in Saul, the Biblical story

He transformed the commedia dell'arte into a comedy by the author, in which the actors' masks became characters, forced to follow basically a written script. Goldoni felt an increasingly strong impatience towards the commedia dell'arte; his eyes saw it necessary to eradicate the improbability and exaggerations typical of the commedia dell'arte by giving the comedy a realistic connotation, transferring men on to the stage, with their behaviour, their defects and normality.

The result of the Goldonian reform is the comedy of character: those who go on stage are not the masks of the commedia dell'arte nor the fixed types of classical theatre, but characters with temperaments and social characterization. The figures in the comedies of Goldoni are exponents of the bourgeois class: like the innkeeper Mirandolina, aristocrats like Don Marzio, and commoners all caught up in the concreteness of their mentality, their social-economic conditions, their customs, their vices and their virtues. Language is the tool to give that realistic reservation so desired by the author.

In his comedies, the writer employs a Venetian dialect. However, Goldoni's reforms raised controversial polemics among his contemporaries, including Pietro Chiari and especially the Venetian Carlo Gozzi (1720–1806), who recovered the character and schemes of the commedia dell'arte, representing fairy tales far from everyday life. According to Gozzi, the task of theatre was to help escape reality, transforming it with imagination. In contrast, a theatre like the Goldonian one, so close to material reality, is characterized by a language full of foreign terms and dialects, opposed to the most elementary rules of classical taste, according to which reality was instead idealized and harmonized in all its contents. Goldoni's work was inundated with enlightenment ideas, and as a result was seen as dangerously immoral. For this reason, Gozzi's works will deal with the scheme of the fairy tale, in order to give viewers the impression of being catapulted into an imaginary world.

Fashion

It is in this period that French fashion is affirmed, and it will remain a reference both for Europe and for America throughout the eighteenth and nineteenth centuries. If France is the master of dictating new fashions, England exerts its influence from the technical-industrial point of view: from the early eighteenth century, there was the discovery of fixed dyes which favoured the industrial production of printed cloth material, as well as the mobile quill in 1733 and the spinning mill in 1760 (which starts the mechanization of the textile manufacturing industry). These innovations, in addition to the importation of large quantities of cotton from India and America, allow the creation of a non-aristocratic and, therefore, non-exclusive fashion. In this century, fashion influences not only the richest social classes, but also the bourgeoisie and the workers of the big cities. The continuous search for novelty becomes the real engine of the clothing industry, and its diffusion is entrusted to modern advertising forms, such as the illustrated tables published with the first fashion magazines. A radical transformation of clothing and its uses then occurs as a result of the revolutionary spirit of 1789. The implementation of the principle of equality influences not only gender fashion, but all customs. In the convention of 1793, which will decide the French constitution, the right to dress according to one's taste is established, without having to respect obligations of any kind.

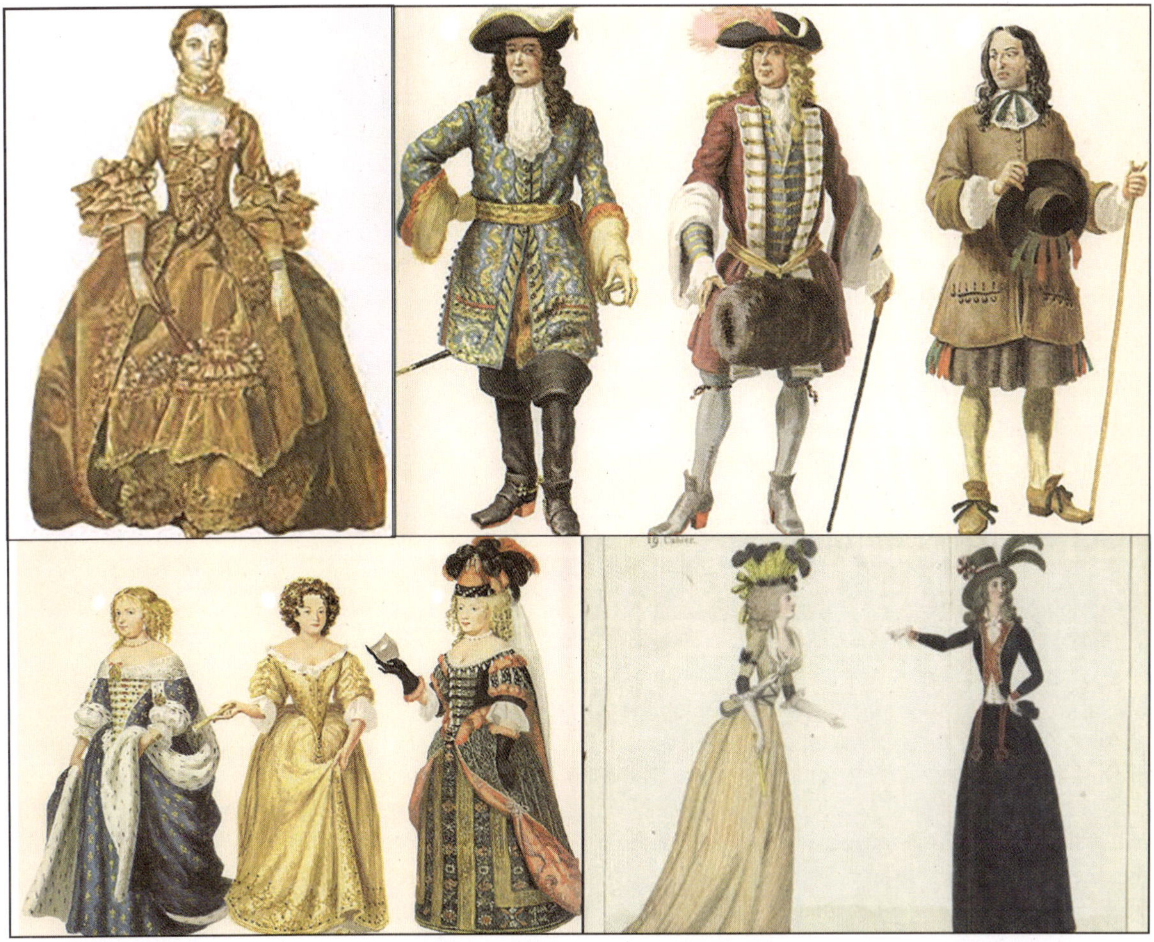

Clothing in Eighteenth Century France

Enlightenment Politics

The term Enlightenment refers to a movement of renewal of thought, science and literature that began in England in the seventeenth century and then spread to France throughout Europe, in a period marked by two major revolutions: the English one of 1688 and the French one of 1789. The chief characteristic of the movement is the absolute confidence in the critical exercise of reason and its ability to enlighten the mind in every sector of life. The product of humanism and the scientific revolution, the Enlightenment transfers the concept of man's centrality and the scientific method on to the concrete level of the transformations of society in opposition to the traditional structures of the church, monarchical absolutism and aristocracy.

Its main features include: progressive rationalism—the idea that culture is no longer the defence of tradition, but it is the search for progress that frees man from the limits of ignorance; cosmopolitanism—man becomes a citizen of the world, subject to the same laws of justice and freedom in every place, without distinction of race, sex, social class, or religion; dissemination of knowledge—the need to make known the progress of the cultural sciences, so that knowledge is not only the privilege of a closed elite, but an instrument of improvement for all men; trust in reason—a fight against prejudice, myth and superstition; an aversion for religions—religion is framed as guilty of having held peoples for centuries in ignorance and in servitude, for cheating reason with the sense of sin, for the punishment of death.

On the strictly political level, the illuminists advocate the theory of enlightened despotism, which disputes the validity of the principle of the divine origin of the monarchical institution, and believes that the ruler should be a man who governs according to the lights of reason—an enlightened sovereign. The most authoritative interpreter is Voltaire (1694–1778), author of poems and works of history, who, as a fervent supporter of the natural religion of freedom of thought, fights against intolerance, superstition, the atrocities of the judicial systems of the time, and the abuses of governments. Rousseau (1712–1778), in his *Social Contract*, theorized a new society in which all men are socially equal and can choose a democratic constitution that makes governors of public officials at the service of the people. He also outlines an innovative form of education based on tolerance and freedom of access to knowledge. We also remember the Scottish philosopher Adam Smith (1723–1790), advocate of the free market, who, with his investigation of the nature and causes of the nation's wealth, developed a text destined to radically transform the European economic world, laying the foundations of the economic science of the industrial revolution.

The Reforms in Europe

Enlightenment ideas spread rapidly in all the major European states, which undertook profound reforms to make the exercise of political power conform to the ideal of reason. In the field of taxation, tools are created that are able to reach the subjects in an organic and fair manner, with plans to ascertain wealth that are valid for the entire national territory. In legal matters, new penal codes are compiled to make the administration of justice the same in all territories. We see the abolition of torture, while the death penalty is used only in serious cases. In religious matters, the power and property of the church is limited, and ecclesiastics is abolished. Anti-clerical policies and the Inquisition tribunals are implemented. On the subject of individual liberties, censorship in the press is abolished and freedom of residence and property are introduced for the non-noble classes as well. In the field of education, there is the regulation of primary education which becomes compulsory and secularized. In administrative matters, the bureaucratic machine becomes more effective and powerful. Protectors and friends of the Enlightenment are Catherine of Russia and Frederick of Prussia, especially in matters of religious tolerance and the rational ordering of the state and society.

The Reforms in Italy

In the fifty years between the end of the war of Austrian succession and the outbreak of the French revolution, Italy experiences a period of uninterrupted peace which favours the formation of active centres of intellectual life inspired by Enlightenment in Milan, Florence, Naples and Parma. A vast work of reforms is promoted by the Austrian government in Lombardy, the Lore Nese government in Tuscany, the Bourbon one in the kingdom of Naples, and the Duchy of Parma and Piacenza.

In the Duchy of Milan, around the periodical *Coffee* of the Verri brothers and at the Accademia dei Pugni, a fervid cultural environment begins, in which the enlightened reformism spreads (it had been already successfully experimented within Austria by Maria Theresa of Hapsburg). Applying the directives coming from Vienna, the ministers Beltrame and Firmian bring the Lombard economy to prosperity. Reformist work and the compilation of a large land recording of the entire state was realized according to the most modern criteria for measuring rustic funds. In the grand Duchy of Tuscany, the second-born of the Hapsburg Empress, Pietro Leopoldo, surrounds himself with men of great genius. In the administrative sector, equalization and equality are promoted as public budgets are publicized. In the legislative field (with the Leopoldino code), we see uniformity of legislation, the abolition of torture and death sentences, the suppression of the majority, the right of progeniture, and the affirmation of equality of all children in the rights of succession of the paternal inheritance. There is also abolition of the Inquisition and the Manomorta.

With the rise to the throne of Naples of the son of the king of Spain (Charles of Bourbon), an autonomous kingdom is established in southern Italy, although it is still dependent on the powerful Iberian ally. Charles of Bourbon's reformism was characterized by a struggle to limit the power of feudalism and the clergy, and it involved a downsizing of the feudal jurisdiction, the abolition of the Inquisition, and the strong limitation of ecclesiastical benefits. The Duchy of Parma and Piacenza is undermined by the Duchy Filippo di Borbone, brother of the king of Naples. Filippo entrusts the direction of the government to Prime Minister Guillaume du Tillot, a skillful man, who summarizes the Duchy's finances, reorganizes the administration according to the most modern criteria, and drastically reduces the power of the Jesuits, whilst also providing a significant boost to the culture.

Italy under Napoleonic Domination

Towards the end of the eighteenth century, Napoleon Bonaparte, appointed supreme commander of the French armies in Italy on 2 March 1796, appears on the scene. On 1 April, he launches a violent attack against the king of Sardinia, Vittorio Amedeo III, forcing him to abandon the first coalition of European states in war against revolutionary France and to sign the Cherasco armistice (28 April 1796) with which Savoy and Nice were sold to the French. Immediately after, Napoleon focused his attention on Lombardy, defeating the Austrians, and forces them to evacuate Milan (14 May 1796), so that all Italian states were at war with France. They hastened to conclude armistices with Bonaparte so that he can safely occupy the cities of Bologna, Ferrara and Reggio. Only the Pontifical State still opposes, but on 19 February 1797, it is obliged to sign the burdensome peace treaty of Tolentino, which calls for the definitive transfer of Avignon to France. Napoleon reports a series of victories against the Austrians; they too were defeated on the western front in the battle of Koblenz, and on 17 October 1797, signs the peace of Campoformio, by virtue of which the territories located along the left bank of the Rhine, Belgium and Lombardy go to France, while Austria recovers the Republic of Venice (which despite its neutrality, was occupied by Napoleon, thus losing, after centuries of history, its independence).

The Jacobin Republics in Italy

The formation of the Jacobin republics in Italy dates back to the period between November and December 1796, with the birth of the Transpadan Republic in Lombardy and of the Cispadan Republic (including Modena, Reggio, Bologna and Ferrara) in July 1797. The Cisalpine Republic, after the peace of Campoformio, Bergamo, Brescia, and the annexation of Valtellina, assumes the new name of the Italian Republic, with Napoleon as president.

Meanwhile, Genoa was built in the Ligurian Republic, in June 1797. In the Papal State, the killing of a French general in the course of popular unrest in Rome offers the transalpine country a pretext to intervene alongside the revolutionaries, and proclaim a Roman Republic in February of 1798. The king of Naples, Ferdinando Quarto, attacks the French outposts of Rome, but the French troops defeat the militias of Ferdinando, forcing him to find refuge in Palermo. This gives way to the Neapolitan Republic in 23 January, 1799, which under a series of absolutely innovative measures in the south of Italy, abolishes feudalism, calls for the redistribution of peasant lands, and comprises a solemn proclamation of the principle of equality of all citizens.

The birth of the Jacobin republics in Italy in the revolutionary triennium (1796–1799) is accompanied by a vast reformist work which leads to the elaboration of new constitutions and the implementation of innovative social and civil programmes. However, the Republican experience lasts for a very brief time throughout the peninsula. Between the spring and summer of 1799, following the attacks brought to Italy by a new anti-French coalition, the other Italian Jacobin republics fall,but the legacy they leave in the country is enormous. The exchanges and relations between the various autonomous republics, united by the affirmation of the values of the French revolution of 1789, will constitute the foundations of the Italian Risorgimento.

The 1800s (Nineteenth Century)

VIII

Edited by
Asra Naaz, Shanfa Rehman

Designed By
Saniya Arshad, Aymun Kaleem Naqvi,
Nikhil Prashar, Ayesha Parveen, Shahzaib Ali Naik

The 1800s (Nineteenth century)

Historical Summary

The period 1815–1830, which goes by the name of the Age of Restoration, is marked by the immediate consequences of the Napoleonic defeats, and also by the decisions taken at the Congress of Vienna (1814–1815). These decisions redrew the geopolitical map of nineteenth-century Italy, and led to the birth of the Holy Alliance (between Austria, Prussia and Russia) for the maintenance of the status quo state established in Vienna. In Italy, subjugated by the Austrians, the secret societies develop into protagonists of the movements of 1820–1821. Between 1830 and 1831, the whole of Europe experiences a crisis that shakes the conservative energies and the bourgeois forces (constitutional and liberal). The most important cultural phenomenon of the first half of the nineteenth century is Romanticism: active in the literary, artistic, historical and philosophical fields. In polemics, with the Enlightenment, the individual sphere, the activity of the spirit, and the idea of nation is exalted. In Italy, the Romantic current is centred in Milan, where the magazine *The Conciliator* extols the project of independence, and the unity of the peninsula after centuries of foreign domination. One of the key aspects of Italian Romanticism is the controversy with the classics, based on the initiative of Madame De Steal, who, in 1816, published her work on public opinion and on the teaching of tradition, inviting Italian intellectuals to enter into conversation with the exponents of foreign literary currents in order to renew and restart their culture.

With Romanticism the question of the language re-emerges. The purist, belonging to the Accademia della Crusca, proposes a Florentine return of the fourteenth century. On the other side, the classicists, led by Vincenzo Monti, propose to take into account the entire national literary tradition (I neotoscani, like Manzoni) for which a live and real language should be used, the one spoken by educated Florentines. The linguistic choice will impose itself upon the literary panorama of the century.

In the beginning of the nineteenth century, the key elements of the genre of romance were a sense of history and nationality. The first edition of Promessi Sposi of Alessandro Manzoni was published in Italy in 1827. Few magazines like *The Conciliator* came into being during 1818–1819 but were later suppressed due to hostilities towards Austria. The autobiographical genre was primarily by Silvio Pellico. Francesco De Sanctis' *History of Italian Literature* could be found in the second half of the century, whereas the most expressive was the work of Giacomo Leopardi.

Detailed History

The period from 1796 to 1799 sees the conquest of most of Italy by Napoleon, and the consequent birth of several democratic republics modelled on the French style. In 1805, when Napoleon became emperor, Italy was transformed into the kingdom of Italy; almost the entire peninsula was under French influence. After the definitive defeat of Napoleon, between 1814 and 1815, a period of restoration of the ancient kingdoms and old systems began. It is one of the most vital times for Italian culture: in a few years we pass from the enthusiasm for the democratic choices of the late eighteenth-century republics to the disappointment of a kingdom of Italy relegated to a satellite of imperialist France and the restoration of the ancient absolutist regimes. But the experience of that period leaves a mark: the conquest of economic power by the bourgeoisie, the development of national consciousness, the legal and administrative modernization, the circulation of newspapers and magazines, and the basis of the Risorgimento, all of which will lead to unity of Italy in 1861. Between the mid-eighteenth and early nineteenth century, the recovery of Classicism characterized the world of art and Italian and European literature. The return to the classical tradition was favoured by the fashion for travel that characterized the 1700s. In 1764, the manifesto of neoclassical aesthetics was published—the history of ancient art by the German historical archaeologist Winckelman. Greek art embodies ideals of grace, serenity, dignity, beauty and harmony, best representing modern taste.

In the Jacobin and Napoleonic period, an idea of art and beauty is affirmed: it is the period not only of Canova's sculptures and of Piranesi's engravings, but also of the paintings of the French David and of the essays of the German Schiller, and of that 'style empire' that generally characterizes the fashion of the costume. The supreme ideal is grace: the ancient, Latin world is transfigured into a world of harmony, serenity, formal beauty and composure. Lost in this ideal vision is the real historical dimension of ancient art, which is often realized in an empty exercise of style and in formal coldness, rather than in real works of art.

At the beginning of the nineteenth century, neoclassicism encountered on the one hand the first signs of Romanticism, on the other, the historical disappointment caused by the sunset of the ideals and hopes raised by the French revolution and the Napoleonic period. The world of antiquity (classical Greece) thus become the nostalgic vision, the ideal for everyone, inspired by high values of heroism and dignity, in which man was in tune with nature. This desire for a possible return to an ideal ancient world is contrasted by the sadness of reality, the greyness of the era of restoration and the destruction of libertarian illusions. The heroic examples of classicism become an alternative, a hope able to calm and inspire consciences tormented by the delusions of history. In this period of encounter between the modern torments of the romantic conscience and the classicist imitations of equilibrium and beauty, we find the literary works of Foscolo.

Vincenzo Monti

The greatest representative of Italian classicism was Vincenzo Mondi (1754–1828), who inspired and was admired by poets and writers such as Foscolo, Leopardi, Manzoni, Goethe and Byron. A poet, theatrical author and a translator of classics, he celebrated in his works the Rome of the popes, Jacobinism, the rise of Napoleon, and the return of the Austrians, managing to maintain a role as a regime poet and an official poet in an era of continuity and changes. His works are rich in mythological references, and reflect the neoclassical taste for formal perfection and a dramatic inclination that hardly exceeds a certain superficiality. His 1810 translation of the Iliad is famous, in which he tries to reconcile the classical ideals of antiquity with the restlessness of modern sensibility.

Ugo Foscolo

Ugo Foscolo was the greatest interpreter of the feelings which characterized the passage of neoclassicism to romanticism. He was born in 1768 in Zakynthos, a Venetian island in the Ionian Sea, to a Greek mother and a Venetian father. An impulsive and passionate man, he intensely lived the contradictions of his age; dominated by deep and devastating feelings, he never ceased to seek a balance of realism, skepticism and pessimism. Although secular, he believes in illusions, and in values such as poetry, beauty, and the homeland, which allow man to rise above barbarism. He died in 1827. His first meaningful work, the epistolary novel, *Last Letters of Jacopo Ortis*, presents some of the main themes of his poetics: historical pessimism, patriotism, and respect for illustrious ancestors. His sonnets, composed after 1802, are among his masterpieces; in a balanced form and a solemn and serene tone, the poet really seems to reach the much desired balance between the desire for classical harmony and the urgency of passions.

In 'Falling from a horse' and 'Her healed friend', he resumed the neoclassical tradition of myth, beauty and formal perfection. The neoclassical themes also dominate the unfinished poem 'Graces'. Foscolo's major work is the poem 'Dei Sepolcri' (1806), a great example of civil poetry; in it the poet celebrates the secular religion of illusions, universal feelings and classical values such as glory, heroism, beauty and art, and civil values such as patriotism, friendship, love, and the ability to make sense of the mechanisms of nature and life.

Foscolo Poems

Alla Sera
Forse perché della fatal quïete
tu sei l'immago a me sì cara vieni,
o sera! E quando ti corteggian liete
le nubi estive e i zeffiri sereni,
E quando dal nevoso aere inquïete
tenebre e lunghe all'universo meni
sempre scendi invocata, e le secrete
vie del mio cor soavemente tieni.
Vagar mi fai co' miei pensier su l'orme
che vanno al nulla eterno; e intanto fugge
questo reo tempo, e van con lui le torme
delle cure onde meco egli si strugge;
e mentre io guardo la tua pace, dorme
questo spirto guerrier ch'entro mi rugge.

Né più mai toccherò le sacre sponde
ove il mio corpo fanciulletto giacque,
Zacinto mia, che te specchi nell'onde
del greco mar da cui vergine nacque

Venere, e fea quelle isole feconde
col suo primo sorriso, onde non tacque
le tue limpide nubi e le tue fronde
l'inclito verso di colui che l'acque

cantò fatali, ed il diverso esiglio
per cui bello di fama e di sventura

To the Evening
Perhaps because of the fatal silence
you are the image I cherish when you come to me,
o evening! and when happily
the summer clouds and the warm breezes court you
or when from the snowy air you lead
restless and long shadows upon the universe
you always descend, invoked by me, and the secret
pathways of my heart you gently hold.
You make me follow with my thoughts in the footsteps
that lead to the eternal void, and meanwhile
this guilty age passes away, and with it the crowds
of cares depart, so that it dissipates with me;
and while I contemplate your peace,
the warrior spirit that roars within me sleeps

No more will I ever touch the sacred shores
where my little boyish body lay down,
My Zakynthos, which you mirror in the waves
of the Greek sea from which virgin was born

Venus, and fea those fruitful islands
with his first smile, so he did not stop
your clear clouds and your leaves
the inclined towards him who waters

he sang fatal, and the different exile
so beautiful of fame and of misfortune

baciò la sua petrosa Itaca Ulisse.
Tu non altro che il canto avrai del figlio,
o materna mia terra; a noi prescrisse
il fato illacrimata sepoltura.

kissed his petrosa Itaca Ulisse.
You only have the song you will have of the son,
or maternal my land; he prescribed for us
the unholy fate burial.

Italy after the Vienna Congress

With the Vienna Congress, the era of restoration begins, i.e., the return of the political situation existing before the arrival of Napoleon. However, the conclusions of the Vienna Congress leave many people unhappy. In Italy, the restoration of the old States brings a slowing of the political civil development begun during the period of Napoleon. The nobility returns to rule and in southern Italy remains the feudal structure of the latifundium, a large agricultural property in the hands of a single owner. In Northern Italy, particularly in Lombardy, returned under Austrian rule, the bourgeoisie is stronger and tries to spread a national resurgence, but with little success.

After Neoclassicism, a great social literary movement was born in Germany at the end of the eighteenth century—Romanticism. This new culture spread thanks to the 'Sturm und Drang' (impetus and assault), a movement born in open polemic against the French Enlightenment. This trend spread in the following decades throughout Europe, until becoming, during the first half of the nineteenth century, a common reference for European culture: from novels to poetry, music to philosophy, painting and architecture. The term 'Romanticism' derives from the ancient French 'romaunt', meaning 'narration'. Narration indicates an adventurous, fantastic genre of literature that arouses particular emotions in the reader, although later the word becomes synonymous with sentimental. After the fall of the myth of the region at the end of the eighteenth century, with Romanticism there is a rejection of previous ideas and the search for an inner security that was lost. Romantic man lives the contrast between ideal and real, and as a consequence his spirit is characterized by his pessimism and individualism, by the desire for freedom and affirmation of the individual with respect to the rules of society. Romantic culture enhances the spontaneity of feelings, the free creativity of each person, but at the same time discovers that man has deep ties with his society in which he lives, shares feelings, culture, and the values of the nation's tradition. In this way the concept of nation is born, which becomes almost a religious value for the culture of the period.

Romanticism also exalts religious values, and in particular, the widespread ones of Christianity. There is a re-evaluation of the Middle Ages, a historical period in which there was the origin of modern Christian civilization, and also of the traditions of different nations. Romanticism considers art and poetry as the most complex form of total expression of the feelings of spirituality; poetry becomes the voice of the soul, the individual confession. The Romantic poet expresses the value of feelings, which have been previously analysed in an exaggerated way, and searches for new forms of poetry to give voice to their sensitivity. His works seeks creativity and feeling, rejecting the rules of traditional literary genres. Romantic literature must be alive, must show the poet's soul and the value of the society and the heroic actions of a people's past. The poems of this period, therefore, unlike the classical one intended for educated people, are naive and popular, written for the people, especially for the bourgeoisie, the new social class active at that time in politics and culture.

In Italy, Romanticism does not reach the excesses of the European one, but reflects the characteristics of the political situation of that time. The new Romantic ideas come to Italy thanks to Madame De Steal, a French woman who writes the article 'On the Manner and the Usefulness of Translations' in an Italian library magazine; this piece opens a debate between three writers in favour of Romanticism. In the beginning, Italian Romanticism spreads in Lombardy, a region where the desire for a national Risorgimento was more present. There is the rebirth of the Italian national consciousness, and a change towards the favouring of a state of unity. The controversy between Classicists and Romantics has the merit of producing the definition of the theoretical concepts of Italian Romanticism. The Romantics are all in favour of new ideas, and reject the imitation of the Classics. In particular, Italian Romanticism places the sense of history, the concept of nation and people, as fundamental. For this reason, the literature of the period is predisposed to the realistic and popular; there is the desire for poetry that shows the concrete historical reality and is written in the spoken language. Poetry must educate the people and form a civil conscience.

In Italian Romanticism, magazines are very important because they become the centres from which new ideas are born and spread. The magazines have the task of deepening the literary, historical, scientific and philosophical studies of that period, and of carrying out the work of social political education. Italian poets, writers and thinkers welcome the stimuli of foreign literature and, writing in literary magazines of the time, help to spread the new culture. Among the most important magazines of that moment are *The Conciliator* of Milan and *The Anthology* of Florence. *The Conciliator* is active from 1818 to 1819 and is directed by Silvio Pellico. He tries to reconcile new ideas with tradition; he wants to stimulate the economic and social development of the country. He also collaborates with Alessandro Manzoni. The magazine, despite having a great success, is closed after only one year of activity due to Austrian censorship. *The Anthology* of Florence, active from 1821 to 1833, aims to spread the culture and main works of contemporary foreign literatures; therefore, it publishes translations of authors such as Byron and Hugo.

Romanticism considers art an absolute expression of man, a divine gift, and painting and music in particular are considered pure arts, capable of expressing sentiment, religiosity and interiority. Romantic painting sees a new relationship with nature, which is now understood as a place for the spiritual experience of every man. For this reason, nineteenth-century paintings often show landscapes with warm colours and cubes. Two Italian Romantics are Francesco Hayes and Antonio Fontanesi. Hayes (Venice, 1791–Milan, 1888) starts as a neoclassical, but in Milan, he comes in contact with new romantic ideas. His paintings often originate from a historical theme inserted in a real landscape. Fontanesi (1818–1882) finds inspiration in nature, so he often paints landscapes with warm and revealed light, thus showing his Romanticism.

Giacomo Leopardi

Giacomo Leopardi participates with interest in the polemics and literary discussions of his time. The first period of his activity is characterized by his interest in the classics, having studied Latin and Greek languages and literature since he was a child. Thanks to his study of the great ancient writers, Leopardi discovers the world of the interior and his vocation as a poet; for this reason, at first he supports the reasons for Classicism. After some years, the poet, suffering from physical pains and the danger of becoming blind, understands that in that historical moment, it is not possible to creates poems of imagination like those of the ancient years, and that the only form of poetry possible for the modern man is that of feeling, in which man analyses his condition with respect to society, to nature.

The main characteristic of Leopardi's poetry is the pessimistic vision of life: the poet meditates on his own unhappiness, and on the fact that pain is the only reality for all men, because to hesitate means to struggle to survive. At first, nature seems good to him, and reason is seen as the cause of man's unhappiness because it allows him to know reality; this phase of his thought was called historical pessimism. However, later, he changes his ideas, and affirms that the true cause of unhappiness is nature, cruel and indifferent to the destiny of man, while reason helps people to become aware of their situation. This is cosmic pessimism.

Giacomo Leopardi is a poet of great and personal romantic sensitivity, continually torn between feeling and reason. He does not accept all the values of Romanticism; he thinks that poetry can not be popular, it can not really show a social commitment. He also does not approach Catholicism as many Romantics do, and instead maintains a secular and materialist position. The poetry of Leopardi in that period has a new and sentimental spiritual content and an originality of language. In fact, little by little, the poet develops a kind of expression which unites musicality with a great clarity of image and form. Words of the literary tradition are used in an original way and applied to expressions of the common language, while the traditional metric is interpreted in a new, more free way.

The word idyll in ancient Greek means 'the small image'; that is, a picture that portrays not just a landscape, but a society, a snapshot of life in the countryside. Leopardi uses this type of composition because it is more intimate and personal, a form of poetry with which he can express his feelings more freely. Leopardi writes his first six idylls between 1819 and 1829; in these poems, he expresses a positive impression of a nature with which he feels in tune, but the protagonist is always the poet in the first person. Between 1829 and 1830, he wrote the great idylls, poems composed during a period of pain in his life, in which the memories of pessimism appear. These poems involve not only men, but the whole cosmos. Here the poet disappears behind the undefined landscape; poetry is no longer graphic, but a complete description of the vision of nature. In the last years of his life, after 1830, Leopardi is increasingly pessimistic and writes poems that are no longer described as idylls, but use the harsh language of reason which coldly contemplates things and silences the feeling.

The songs that he writes in this period, 'Love and Death', have as main themes: the farewell to memory, illusions, and death as liberation from suffering. In 1835, he wrote some operetta and prose. They are philosophical meditations on the unhappiness of man in an original form; that is, dialogues between imaginary characters on the model of Luciano's Greek dialogues.

'The Infinite' (1819) is one of Leopardi's most famous idylls. The poem reflects on the infinity of time and space, and nature becomes one with its soul and its inner vision. The meaning is fairly straightforward. We can get a literal rendering easily enough with a dictionary.

L'infinito

Sempre caro mi fu quest'ermo colle
E questa siepe che da tanta parte
De'll ultimo orrizonte il guarde esclude.
Ma sedendo e mirando interminati
Spazi di là da quella, e sovrumani
Silenzi, e profondissima quiete,
Io nel pensier mi fingo, ove per poco
Il cor non si spaura. E come il vento
Odo stormir tra queste piante, io quello
Infinito silenzio a questa voce
Vo comparando; e mi sovvien l'eterno,

Always dear to me was this lonely hill,
And this hedge, which from so much part
Of the ultimate horizon the view excludes.
But sitting and gazing, boundless
Spaces beyond that, and more than human
Silences and profoundest quiet
I in thoughts pretend to myself, where almost
The heart is overwhelmed. And as the wind
I hear rustle through these plants, I such
Infinite silence to this voice
Go on comparing: and come to mind the eternal

E le morte stagioni, e la presente E viva, e'l suon di lei. Così tra questa Immensità s'annega il pensier mio: E'l naufragar m'è dolce in questo mare.	*And the dead seasons, and the present* *And the living, and the sound of it. So through this* *Immensity is drowned my thoughts:* *And being shipwrecked is sweet to me in this sea.*

Giacomo Leopardi to Silvia

In 1818, Teresa Fattorini, the young daughter of the coachman of the Leopardi family, died of illness. Ten years later, in 1828, the poet wrote a song for her in six free strophes, calling the girl Silvia, like a character in a famous work by Tarquato Tasso. In this poem, Leopardi sings the pain of betrayed youth, showing in parallel the figure of the girl and the poet himself.

A Summary of the Late 1800s

The spread of capitalism internationally results in extraordinary growth in production and technological development. The era of free competition ends and industrial concentration intensifies, with the state intervening heavily in the economy. In the political sphere, the strengthening of governments leads to authoritarian rule, to the crisis of liberal movements, and to the emergence of anti-parliamentary tendencies. The condition of the proletariat is affirmed as a social issue, and we see numerous migratory movements. The so-called 'mass society' emerges with the birth of a new form of entrepreneurial bourgeoisie, the management of finance and credit widening of the middle classes, and also by virtue of the bureaucracy. We witness the growth of schooling and the development of traditional means of communication: newspapers, magazines, books etc., in relation to an ever-expanding market and a predominantly bourgeois public.

On the international level, the so-called 'Age of Imperialism' sees the great powers involved in a contest of colonial expansion that has economic, political, but also cultural and ideological motivations. The literary current which dominates the Italian scene in the first years of national unity is the scapigliatura, a term used for the first time by Cletto Arrighi in the novel *La Scapigliatura and 6 February* (1862). Many nonconformist, rebellious young authors join the movement, impatient with every form of bourgeois life. At the same time, there is also a classicist tendency, one exponent of which is Giosuè Carducci. The main literary currents in the second half of the century are realism and decadentism, but the effects of the latter will fully be manifested only at the beginning of the twentieth century.

Verist Literature

In the middle years of the century, positivism prevails in the philosophical sphere, favoured for the application of reason, and in science the will to extend the experimental method and other fields of knowledge led to the foundation of new disciplines such as sociology. In France, on the heels of positivism, naturalism develops: literature is characterized as an activity capable of cooperating in cultural social development. Moreover, the place of the omniscient narrator, dominant in the early nineteenth century, takes over the canon of the impersonality of the narration. For the French, naturalism corresponds to the Italian verismo, that has Giovanni Verga among its top representatives.

La Carboneria and Giuseppe Mazzini

After the Vienna Congress, no one could freely pursue political activity, spread liberal and democratic ideas, or seek independence from the homeland. For this reason, many politicians organized themselves into secret societies: associations of people who share the same political ideas. In Italy, one of its most famous secret societies was born in the kingdom of Naples, called 'Carboneria' because it used the language of Carbonari, i.e., the coal sellers. Comprising mainly the military bourgeois, they fought in secret to obtain the constitution of national independence. Giuseppe Manzini (Genoa, 1805–Pisa, 1872) began his political activity as a Carbonaro, but soon realized that he had to change the way he acted in order to make the organization of the secret society more effective, with clear objectives for everyone. In 1831, he founded a new society called 'The Young Italy', which had as its goal the unity and independence of the nation.

Alessandro Manzoni

Alessandro Manzoni, born in Milan in 1785, was a noble man living in the lively Milanese cultural environment. In 1805, he joined his mother, Giulia Beccaria, in Paris, where his studies helped him to form his historical consciousness. In 1810, he converted to Catholicism. He died in Milan in 1874. In his youth, Manzoni accepted the Enlightenment ideas thanks to contact with his maternal grandfather, Cesare Beccaria, and his friends from the Enlightenment magazine *Il Caffe* (although his first works tend toward neoclassicism). His great moral commitment soon turned him away from neoclassicism and prepared him for conversion to Catholicism in 1810 (due to the influence of his very religious wife, Enrichetta Blondel). The conversion to Catholicism was, for Manzoni, the reconfirmation of those spiritual values: freedom, equality and brotherhood among men, which the French revolution had taught him and that he felt as a religious duty.

His religious and political convictions gave him a great sensitivity to the sufferings and hopes of the common people, whose sentiments he became a spokesman for. Romanticism for Alessandro Manzoni is found in the need to understand and love men, to show their pain, joy, desires and disappointments. With Italian people he shares the love for freedom and national independence: he participates in the debate in the magazine *The Conciliator*, and he is recognized as the main representative of the Romantic movement in Milan. However, he thinks that art and literature must be popular, historically accurate, and nationalist, and also that it must show a moral and civil commitment. This means that it must use a new language, one which speaks from the heart, to the conscience of the people.

Manzoni is interested in the problem of language in many of his writings, right up to the last years of his life. The rigid and cold language of the classicists is in opposition to the spoken language used by the educated class of Florence. Manzoni thinks that language should be national and contribute to the unity of Italy, therefore it must be based on usage and be close to the historical and social reality of the moment. While in Italy Romantic ideas are discussed, Manzoni emphasizes his interest in aspects of human weakness: he begins to compose some tragedies, trying to create a new model of theatre based on historical and political inspiration. In the theatre, Manzoni seeks contact with the public and tries to renew the contents and theatrical forms: in the tragedies, he inserts decorations as a moment of moral, political, and religious meditation on facts present in the scene. In the 'odes', the poet tries to reconcile the political commitment with the religious vision of history. In 'Ode March' (1821), written for the Carbonari motions of that year, Manzoni exalts freedom as a gift from God, but one that man can conquer only through personal sacrifice.

Alessandro Manzoni's most famous work is the novel *I Promessi Sposi*, in which he realizes his intentions: to create a pedagogical historical novel, to entrust the role of protagonists to popular characters, and to create a simple language able to interest a broad public. Against the background of the historical events of the seventeenth century (the popular revolt in Lombardy, the famine, and the Thirty Years War), Manzoni inserts a love story between Renzo and Lucia, a love hindered in all ways by a powerful man, who in the end is defeated. Manzoni writes three versions of the novel before arriving at the definitive one in 1840.

The historical novel was born in England at the beginning of the nineteenth century, continuing the tradition of the eighteenth-century Russian realistic novel. The narration is set in the past, especially in the Middle Ages with its idealized model of society, and for this reason it becomes a characteristic form of Romance literature. The characteristics of the historical novel are based on the precise reconstruction of the historical epoch, but the real events are mixed into invented events, and with real and imaginary characters. From a stylistic point of view, the historical novel uses the descriptions of landscapes to create the framework for history, and also employs material belonging to the traditions of a people: legends, fairy tales and proverbs.

Giuseppe Garibaldi (1807–1882)

Garibaldi had a life full of adventure. He shared Mazzini's ideas, and struggled for the unity and independence of Italy. He took part in the riots of 1834 in Piedmont, but was arrested and took refuge in Latin America where he fought for the independence of the South American countries. He returned to Italy in 1848 to take part in the first war of independence, but again was forced to escape from the country. In 1854, he returned definitively, and participated as a general in the second war of independence. In 1860, he organized the Expedition of the 1000, so called because it had about 1000 volunteers (also called Garibaldini). They departed from Quarto, near Genoa, and landed in Marsala to conquer Sicily. The Piedmontese army then headed south to reunify Italy: Garibaldi met Vittorio Emanuele II at Teano, near Caserta in the countryside, and handed over the territories he had conquered.

Romanticism and Risorgimento

The Italian literary history of the first half of the nineteenth century reflects the characteristic aspects of the contemporary political and social situation. This close link between Romanticism and the Risorgimento allows us to define the ideal of the new literature: it must be nationalist, popular, risorgimento, historical and bourgeois. The civil and moral tension of the early nineteenth century produced a literature inspired by patriotism, reflecting the ideology of the two political currents of the time: moderate and democratic. The Risorgimento influenced literature not only in terms of themes and character, but it also determined some characteristics of the typical genres of the new movement, such as the novel, the historical drama, patriotic poetry, memoirs, and the historical ballad.

The climate of the riots, from 1820-21 to 1848, is represented in the Risorgimento literature via the themes of the denunciation of oppression, the desire for freedom, the explosion of hope, the nostalgia for the distant homeland, and the memory of the sufferings of prisoners.

Patriotic Poetry

The patriotic poetry of the Risorgimento was intended to arouse love, a spirit of struggle for the homeland, a hatred of the foreigner, and the desire for independence and national unity. This was expressed through an easy but musical language, very close to the spoken word. Among the authors of this genre is Giovanni Berchet (Milan, 1783–Turin, 1851), the first and greatest patriotic poet. He wrote for *The Conciliator* as a theorist of Romanticism, but was forced into exile after the revolts of 1821. His works were intended as a form of patriotic and civilized propaganda, expressing themes such as melancholy, the pain of exile, love for the homeland, and the desire for freedom. Goffredo Mameli (Genoa, 1827–Rome, 1349), who died of a leg injury during the defense of Rome, was also active in creating poetry aimed at interpreting the spirit of the people. He was the author of the song 'Brothers of Italy', which is the national anthem of the country today.

Brothers of Italy

Fratelli d'Italia, l'Italia s' desta
dell'elmo di Scipio se' cinta la testa
dove' la vittoria? Le porga la chioma:
ch schiava di Roma Iddio la creo.(rit.)
Stringiamoci a coorte, siam pronti alla
morte, siam pronti alla morte, l'Italia chia-
mo. Stringiamoci a coorte, siam pronti alla
morte, siam pronti alla morte l'Italia chiamo
si.2) Dall'alpe a Sicilia, dovunque
Legnano; ogni uom di ferruccio ha il core,
ha la mano. I bimbi d'Italia si chiaman
Balilla il suon d'ogni squilla i vespri sono.
Noi fummo da secoli, calpesti e derisi,
perche non siam popolo, perche siam
divisi. Raccolgaci un'unica bandiera, una
speme: di fonderci insieme gi l'ora suono.
(rit.)4 Son giunchi che piegano le spade
vedute, gi l'aquila d'Austria le penne ha
perdute il sangue d'Italia il sangue polacco
bev col Cosacco, ma il sen le brucio.(rit.)5)
Uniamoci, uniamoci l'unione e l'amore
rivelano ai popoli le vie del Signore.
Giuriamo far libero il suolo nato.
Uniti per Dio, chi vincer ci puo?(rit.)
Evviva l'Italia, dal sonno s' desta,
dell'elmo di Scipio s' cinta la testa.
Dov' la vittoria? Le porga la chioma:
ch schiava di Roma Iddio la creo.

Brothers of Italy, Italy is awakening
of the helmet of Scipio if his head is wrapped
where is the victory? Give her the hair:
ch slave of Rome God I create it (rit.)
Let's join a cohort, we are ready to die,
we are ready to death, I call Italy.
Let's join a cohort, we are ready to die,
we are ready to death Italy I call si.2)
From the Alps to Sicily, wherever Legnano;
every man of ferruccio has the core, he has the hand.
The children of Italy are called Balilla
the sound of each ring is vespers.
We have been for centuries, trample and laugh,
because we are not a people, because we are divided.
Collect only one flag, one spied:
to merge the sound hour together. (rit.) 4)
They are rushes that bend the swords,
already the eagle of Austria has lost its feathers
the blood of Italy the Polish blood
drink with the Cossack, but the sen bruci. (rit.) 5) Let's join, let's
unite the union and the love
reveal the ways of the Lord to the peoples.
We swear to free the born soil.
United for God, who can win us? (Rit.)
Hurray Italy, from sleep s' awake,
of the helmet of Scipio's head.
Where's the victory? Give her the hair:
ch slave of Rome God I create it. Let's draw ourselves

Stringiamoci a coorte, siam pronti alla morte, siam pronti alla morte, l'Italia chiamo. Stringiamoci a coorte, siam pronti alla morte, siam pronti alla morte, l'Italia chiamo.	*to a cohort, we are ready to death, we are ready to death, I call Italy. Let's join a cohort, we are ready to die, we are ready to death, I call Italy.*

Many compositions of Risorgimento authors are still remembered emotionally today by Italians. Although the production did not reach other artistic levels, it was a faithful reflection of a heroic feeling and a sincere enthusiasm, and thus deserves an important place in the history of Italian poetry.

The Autobiographical Writers

During the Risorgimento there was an increase in the production of autobiographical literature by patriotic political characters. This genre corresponds to the romantic taste for autobiography, and tends to propose models for behaviour whilst provoking the emotional participation of the reader.

Silvio Pellico (1789–1854)

Silvio Pellico was one such writer. Editor-in-chief of the magazine *The Conciliator*, he was also part of the carboneria, and for that reason arrested by the Austrians. He remained in prison in a fortress in Moravia for fifteen years, and when back in Piedmont in 1832, he wrote the memoir *My Prisons* based on his experiences. It is a simple book, which never condemns the Austrians openly, but is very vivid in its descriptions of the characters that appear, and is renowned for the humanity with which the author looks at the world and himself.

Historical and Political Writings

In the historical and political thought of the Risorgimento we can identify two tendencies: one of a liberal Catholic type, the second with a secular and democratic inspiration. The first current advocates the need to consider the church as the centre of the process of civil political development (as had already happened in the Middle Ages). This is part of Vincenzo Gioberti's work, *Moral and Civil Primacy of the Italians*. This Piedmontese priest (1801–1851) proposed the birth of a united state from a confederation of Italian states led by the Pope. However, after the failure of the revolution in 1848, he saw Piedmont as the only state capable of leading Italy to independence and unity. The second current, on the other hand, wants to see a rebirth of Italy by popular initiative, and to achieve independence with revolutionary methods.

Among the authors working in this current is Giuseppe Mazzini (Genoa, 1805–Pisa, 1872). He is not only a politician, but also writes essays in which he states that his ideal is a literature that acts as a guide, leading to an awareness of the people and of one's own society. Ippolito Nievo (Padua, 1831–Tyrrhenian Sea, 1861) has ideas close to those of Mazzini. He participated in various revolutionary conspiracies alongside being part of the Garibaldi 1000 expedition. He died when the ship bringing him to Naples in 1861 sank. His literary activity was very intense, his masterpiece being the novel *The Confessions of an Italian*, published in 1867 after his death. In it, which was extremely famous during the nineteenth century, Ippolito Nievo tells the story of an elderly man, Carlo Ippolito Nevio, from his childhood until the revolution of 1848, mixing the private events of the protagonist with some key events in Italian Risorgimento history. It has been noted through historical and political writings that in the nineteenth century, people gradually started opening up towards freedom and politically matured since the Sacrifi Independence.

On 17 March 1861, the Parliament of Turin proclaimed Vittorio Emanuele II the first king of the Kingdom of Italy. At this moment, Italy became one, just as Mazzini wanted. It was not federal, it was monarchical (as the bourgeois wanted), but Venice (still under Austrian rule) and Rome (governed by the Pope) were still absent from the union. In order to address this, in 1866, Italian forces joined with Prussia to begin the Third War of Independence. They succeeded in gaining Venice and its territories after a few months, but at this point, relations between the Catholic Church and the Italian state were very tense. The government wanted Rome as the capital of the nation, while the Pope did not want to renounce the possession of the city. On 20 September 1870, the Italian army entered Rome by force, and in 1871, the city became the new capital of Italy.

Verism (Realism)

Verism is the most significant movement of Italian culture at the turn of the century. Like the scapigliatura, it develops in a Milanese environment, but the Veristic writers are of Southern origin, and describe the difficult life of the people of the South. Verism is influenced by English and Russian narrative realism, but even more so by the French naturalist novel. Within the Italian experience, it is linked to Mazzini's realist Romanticism and to the scapigliatura.

Two historical cultural situations influence the movement in particular: the spread of positivist doctrines and the Italian social question. Realism is influenced by positivist determinism, by the historical moment and by the social environment. Like other realities, it is proposed that humans can be analysed scientifically. Even the psychological aspects and the vices and virtues are observable through the magnifying glass of the narrator in such a way that they can be analysed and known. The work of art, therefore, must study man with the methods of the natural and social sciences. The negative and positive aspects of human reality must be subjected to a rigorous scientific study. The novel is the most suitable literary genre for this study.

The Veristic novel always has a contemporary subject. The environment is often restricted to the regional. There are very precise descriptions of natural and human situations, and the characters are observed by means of generic psychological reflections. The writer seeks literary impersonality: his point of view should not prevail, he must let things and people speak. It is important for the Veristic author to disappear from the text, i.e., to respect the reality described and not to elevate it to the level of high literature.

Verism poses the problem of language. The writer seeks the most appropriate linguistic style to represent this new social reality, and endeavours to remain as faithfully similar to the spoken language of the men of his time with dialectal expressions. Verism expresses disappointment at the partial failure of the hopes raised by the unification of the peninsula: the ruling class proves unable to resolve the conflict between North and South, or to improve the conditions of misery and backwardness of much of the peninsula. There is emphasis of the most disheartened, skeptical and mystical aspects without a satirical polemical attitude. There is a real interest in the vanquished, the defeated, those who struggle hard for survival, and those who accept fate with resignation.

Verists have a pessimistic view of life. They do not believe in providence (God is absent in their stories), just as they do not believe in social progress or the possibility of change. The most important Verist storyteller is the Sicilian Giovanni Verga.

Giovanni Verga

Born in Catania in 1840, he spent his first years in Sicily writing for local newspapers and composing the first historical novels: *The Carbonari della Montagna* and *Amore e Patria*. Between 1865 and 1871, he lived in Milan, where he worked to mature the experience of scapigliatura. Between 1880 and 1894, however, he wrote his masterpieces: *The Bad Things* and *Mastro-don Gesualdo*. He died in Catania in 1922.

In the artistic production of Verga, two phases are distinguished. In the first phase, he focuses on high society and artistic environments. There are autobiographical elements, and we note his desire to denounce the defects of contemporary society, especially those of the upper classes. His characters belong to high society: you meet the young woman from a good family forced to become a nun, the artist who can not succeed, the lover who refuses to commit suicide. In 1884, he begins the truly 'Veritable' phase, during which he tells the story of a poor peasant victim of poverty. It seems that Verga is tired of the frivolous world of early stories, and prefers characters who struggle hard to survive. For a time, he still writes worldly novels, but his interest has already shifted to the more humble classes. In 1880, he wrote *The Life of the Fields*; in 1881, *The Bad Things*; in 1893, *Mastro-don Gesualdo* and *Novelle Rusticane*. These works are set throughout the Sicily that Che Verga knew, and the protagonists are farmers, shepherds and fishermen.

I Reluctantly, along with *Mastro-don Gesualdo*, is part of a collection of five novels entitled *The Vanquished*. *I Reluctantly* is the story of a family struggling to get out of poverty. The values of the family are very important. It is a story about a group rather than about single individuals, which covers tradition, work, the home, and worship. The family face the risks of the sea every day in return for very little money. Theirs is a miserable and difficult life. 'Ntoni, the nephew of patron' ntoni, the head of the family, does not accept this hard and poor life. He did his military service in the great cities of Italy, and noticed that people live differently. There were rich people who do not have to fight for a piece of bread. 'Ntoni no longer wanted to live in Aci Trezza; he leaves in search of fortune.

Mastro-don Gesualdo represents the struggle of the protagonist who overcomes his misery, but fails to improve his social position. He is also a loser. In the Verist genre, there is a great respect for the seriousness and the values of men. Verga no longer paints the poor with paternalism, he recognizes their strength and dignity. He has a very pessimistic view of life: he does not believe in God or providence, and he is not a socialist who fights for social change. He is the poet of the vanquished, of those who can accept destiny with resignation. This is a bourgeois vision of life, a positive rejection of sentimentality and paternalism. The discovery of the dignity of the poor was positive. His attitude is resigned and conservative. Verga accepts the general lines of French naturalism, but he is not so attentive to the psychological analysis of the characters as to their actions towards the environment. He believed that the novel should deal with the whole society of the lower classes and accept the principle of the impersonality of the work of art.

Whilst French naturalists had a homogeneous national public, Italians did not speak a national language, but regional dialects instead. This is why the revolutionary solution of Verga was to write his with dialect expressions that faithfully represented the reality of the characters. Verga had immediate success, and soon became a classic author: his novels were adopted in schools as textbooks.

The South in the Nineteenth Century

When the unification of Italy took place, the so-called 'southern question' was posed: the problem of poverty, illiteracy and southern brigandage. Poverty and illiteracy were naturally also problems in the North, but in the South, they were particularly serious. Both urban centres and the countryside had an impoverished population. In the towns, the landowners forced the peasants to live a life of poverty. In 1799, a peasant uprising exploded: the brigandage, which had developed throughout the nineteenth century, expressed their great discomfort over the lack of agrarian reform. The mafia was born during this period.

The term mafia originally meant the practice of brigands employed by landowners to protect their lands. During the 1800s, these brigands became very powerful, and around 1900, the mafia families were so influential in the South, that they controlled almost every economic activity in their territory. After the unification of Italy, in 1863, the Pica law was passed, declaring a state of war in the south, entrusting the brigandage trials to the military tribunals. The war between the gangs did not solve the problem of the discomfort of the peasants; rather, it confirmed the dominion of the landowners. The group of so-called meridionalists was formed to devote themselves to the problems and the fate of the South, but there were also intellectuals who explained the southern question in racist terms, fuelling hostilities and prejudices still perceptible today.

The Macchiaioli

The artistic movement of the Macchiaioli developed in Florence around the middle of the nineteenth century, and is considered the most important artistic movement of the century in Italy. Young artists flocked to the city from every part of Italy, and their meeting place was the Michelangelo Cafe. Here they discussed historical and contemporary artistic events. In 1856, Domenico Morelli arrived in Florence from Paris, and he enthusiastically recounts the cultural events he had witnessed in the French capital; this year is considered the official beginning of the movement. Morelli, in a conference in 1877, explains that the stain is the weapon with which the new painting fights tradition. Isolated shapes are not important, because in reality, we do not perceive isolated images. What counts is the light, and the stain of colour that light produces. There is an obvious analogy between the movement of the Macchiaioli and the French impressionists. The most brilliant exponent of the group is Giovanni (1825-1908); like many other Macchiaioli, he participated in the Risorgimento movements for freedom and unification.

Scapigliatura

The term scapigliatura is mentioned for the first time in an 1862 novel by the Milanese Cletto Arrighi. He was referring to a rebellious and marginalized lifestyle, both restless and disorderly. The scapigliatura style flourishes in the Lombard environment after 1860, after the union of Italy. The first proponents include Milanese narrators such as Arrigo Boito and Emilio Praga, and they are later joined by writers from Piedmont. In those years, first Piedmont and later, the rest of Italy began to become a modern state, giving life to the first forms of industrial agrarian capitalism. This means progress and wealth for many, but poverty and marginalization for others. The poor, those vanquished and defeated from a moral and material point of view, are excluded from the new economic development. Even the scapigliati are vanquished: they reject progress and positivist thinking, the success of science, and bourgeois structures, all of which they see as the negation of their artistic ideals. They rebel against society but do not produce another social model. The Scapigliatura develops in Milan, where the social and economic changes were faster and more intense, and where there was a contrast between the rich, the bourgeois, and the intellectual dreamers. The movement is therefore not only literary but also social, the first manifestation of the intellectual discomfort in a bourgeois capitalist society.

The scapigliati did not limit themselves to writing, but they lived in first person the discomfort of the artist, often leading a life on the margins of society. The scapigliati writers wanted to scandalize the bourgeois class with their unruly lives, lived in poverty and drunkenness and sometimes ended with suicide. They also aimed to scandalize with their literary work, with their immoral themes, and with their anarchist socialist polemic. Their style was bizarre, their metre anti-traditional, their language irreverent. The scapigliati also felt attracted to the other arts. They wanted to represent human reality as it really was, even in its most ugly, painful, squalid and mundane aspects. They rejected all conventions. The influence of Baudelaire is evident, but also that of French decadence and of naturalism and philosophical positivism, which translate into the search for realistic motifs that are often squalid and mundane. The literary results from the movement are mediocre, but they are important because they prepare the ground for the development of realistic tendencies.

History from the Unity of Italy to 1901

In 1876, the parliamentary Left gained power in the newly united nation, and with the electoral law of 1882, the right to vote was extended (but the illiterate and those who did not own property were still excluded). After unity, a policy of colonial expansion begins in Africa, Eritrea and Somalia. In 1892, the Italian Socialist party was born. In this period, the economic crisis and the strong political opposition between conservatives and liberals caused many protests, especially amongst the poorer classes. In 1898, riots broke out against the high cost of living. The reaction of the Rudinì government was very harsh, and in Milan, many demonstrators were killed. The person responsible for the massacre, General Beccaris, was rewarded by King Umberto I. Many socialists were arrested. On 28 July 1901, the anarchist Gaetano Bresci came from America to avenge the killings in Milan, and he killed King Umberto I. Umberto was succeeded by Vittorio Emanuele III, who gave the task of forming the new government to the liberal Zanardelli. The following period was characterized by a liberal policy and intense economic development due to the spread of industry.

Giosuè Carducci

Carducci's personal history is very closely tied to Italian political events. He participated intensely in the events that followed the union of Italy, and was an opponent of the government. He supported the Republican party, rejected the monarchical solution given by unification, and was anti-clerical. Following his sectarian positions, as a populist and a supporter of the rights of the plebs, he became closer to the bourgeois position and eventually became part of the bourgeoisie. After his meeting with Queen Margherita in 1878, his republicanism was abandoned and he became a supporter of the monarchy, causing great scandal in the Republican youth circles. Even his anti-clerical position weakened as he recognized the historical and civil value of Christianity and of Catholicism.

Carducci's education was essentially classical, based on the Greek and Latin senators and on the Italian tradition. He despised modern Romantic writers, and exalted Italian authors by rejecting the foreign model. Only later did he come to appreciate Hugo and Baudelaire. A constant of his thought is love for his country, sometimes expressed in rhetorical form, but always intense and sincere. Another constant is the total dedication to poetry, which he allowed to express his personality. Carducci was a lively man, but also melancholic; combative, but also solitary.

The beginning of his poetic production coincided with a profound interest in the classics. Expressions of his classicism are the collections *Juvenilia* (1850–1860) and *Levia Gravia* (1861–1871). In a second movement, he combines the classical model with ideas of the modern world, and expresses his impatience for the ruling class and its hypocritical clericalism. In contrast to the present are the greats of the near past: Garibaldi, Mazzini, the heroes of the Risorgimento; later, he approaches the Modern writers, from whom he seeks an expression closer to the spoken language.

In *New Rhymes* (1887), his poems are inspired both by the classics and by intimate poetry. In the former, the inspiration comes from great personalities of the past such as Homer, Virgil, Petrarch, Dante and the historical moments that he recalls. In the latter, he recalls events in his private life, such as the death of his son Dante, a trip to the Maremma, and a memory of a woman he loved in his youth. Taking a melancholy and sad mood, he evokes historical actions, like the legend of Theodoric, and celebrates the French revolution, which he considers one of the highest moments in contemporary history.

There is also poetry; in which he recalls the Hellenic past, representing a refuge in a world of pure beauty far from the sad present. The more he becomes part of the new Italian state, the stronger his suffering for the mediocrity and misery of his time becomes, and he seeks refuge in art. He write rhymes which make a rhythm out of the Latin verses, but which must be read according to the accent from modern languages: this is why he defines them as barbarous—'ododi barbare'.

Between 1897 and 1898, his last collection *Rhymes and Rhythms* is composed, in which one perceives an anxiety, a nervousness, behind his official optimism, anticipating the climate of decadentism. The barbaric metric forms are re-proposed, opening the way to the unhinging of traditional metric forms. Behind that classical solemnity is the free verse that will be used in the twentieth century to express the restless sensibility of the period in new metrical forms.

Decadentism

Towards the end of the nineteenth century, the term 'decadentism' was used in a negative sense: to define the characteristics of a movement of thought that was developing in reaction to positivism and naturalism. The term was adopted and transformed in a positive sense by those who experienced the crisis which dominated that period. At the end of the nineteenth century, a period of profound historical, social and economic crisis began all across Europe. It marked the sunset of the positivist faith in reason and progress, and also the conviction that it is possible to investigate and analyse reality in an objective way.

Reality no longer appeared as an object to be explored with instruments of reason, but as a universe of different facets, in which there was something which escaped logical thinking. Here, demand developed for an investigation of what was beyond visible reality, to discover the hidden mystery, beyond the real, which escapes the common man. For this task, new instruments were needed: intuition and imagination, an exceptional sensibility, a disposition to listen to reality in order to grasp the most hidden messages, a feeling of tension and of anxiety, and a restlessness which never finds peace. The crisis of reality also soon became a crisis in the personality of man. Man, like reality, was now also considered to be made from 1000 pieces. The spread of the feeling of anxiety and the discovery of the unconscious were evidence of irrationalism.

Decadentism was a movement that impacted all of Europe, finding expression not only in poetry but also in theatre and music, in philosophy, and in the figurative arts. The artist and the writer lose their certainty in their task of analysing and critiquing reality and being the interpreters of bourgeois society. The decadent artist feels increasingly distant from society and the common man: the inability to fit into common reality reopens different paths.

The writer can be identified as the only exceptional person able to grasp the mystery, the hidden message of reality: in order to do this, he must isolate himself from the social and historical context, from the common world, closing in on himself, cultivating his exasperated sensitivity, in order to explore through the art the most unknown and mysterious aspects of the nature of man and the symbols of the universe. Here the poet seers are born, the symbolists, the singers of aesthetics, and the theorizers of identity between truth and art. The sense of isolation can lead the artist to an existential crisis, characterized by anxiety, the inability to communicate or to maintain relationships with others.

In Italy, Giovanni Pascoli and Gabriele D'Annunzio worked within the late nineteenth-century decadentism, alongside Svevo, Pirandello, and Montale. Within their interpretation of the crisis, and in their artistic and stylistic research, the roots of movements such as the avant-garde and corpuscularism can be seen. Decadent themes can also be found in the artistic movement of the Milanese scapigliatura, characterized by an attitude of violently breaking with tradition and a rebellion against the conventions of the bourgeois world.

More History

The last decades of the nineteenth century and the first decades of the twentieth century throughout Europe are a complex and difficult period on the historical and social level, characterized by great international tensions, strong colonial imperialist pressures, and a deep economic crisis (The Great Depression). Italy is also affected by the general crisis, the government responding with the closure of the protests of workers, and with the introduction of a series of protectionist measures to defend national agricultural products, measures which harm small-scale farmers. There is a mass-migration: over a span of thirty years, Italians are forced to leave their homeland to emigrate to northern Europe and America in order to flee from poverty.

In this context, the poet Giovanni Pascoli stands out. He was born in San Mauro di Romagna on

31 December 1855, and he died in Bologna on 6 April 1912. Pascoli was a lonely man, marked by the trauma of his parents' death. Without any trust in man and without the support of an ideology, he closed in on himself to cultivate his personal myths: the family nest, the countryside, childhood. Pascoli began to compose poetry in his youth, but began to publish them only quite late in life.

His first collection came out in 1891; titled *Myricae* (a Latin word referring to the tamarisks—simple, wild, countryside plants), the book was organized as the diary of a day in the countryside. In 1897, the *Poemetti* came out, in which the poet brought suggestions from his foreign poetry, in particular English, into the history of a peasant family. In 1903, the *Cantos of Castelvecchio* are published; in 1904, the *Convivial Poems* (in which characters and events of antiquity and classical mythology can be found), and two years later came *The Hate and the Hymns.*

Alongside poetry in Italian, Pascoli composes lyrics in Latin and is also notable as a literary critic. The main themes of Pascoli's work are the simple things: the countryside, the family, the everyday world, and childhood, but also the idea of the evil of irrationality always present in man and in society. These are elements that the poet recounts and rediscovers with an amazement, a melancholy, a subtle restlessness which runs through his entire production. His is not descriptive poetry; the little things are symbols to be investigated in the most hidden parts in order to reveal the mystery, the secrets which they keep and which escape the common man. The poet escapes from reality to take refuge in an inner world, in the myth of childhood and the family nest, the places which can offer the protection of human values against an irrational and violent history and society which offend the poor, the humble and the simple.

Faced with this pessimistic view of social life, Pascoli returns to the innocence of childhood; he theorizes in a famous essay that poetry comes from the ability of children to notice, to study the simplest and smallest things. He theorized that a little boy is inside us; we grow up and he remains small ... And without him, not only would we not see so many things, but we could not even think about them and give them back. The poet is the one who discovers and listens to this little boy, this child, hidden in all men, and who is capable of overcoming the injustice of the contemporary world to inspire piety and brotherhood. In this sense, poetry has a profound moral and social value.

Pascoli's poetry is also influenced by his classical culture: he does not resume, like Carducci, the style and contents of the ancient world, but he makes the great characters of myth and history the protagonists of his verses, giving them feelings of restlessness and amazement. The rejection of society, the flight from reality, and the sensation of the continuous presence of mystery and irrationality make his work fully representative of European decadentism.

Pascoli's poetry is characterized by a particular symbolism typical of the symbolist tradition: the small and humble things that he likes to describe in the most particular detail are deformed and transfigured to represent the mystical torment of the poet's soul. The music of the words of the verse is very remarkable: he uses rhyme, alliteration, onomatopoeia, and the reproduction of the sounds and noises of nature. He also uses the synaesthetic, realized by putting one beside the other words that refer to different senses: images, sounds, smells.

Also interesting is his ability to combine words from different sectors and languages: technical terms of the campaign world, dialect expressions, courtly forms and foreign words. The language of Pascoli definitively breaks the overwhelming tradition of syntax, shattering the sentence and creating a complex set of flashes, immediate sensations, and fragments of music that are sometimes excessive.

Il gelsomino notturno di pascoli

Il gelsomino notturno

E s'aprono i fiori notturni,
nell'ora che penso a' miei cari.
Sono apparse in mezzo ai viburni
le farfalle crepuscolari.
Da un pezzo si tacquero i gridi:
là sola una casa bisbiglia.
Sotto l'ali dormono i nidi,
come gli occhi sotto le ciglia.
Dai calici aperti si esala
l'odore di fragole rosse.
Splende un lume là nella sala.
Nasce l'erba sopra le fosse.
Un'ape tardiva sussurra
trovando già prese le celle.
La Chioccetta per l'aia azzurra
va col suo pigolio di stelle.
Per tutta la notte s'esala
l'odore che passa col vento.
Passa il lume su per la scala;
brilla al primo piano: s'è spento . . .
È l'alba: si chiudono i petali
un poco gualciti; si cova,
dentro l'urna molle e segreta,
non so che felicità nuova.

The nocturnal jasmine

And the night flowers are open,
in the hour that I think of 'my dear ones.
They appeared in the middle of the viburnum
the crepuscular butterflies.
For a long time the cries were silent:
there alone a house whispers.
The nests are sleeping under the wings
like the eyes under the eyelashes.
From the open glasses it is exhaled
the smell of red strawberries.
There is a light shining in the hall.
Grass is born above the pits.
A late bee whispers
finding the cells already taken.
The Chioccetta for the aia azzurra
he goes with his peep of stars.
Throughout the night he gets excited
the smell that passes with the wind.
Pass the light up the ladder;
shines on the first floor: it's off. . .
It is dawn: the petals are closed
a little crumpled; he hates,
inside the soft and secret urn,
I do not know what a new happiness.

The International Panorama in the Nineteenth Century

In the first half of the nineteenth century, Romanticism spread into French territory. The most prominent storytellers were Victor Hugo and Honore de Balzac (author of Comedie Humaine), both proponents of the realistic novel and of the narrative module based on the omniscient external narrator. In the second half of the nineteenth century, a large group of novelists emerged. Among them was Charles Baudelaire, also known as the cursed poet, who paved the way for the symbolist and decadent poetry of the end of the century. Meanwhile, the tradition of the realistic novel, inaugurated by Balzac, continues with Victor Hugo's *Les Miserables* in 1862. When realism is enriched by naturalism, it becomes able to represent reality in literary production with the utmost objectivity. This is achieved by resorting to precise scientific rigour. A vanguard of this genre was Emile Zola.

In England, Romanticism is preceded by a movement which nourishes popular interest in traditional and epic themes, the highest example of which is James Macpherson's songs. This lasts until the publication of Samuel Taylor, which marks the beginning of the great Romantic season. The underlying commonality of this season is the vision of the mystical individualistic life. This shines through the production of Lord Byron and the exotic visions of William Blake. Their poetry is flanked by historical novels (such as those by

Walter Scott) and tales of domestic life (Jane Austin).

In the second half of the century, the evolutionary theory of Charles Darwin is affirmed in the field of science. Darwin's work of 1859 entitled *On the Origin of the Species* shakes traditional religious beliefs. Novelists, including Charles Dickens, create the so-called 'Victorian novel', which mixes ironic and dramatic tones with psychological and social analysis. Towards the end of the century, there was a return to an art free of any social or moral implication, in particular in the work of Oscar Wilde, who was a bitter witness to a world in the process of disintegration and in the grip of a profound spiritual crisis. This is clearly seen in the his most important work, *The Picture of Dorian Gray* (1891).

During the early nineteenth century, Germany became a centre for the irradiation of romanticism through the movement of the Sturm und Drang. In this movement, the influence of the sepulchral and ossianic poetry of English derivation was combined with mysterious Nordic atmospheres, enabling the mitigation of the passionate nature of the conventional romantic hero. The first members of the romantic school, called 'Cenacolo di Jena', were Goethe and Frederic Schlegel. In the second romantic school, the Grimm brothers stand out. Towards the end of the century, there was also an affirmation of the naturalism of French derivation (in particular with Thomas Mann), while other authors, under the influence of the philosophy of Frederic Nietzsche, turned towards a literature in line with European decadentism. Franz Kafka's novels (among others, *The Trial, The Metamorphosis*) gave voice to the existential anguish that now possessed the human being.

Art

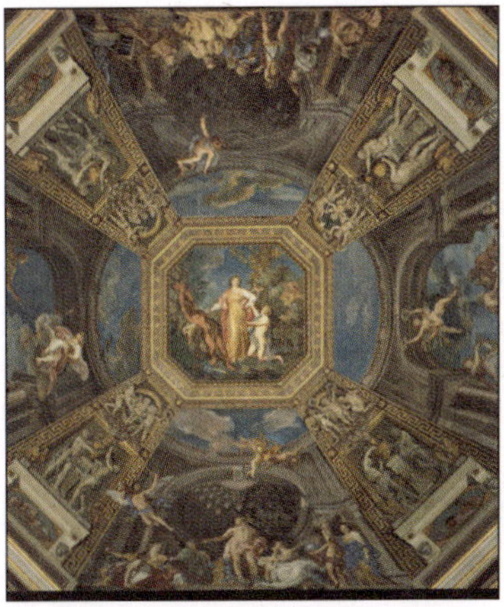

Neoclassical Art

The Napoleonic empire (which was established between the French Revolution and the subsequent restoration of the monarchy) was characterized by the rise of the bourgeois class, the birth of capitalism and strong industrial development. At the same time, a new class developed political consciousness: the workers, who increased in number and began to change their living conditions.

In the domain of art, several trends coexisted. The first of these was Neoclassicism, which was a decorative trend (as opposed to the Baroque), trying to reach a formal perfection through the inspiration of models from classical Greece. The spirit of Renaissance (rebirth of art and culture) led nazarene art and purism to go out together in search of their artistic spirit. Romanticism was the predominant current that manifested throughout Europe during this period. In literature and philosophy, we see two trends—one toward the medieval traditions, the other revaluing the nationalist artistic forms and expression of feeling of neoclassicism.

The neo-Gothic, which has been evident in England since the beginning of the seventeenth century, now spreads to Europe along with the Romance style. Impressionism arises from the interest of some French painters in landscape painting and post-impressionism. Paris is the art capital throughout the nineteenth century, while Italy has to settle for a minor role in the European art scene. In this period we see the rise of art movements based on the intent of different artists working under the joint program guidelines explicitly formulated via posters (in the early twentieth century, this term was used to indicate a writing of political and artistic character, a clear statement of intent, often heated and controversial). These movements developed a lively dialectics, which often saw new movements opposing the dominant artistic schools.

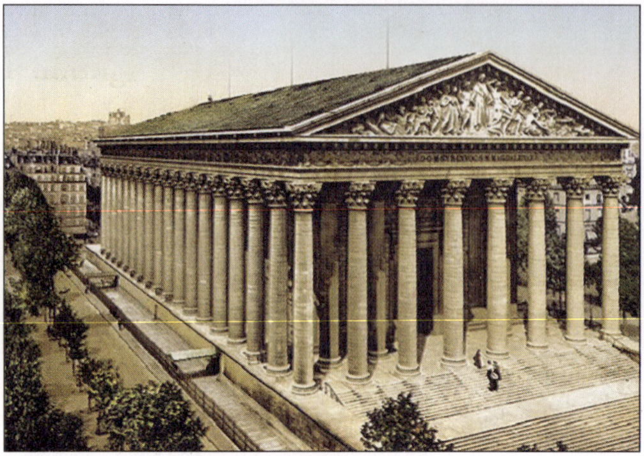

La Madeleine, Paris

Neoclassicism

This current develops between 1750 and 1830, and is based on the theories of Winckelmann, a German architect and author of *The Ancient History of Art*. He considers the history of art to be the result of certain political, social, and intellectual forces placed at the base of creative activity, and thus the result of successive evolutions. A significant boost to this current comes from the archaeological excavation carried out in Pompeii and Herculaneum.

The principles of neoclassical art are the balance and stability of the forms; this equilibrium model defines Greek-Roman art. The neoclassical cultural centres in Italy are in Rome, and also with Canova in Milan. In France, we have Jacques Louis David, and Francisco Goya in Spain.

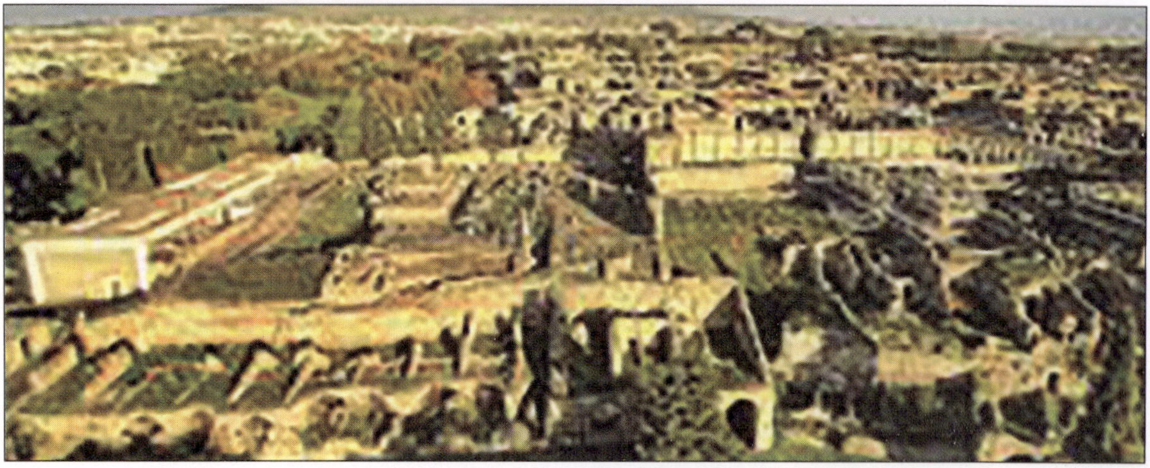

Pompeii was inhabited by wealthy Romans

Pompeii and Herculaneum

The archaeological excavations in Pompeii and Herculaneum uncovered the remains of those ancient cities destroyed in 79 CE by the eruption of Vesuvius. The first excavations in Pompeii were actually in 1749 by order of Charles III of Bourbon, but because of the poor recoveries, they were soon abandoned. They were then resumed in 1754 until, in 1763, there was the discovery of an inscription bearing the words 'Res Publica Pompeianourum' and it was realized that it was ancient Pompeii. At the behest of Maria Carolina, wife of Frederick IV, the city was brought fully to light. During the period of French rule in Italy, there was a continuation of the excavations, and this led to the uncovering of the city walls and the Herculaneum Gate area, as well as to an increase in the fame of Pompeii across Europe. It became a mandatory stop on the so-called 'grand tour' of Europe (a lengthy trip which many young members of the European Aristocracy undertook).

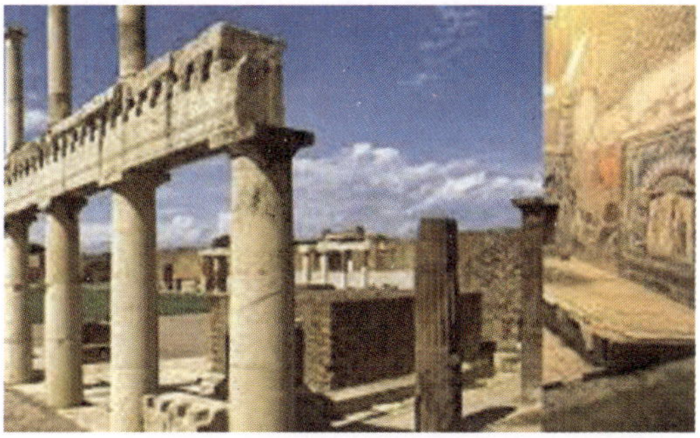

Herculaneum was a resort to 5,000 inhabitants

With the return of the Bourbons in Naples, excavations halted and the ruins were only accessible and visible to guests of the court, but after the unifica-tion of Italy, under the coordination of Giuseppe Fiorelli, there was the first division of ancient Pompeii into regions and islets, so that from 1870 to 1885, the first map of the entire Pompeii area was produced. In 1997, the ruins of Pompeii were included in the UNESCO list of World Heritage sites, and the European Union gave special resources to fund the protection of excavations through the so-called 'big project of Pompeii'.

Archaeological excavations of Herculaneum—an area much smaller than that of Pompeii—began by chance in 1709, when a farmer engaged in the extension of a well for irrigation of his gardens found some fine marble pieces. These attracted the attention of Prince Emanuele Maurizio d'Elbeuf, who bought the well and performed a series of investigations that led to the discovery of several artifacts belonging to the Herculaneum theatre scene.

Antonio Canova

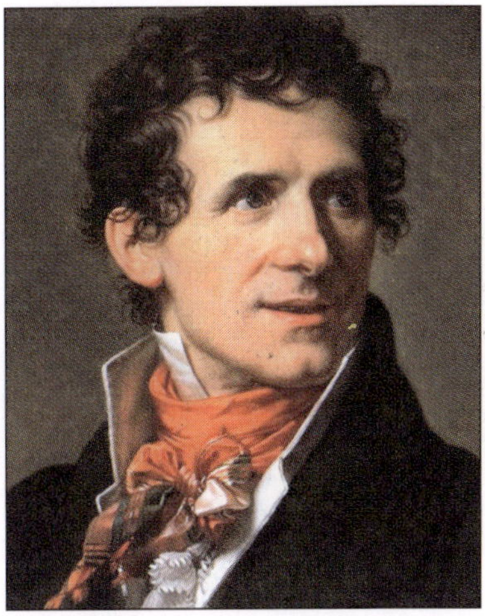

Antonio Canova

Canova was born in 1757 in Treviso, into a family in which stone work was an ancient tradition. He completed his apprenticeship in Venice, where he made his first sculptures of classical subjects, and at sixteen, he had his first commission, 'Orpheus and Eurydice'.

At eighteen, he opened his own studio where he created 'Daedalus and Icarus'. The work triumphed in Venice, and with the money he went to Rome, where he studied the works of antiquity and came into contact with neoclassical circles. The neoclassical style tends to a smaller representation and is sometimes idealized, inspired by Greek mythology and Greek and Roman sculpture.

In 1781, he decided to settle in Rome, creating beautiful sepulchral monuments to Clement XIII and XIV. He died in 1822 in Venice.

Daedalus and Icarus

Canova's famous work was based on the story of a maze which Daedalus, a skilled artisan in Athens, had built for the King of Crete, a building from which it was impossible to escape: the labyrinth. This complex imprisoned the Minotaur, a monster who was half-man and half-bull, the son of Queen Pasiphae. The

Athenian hero Theseus entered the labyrinth and killed the monster, but in revenge, the king locked Daedalus in the maze, along with his son Icarus. To escape from there and from the island of Crete, Daedalus creates a pair of wings made with wax and bird feathers for himself and Icarus. The father and son manage to fly from the island, but although his father advises him to fly low, Icarus ventures higher and higher until the heat of the sun melts the wax of his wings and Icarus falls into the waves. That sea bears his name: the Icarian Sea near the island of Samos in Greece.

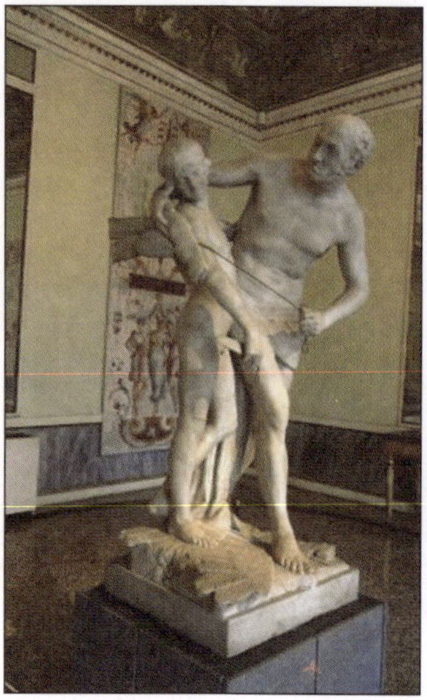

Daedalus and Icarus (1779)

The statue of the mythical father and son is based on the juxtaposition of the naturalist father figure and the idealized, perfectly harmonious young boy. The faces and positions are not expressionless—Daedalus shows attention and effort while his son is smiling. Counter to the usual figure centrality, the center of the composition is empty; the carvings are placed around this space. The thread that binds and encloses the two figures is an ideal circle. Other interesting details are the sculpted objects at the feet of the figure—the slabs and the mallet, which Canova decides to leave in a corner of his work. This may mean that the work itself should be interpreted as an allegory of sculpture. The marble statue was created from a plaster model. The figure of Daedalus and Icarus was sculpted by Antonio Canova in the year 1779. It is a form of kinetic art under Neoclassicism. This sculpture is marked by Baroque abundance of movement.

Jacques Louis David (1748–1825)

Jacques Louis David (Paris, 1748–Brussels, 1825) was probably the greatest interpreter of the neoclassical painting style, creating large paintings of classical subjects and historical events, with the intent to become the official painter for the French revolution and then Napoleon. Among his works is 'The Oath of the Horatii', a celebratory framework of civil virtues. It was created in 1784 with oil paint as medium. It is one of the best specimens of the Neoclassical style.

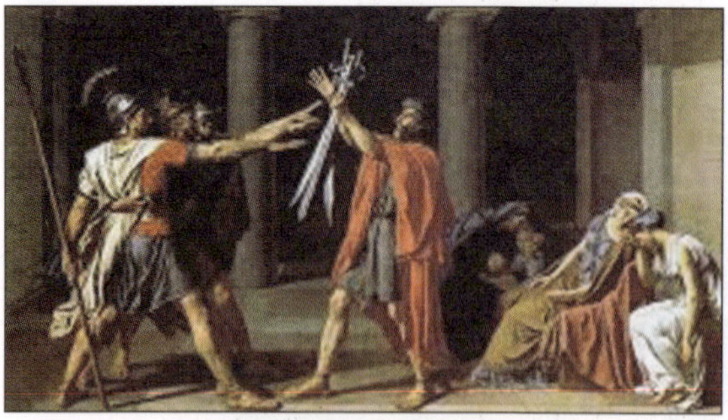

The Oath of Horatii

Nazarenes and Purists

In addition to neoclassicism, other past artistic styles provided inspiration for the artists in the nineteenth century. The German painter Frederic Overbeck (1789–1869) gave birth to the Nazarenes group, active German artists in Rome whose aim was to regenerate German painting by returning to the purity of the early Renaissance.

In June of 1810, Overbeck and his associates arrived in the capital city and obtained permission to stay in the monastery of St. Isidore. Here they led shared lives, painting during the day in the refectory and then discussing their works in the evening. They never painted from live female models; they did not feature mythological subjects or contemporary historical events, but the events of the ancient New Testament or from the lives of saints. They were baptized Christians.

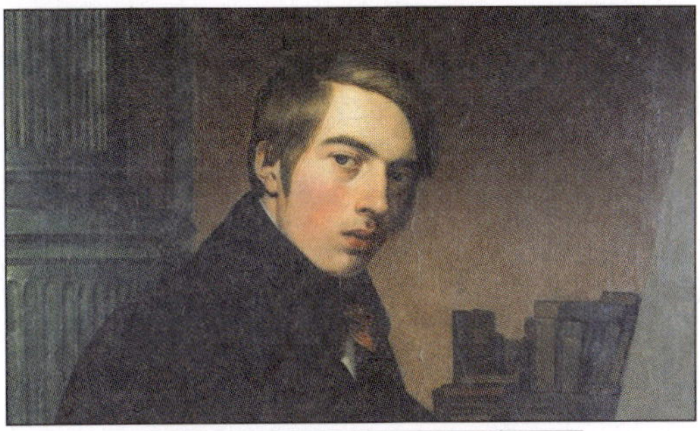

Frederic Overbeck (1789–1869)

In the wake of the Nazarenes developed Rome purism: a movement which proposed a return to the art of religious inspiration, from Cimabue to Raphael. This was analogous to what was happening in the literary field, where authors were being inspired by the Tuscan writers of the fourteenth century. Classicist and painter Antonio Bianchi (1803–1884) was the editor of the official manifesto of the movement, entitled 'Purism of the Arts', published in 1843 and also signed by the painter Tommaso Minardi.

Appreciated by his contemporaries as a miniature painter and watercolourist, Bianchi was also the creator of paintings in oil on more religious themes: we remember the great altarpiece of 'St. John Baptist de' Rossi' in the Most Holy Trinity pilgrimage church in Rome. The main interpreter of the purist movement in Rome was Tommaso Minardi (1787–1871), who did not paint much but instead created numerous designs focused on literary and historical themes. He was director of the Academy of Fine Arts in Perugia. Among his works, one to remember is 'The Supper at Emmaus'. The painting is said to revolve around the time when Jesus revealed himself to his two disciples in the town of Emmaus.

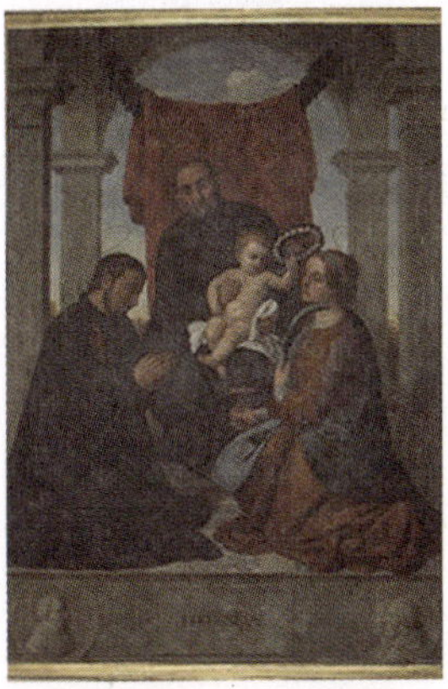

St. John Baptist de Rossi

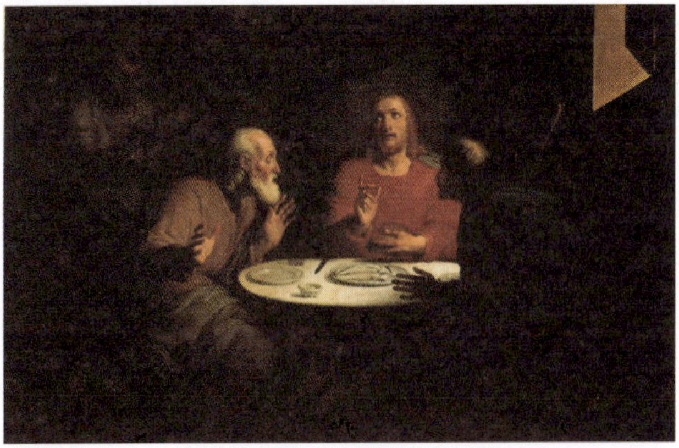

'The Supper at Emmaus' by Tommaso Minardi

The Romance Art

Against the uniformity of the culture imposed by the Napoleonic period, various European states each sought value in their own history. So when the Romance style spread throughout Europe, it was characterized by an emphasis on human values, sentiment, and love for one's country. Painting is the most important innovative form of art during this period, and is based on the great historical themes, with preference for the moments of popular patriotic struggle. It embraces the representation of landscapes. Romantic painting was more communicative than the neoclassical style: the artist wants to express feelings and emotions;

his brush strokes are fluid, the colours are alive, the contours are less defined contours, the contrast of the light is often dramatic.

German Romantic painting develops towards the start of the nineteenth century, in relation to the literary movement of the Sturm und Drang and the music of Goethe and Beethoven. The painter David Frederich (1774–1840) portrayed nature and nocturnal atmospheres which were corpuscular, melancholic, and often in connection with the idea of death. An example is 'The white cliffs of Rügen' (1818). This oil painting depicts Stubbenkammer which was one of the well-known lookout points in the nineteenth century.

In England, the poet, painter, and draftsman William Blake (1757–1827) also used new engraving techniques. These can be seen in his illustrations from the *Divine Comedy* and Milton's *Paradise Lost*. In 1824, Blake was commissioned by John Linnell to paint an illustration of Dante's work.

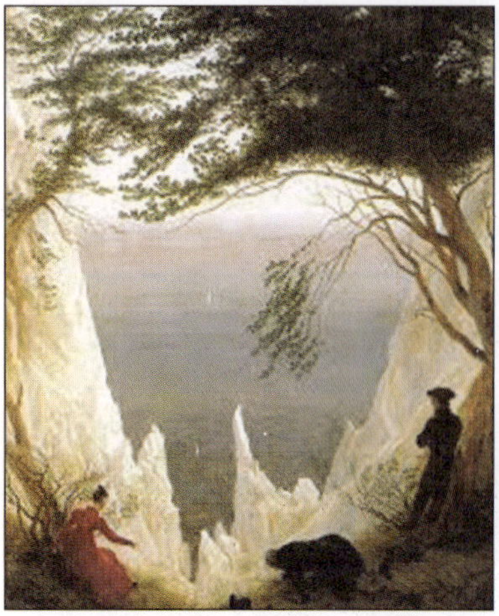

Chalk Cliffs of Rugen

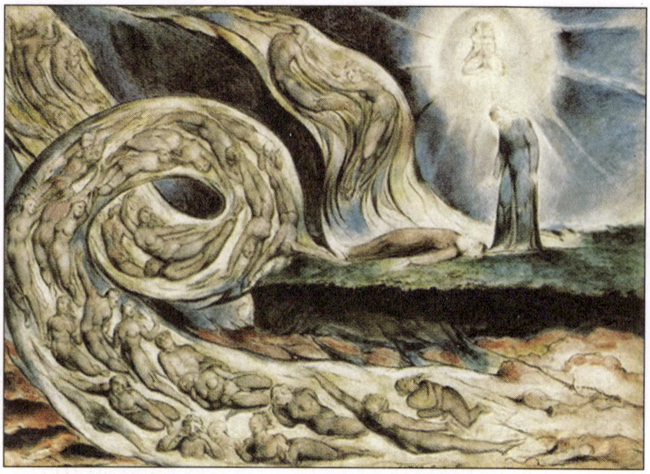

Divine Comedy by William Blake

Realism and Naturalism

The term 'realist' was often used to describe works in which the representation of objects and figures was so faithful to the truth as to sometimes be unpleasant, especially when considered in relation to the beauty of classicism. Realist art often featured subjects from the lower social classes, and often denoted a strong social criticism, with the movement openly placing itself at odds with the idealistic painting style. The promoters of the style were the French painters Gustave Courbet, Honore Daumier and Jean-François Millet, who debuted at the Paris Exposition in 1855. Amongst the works that are considered representative of this so-called social realism are the painting 'Gleaner' during the growing movement of Socialism.

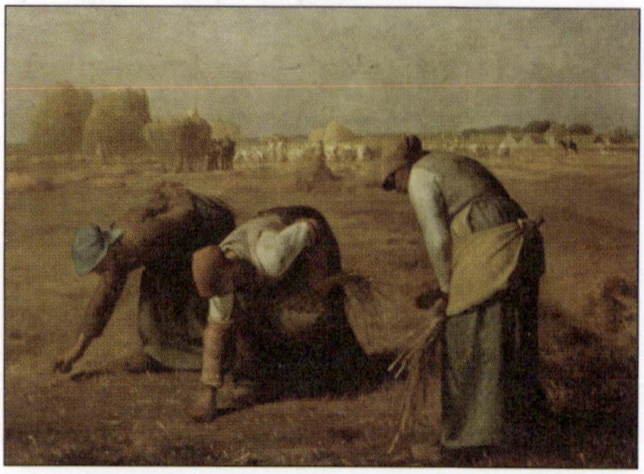

The Gleaner by Jean-Francois Millet (1857)

The Neo-Gothic

As part of the general interest in the romantic culture of the medieval world, the Gothic period (understood as the height of Nordic civilization) became the object of study and historical reenactment. Thus was born the neo-Gothic- or 'Gothic Revival' as it was called in England. Its main exponents were:

Augustus Welby Pugin, who undertook the construction of the London Houses of Parliament in Gothic style. Augustus Welby Pugin assisted Charles Barry in the construction of Palace of London which mainly included details, fittings and furnishings.

Eugene Viollet-le-Duc (1814–1879), a French architect, engineer and theorist who restored the Notre Dam de Paris. It is one of the finest examples of French Gothic Architecture.

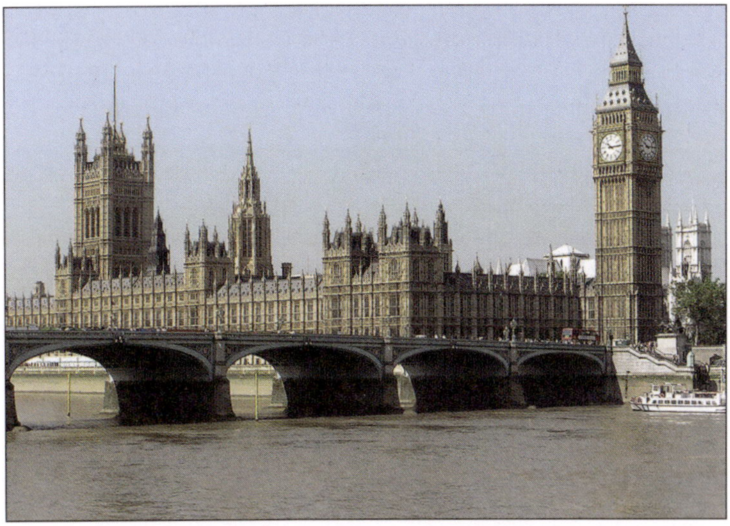

London Houses of Parliament

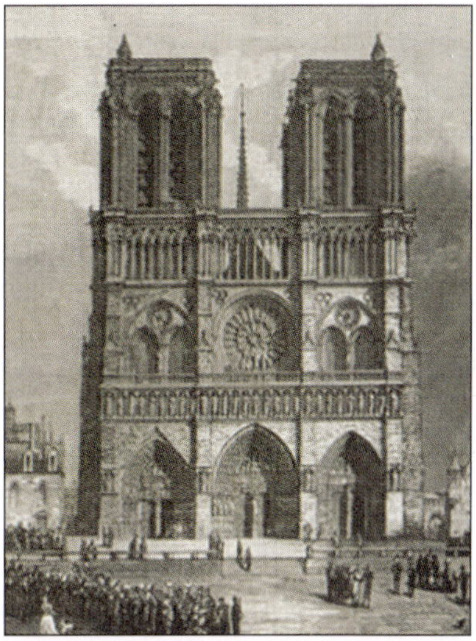

Notre Dam de Paris

Pre-Raffaelite Movement

The Pre-Raphaelite Brotherhood was founded in 1848 in London for young painters interested in the Italian primitive paintings and for the Gothic Middle Ages. The founders were William Holman Hunt and Dante Gabriel, who had the intention of recovering the ethical sense of the primitive art produced before Raphael—art inspired by nature, and with themes of the medieval, symbolic and archaic (opposing the official academicism of industrial society). Pre-Raphaelite J. Everett Millais produced the famous painting 'Ophelia', an oil painting by Sir John Everett Millais completed in the year 1851 and 1852. It is currently located in Tate Gallery, Britain.

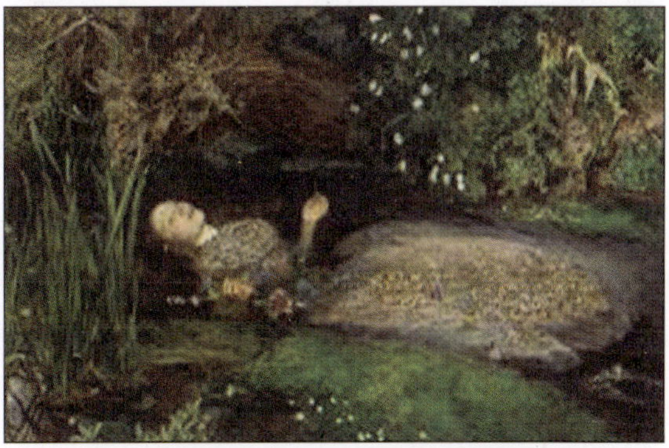

Ophelia by Sir John Everett Millais

Impressionism

Impressionism was a painting movement that developed in France in the second half of the nineteenth century, born from the rejection of both the contemporary pictorial traditions and the classic sentimental subject (which were both styles promoted by the Academy of Fine Arts in Paris, technically meticulous and focused on the work of study). Traditionally, the Academy imposed models with which the entire world of French art would have to comply, and promoted the official exhibition of the Paris show, through which these models were made popular among the general public. The Impressionists rejected these dictates, preferring to paint landscapes, street scenes and aspects of everyday life, instead of episodes relating to classical history. They wanted to paint outdoors in 'plein-air' rather than in the studio, as they were interested in natural light effects rather than the exact design and description of the objects.

By observing how the light reflects the colours, almost breaking them down, they put on the canvas short strokes of pure colour, juxtaposing the primitive primary colours (red, yellow and blue: from their mixing arise complementary secondary colours—green, orange, purple and indigo) so that they mingled in the visual perception only from a certain distance. The primary colours were placed in contrast with the complementary to enhance the intensity. In this way, they obtained a higher brightness than what is usually produced by mixing the colours before applying them to the canvas. Among the most significant artists was Edouard Manet (1832–1883), who was influenced by the colours of Venetian art and Japanese prints. In 1863, he exhibited in the 'salon des refuses' the painting 'The Dejeuner sur l'Herbe', which had been rejected by the official salon.

'The Dejeuner sur l'Herbe' or The Luncheon on the Grass is an oil painting by Edouard Manet created in 1862 and 1863. It has been said to be inspired from 'The Pastoral Concert' by Giorgione or Titian, Louvre, Paris.

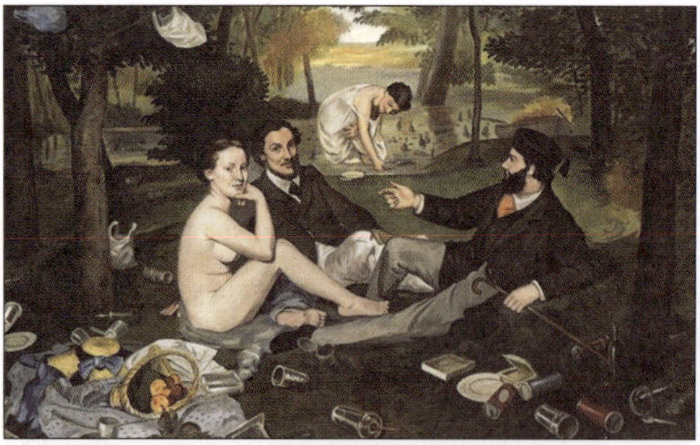

The Luncheon on the Grass by Edouard Manet

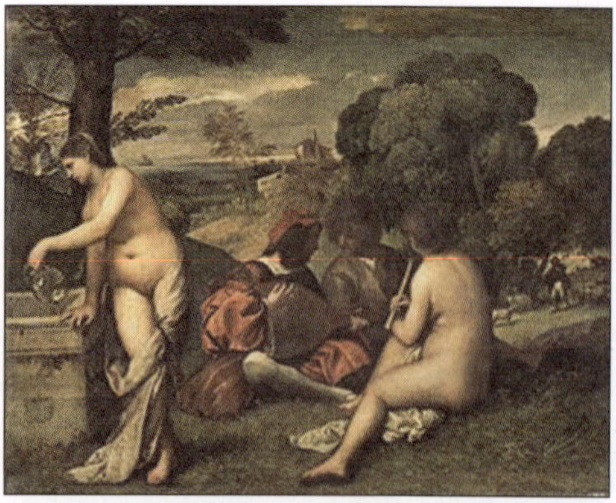

The Pastoral Concert by Giorgione or Titian

Some critics mark this episode as the beginning of modern art. The painting 'Olympia', exhibited at the Paris Salon in 1865, similarly arouses a short scandal. Edouard Manet painted 'Olympia' in 1863, which is a fine example of Modern Art. It is said to be inspired by Titian's 'Venus of Urbino'.

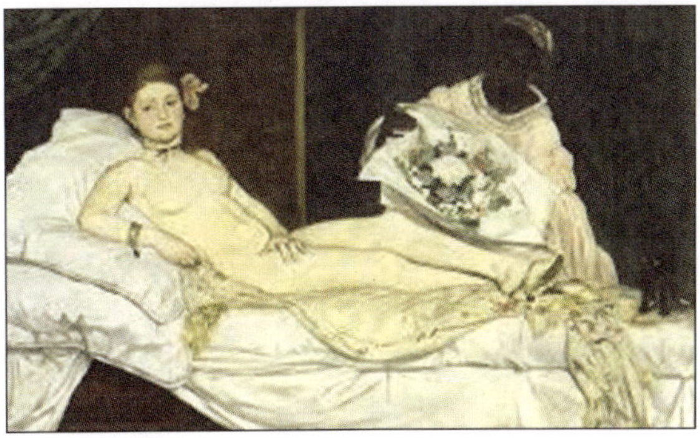

Olympia by Edouard Manet

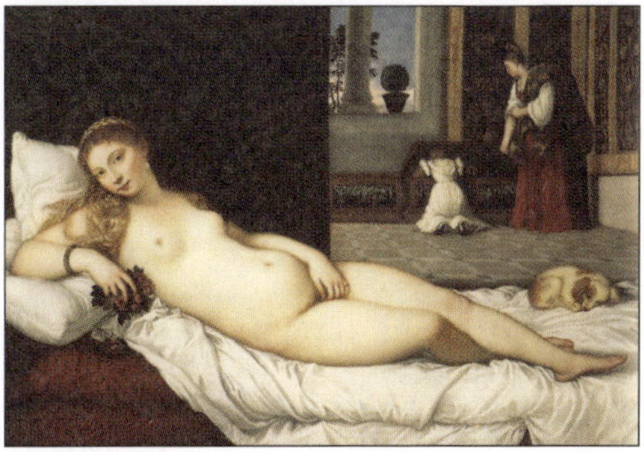

Titian's Venus of Urbino

Both works were inspired by Renaissance models: the 'Concert Country' by Giogione and the 'Venus of Urbino' by Titian. However, Manet distorts the conception, abolishing the sense of the volumes, the light and dark, and the perspective by using flat colours in strident combinations. The nudity of both women is provocative and disturbing owing to the unreal settings and contexts.

Post-Impressionism

This term is used to indicate the variety of painting styles that spread after Impressionism (particularly in France) between 1880 and 1905. The definition was coined by the critic Roger Fry in 1910, on the occasion of an exhibition held in London in which there were works by Van Gogh. Paul Signac is often placed as an artist of post-Impressionism. Although, in fact, their work was based on technical research and the colours of the Impressionists, post-Impressionists did not reflect the texture of the objects of nature through colour and light effects; instead, they tried to embody a more subjective worldview.

Pointillism

This is a painting technique based on the combination of many tiny dots of colour that, when viewed from distance, create a sense of fusion which produces a chiaroscuro effect. Georges Seurat (1851–1891) was a theorist and promoter of the movement, and produced the work 'A Sunday on La Grande Jatte', in which the figures composed were from aggregate colour dots (reminiscent of a painting by Piero della Francesca). 'A Sunday Afternoon on the Island of La Grande Jatte' was painted in 1884 by Georges Seurat. It depicts a popular retreat for the middle and upper class of Paris in the nineteenth century.

Paul Signac (1863–1935)

After the death of Seurat, finds himself at the head of the neo-Impressionist movement, continuing to paint with the pointillist method. An example is 'The Entrance to the Port of Marseilles' (1911). In the year 1911, Marseille is the third biggest city in France, known for being the biggest port in France, with its strategic location on the Mediterranean sea.

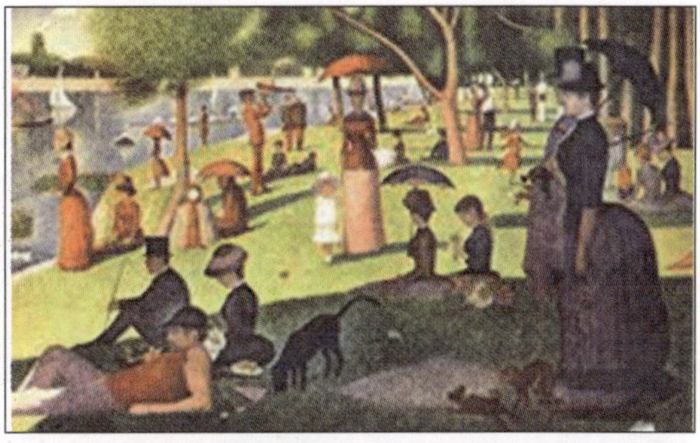

A Sunday Afternoon on the Island of La Grande Jatte

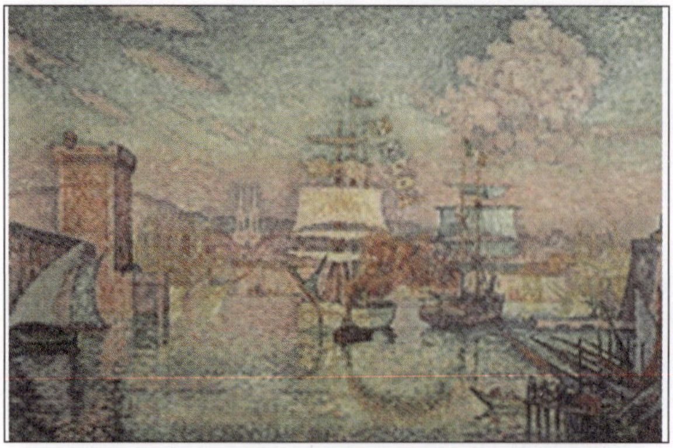

The Entrance to the Port of Marseilles by Paul Signac

Vincent Van Gogh (1853–1896)

Vincent Van Gogh approached nature using vivid colours, often strident, intended to produce very intense emotions. At first he turned to social themes, such as 'The Potato Eaters', and then moved into an introspective pictorial discourse in which both the brushstrokes and the colours of the composition conveyed his inner moods. He later entered into a living relationship with nature: seen in 'In the Cornfield with Crows' and 'Starry Night', in which nature seems to come alive in a whirling and dramatic movement. Later in life, he falls into a deep depression; he mutilates a ear and is interned in a hospital before he commits suicide in 1890.

'The Potato Eaters' by Van Gogh in the year 1885 is said to be one of his finest paintings; the painter is said to have deep affinity for the poor. Van Gogh's magnum opus 'Starry Night' was painted in June 1889. Although the painting was painted from memory during the day, it depicted the view outside his sanatorium room window at night. Vincent Van Gogh's 'Wheatfield with Crows' in July 1890 has been cited as one of his greatest works. It is said that this was Van Gogh's final painting.

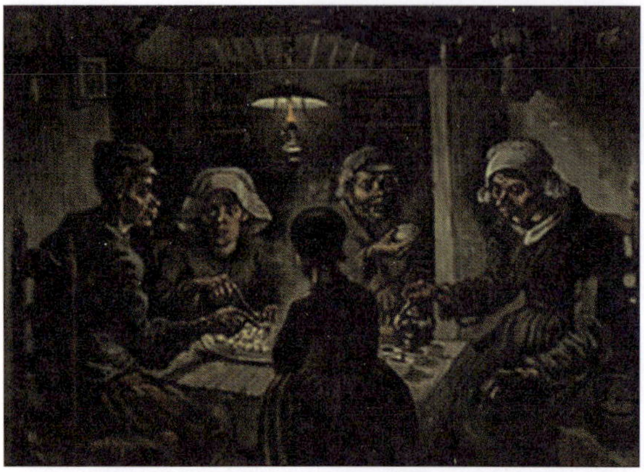

The Potato Eaters

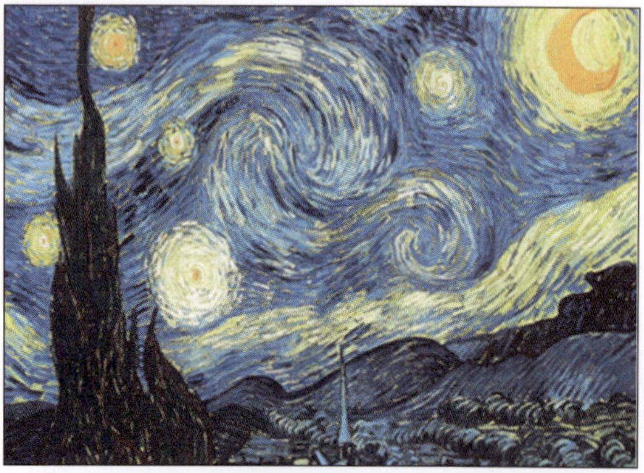

Starry Night

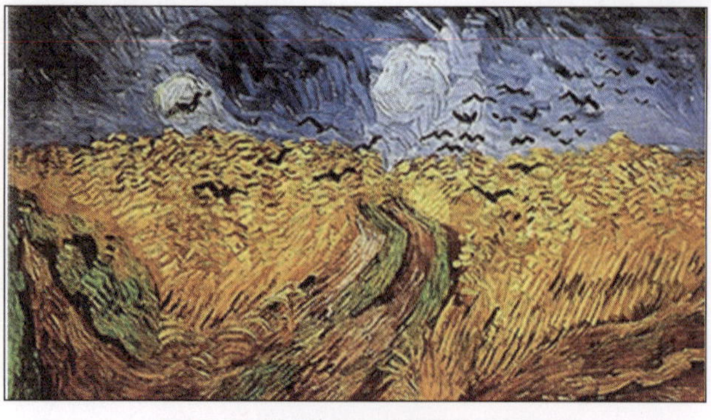

Wheatfield with Crows

Symbolism

The term 'symbolism' refers to the artistic movement started in France in 1880, which interpreted the same attitudes of taste and sensitivity that characterized the symbolism of the literary field. In contrast to impressionism and naturalism, symbolists conceived art not as a result of natural phenomena, but as a synthesis between sensory perceptions, thus a manifestation of the spirit. They shifted the interest from the object to the subject, from a passively perceived to a re-elaborated reality of the artist's spirit. They used brilliant colours and strongly expressive lines to represent oneiric visions of remarkable emotion, sometimes tending to the macabre, and inspired by literary subjects and mythological religions.

The Nabis (Prophets)

Part of the second symbolist generation, these were a group of painters who ironically defined themselves 'the prophets'. In the same period, the Norwegian Monch developed a symbolic style of painting characterized by strong expressive charge and dedication, and in 1884, he formed Societe des XX in Brussels, which later gave impulse to the birth of art nouveau in Belgium (Modern Art).

Art Nouveau

The term 'art nouveau' refers to a set of artistic movements which developed between the late nineteenth and early twentieth centuries. Here, decorative styles find expression across a wide range of artistic forms: architecture, interior design, production of furniture, posters, metalworking, glass, ceramics, fabric, and book illustration (where the influence of Japanese prints is evident). The dominant elements are the wavy curved lines, often called 'whiplash', inspired by the sinuous forms of the natural world and combining elements of fantasy. The term 'Modernism' is generally used to indicate such artistic currents that, amid a rejection of the ancient models, tend to build an international style based on the functionality of the decoration and on a general re-evaluation of the so-called 'minor arts'.

This conception of art applied to the objects of everyday life, already developed in England by William Morris, is taken up again by the Art and Crafts movement, which promoted decorative design for furniture and household artisan artifacts. In Spain, Morris' most imaginative interpreter is Gaudi. In Austria and Germany, artists participating in the modern movement are organized into successions: secession of monk (Von Stuck) dating back to 1892. Secession of Berlin (Otto Wagner) dating back to 1893, and the Vienna Secession (Gustav Klimt) dating back to 1897.

Gustav Klimt (1862–1947)

He adopts an elegant decorative style, rich in symbolic references, using precious materials such as mosaics. His work includes the frescoes of the University of Vienna and the frieze of the Stoclet Palace in Brussels.

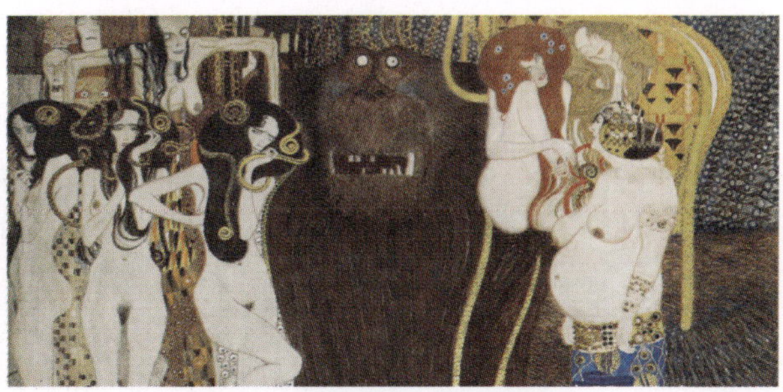

The Beethoven Frieze

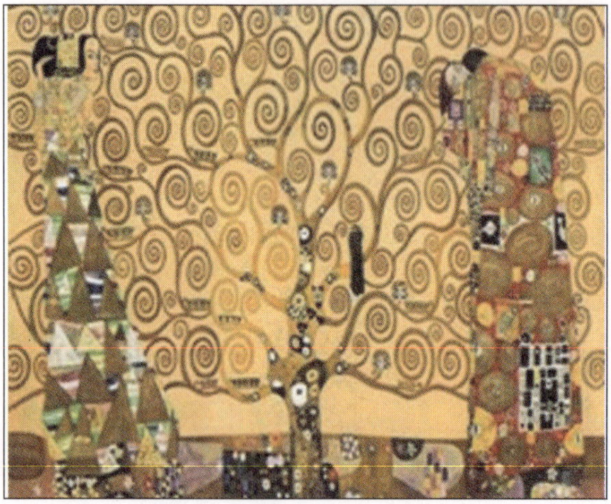

The Tree of Life, 1905 by Gustav Klimt

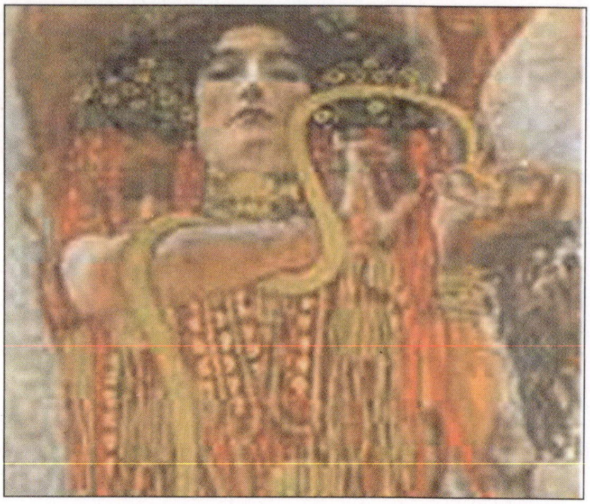

Gustav's University of Vienna Ceiling Paintings

'The Tree of Life', 1905, by Gustav Klimt signifies the connection between heaven and earth, the branches symbolizes the perpetuity and complexity of life.

Gustav's University of Vienna Ceiling Paintings (Medicine) showing Hygieia was painted from the year 1900 to 1907; the painting represented the river of life but was subject to a lot of criticism and was even burnt to the extent that only one photograph remains of the complete painting of Medicine.

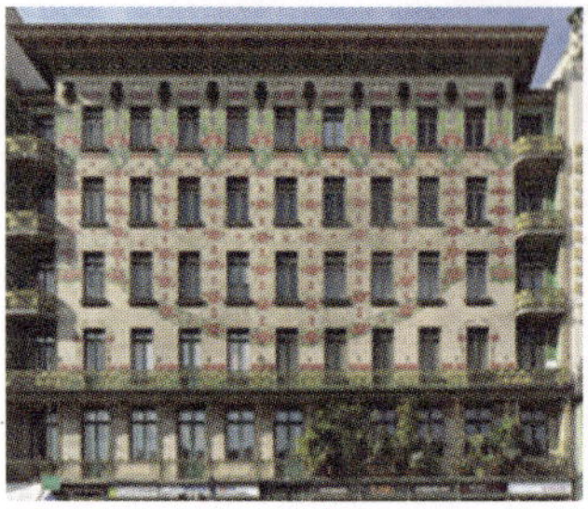

La Casa della Maiolica

Otto Wagner (1841–1919)

Otto Wagner created the famous 'La Casa della Maiolica' in 1899, a textile-like decoration in Vienna, Austria.

Gaudi (1852–1926)

A Spanish architect who created the Güell park and numerous buildings in Barcelona using a characteristic and imaginative decorative style. Featuring bold lines and plastic, rolling surfaces, his masterpiece is the Segrada Familia Cathedral. The cathedral of the poor created by Spanish architect Antonio Gaudi is a prime example of modernist architecture; it was intended not only a as place to reach God but also as a place to dignify the industrial workers.

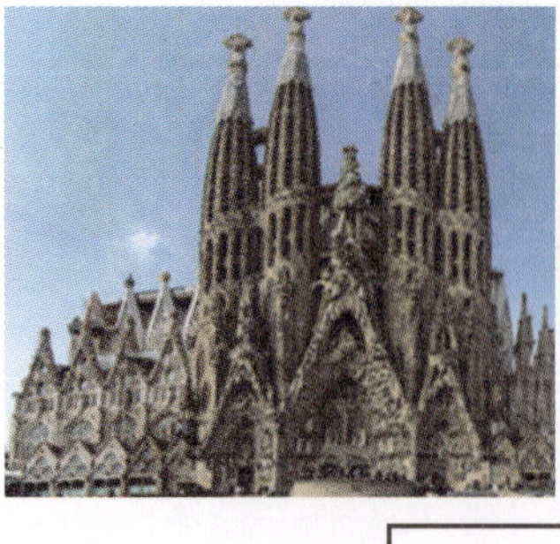

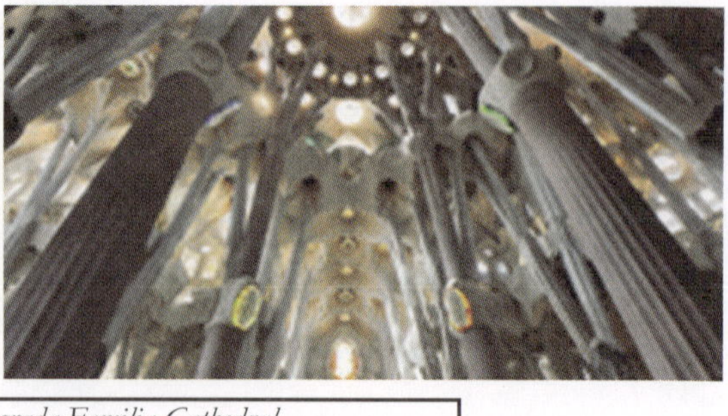

Segrada Familia Cathedral

Art Nouveau (New Art)

Inspired by Morris' Art and Crafts movement in England (which was fighting against industrialization and loss of quality in material goods), Art Nouveau favoured the use of steel very much. Steel was a new material, which began to be used extensively during the nineteenth century. Examples of early steel construction are the Luís I Bridge in Porto, Portugal, the Tour Eiffel in Paris, the Galleria Vittorio Emanuele in Milan, and railway stations all over Europe. The idea of 'total artwork' is proposed, in which fine arts and decorative arts are not seen as different or one more valuable than the other.

The effort of building a style which combines architecture, interior design, furniture and industrial design gives value and importance to details and crafts. The movement is also inspired by nature and is trying to build a link with it. Architects of this period include: Victor Horta (see his houses in Brussels) and Frank Lloyd Wright (see Robie house in Chicago) although Wright, part of the Prairie School, produced work much later and in a style markedly different from Horta's.

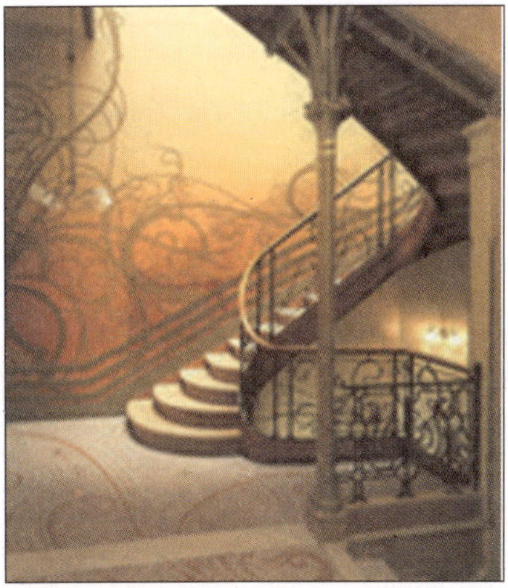

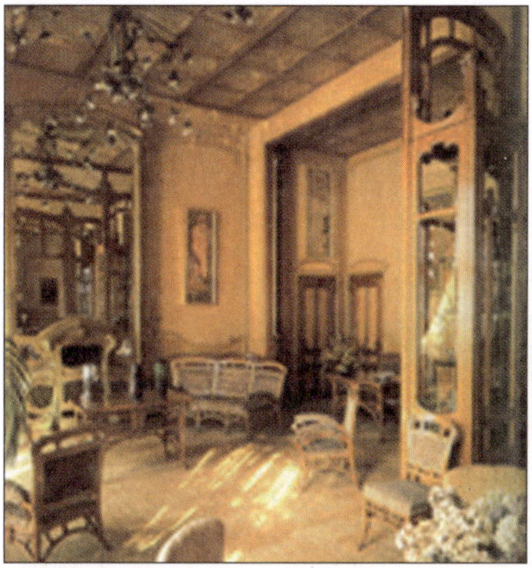

The extensive use of steel as a part of New Art

The Nineteenth Century in Italy

Neoclassical Architecture

Based on the classical style, the neo-classical architecture of eighteenth-century Italy is expressed through the works of the following artists:

Giuseppe Piermarini (1734–1808) worked in Milan, renovating and constructing the Teatro alla Scala. Funding for the construction of the theatre came from a group of Milanese families who continued to support Piermarini. He began in 1776, when a fire destroyed Teatro Regio Ducal in the courtyard of the royal palace. By the decree of Empress Maria Theresa of Austria, Giuseppe Piermarini was commissioned to build a new one. The site chosen was that of the church of Santa Maria alla Scala, which was was demolished in order to make way for the theatre. It was used not only as a place of entertainment but also for the public life of the owners who used it to host their guests, to enjoy their meals, and to enjoy gambling. The theatre was inaugurated in 1778, and hosted a debut performance of the work of composer Antonio Salieri. The theatre represented the works of the best composers of the time, and became a location of choice for the performances of Italian opera: Here premiered Rossini, Donizetti, Bellini and Giuseppe Verdi.

In 1898, the Scala became a public company led by Guido Visconti di Modrone. The artistic direction was entrusted to Arturo Toscanini, who was able to stage Wagner's operas as well as contemporary authors. In 1920, following the surrender of the property rights of the boxes, Teatro alla Scala was founded as an autonomous body. The orchestra of La Scala Theatre was composed of musicians selected with strict criteria and employed on permanent contracts. All the musical direction remained under Toscanini. In August 1943, the theatre was largely demolished by bombing, but rebuilding was immediately started, and was completed in 1946.

The inauguration of the new Scala was overseen by Toscanini, who organized the 'concert of reconstruction', intended to be a mark in the history of Milan. In 1996, the Italian state law transformed the foundation Teatro alla Scala into a non-profit foundation. From 2002 to 2014, the theatre was extensively renovated with an innovative design from architect Mario Botta. It was again inaugurated with a performance of Salieri's *L'Europa Riconosciuta* (Europe Revealed). The theatre represented the works of the best composers of the time, and became a location of choice for performances of Italian opera.

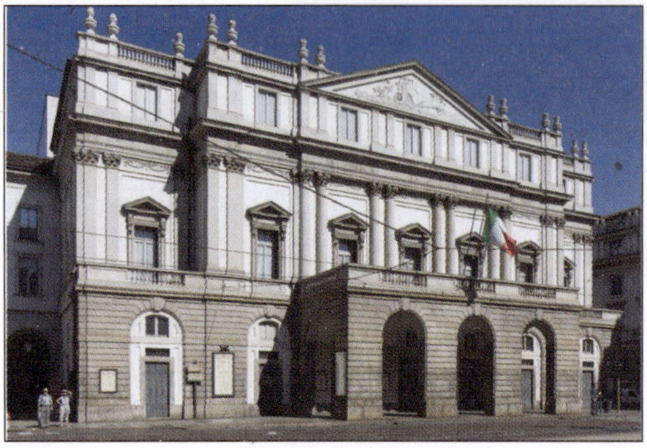

Teatro alla Scala

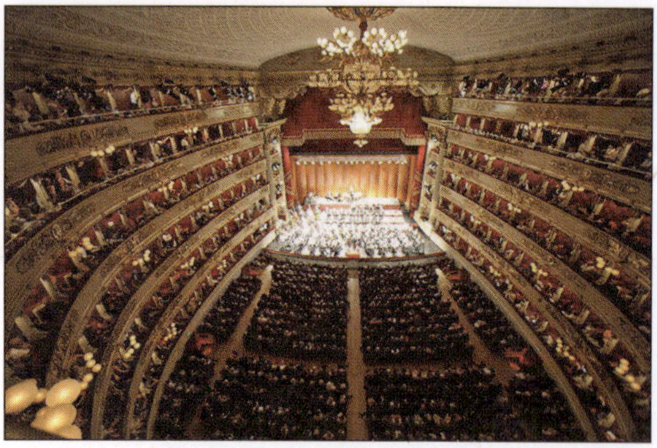

Opera at La Scala

Neoclassical Painting

The return to the classical style in painting developed in Italy with Andrea Pagliani (1754–1817), the Milanese favourite of Napoleon, who created 'Stories of Love and Psyche' and 'Portrait of Ugo Foscolo'.

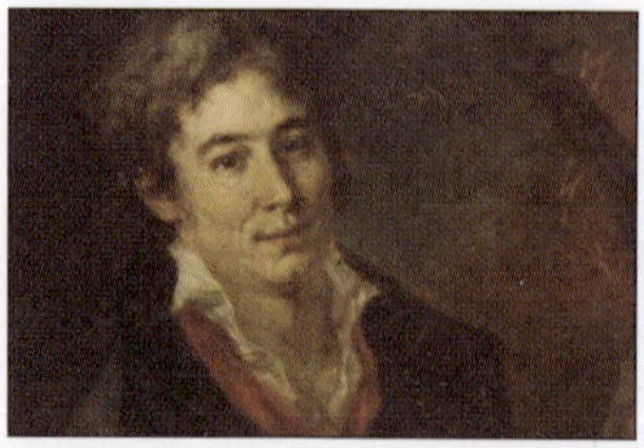

'Portrait of Ugo Foscolo' by Andrea Pagliani (1801–1802)

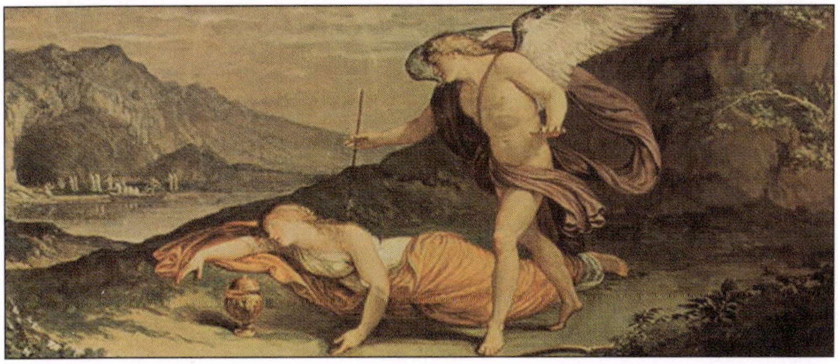

'Stories of Love and Psyche' by Andrea Pagliani

The Historical Romance

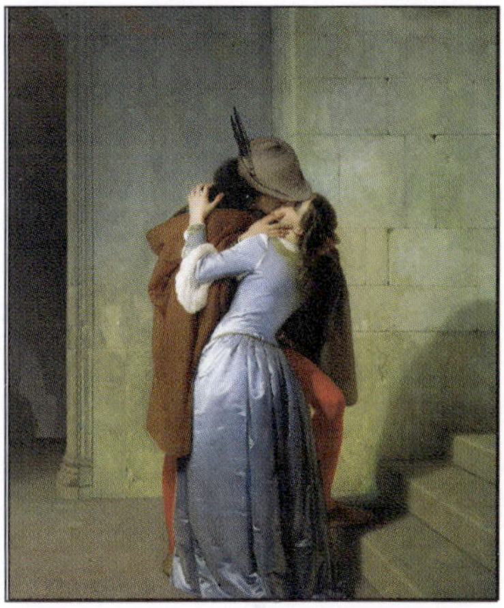

Last Kiss of Romeo and Juliet by Francesco Hayez

Also in Italy, around 1820, a reaction against academic neoclassicalism resulted in adherence to the Historical Romance, a connection of the literary trends to emerging political events. Among the artists inspired by Romanticism was Francesco Hayez (1791–1882), a Venetian painter who was active in Milan and the greatest exponent of Italian Romantic painting. One of his works was 'Last Kiss of Romeo and Juliet' in the year 1791–1882 is considered a complex work of art.

The School of Posillipo

This was a group of artists working in Naples in the second decade of the nineteenth century, all of who were devoted to landscape painting. The school was born in 1820, when Anton van Sminck Pitloo (1791–1837), a Dutch landscape painter residing in Naples, became the first to paint outdoors. The school became a meeting point for many young artists. At the start, the school turned to the style of the vedutismo and picturesque, focusing on lyrical elements and the landscapes of romantic atmosphere. They also took advantage of a greater freedom by virtue of the fact that landscape painting was considered a minor genre. On the other hand, it was precisely the emancipation of academic constraints which allowed them to more easily adopt European trends, so the school was later strongly influenced by the foreign artists present at that time in Naples, such as the Englishman William Turner. The brothers Giuseppe and Filippo Palizzi took their cue from the Posillipo school.

The Macchiaioli

One of the most important Italian artistic movements of the nineteenth century, the Macchiaioli was born in Florence. The term was used for the first time in the Gazette of 1862. In those days, Cafe Michelangelo was crowded with young talent, and Florence was a place where artists loved to share their ideas in a restive atmosphere full of creative ideas. The art of these painters aimed to replicate the impressions they received from observation by means of patches of colour and shadow. On his return from Paris, the critic Diego Martelli spoke in Livorno in 1879, at a major conference on the Impressionists. He described Café Michelangelo as a place full of discussions about the problems of art. These artists claim that the form does not exist, as it is through the light that man sees the world around him, not through forms isolated from nature, but as distinct coloured spots and other spots of colour, because light hitting the objects is sent back to our eye as colour. Therefore, colour is the only way for man to get in touch with reality. This theory underpins the whole Macchiaioli movement, which is later influenced by the French impressionists and is informed of the new trends by the frequent visits of artists to Paris.

The Macchiaioli also gave rise to a marked 'anti-academic' movement in the realist sense, as it was argued that the true image of correspondence to a contract of light, shade and colour obtained by means of the 'black mirror technique' (using a mirror blackened with smoke to enhance the light and shade contrasts within the framework). Among the exponents of this style was Telemaco Signorini (1835–1901), who was born in Florence in 1835. After studying drawing at the Academy of Fine Arts, he began to frequent Café Michelangelo. In 1858, he went looking for an environment that would make it easier to represent the contrast between light and shadow, and which would help him paint the surrounding environment by means of colour. In 1859, he participated in the military events and left for the front. When he returned from the war in 1860, he began again to paint the countryside from life.

Giovanni Fattori John Bellboys (1825–1908) was the most outstanding artist of this period. He was considered the greatest exponent of the Macchiaioli. Born in Livorno, he began his training in Florence. His first paintings had historical subjects, according to the romantic tradition. He entered into contact with the Cafe Michelangelo artists, and in his paintings one can see that effect of colour stain which characterized the group. He took part in the battles for the unification of Italy in 1862, and this was the inspiration for his painting 'The Italian Camp after the Battle of Magenta'. The subject, presented in the merciless harsh reality of a military confrontation, is one of the many men who are injured and picked up by a chariot led by nuns. Fattori mainly produces military subject paintings: depictions of soldiers, battles and Italian landscapes.

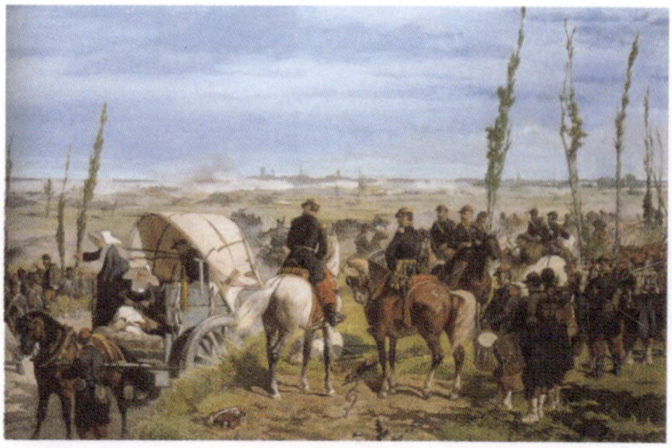

The Italian Camp after the Battle of Magenta' fought after the second Italian war of Independence

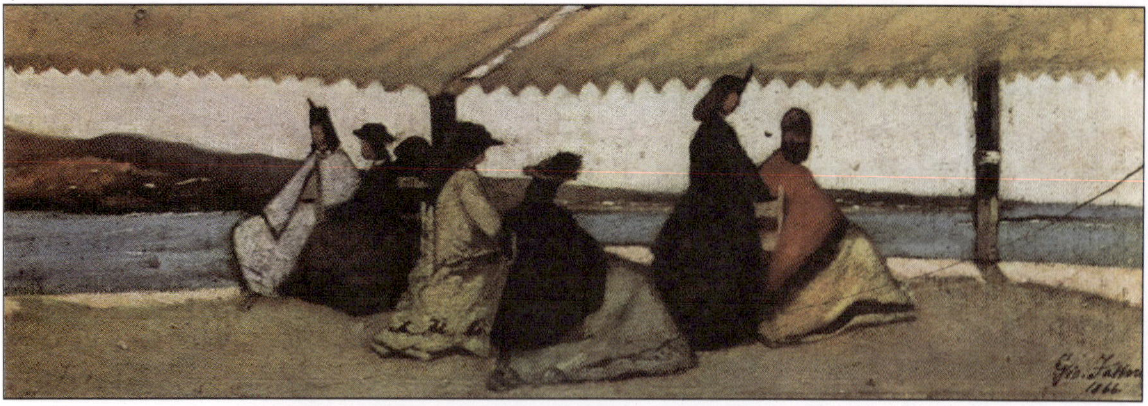

Rotonda di Palmieri (La rotonda dei Bagni Palmieri)
The pictures depict the harsh realities of wartime

The Divisionists

Divisionism indicates the pictorial movement formed in Italy in the last decade of the nineteenth century, characterized by the separation of colour into individual points or lines which interact with each other in an optical sense. Therefore it can be considered, from a technical standpoint, as a specific variant of the French pointillism. The technique of pointillism, derived from the Impressionist current, approached the canvas, through dots, strokes and pure colours (without mixture). This procedure not only allowed one to obtain maximum brightness and colour complementation, but also presupposed a precise scientific interest; with this technique, the artist sought to obtain a colour decomposition similar to that which was then believed to be, on the basis of the latest scientific investigations, the composition of the acquisition of natural colours at the level of the retina. According to this principle, it was precisely the observer's retina which must recompose the shades and nuances derived from paint dots.

The pictorial representation of new scientific discoveries about the colour did not adhere to the laws of optical mixing and principles of form (as it had in France), so the dots of pointillism became ragged filaments, which already seemed to direct towards futuristic dynamism.

The Music

In the nineteenth century, instrumental music acquired unprecedented importance, especially in German-speaking countries. It developed according to two trends, corresponding to different methods of listening. For the execution of large scale concerts, oratorios and symphonies were composed, but for more intimate living-room performances, elegant piano pieces were performed. Although musical forms remained the same, on the level of content, music production expressed the guidelines of the other arts, affirming the taste for the fairytale, the exotic, and the fantastic. This led to a return to primitive medieval themes, emotional and popular.

These trends are evident in all the composers of the early nineteenth century, but a romantic sensibility is already evident in the work of some composers who lived in the previous century, such as Mozart, who in the latter part of his life indulged in a melancholy and fantastic mood. Beethoven was an heir of Haydn and Mozart (of whom he was a student), but he was also an interpreter of this era of profound change. In his works, classical composure gave way to the feeling of pain—not on the individual level but for all mankind—and the heroic power of those who proposed to overcome it. The dramatic contrast between the two is expressed in the new sonata form. With Beethoven ended the classical age, and thus began the new romantic sensibility.

The nineteenth century was a century of great changes in music, not only from the point of view of the composition of the equipment, but also with regard to the social context. Until 1700, musicians exercised their activities almost exclusively for the service of wealthy aristocrats. Every court, every palace, had its choirmaster. However, there was now a musician who composed and performed music when requested, on various occasions, and in exchange for a salary. The musical composition had to meet the precise demands of the customer and adapt to the circumstances for which it was made. Of course, this restricted the freedom of choice and the creative spontaneity of the musician. The French Revolution and the rise of the bourgeoisie marked the decline of the institution of patronage, and instead paved the way for the figure of the independent musician who composed and performed his music not for the nobles of the court, but for the paying public. With the affirmation of bourgeois society came a chance in the relationship between music and audience. Many music halls opened in cities across Europe, welcoming thousands of listeners to appreciate the musical message.

In the romantic atmosphere of the nineteenth century, music became the preferred language in which to express emotions, feelings and inner conflicts. The new dimension allowed it to break free from traditional rules: forms and harmony were used more freely, the contrasts were accentuated, and the expressive resources of tones, colours, and rhythms took on a greater significance. The philosophical and aesthetic validity of music is recognized, and instrumental music is no longer bound to the verbal support. With Beethoven, technicality as the main theme of the instrumental composition is replaced by ideas and thematic material. Romance spreads with a special intensity in the Latin countries, where there is a stronger instrumental tradition and where the melodrama was the most beloved musical form by the public.

The Opera in the Nineteenth Century: Classicism and Romanticism

The most emblematic musical personality between 1700 and 1800 is Italy's Gioacchino Rossini. The relationship between Classicism and Romanticism in the work of Rossini is analogous to that in the poetry of Foscolo and Leopardi. In the course of the classic form of Rossini's music emerges many elements of romantic sensibility. A pathos and romance pervades all the works of the musician, especially 'William Tell', in which the aspirations for freedom of the Swiss people is a theme which anticipates the subjects of the patriotic nineteenth-century melodrama.

It can be said that the Rossini completely transformed classicism and adapted it to the needs of the new culture. As for the structure, the comic opera by Rossini does not deviate substantially from that of the eighteenth century, but it takes up new subjects and situations. The author's humour has a quaint and realistic tone which reflects the reality in all its aspects, and anticipates the descriptive study of Romantic opera. With the Romance, which coincides historically with the rise of the liberal bourgeoisie, there is also a change in musical production.

Melodrama is the style preferred by the public: the masses flock to theatres and applaud the works of composers. Music also enters private life: the piano is replaced by the eighteenth-century harpsichord in the houses of the nobility and bourgeoisie. The music of the nineteenth century is no longer a means of entertainment, but a cultural operation which the audience watches with interest. With the spread of music to a wider audience, a new figure emerges—the music critic—as an intermediary between the work and the audience.

A special theatrical structure which spread in Italy from the eighteenth to nineteenth century was the 'CD', characterized by a horseshoe-shaped rather than rectangular seating area. Such a structure ensured greater visibility to the public, who were seated on separate platforms and divided by orders of height. In addition, the stage is given greater depth to allow the actor to recite whilst standing on it (and no longer in front of the stage as it happened in ricon precedente theatre).

The Romantic Musical Theatre

In the Romance period, melodrama, like instrumental music, experienced the revaluation of sentiment against reason, and a rediscovery of national and popular traditions. The musical Romanticism assumes different aspects in different countries of Europe: the Romantics in France rediscovered Gothic art (which for centuries had been considered barbaric); in Russia and the Nordic countries, the composers are inspired by the ancient traditions; while in Italy (a country oppressed by foreign domination), Romance coincided with the national Risorgimento and with the fight against tyrants. If Rossini marked the transition between eighteenth-century taste and the new romantic sensibility, Bellini and Donizetti can be defined completely romantic composers. Bellini's melodies are passionate, express inner conflicts of the human soul, and are veiled in a melancholic languor. The romantic mood for Donizetti is shown by his choice of characters, drawn from the popular historical tradition, and by the melodies and the description of environments and characters.

However, it is Giuseppe Verdi's Italian opera which implements the romantic poetry in full, expressing a musical language with feelings of freedom, national dignity, and civil consciousness (as had become the ideals of Italian society). At the time of the first Verdi operas, the turmoil which agitated the Italian people found expression in musical theatre. The rulers encouraged performances in the belief that it would distract their subjects from the policies, but in reality, the artists were using the performances as a means of transmitting ideas. The public, for its part, was ready to implement even the vaguest political intentions. The theatres were the haunts where people chatted, conspired, and where ideas matured. The works of Verdi showed continual references to the Italian political situation, and very often, there were problems with the censorship of such pieces.

In the 'Nabucco', patriots identified with the enslaved Jewish people, and in the 'Lombards in the First Crusade', Verdi created a parallel between the liberation of the peninsula from the foreign yoke and the liberation of the Holy Sepulcher. Any hint of melodrama in the political situation was immediately applauded by the audience, and thus Verdi was the author who best interpreted the spirit of the Risorgimento, not only for the subjects of his works but also for the vehemence and the lyricism of the music. 'Cavalry Rusticana' by Pictro Mascagni used to be a musical theatre in Italy in 1890. It was welcomed in triumph by public criticism after Mascagni participated in a competition in 1889 organized by Sonzogno. Mascagni was the sole representative musician delegate in Vienna to celebrate the Victorian centenary in April 1927.

Popular Music

In the Italian popular music tradition, we see underlying trends which correspond to the two main language areas: in the north, polyphonic song prevails, with a dominant melodic system, while in the south, the Opera Monostrofico and modular rhythmic sense are most popular. An exception is Sardinia, which has a completely independent musical tradition as well as its own peculiar linguistic identity. The singing there is strophic, a typically Italian genre influenced by a tradition present in the Mediterranean area. It is a descriptive composition in which each verse appears poetically accomplished and independent of the others.

Despite the overarching trends, Italian folk music has a variegated panorama with regional and sub-regional connotations. These are very interesting because they reflect the historical events and the peculiarities of each territory and culture.

Theatre in the Late Nineteenth Century

In the early nineteenth century, Italian drama remained under the influence of Goldoni (for comedy) and Alfieri (for tragedy). Later on we see new instances of the influence of German Romanticism, such as in the work of Ugo Foscolo (1778–1827), whose works—*Thyestes and Ajax*—seemed to contain allusions to the contemporary political situation (and were censored). His tragedies were more akin to the taste for sentimental poetry and medieval settings. Attentive to the innovations introduced by European drama and taking Shakespeare as a model, Alessandro Manzoni (1785–1873) wrote two tragedies in five years: *The Count of Carmagnola* (1820) and *Adelchi* (1822). In reality, these are works that have more literary value that theatrical, intended to be read rather than performed. However, they are remembered for some famous songs of pure poetry.

In the two tragedies, Manzoni violates the Aristotelian unities of time and place, in accordance with the romantic ideas of the time. He introduces between one act and another a chorus that, unlike those of ancient Greece, was a moment of reflection on the narrated facts. For Manzoni, the viewer must first be emotionally involved in the action. He feels the need for a drama centred on the pain suffered by the person, as in *The Count of Carmagnola.*

We also remember the works of minor authors, such as the *Francesca da Rimini* by Silvio Pellico (1789–1854) and *Arnold of Brescia* by Gian Baptist Niccolini (1782–1871), both openly patriotic and nationalistic pieces. Pellico wrote historical tragedies in the manner of Alfieri, but inspired by the themes of the Renaissance medieval trend. *Francesca da Rimini* was staged in 1815 with great success, and the tragedy becomes a poignant story in which love meets death according to romantic tastes. Other typically romantic themes are a mysterious setting and patriotic love.

The structure of the drama is linked to Alfieri's model: the tragedy is in five acts and takes place quickly without interweaving deviations. There is no distinction between major and minor characters, and there are four protagonists on whom the author focuses the tension. This leads to drama and the inner conflicts are revealed in high and abstract language.

In Search of the Truth

After the unification of Italy in 1861, theatre is oriented more toward the taste of the new bourgeois audience. A critical and scientific attitude towards social reality began to establish itself in the theatre, and analysis was aimed at the demystification of each convention. The theatre which formerly entertained and amused was replaced with one looking for the truth, which was to be judged and contended. From such a perspective, verism derived different orientations. The first orientation was one which critiqued the mechanisms of bourgeois society: the lust for money, respectability, and authenticity of feelings. A representative of such an orientation was Paolo Giacometti (1816–1882) who in *Civil Death* (1871) presented a pathetic story in strong colours, railing against the indissolubility of marriage. He advocated the need for religious divorce if one spouse was excluded from human society on account of committing a crime with a severe penalty.

A second approach was one in which attention was given to the antagonist of bourgeois society—the proletariat—to its past struggles and the new values proposed by the socialist thinkers. A third approach was to represent regional realities in terms of their values and behaviours. An example was the opera *Cavalleria Rusticana* (Mascagni, 1894).

Neapolitan Theatre

In the second half of the century, theatre in the Neapolitan dialect became important, especially the works by Salvatore di Giacomo (1860–1934). At the centre of the production of this poet and writer are always the poor people of the city of Naples, their superstitious faith, their misery, the scenes of violence, and their extreme generosity. *Play or Vote* (1889) focuses on a vow made by a craftsman that if he recovers from a disease that is gripping him he will marry a prostitute. He does not keep the promise because of social conventions.

Opera Theatre

The nineteenth century was undoubtedly the century of the melodrama. This type of show enjoyed extraordinary success, managing to attract diverse audiences within the middle class, the most popular social strata. In the course of the nineteenth century, the relationship between music and libretto develops in a completely new way compared to the 1700s. The reform of Metastasio text gave supremacy to music, which acquired increasing importance, confining the booklet to a secondary, not autonomous, role. There emerged great musicians like Rossini, Bellini, Donizetti and Verdi. Among librettists, Cesare Sterbini (1784–1831) stands out, author of *Barber of Seville.* Also *Sonnambula* by Bellini, and various works by Verdi, including the *Rigoletto* and *La Traviata.*

The Language of the Theatre

The term scenography came to mean the art and technique of organizing the theatre space. In addition to the actual scenery, there was installation of stage machinery, and a new interest in the play of light and the spread of sound—generally the whole dynamic of the stage. In the past, the function of the scenery was different: for the ancient Greeks, it was the drawings with which the scene was upgraded, whilst in the Renaissance, thanks to the perspective, the scenery was enriched with drawings or paintings on canvas—backdrops on which were depicted idealized cities or beautiful landscapes. Great painters such as Raphael produced lavish backdrops for court theatres, and these became more and more adorned and opulent.

Quite different was the Elizabethan stage in England which dealt with drama based on the Jacobean and Elizabethan era, believing in quick transformation scenes, less focus on backdrop and more emphasis on poetry. The rear part of the stage was constituted by two columns supporting a roof, and the ceiling was a tent (and an open sky during the summer performances). In the background, you could see the outdoors, with a tree or a well, or the viewer could imagine it with simple allusions and author descriptions. In the nineteenth century, with the spread of bourgeois realist drama, set design began to imitate reality more and more. And, just as in a middle-class dwelling, the stage was filled with furniture. Since 1900, there was a remarkable evolution: the scene has been transformed into a dynamic and functional element.

The younger generation of designers are intolerant of the traditional natural environments, and eliminate volumes and dimensions, using only one object—the symbol of wider reality and more extensive meanings. This change is representative of the disintegrated conception of personality, crushed and lost in an increasingly diverse society. After 1900, there are three types of staging: the imagined background, the open space, and the de-materialized scene. In the first case, the scenic backdrop takes shape in the imagination of the viewer—through the words and gestures with which the actors allude to scenic elements (which are not really present). In the second case, the place of the theatrical event expands to encompass the audience. This multiplies the points of view, and relativizes the traditional uniform, motionless audience perception. Finally, the de-materialized staging makes use of lightweight materials, and the scenery acquires fluency, plasticity, and mobility. The play of light by means of projectors and filters enables the appearance of rarefied presences and suggests atmospheres which can be quickly dissolved.

Going to the theatre in the nineteenth century was a common social habit, almost a requirement. The split in Italy's political situation gave rise to a cultural polycentrism. To get an idea of the dimension of the phenomenon in Italy, consider the fact that about fifty new scores were produced annually, of which some would enter Italian cultural heritage for posterity. Naples alone offered a total of 700 performances a year. Some theatres, like the Scala of Milan and the San Carlo in Naples, became places of worship of the melodrama. The Phoenix of Venice was also one of the sacred theatres of opera, founded in 1792 and rebuilt after a fire.

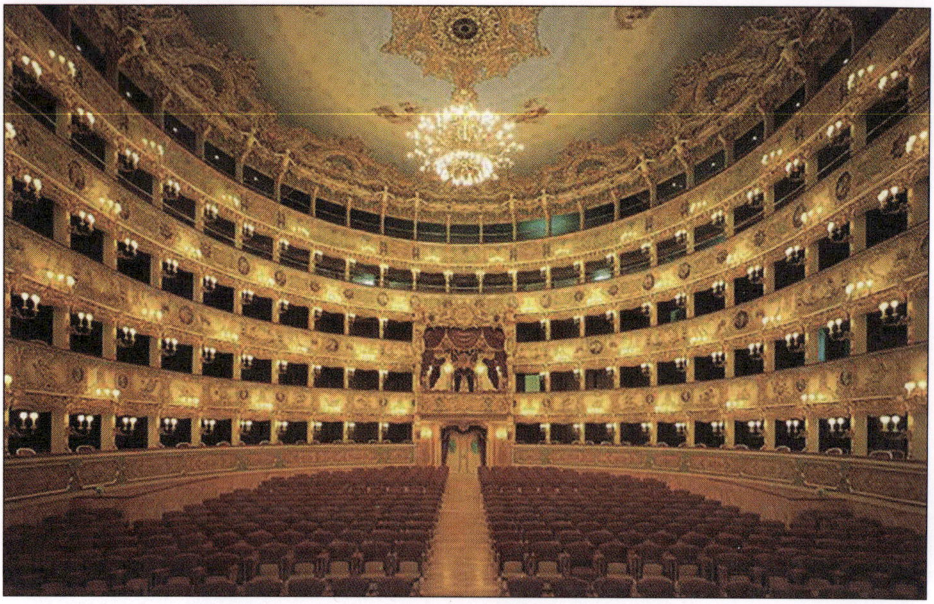

The Phoenix of Venice was also one of the sacred theatres of opera, founded in 1792 and rebuilt after a fire

Vincenzo Bellini

Born in 1801, the son of musicians, Bellini manifested great musical gifts; at six, he wrote his first composition. After studying at the Conservatory of Naples and pursuing further studies on Neapolitan opera and the instrumental works of Mozart and Haydn, Bellini moved to Milan, where he began a long collaboration with the librettist Roman Felice who scripted words for musical works. This way, Bellini began his new venture with Felice. The largest body of production by Bellini was concentrated in eight years, 1827–35. In 1833, he went to London, and also spent a few months in Paris.

Gaetano Donizetti

Born in 1797, to a very humble family, in 1806, he was admitted to charitable music lessons and there he received a musical education. In 1838, he went to Paris, and finally arrived in Vienna, where he became the music director of the Italian season and the choirmaster of Emperor Ferdinand I Augustus. His production included more than seventy works.

Giuseppe Verdi

He was born in 1813 near Parma, to a family of modest origins. He began studying music with the organist of the country. He was admitted to the Milan Conservatory, and in 1836, he won the post of music teacher in the town of Busseto. Verdi went through periods of crisis, sorrow and despondency after his wife and his son's death. In 1842, he reached great success with *Nabucco* and *Lombards in the First Crusade*. Of great importance was his meeting with the librettist Francesco Maria Piave, with whom collaborated on major works such as *Macbeth* (1847), *Rigoletto* (1851), and *La Traviata* (1853). The great Verdi opera productions coincided with the Risorgimento era of awakening, with which he became synonymous due to his realization of musical drama with very deep and complex connotations. After *Aida* in 1871, Verdi collaborated on works by Shakespeare, including *Othello* in 1887. He died in Milan in 1901.

The music opera was born in Italy, and is now one of the best-known artistic and cultural symbols in the world. The opera's origins date back to the Italian musical traditions of the late sixteenth and seventeenth century. Very important here was the musical genius of Claudio Monteverdi (1567–1643).

In this age, the representation of entirely sung dramas began, featuring reciting and singing based on the metric system used in the literary scene of the time. The process was in fact used, in keeping with the paradigms of the various eras, as the base model of the libretto (the literary text of the work in music). The production of the operatic genre reaches its heyday in the nineteenth century, when works of great writers such as Hugh and Shakespeare are put to music.

The 1800s leave behind the eighteenth-century opera buffa (which Gioacchino Rossini will parodize with *The Barber Saviglia* (1816). Later, he devoted himself to composing opera seria. The work is a succession of blank verse that matches music to recitative and measured verses, lyrical, in verses that give life to the aria and the other closed forms, through which generally is expressed the particular pathos of the characters.

Two other characteristics that remain substantially unchanged in the new opera are: the subject of the drama (which are never fantastic fairytale characters but are geared towards realism), and the representation of the discomfort of passion and emotional human stories.

Nineteenth-century melodrama establishes a deep relationship with the public, who identify themselves in the characters, in their feelings, in their stories. The tensions and the exaltation of the romantic sentiment of man break the rational architecture of the 1700s. And, if the comic opera was also a moment of relaxation, the romantic melodrama necessitates emotional involvement. However, while German romanticism (the reaction to classicism) turns to nature and the mystery, in Italian opera, we find passion and love.

In the romantic melodrama of the first half of the century, there are two figures: Gaetano Donizetti and Vincenzo Bellini. In the works of these artists we find a strong romantic style, and lyrical emphasis translates into melodic episodes and a taste for folk tradition. With the birth of the Kingdom of Italy in 1861, the melodrama is embodied in the great genius of Giuseppe Verdi. The musical and intellectual development of Verdi is very complex; however, you can outline the main phases. In the first period, he devoted himself to historical romantic subjects such as *Nabucco*, which becomes a symbol of the Risorgimento battles for freedom and is chased by censorship. In a second phase, the master, after the failure of the actions of 1848 and 1849, is dedicated to the psychological depth of the characters. This phase results in the popular trilogy *Rigoletto. Il Trovatore* (1853) is set in fifteenth-century Spain and is a highly dramatic work of melodic intensity. *La Traviata* is composed in 1853.

The social theme is always present in works of Verdi. *La Traviata* tells the story of a French whore, Violet, and her love for Alfredo. This love is not placed in the distant Middle Ages, but set in the contradictions of contemporary bourgeois society. So much so that the protagonist actually existed! It is one of the most intense works of all the romantic era. Finally, after the majesty *Aida* (1871) was staged for the first time in Cairo for the opening of the Suez Canal, Verdi turned to Shakespearean dramas with two booklets—*Othello* and *Falstaff.*

In 1890, Pietro Mascagni (1863–1945) achieved great success with *Cavalry Rusticana*—a work in a single act, in which the subject is taken from a novel by Giovanni Verga. Born verism, melodrama places much highlight on the element of lyrical expression rather than the recitation and melodic invention. The subjects are taken from contemporary reality, and are narrated as news stories. It shows the influence of literature, especially Zola.

Giacomo Puccini

Puccini was born in Lucca in 1853 to a family of musicians. Despite financial difficulties, he completes his musical studies. In 1876, he goes to Pisa to attend the first opera *Aida* by Verdi. He then moves to Milan, where for a period of time he shares his apartment with Mascagni. He produced *Tosca,* inspired by the realist models. For a time, Puccini opera succeeds in the public but does not receive critical acclaim, although today he is recognized as the greatest star of the Italian twilight period. Puccini's work is divided along a path which goes from a romantic bourgeois first phase to a phase of renewal, which takes him to scapigliatura and twentieth-century modernism.

On 1 February 1893, at the Teatro Regio in Turin, Puccini staged Manon Lescaut, and was confirmed as one of the greatest composers of the opera house. He then dedicated himself to the composition of *Turandot,* a subject taken from a theatrical tale of Gozzi. However, the work remained unfinished and Puccini died in 1924. Turandot was eventually staged in 1926 at Las Scala in Milan, directed by the great maestro Arturo Toscanini.

E lucevan le stelle
This work is set in Rome in 1800 against the the background of the Napoleonic events which upset the political order. The love of the painter Mario Cavaradossi (tenor) for the singer Tosca (soprano) is opposed by the Baron Scarpia. He manages to get a conviction against Mario, while Tosca, desperate, throws herself from the battlements of the castle.

E lucevan le stelle ...
ed olezzava la terra
stridea l'uscio dell'orto ...
e un passo sfiorava la rena ...
Entrava ella fragrante,
mi cadea fra le braccia.

The stars were shining
(Literal translation)

And the stars were shining,
And the earth olezzava
Stridea the orchard door

O! dolci baci, o languide carezze,
mentr'io fremente le belle forme disciogliea dai veli!
Svanì per sempre il sogno mio d'amore.
L'ora è fuggita, e muoio disperato!
E muoio disperato!
E non ho amato mai tanto la vita,
tanto la vita!
.

And a step brushed the sand.
He entered her fragrant,
I entered and fell into the arms of.
Oh sweet kisses and soft caresses,
While I was quivering beautiful forms removed the veils from!
Vanished forever is that dream of love.
The time has fled, and die in despair!
And I die in despair! And I never loved life so much!
So much life!

And the stars were shining,
And it smelled the earth
Stridea the garden door
And one step touched the sand.
It was fragrant,
He fell into my arms.
Or sweet kisses, or languid caresses,
Whence the beautiful quivering forms dissolved by veils!
My dream of love vanished forever.
The hour has escaped, and desperately I die!
And I desperately die! And I have never loved life so much!
So much life!

Giuseppe Verdi

Tacea la Notte Placida
From the first act of *The Troubadour*, an the opera set in fifteenth-century Spain. A gypsy is sentenced on charges of having bewitched one of the two sons of Count Luna. The daughter of the gypsy throws the son of the count on the same fire her mother is burned on, but makes a mistake and burns her own baby instead, meaning that she raises the count's baby as her own. The son of count therefore grows with the gypsy's daughter as Manrico, the troubadour. Fate has it that he and his brother, another son of the count, fall for the love of the same woman: Leonora of Aragon. Leonora tells of a troubadour who has never forgotten...

Ascolta.
Tacea la notte placida
e bella in ciel sereno
La luna il viso argenteo
Mostrava lieto e pieno...
Quando suonar per l'aere,
Infino allor sì muto,
Dolci s'udiro e flebili
Gli accordi d'un liuto,
E versi melanconici
Un Trovator cantò.
Versi di prece ed umile
Qual d'uom che prega Iddio
In quella ripeteasi
Un nome... il nome mio!...
Corsi al veron sollecita...
Egli era! egli era desso!...

Listen!
The serene night was silent
and, lovely in the calm sky,
the moon happily revealed
its silvery and full face!
When, resounding in the air
Which till then had been so quiet,
sweet and sad were heard
the sounds of a lute,
and a troubadour
sang some melancholy verses.
Verses, beseeching and humble,
like a man praying to God:
and in them was repeated a name,
my name!
I ran eagerly to the balcony ...

Gioia provai che agli angeli
Solo è provar concesso!...
Al core, al guardo estatico
La terra un ciel sembrò.

There he was; it was he!
I felt a joy That only the angels
are allowed to feel!
To my heart, my ecstatic eyes,
the earth Seemed like heaven!
To my heart, etc.

The production of each work, new or old, began with formation of the cast of artists. Mid-century, the singers were signed to according to the repertoire, but very often impresarios and composers chose the subjects and the structures of their works based on the type of cast that could be formed. They were forced to comply with theatrical conventions, and had to take into account the distribution of the solos and choral parts in order to be in compliance with the vocal characteristics of the dramatic artists. In the nineteenth century, they become stars and the first women to impose their warhorses. The bel canto audience goes to the theatre to listen to the voices of their heroes and often tie their affections to a certain character at the beginning of the season. The great contemporary interpreters of opera include two artists: the Italian tenor Enrico Caruso (1873–1921), and the Greek soprano Maria Callas (1923–1977). Today we also remember Luciano Pavarotti.

Fashion

Paris in this period remained the centre for European fashion. In 1824, Pierre Parissot, began the first clothing production enterprise; his designs could be reproduced for the mass market. Pierre, a modest textile merchant, had an innovative idea: the production of a series of dresses available in different types and sizes. These became popular amongst his clientele, who liked the fixed price and the good relationship between quality and price. This production method simplified organization and began to increase sales, whilst the introduction of a fixed price marked a change in the new retail trade, excluding the lengthy negotiations on the price of the goods between the seller and the customer.

A further thrust in the direction of industrialization of the sector came in 1829, with the invention of the Della sewing machine by Barthelemy Thimmonier. Mass production of clothing started for the French army uniform and other work clothes, followed by other men's clothing. In the domain of women's fashion, industrial technology was first only applied to accessories such as shawls, coats, and linens that did not require precise measurements. Meanwhile, the demand for new clothes at a good price from the lower end of the bourgeoisie is answered through the new marketing mechanisms. Focusing on large quantities, traders are able to decrease the cost of buying their goods, allowing them to market the product to the customer at a lower price. Their initiative is rewarded with a consequent increase in profits owing to increased sales. The truly significant innovation is the opening of A la Ville de Paris in 1841: with the new fixed price trading system, the vision of the goods on display is disconnected from the act of purchase; you can freely browse through the wide variety of products with no obligation to buy. This starts the process of depersonalization of the store.

This new model, a result of the modern capitalist system, explodes during the Universal Exhibition in London (1851–1862) and Paris (1855–1867), and the logic is replicated in the new department stores in the streets of Paris. Paris is also renovated by Haussmann's urban planning, and the new commercial spaces represent the evolved form of 'magasinis de nouveautes', which involved a mega store with sub stores that had different departments for all kinds of goods, common in the first two decades of the nineteenth century (long passages and streets). The goods on offer vastly diversified, guaranteeing novelty. The clothes were spectacularly displayed on headless mannequins, and the stores' interiors were fitted out with colourful upholstery, marble, crystal, and everything was designed to make them absolutely spectacular places worthy of being described by Emile Zola in 1883 as a 'paradise for ladies'. It is in this period that there is differentiation between youth fashion, popular fashion, high fashion and luxury.

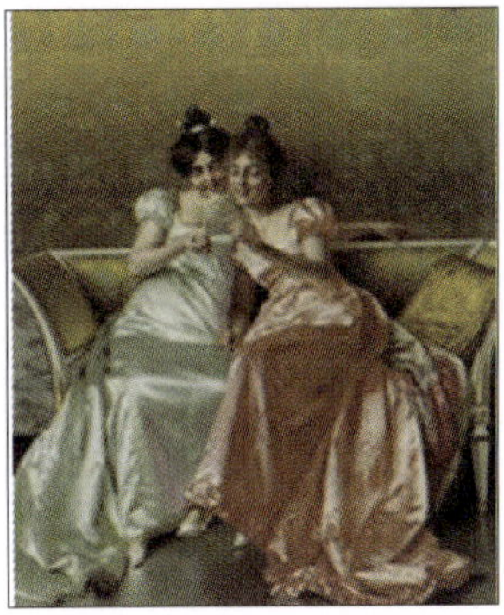
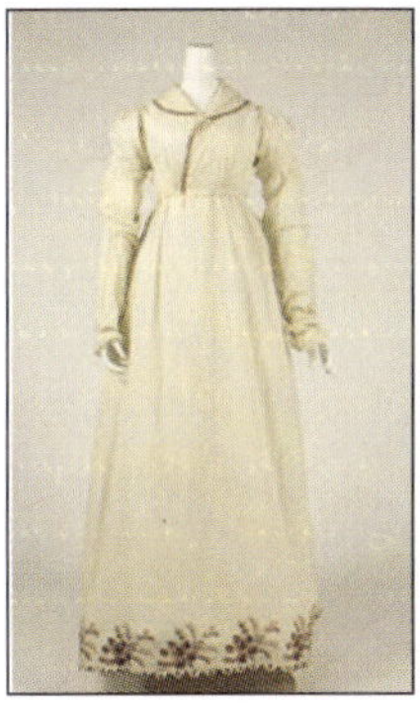
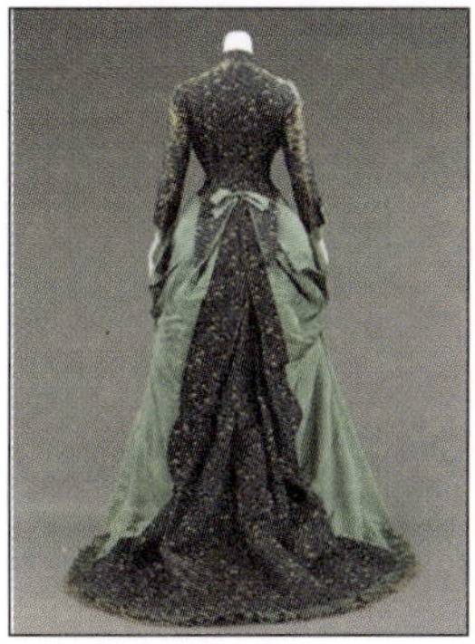
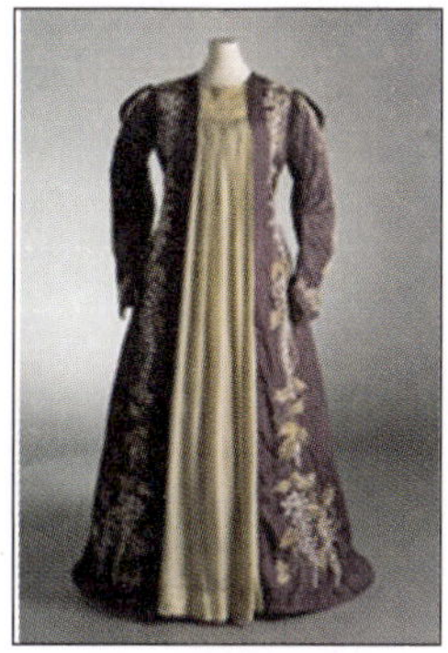

Fashion, a paradise for ladies

Photography

The birth of photography is conventionally marked as 7 January 1839: the date of the official presentation of the daguerreotype at the Academy of Sciences of Paris. This invention comes from the union of two distinct streams of studies: the first leading to the evolution of the darkroom and the second resulting in the development of chemicals which changed when exposed to light. However, Louis Jacques Mande Daguerre, the man from whom the daguerreotype takes its name, is not the only father of photography. His invention required the contribution of the eliografia (by Joseph Nicephore Niepe). Furthermore, the invention of the positive/negative procedure is credited to William Henry Fox Talbot (who perfected the talbotipia in calotype), who was also indebted to the suggestions received from John Herschel, the inventor in turn of the fixing procedure and the terms 'photography', 'positive', and 'negative'.

Daguerre's invention was greeted with great interest in Italy, where the press acted as a sounding board. *Lucifer*, a Neapolitan newspaper, announced the invention on 6 February, while the *Piedmontese Gazette* dedicated the entire issue of 6 March to the new technology. Talbot arranged to personally disseminate his findings in Italy where, thanks to frequent trips, he had many contacts in scientific fields. In June 1839, he sent six photogenic drawings of a windmill to the botanist Antonio Bertolini in Bologna. He also sent drawings of plants and flowers. Demonstrations related to daguerreotype were held in Turin, Trieste, Milan, Rome, Naples and other Italian cities. There were immediate commercial prospects, especially because of the many travellers who wished to keep some souvenirs of the places they visited. The need to accurately and easily reproduce images of the many national monuments gave great impetus to the development of the new technique. In Milan, the photographer Alessandro Calluses began to take different shots of the city in 1839. The first Italian to achieve the production of a series of views in a systematic way was the publisher Ferdinando Artaria. Between 1840 and 1844, he produces a series of 119 Vues d'italie d'après using the daguerreotype. The pictures were produced by a fine coloured engraving drawn to water. The work is a veritable catalogue of images of the most beautiful places of the country—Milan, Monza, Pavia, and the lakes of Lombardy, followed by the most important tourist destinations—Venice, Florence, Rome and Naples.

The Portraiture and Vedutisimo

After chemical improvements which sped up the development process, portrait photography became popular in Italy. The first portrait artists were versatile and available to customers: in addition to providing their own equipment and traveling to the homes of the client, they also ran stores selling machines and optical instruments of all kinds, plus accessories and chemical supplements, and sometimes gave lessons. Among the first portrait photographers was Ferdinand Brosy. He was German-born with a base in Venice, but moved around frequently in Trentino, Austria and Germany.

Some artists used retouching methods to enrich standardized photographic practice with their own expressiveness. Stefano Stampa, a painter and photo lover, stepson of Alessandro Manzoni, created portraits of his loved ones. Antonio Sorgato used images of common people as models for his artistic activity, and the Alinari brothers (and Giancoma Brogi) started a trend for photographs of city scenes. Although not intentionally, their pictures are a documentation of the urban transformations which occurred during the first seventy years of the nineteenth and early twentieth centuries.

Their images showed the results of the work carried out to build new roads and neighbourhoods, illustrating changing landscapes and views. In the choice of subject matter, the photographic production of southern Italy was strongly influenced by international tourists. There were not yet huge in number, but showed a remarkable consistency, a new crowd of visitors replacing the elitist tradition of the Grand Tour. The foreigners bought souvenirs of engravings and drawings on paper. Now, photographs depicting popular life scenes and crafts could be chosen from rich catalogues, lime glued on cards, and bound in precious album. In these same years, the imagination of tourists was captured by the photographic campaigns carried out on the archaeological finds from Pompeii and Herculaneum.

The Alinari brothers—Romualdo, Leopoldo, and Guiseppe—were born in Florence. In 1852, Leopoldo opened a workshop in Via Cornus where he started to take portraits, and in 1854, he founded the company Fratelli Alinari. His orders grew so dramatically that he had to move to new premises in 1863: a great establishment, purpose-built, and which became the historic headquarters of the company. The fame of the Alinari brothers is remarkable, even abroad. The work commissioned required technical skills and a particular artistic taste. They worked with slabs of extraordinary size: 1.15m high by 85cm wide, which had to be prepared one by one, put to dry, and then sensitized in a darkroom.

The Alinari brothers dealt with all the procedures in their own laboratory. Their sheets were kept in a very organized archive, and they routinely advertised their works in printed catalogues. New initiatives included the famous 'photographic walks' to inaugurate the photographic teamwork: carriage expeditions were organized by team members, during which group photographs were taken and then developed in the company's laboratories.

In 1893, the son of Leopoldo—Vittorio—published an article in the *Bulletin* against a new state regulation regarding the taxation of people who photographed paintings and objects in museums and state institutions. His photography shows were always crowded and in full swing, while the work he presented at international exhibitions obtained diplomas, medals and prizes. The beautiful pictures represented a new way of creating culture; one which affected and stimulated art scholars. His photographs did not just portray paintings, sculptures and architecture, but also bound them to the interpreter. The photos were easier for the public to interpret than the traditional paintings of artists.

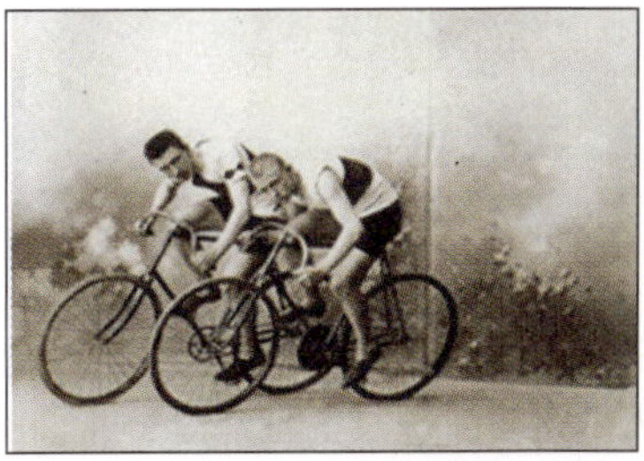

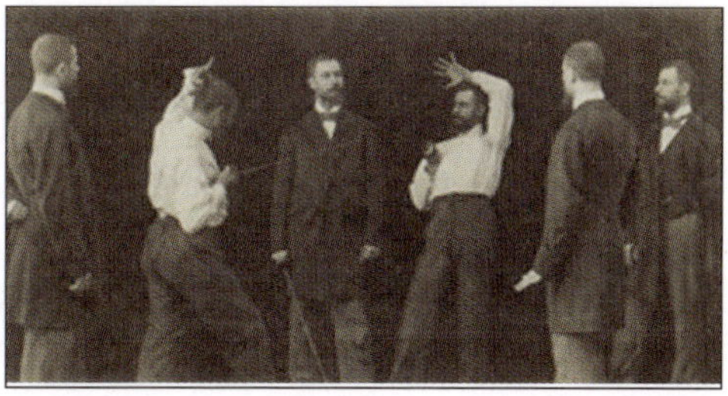

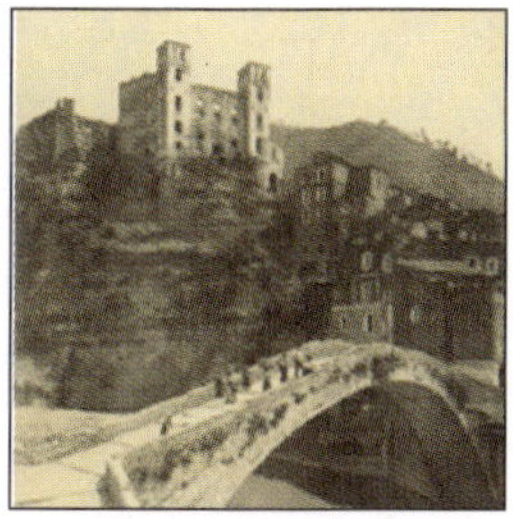

No sooner was Italy gripped by the passion of photography, than the Alinari brothers undertook several exhibitions to showcase works of photographers in Florence

Work of some of the photographers seemed to be cloyed, but was actually a creative take. They tried to capture the description and details through the image.

In 1873, the Fratelli Alinari, whose activities in the field of photographic production had thus far been characterized by images of sculptures, began to dedicate themselves mainly to images of contemporary paintings. The Alinari house became the focus of artists, critics, writers and scholars. Their family villa in Florence, 'the quartino', gradually turned into a very popular cultural salon. Vittorio Alinari, under the patronage of the Italian company for public art, organized an international competition, with prizes for original pictures of religious subjects. The purpose was to achieve a mixture of cultural and commercial images, and to acquire exclusive photographic productions of paintings.

The most popular formats at the time were the large format (perfect for decoration in the home), and the album (suitable for small collections of artistic reproductions). Vittorio himself, through these competitions, began a personal collection of paintings: the participation clauses provide more than the right to free reproducibility, they also confer the right of first refusal of their purchase on the organization. In 1901, the competition award was to illustrate the *Divine Comedy*. The work is printed in three tomes between 1902 and 1903, and is accompanied by 388 illustrations.

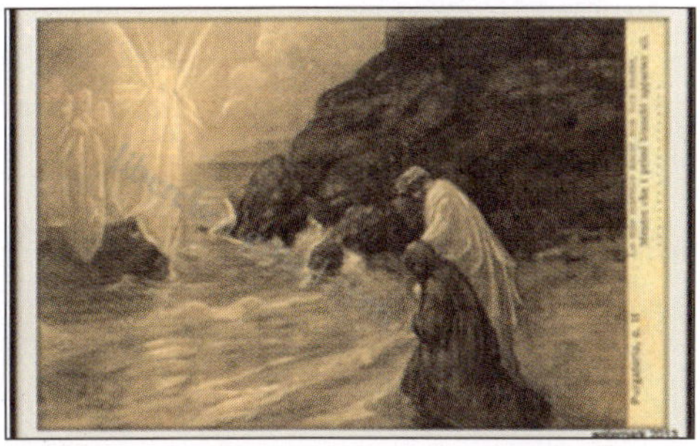

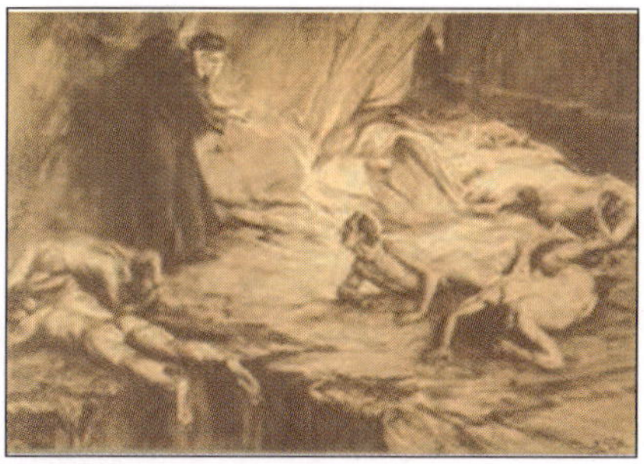

Fratelli Alinari is the world's oldest photographical firm that possess the photographs which serve as a witness to the history of Italy

In the early years of the twentieth century, the Alinari house ran a series of photographic campaigns, documented by catalogues and the press. In 1909, they began the publication of the *Decameron*, which continued till 1915.

Meanwhile, in 1920, against the advice of his children and grandchildren, Vittorio created the limited company 'Fratelli Alinari Institute of Art Editions'. This was a publishing house which bought a diverse collection of negatives, reaching 6000 subjects with thousands of slabs uncatalogued. The catalogued reproductions of works of art were divided by country, region and city.

In this school we see how the ability of the camera to reproduce photographic works with complete accuracy completely overwhelms the method of art, where disciples would spend years to be able to accurately replicate what they saw. The photograph can be analyzed and the images represent a more faithful reproduction of design.

The Englishman John Ruskin, the first critic and historian of art that uses the daguerreotype, is fascinated by photography. In the fall of 1845, in Venice, he buys some beautiful daguerreotypes depicting palaces from a Frenchman facing financial difficulties.

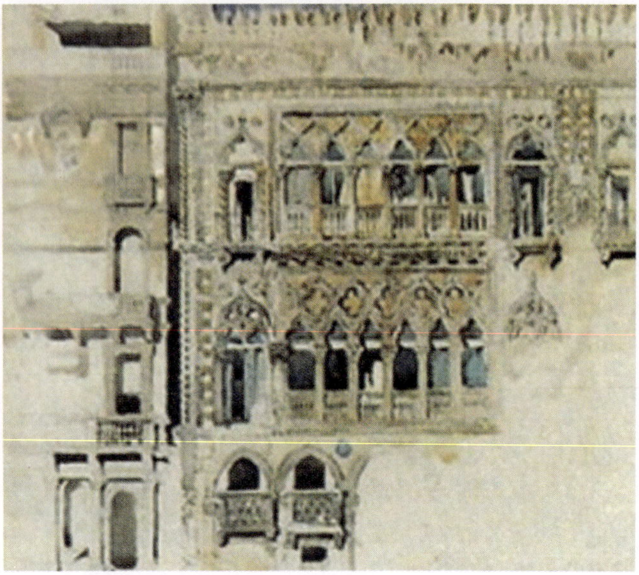

John Ruskin (1845) Casa d'Oro, Venice.
Graphite, watercolour and body colour on toned paper.
The Ruskin Library and Research Centre, Lancaster University.

The Origins of the Cinema

The first official presentation of the Lumière Cinema in Italy takes place on 13 March 1896, at a photography studio in the alley Mortar in Rome. There are other brief screenings in Milan, Turin and Naples. The Milanese architect Italo Pacchioni makes several attempts to photograph the animation in the early months of 1896, trying in vain to copy the Lumière cinema. Back in Milan, on the basis of what he had seen in Paris, he builds an appliance socket E projector using film and two lateral perforations, equipped with two small windows and paired targets for shooting with the stereoscopic effect. He manages to produce 'Train Arriving at Milan Station'. Here are some comic characters, including 'the cage crazy' and 'fake cripple'.

In the Italy of the late nineteenth century, Lumière films are seen on the streets or in exhibitions. In the early 1900s, there are many great contributions to Italian cinema, which spreads as a public spectacle. Permanent rooms are opened in major cities, eleven in Turin.

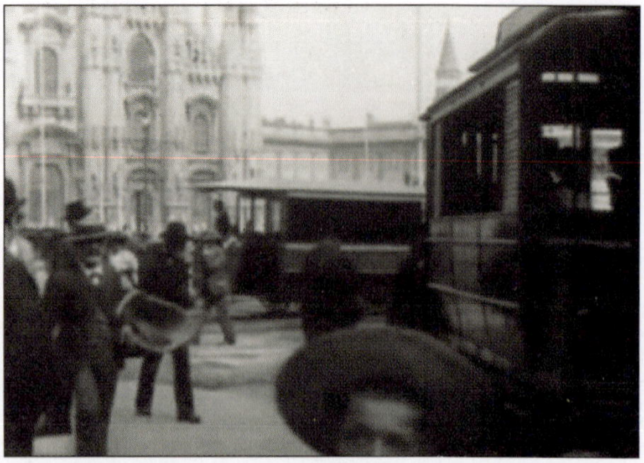

Italy's new found love for cinema and photography

Here Vittorio Mortar becomes an official operator of the royal house, Roberto Omegna opens the scientific cinema, while Arturo Ambrosio (1882–1960) produces a documentary about the first car race, *Susa Moncenisio* (1904). These pioneers lay the foundations of the industry.

The 1900s (Twentieth Century)

IX

Edited by
Ridha Akhoon, Fateh Veer Singh Guram,
Rishabh Jain

Designed By
Shahzaib Ali Naik, Ayushi Malik,
Rushda Anwer, Yumna Ahmad, Aatif Nawaz,
Amina Razzack

The Twentieth Century

Summary of Historical Context

In the late nineteenth century and the first decades of the twentieth century, the international scene was radically transformed by the development of capitalism. Capitalism, and imperialism before that, eventually trigger the First World War. In Italy, the first decade of the twentieth century goes down in history as the 'belle epoque': the transformations in the field of industry and technology enable the emergence of so-called 'modern society', which among other things drives an increase of production and consumption, the bureaucratization of state organs, the spread of education, and expansion of the electoral base. Improvements in well-being during this period remain limited only to the upper classes. In the last years of the nineteenth century, culture goes through a period of crisis and profound loss due to the crumbling of certainties fed by positivism.

The cultural movement that best expresses the existential malaise of this era is 'decadence', whose birth dates back to 1886, when the magazine *The Decadent* was founded in France by Anatole Baju. The keynote of text of the decadent aesthetic is the *Picture of Dorian Gray* by Oscar Wilde. In Italy, there is *In Pleasure* by Gabriele D'Annunzio. The general feeling of fracture between the individual and the decadent bourgeois society is expressed and inherited between the first and second decades of the twentieth century, starting with Futurism. This arises precisely with the manifesto of Futurism, published by Filippo Tommaso Marinetti in the Parisian newspaper *Le Figaro* in 1909, which contains the ideological programme of the movement. This included criticizing tradition/the past in general, the enhancement of industrial technological progress, the need to renew society and art, and the dramatic boost of war. From the first decade of the twentieth century, the avant-garde cultural movement spread throughout Europe: proposing to break with tradition, and by virtue of experimentalism to seek new forms of literary artistic expression. Forms taken include surrealism, dadaism in France, expressionism in Germany, and futurism in Italy and Russia. In most fields of knowledge, the only possible point of reference is, paradoxically, relativity: as in the natural sciences with Einsteins's theory of relativity, and in the human ones with the discovery of the unconscious by the Viennese physician Sigmund Freud.

Giovanni Giolitti (1842–1928)

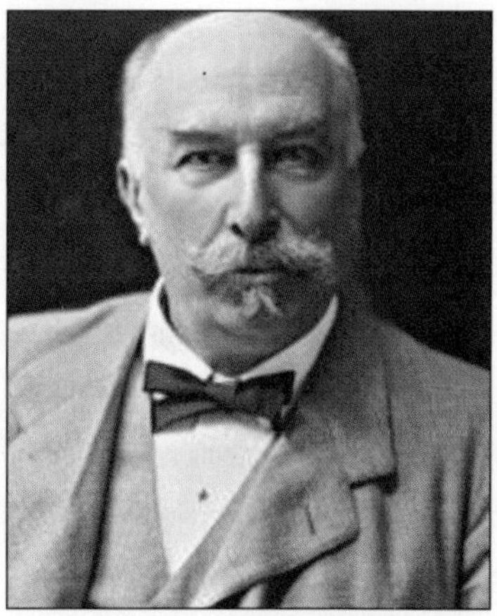

Giovanni Giolitti

He led Italy for about a decade, from 1903 to 1914, and heavily influenced the country's politics before the war. He had inherited an Italy in deep crisis, crossed by strong social tensions, with a dramatic difference between the north and the south of the country, and bankrupt from the colonialist expansionist policy. Giolitti, in a few years, manages to develop an economy with a strong industrial expansion recovery policy, which is carried out thanks to an open and cooperative attitude towards the socialist liberal forces, whose more moderate wings can ally with the enlightened bourgeoisie to ensure for Italy a decade of development. Giolitti sought to strengthen the liberal state and to dampen social conflicts by promoting economic development. He encouraged the free play of opposing forces since the government did not identify with either party but facilitated the meeting. The development of industry led to urban concentration in the industrial triangle: Milan, Turin and Genoa. The increase in the gap between the north and the south led to growing social tensions and a fully-fledged mass emigration. The tension generated by uneven social development and the appearance of new classes (such as the proletariat) fostered an intense cultural debate. It was marked by the growth of intellectual and moral concern, and a trend towards a vision of a kind of spiritualistic life, at odds with the ideological currents that characterized positivism. At the same time, the most extremist parties of the nationalist right and the revolutionary left are already working to bring the country into the catastrophe of the First World War.

Italy in this period was a lively theatre of ideas, and the magazines were a natural place of ideological confrontation: assuming an importance hitherto unknown. The third page of the newspapers became an important place for dissemination of ideas and debate. The establishment of a larger and more articulate middle class and the spread of reading and culture even among workers' groups expanded the audience for literature. The consequence of this was the stratification of literary works on different levels; this forced the writer to become aware and to make his own choices.

The richest literary genre of works was the narrative. Especially the novel, which managed to meet all the needs of the reader: being both decent entertainment and providing an interpretation of the world. Fiction was no longer based on the dissolution of naturalism, but the invention of an entirely different novel, based on other artistic principles. Writers stepped toward the realist novel, because if man's condition was what it was, tragic and painful, then what was the point of the analysis, the telling of a story? The novel could only be man's analysis, the consciousness of his misery, the polemic against common sense. A new style of narrative was conceived as a tool for the dissemination of ideas, allowing the accentuation of a character who becomes the author's spokesman. It operated by the breaking of the relationship between the characters and society, and the author of the story infers through new procedures and different techniques, including recovery through memory.

The Crepuscular Poets

The early years of the 1900s in Italy are marked on one side by social ideological tension, and on the other by the development of an industrial bourgeoisie focused only on profit and money. In this context, even the hopes for development and social peace (represented by Giolitti) stop the discomfort and the rebellion of many of the cultural Italian intellectual circles. These signs of disappointment and existential malaise are in a confusing and contradictory relationship, but they are expressions of the new twentieth-century sensibilities which are common to most of the literature of these years in Europe. Among these reactions is the refusal of the literary tradition represented by Pascoli, D'Annunzio and Carducci; this characterizes the two most important literary movements of the twentieth century period: crepuscularism and futurism.

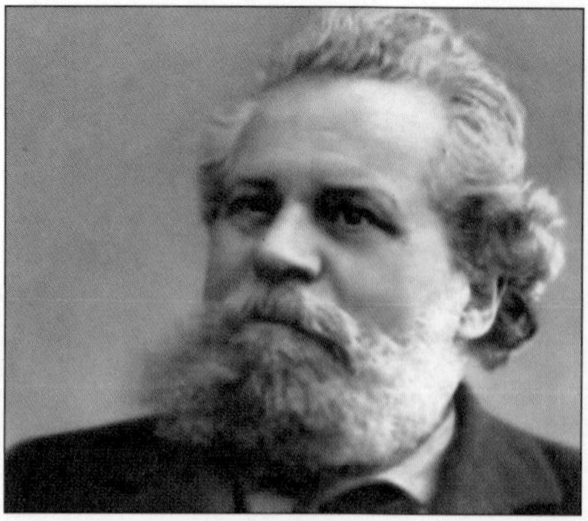

Giosuè Carducci

The crepuscular is not a real literary movement as futurism was, but under this name, several poets are united by the rejection of what had established itself as the era's literary tradition, specifically:

hero worship of the poet-bard, typical of D'Annunzio, the lofty rhetoric of Carducci and the earnest austerity of Pascoli. These poetic traditions, connecting directly with the Belgian franc symbolism, also oppose the romantic passions. They are characterized by feelings of existential boredom, anxiety, a lack of ideals, and by a sense of deep disappointment, both existential and historical. The tone is off, low, pushed to the trivial, the quotidian; the estrangement from modern times implies the rediscovery of childhood and the memory of past moments. The role of the poet is stripped of any exceptional connotation: the only possibility is to take refuge in a humble and unassuming province, from which the poet tells of deserted places, sad gardens, monasteries, dusty lounges: in the words of Gozzano, 'good things in bad taste'.

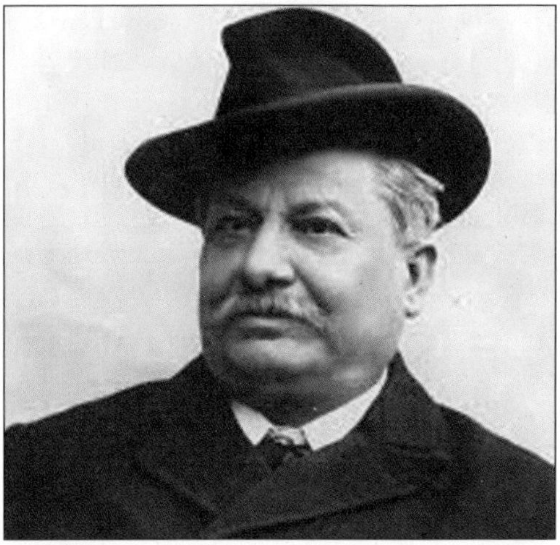

Giovanni Pascoli

For crepuscular poets, there is a chance of a consolation, of hope, of a ransom to their status as outcasts, but they can only describe it with pathetic tones and ironic lucidity. Among the different authors, one of the most important was Guido Gozzano, born in Turin in 1883 to a wealthy family. His poetic masterpiece, presented to the public in 1911, is titled *Talks*. In his work, the themes common to other crepuscular poets (the sense of isolation, melancholy, existential and historical disappointment, folding in on oneself, regression into the past) are characterized by a disenchanted. lucidity and a strong irony, which is often directed at himself, becoming self-irony that takes away all hope. He died in 1916 from tuberculosis.

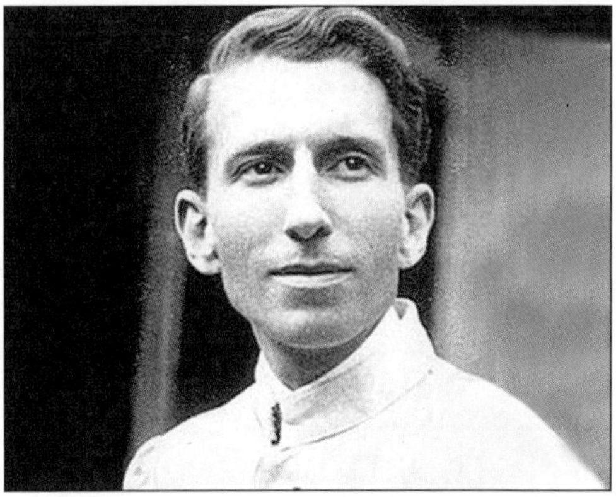

Guido Gozzano

More History

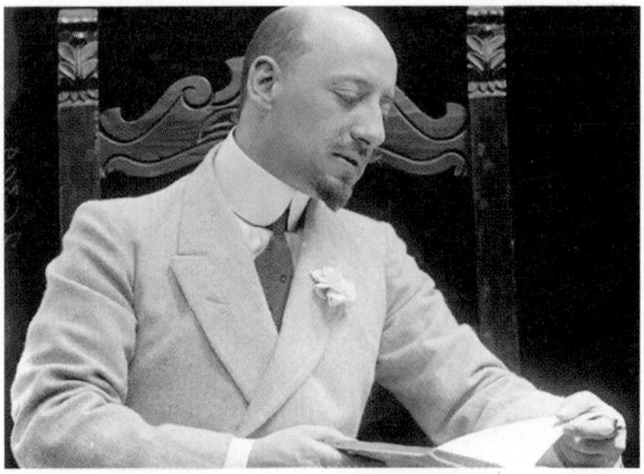

Gabriele D'Annunzio

Gabriele D'Annunzio

Gabriele D'Annunzio is one of the most representative writers of the turn of the nineteenth and twentieth century. From the artistic point of view, he embraces different genres: prose and poetry, dramatic theatre, opera, novels and news, speeches and newspaper articles. He combines excessive attitudes and radical values, with fascist ideology, not always shared, but mostly upfront, with its passions always exhibited. The young poet does not only represent Italian culture, but also that of Europe. His style emphasizes sensuality and physicality, very opposed to the stories of realistic type which go back to French naturalism.

In 1889, *Pleasure* is released, the first novel by D'Annunzio, with lyrical prose and a refined plot revolving around the dissolute life of the protagonist. His poems, 'Roman Elegies' in 1892 and 'Heavenly Poem' in 1893, are influenced by French decadent symbolism, and notable for their lyrical music style. D'Annunzio's work was influenced by a version of the myth of the superman. Starting from Nietzsche and Wagner, he follows the cult of beauty of art, the vitality of sensuality, and the exaltation of race, violence and modern technology.

The sense of decay of the contemporary age has a strong hold on the bourgeois society of the time, and this helps to expand the popularity of D'Annunzio. His novels of the late nineteenth century are centred on the myth of the superman, and his works written for the theatre are characterized by intrigue, lust, cruelty and rhetorical language. Among his masterpieces are *Praise*, consisting of three books: the first two, *Maia* and *Electra*, are related to a nationalist patriotism and anti-democratic theme; the third, *Alcyone*, is an immersion in nature through the description of a summer, expressed with a refined original musical language. After the first decade of the twentieth century, D'Annunzio finds himself in a melancholy mood. This period of his life, called 'Night', leads to the birth of an autobiographical diary based on the period of the 1916 war. The piece is a nostalgic prose about the past, written with the awareness of being an exceptional artist.

The evening fiesolana
La sera fiesolana
fresche le mie parole ne la sera
ti sien come il fruscìo che fan le foglie
del gelso ne la man di chi le coglie
silenzioso e ancor s'attarda a l'opra lenta
su l'alta scala che s'annera
contro il fusto che s'inargenta
con le sue rame spoglie
mentre la Luna è prossima a le soglie
cerule e par che innanzi a sé distenda un velo
ove il nostro sogno si giace
e par che la campagna già si senta
da lei sommersa nel notturno gelo
e da lei beva la sperata pace
senza vederla.

Laudata sii pel tuo viso di perla,
o Sera, e pe' tuoi grandi umidi occhi ove si tace
l'acqua del cielo!

Dolci le mie parole ne la sera
ti sien come la pioggia che bruiva
tepida e fuggitiva,
commiato lacrimoso de la primavera,
su i gelsi e su gli olmi e su le viti
e su i pini dai novelli rosei diti
che giocano con l'aura che si perde,

The evening fiesolana fiesole evening
fresh my words in the evening
it is like the rustling that fills the leaves
of the mulberry in the man who catches them
silent and still lingers
at the slow opra
on the high-pitched staircase
against the stem that is silvery
with its bare copper
while the Moon is close to the thresholds
cerule and par that
a veil is extended before him
where our dream lies
and it seems that the countryside is already feeling
she submerged in the nocturnal frost
and from her drink the hoped for peace
without seeing it.

Praise be to your pearl face,
o Evening, and for your big wet eyes where you keep silent
the water of the sky!

My words are sweet in the evening
it was like the rain that was beating
tepid and fugitive,
farewell tearful de la spring,
on the mulberries

e su 'l grano che non è biondo ancóra
e non è verde,
e su 'l fieno che già patì la falce

e trascolora,
e su gli olivi, su i fratelli olivi
che fan di santità pallidi i clivi
e sorridenti.

Laudata sii per le tue vesti aulenti,
o Sera,
e pel cinto che ti cinge come il salce
il fien che odora!

Io ti dirò verso quali reami
d'amor ci chiami il fiume, le cui fonti
eterne a l'ombra de gli antichi rami
parlano nel mistero
sacro dei monti;
e ti dirò per qual segreto
le colline su i
limpidi orizzonti
s'incùrvino come labbra che un divieto
chiuda,
e perché la volontà di dire
le faccia belle
oltre ogni uman desire
e nel silenzio lor sempre novelle
consolatrici,
sì che pare
che ogni sera l'anima le possa amare
d'amor più forte.

Laudata sii per la tua pura morte,
o Sera,
e per l'attesa che in te fa palpitare
le prime stelle!

and on the elms and on the vines
and on the pines from the new pink fingers
who play with the aura that is lost,

and on the wheat that is not blond yet
and it's not green,
and on the hay that already suffered the scythe
and he is
and on the olive trees, on the olive brothers
what a pale fan of sanctity
and smiling.

Laudata be for your lustful clothes,
o Evening, and the girdled belt that surrounds you like the salt
the fien that smells!

I will tell you to which realms
of love call us the river, whose sources
eternal in the shadow of the ancient branches
they speak in the sacred mystery of the mountains;
and I'll tell you for what secret
the hills on the clear horizons
s'incùrvino like lips that a ban
close, and because the will to say
nice faces
beyond all human desire
and in their silence they are always new
consoling, yes, it seems
that every night the soul can love them
of stronger love.

Laudata be for your pure death,
o Evening, and for the wait that makes you palpitate
the first stars!

More History

This refined and sensual poet devoted himself to his social life and romantic pursuits, thus leading a dissolute and disorderly life. He left his wife heavily in debt to pursue his own adventures. When the outbreak of World War I brought him back to Italy, he was able to realize in action the role of the heroic bard poet. At the end of the global conflict, D'Annunzio moved to Lake Garda (staying in the villa 'Vittoriale of the Italians'). However, with the rise of fascism, he found himself an outcast from society and spent his final years locked in his house museum with a few friends, devoting himself to art and literature.

The Italian political situation at the end of World War I is very much changed: it is experiencing a rapid process of unionization. The socialist party was a revolutionary party that refused any collaboration with bourgeois governments and aimed to socialize the means of production, to distribute all property collectively, to abolish the military draft, and to promote universal disarmament as well as to unite all the international proletarian republics. After the war, Pope Benedict XV authorizes Don Luigi Sturzo to found a Catholic party.

Thus, in 1919, he founded the Italian People's Party, which fought for the end of the landowners, for the defense of small and medium-sized property owners, for administrative decentralization, and for the freedom of teaching in private schools. In 1921, in Livorno, the seventeenth congress of the Socialist Party met, in which the dissidents, led by Antonio Gramsci, left the party and founded the Communist Party of Italy. This party was to have highly centralized organization, meaning that it had to periodically expel petty bourgeois suspects and opportunists in order to establish a dictatorship of the proletariat.

Luigi Pirandello (1867–1936)

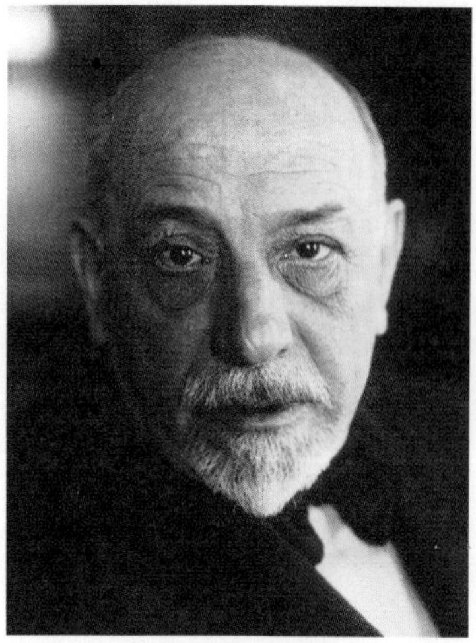

Luigi Pirandello

Born in Agrigento, Pirandello dedicated himself to literature and journalism (and after a financial crisis, to teaching). After World War II, his activities turned almost entirely to the theatre: for example, the 1921 'Representation of Six Characters in Search of an Author'. In 1934, he was awarded the Nobel Prize for Literature.

Pirandello was formed in the positivist culture, participating in the new trends whilst complaining about the failure of the ideals of the Risorgimento. His stories 'Bagpipes' (1909) and 'Old and Young' railed against the Italian businessman, lamenting the corruption and decadence. With the 'Late Mattia Pascal' (1904), Pirandello cast a critical eye upon democracy; he saw the socialist leagues of the executives as ambitious and rabble-rousing. For him, to want to change class relations was not only unnecessary but also harmful. His outlook on life was based on the contrast between life as a continuous flow and the forms in which man is forced to fix it.

He believed that man is a prisoner of schemas, and the only solution is the destruction of himself. In the essay, 'Humour' (1908) Pirandello defines humour as the feeling of the opposite, i.e., the presence of the critic and the poet in the same man, who is the victim of a malicious imp who disassembles the mechanisms to see how they are made. We are warned of the contrast between being of sound substance and form, and this contrast makes us laugh. The audience are moved to laughter not from a sense of comedy but from a sense of pity. Pirandello gradually passed the other realist models of the twentieth century.

His first novel, *The Excluded* (1983), although it seems realistic, really breaks the mould for the novelty of the invention of grotesque style. *Late Mattia Pascal* is the story of a man who is presumed dead; he takes the opportunity to start a new life in another city but, stifled by social conventions, he fakes a second death to return to his old life. However, he finds his family have moved on, and he is resigned to remain on the sidelines of life. With this work ends the 1800s realism, and the tormented world of the 1900s is born. The *Old and Young* (1913) is a vast fresco of the nineteenth century, while *One, Nobody, 100000* (1926) is the synthesis of all the relativistic theory.

Under the 'novel' heading is included a number of short stories—these can be ordered according to a criterion: first regionalism, then social, and finally surrealistic type novels involving the invention of images of reality. Pirandello theatre is defined as a negation of the naturalist. With 'The Reason of Others' in 1889 started a different way of looking at life: things seem to change meaning with the passage of time. In 'The Cap and Bells' in 1917 and 'Think Jack!' in 1916, new perspectives are suggested, involving the characters in revolutionary and absurd gestures. Pirandello aims to unmask the belief system within which men live their lives. The work 'So It Is, If You Like' (1917) affirms the impossibility of knowing the truth, claiming that piety is the only remedy. The theatre becomes a place of representation of the conflicts of human life.

More History

Fascism emerges on the political spectrum as a kind of new and original totalitarianism. It does not rely only on the police and army, but invents a demagogic scenario which allows leaders to organize mass support, especially from the lower middle class. The economic policy of Fascism goes through several phases: liberal in the years 1922–1925 (with strong growth in production), then interventionist after 1925. The international crisis of 1929 increases the public-sector interventions in the economy, forcing the state to become the lender-banker of big business. After the war and sanctions, austerity is promoted and the state supports domestic demand. In short, Fascist economic policy is based on the suppression of wages and the destruction of the trade unions and working class policies. In foreign policy, Fascism must moderate its demands for power. The culture of the past twenty years is bourgeois: that is, made by the bourgeois and bourgeois-facing. Italy is divided into two layers: the upper (aristocratic and bourgeois), and the lower (the lower middle class and the workers). The first Fascist regime in Italy is able to plan and implement a totalitarian political sphere through the liberal use of all possible instruments: from print to film.

Literature between Wars

In the twenty years between the two world wars, Europe is divided between communism in the Soviet Union, liberalism in France and England, and the totalitarian regimes in Italy (facism), Germany (Nazism), and Spain (Franco). Around 1930, the Great Depression (a severe economic crisis caused by excessive industrial production and the consequent fall in prices) caused a steep rise in unemployment. In Italy, where there was a huge gap between the industrialized north and the agricultural south, the facist regime aimed to bring the entire country round to its ideology via a highly repressive policy against any form of dissent, as well as through propaganda in the mass media, radio, cinema, and print media. In the early 1920s, the development of cinema attracts spectators to the theatre, thanks to technical innovations such as sound and colour.

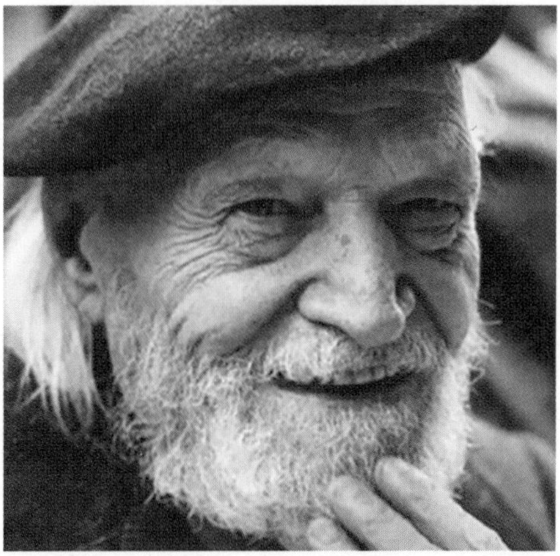

Giuseppe Ungaretti

These obsecurities in Italy start from Carlo Bo's easy's title 'Literature as a Life' that was published in the journal in 1936. Bo gives a definition of the new opera in which he intends to testify the existential restlessness of man. Hermeticism originated in the nineteenth-century poetry. The elements that are used in this hermetic style are the essence of the words, the abolition of syntactic logical connections. The term was particularly applied to the twentieth-century Italian poets whose forerunner was Arturo Onofri and whose primary exponent and leader was Giuseppe Ungaretti. The formalistic devices of Hermeticism were partly an outgrowth of Futurism, a short-lived but influential movement that encouraged innovation in literary language and content. Giuseppe Ungaretti, Eugenio Montale, Salvatore Quasimodo, were the main poets of the period while still preserving a strong link with the tradition of another great poet of these years known as Umberto Saba.

The Obscurity

The lyrics of the 30s, from 1935 to World War II, were baptized with the term 'hermetic', indicating not only a way to represent but also to look at it in a way that it can also be extended to prosatorie essayists. The hermetic, also called 'new opera', makes up a new school of thought for the common masters, in which they all represent the contrast between the real world, disjointed and inorganic, and a fairy-tale dream. At the root of this poem is a strong autobiographical need. The most desolated loneliness and awareness, are the conditions of all modern opera. In this solitude, the poet explores his conscience and brings out the darker and real data: hence there is a dominance of the subconscious and dreams. The poetry of this generation tends to a high pitch, and it is in open conflict with all the recent traditions: against the rhetoric of D'Annunzio, the sentimentality of Pascoli, and the revolutionary spirit of the Futurists. It points to a poetic essence that represents the tragic existential condition: while on one side there is a defense of poetic values, on the other there is an evasion of reality that denounces the tragic situation of past years. It employs a technique that uses all the achievements of the Symbolists: Ungaretti and Montale. Use of the analogy is replaced with the identity (eliminating the word 'like') and with synaesthesia (an association between two words relating to two different sensory spheres; warm words, green silence, etcetera).

There is a belief that poetry becomes greater the more you move away from the common language and the common way of seeing and feeling. So the writer writes in order to ward off reality in a world of myth: with the careful choice of words, by the deletion of the article, with the use of a sententious tone. A series of technical artifices are used to obtain an identical effect. This type of lyricality expresses precisely the feeling of the era: a repressed freedom. Literary forms are the supreme human activity, the pursuit of form as morality. This art is understood as a craft, and the exercise of this job is a full task that surpasses any other duty. This attitude leads us to consider poetry as an alibi used to covered the poet's disinterest in the events of the world and the fate of men. They were self-absorbed. The hermetic man's experience of conflict, and the new values introduced by the resistance, led many writers to change their subjects, entering a post-obscurity in which they express social issues with modules and typical hermetic techniques.

Key poets of this era

Salvatore Quasimodo

Born in Modica in the province of Ragusa in 1901, this journalist and professor of Italian literature died in Naples in 1968.

Giuseppe Ungaretti

Born in Alexandria in 1888 to Luccan parents, he lived for several years in Paris and Brazil.

Chiaroscuro

Anche le tombe sono scomparse
Spazio nero infinito calato
da questo balcone
al cimitero
Mi è venuto a ritrovare
il mio compagno arabo
che s'è ucciso l'altra sera
Rifà giorno
Tornano le tombe
appiattate nel verde tetro
delle ultime oscurità
nel verde torbido
del primo chiaro

Night has absorbed the white of the tombs
Infinite black space fallen
From his balcony to the cemetery
My Arab companion has come to find me
Who killed himself last night
Who when he used to meet my eyes speaking to me with those pure and carven phrases of his
There was a dark voyaging in the gentle blue
He has been buried at ivry
With his splendid dreams
And I bare his shade
Day come again
The tombs reappear
Flattened out in the gloomy green of the last obsecurities
In the turbid green of the first clearing

Clear blatent sadness of the emptiness that death creates for human souls only. The dense black darkness which falls on the tombs and covers them is to hide the sad panorama of what has remained of the dead. The dry monuments and those who live there reappear in their darkest appeareneces which are the recollection of what was alive in the light of the sun.

Filippo Tommaso Marinetti

Born in Alexandria, Egypt in 1876, his first language is French. He participated as a volunteer in the First World War, and after the war, is linked to the fascist regime. All his work is still highly experimental, aimed to enhance modern living and styled on the D'Annunzio myth of the superman. He publishes the manifesto of Futurism in 1909.

Futurist Art

Founded by Filippo Tommaso Marinetti in the first decade of the twentieth century, Futurism was a Europe-wide movement which involved not only literature, but all fields of art: painting and sculpture, music, dance, cinema, theatre, and architecture. In line with the various branches of avant-garde contemporary art (all refusing the naturalistic representation of reality), futurist art proposes the idea of a space in which it must seize the movement, the action and the flow of life. It makes use of new materials, and juxtaposes bright colours, impetuous lines, and dynamics in an original way. Just like the crepuscular, it rejects the tradition of the past, not to retreat into an intimate everyday world, but to bring out all that is new, modern and spectacular.

We see the glorification of war and struggle, a love for danger, for speed, for the industrial world, and a contempt for tradition, morality, for the academy and the museums. To spread their ideas, the Futurists used a new instrument: the manifesto. Via this method, they were able to reach the public in a direct and highly controversial way. The first poster is the Manifesto of Futurism by Marinetti, published in the French newspaper *Le Figaro* in 1909. The Technical Manifesto of Futurist painting was published in 1910, and The Manifesto of Futurist sculpture in 1912.

Italian Futurism has great influence abroad, particularly in Russia. During the October Revolution of 1919, Russian Futurism develops as a cultural and political movement to break with tradition. But the

Russian Futurism, unlike the Italian movement, is not just a controversial break with the past, but also a strong link with the political and social action of the era. The art and expressive techniques of Russian Futurists are intended as a means to act; the precious language of symbolism (the conventional tradition) is replaced by the language of the street, aggressive, but capable of interpreting the problems of the people, the real protagonist of the story.

The inability to describe organized reality rationally brings poetry and futurist prose to the destruction of the metric, the breaking of the syntax, the abolition of the adjective and the adverb, and the abandonment of punctuation. This is replaced with the use of free verse, analogies, onomatopoeia, noises and sounds, mathematical signs, and graphic organization in visual poetry. The Futurist literary techniques are summarized in two expressions: 'Paroliberismo' (or 'words to freedom') and 'Wireless Imagination' (the creation of unexpected analogies through a succession of images not linked to each other logically, representing the poet's feelings directly). This leads to the birth of the synthetic novel, in which words are transformed through the techniques of Paroliberismo and Wireless Imagination.

The importance of Italian Futurism lies in it being a genuine movement to break with tradition and experiment with new artistic techniques. The best results can be found not so much in literature but in painting and the visual arts. In such domains, the significant foreign influence drives development in dadaism and cubism, leading to the artistic avant-garde of the 1960s.

More History

Due to its developed industries, the Germans demonstrated a great resilience after the First World War. However, the strong depreciation of the currency during the Depression led to the advance of reactionary nationalistic currents. In Russia, after the October Revolution of 1928, the policy of five-year plans begins: Russia managed to modernize its production facilities; however, it paid the price of Stalin's dictatorship.

Meanwhile, in America, the prevailing philosophy was that of isolationism. In this context, the Italian political attempt to invade Ethiopia led to international tension, as did the pro-Nazism and German expansion in Central Europe. The Spanish Civil War, in which Italy and Germany intervened, defended by General Francisco Franco, was the first act of aggression that fascism and Nazism implement against democratic Europe.

Eugenio Montale

Born in 1896 in Genoa, Montale was enlisted in 1917 to fight in WWI. In 1925, he published *Cuttlefish Bones*, his first major collection of poems. He then sided with a group of anti-fascist intellectuals and wrote literary essays. After World War II, he began working with the newspaper *Corriere della Sera* as a journalist, literary and music critic, special envoy and prose writer, until his death in Milan in 1981.

In his early work, he is opposed to the poetic traditions of Carducci and D'Annunzio, composing stripped-back poetry in which he recovers Dante, the stilnovisti, Leopardi and Gozzano. He also references the metaphysical poetry of European and Anglo-American opera. The theme which dominates his work is the impossibility of knowing the reality of history (owing to its upheavals), and the pain of belonging to a society which is lacking deep values. Poetry can not give a solution to this pain, it can only register it with lucidity and coherence. But this does not stop man from trying to find the weak link in the chain, the miracle that can offer a way out of his dramatic existential situation.

This, however, can never be found; there is only emptiness. Yet, the poet identifies two possible escape routes: one is constituted by the figure of the woman, the other is the memory. The female figures present in the poetry of Montale are seen as consoling, angelic, built on the model of Petrarch. They guide the poet who asks to cross the darkness of life, acting as messengers of hope. The memory is presented as a consoling feature: as a defence against the lack of meaning in the present.

Cuttlefish Bones, Montale's first collection of poems, consisted of five sections, each of which revolved around common themes such as the sea, and the arid, rugged and rocky terrain of his native land, Liguria. These were metaphors for the pain of existence and the incomprehensible, illusory nature of reality. Montane represented man as a being in crisis, who feels all of the suffering and the pain of living, while always hoping for a miracle which might save him.

Another work from Montale to remember is 'Opportunities' (1939). In this work, he moved away from the environment of Liguria in order to dwell on random situations, opportunities which set in motion the feelings and the memory of the poet. Here appears the woman—as an angel/demon/saviour/messenger—full of light in a dark and gloomy world. In his other work 'The Storm and More' (1956), next to the female angel appears a new, dramatic, violent element from hell: the war. World War II is portrayed not only as a historical phenomenon, but as the symbol of the tragedy and the pain of humanity. In an interview in 1951 about the relationship between poetry, politics, art and history, Montale declared that his poetry was concerned only with the human condition:

The subject of my poetry is the human condition considered in itself. This is not a matter of what happens in the world; it only means becoming aware that we share an essence with the transition. An artist brings a particular attitude towards life, and a certain formal attitude, and interprets it in patterns that are proper ... Having sensed from birth a total disharmony with the reality that surrounds me, the matter of my inspirations could not be that disharmony. I do not deny that fascism and war have made me unhappy; However, there are reasons for my unhappiness that go far beyond these phenomena; it is a psychological and moral maladjustment that it comprises my poetic nature. Those artists who consider art as a product of the environmental and social conditions will argue that you have to opt for one or the other of the warring parties ... I respond that I chose as a man—as a poet—and I immediately felt that I was fighting on another front which was just as significant as the external warring front.

The Novel in the 1920s and 30s

In this period came the final disintegration of the nineteenth-century novel; novels now generally offer a story which revolves around one or more characters who express, in various forms, the crises of the present age. We see the vein of magical realism inaugurated by Bontempelli, with novels like *Eve Last* (1923), *The Son of Two Mothers* (1929), in which the author strives to discover fantastic plots and magical aspects of reality. Examples of the surrealist narrative are the works of Alberto Savinio, and the trend for fantastic fiction is followed by authors such as Dino Buzzati (with *The Desert of the Tartars* Milan, 1940).

In the 30s, the magazine *Solaria* promotes a novelistic style inspired by new realism and modelled on the US/European narrative. These authors are distinguished by a production based on the recovery of the memorial dimension. Alberto Moravia's novel *The Indifferent* of 1929 is proposed as a precursor to neorealism.

History

World War II began on 1 September 1939, with the invasion of Poland by Hitler's German army. It was a truly global conflict: in only two years, all continents were involved, owing to the opening of a range of fronts. Over the course of six years, a 'total war' took place, involving not only the military but also civilian populations. This period was a time of tragedy for the Jewish people, and with the launch of the first atomic bomb on Hiroshima, it began an era of nuclear terror. It was not only a war between nations and peoples, but also an ideological clash between states such as Germany, Italy and Japan, who wanted to create a new order at the expense of the Jewish people. In the Fascist period, literature in prose was guided by the same psychological attitudes which characterized poetry: an overvaluation of literature, a reality filtered through memory, the use of fantasy and dreams.

The Rondisti

This style of literature was followed by 'Rondisti': writers who published in the journal *Patrol*.

The Solarian

This defines those who collaborated with the literary magazine *Solaria*. The prose writers tended to represent themselves via their narrators.

The Novel

On the one hand, the novels in this period were aimed at the disintegration of the narrative fabric, but on the other, there was a real and proper return of the traditional style. Since the dissolution of the nineteenth-century novel had been caused by psychological and cultural processes of time (and by authors like Joyce and Wolff), it was impossible to go back. So the new novels were not like those of the nineteenth century; the attention was instead dedicated to man in his dramatic solitude. The technique used was that of deformation, which represented a world ruled by irrationality and chance.

Italo Svevo (1861–1928)

Svevo was a novelist from Trieste, linked to the Central European, Austro-Hungarian Empire and Europe. A friend of James Joyce and a great innovator, his sophisticated and refined writings were not popular initially, but today they are much appreciated; among his masterpieces are *Lives* (1892), *Senility* (1898), and *The Confessions of Zeno* (1923).

The Surrealists

The surrealist movement exploded in the early years of the century in France and Spain, and radiated throughout Europe. The expression of the surrealists is marked by strong symbolic representation. One of the most significant surrealists was Dino Buzzanti.

Buzzati

Dino Buzzati was born on 16 October 1906, in Belluno, Italy and died on 28 January 1972, in Rome. He was an Italian journalist, dramatist, short-story writer and novelist, internationally known for his fiction and plays. Buzzati began his career in the *Milan daily Corriere della Sera* in 1928. His two novels of the mountains, written in the style of traditional realism, *Barnabò delle montagne* (1933; 'Barnabus of the Mountains') and *Il segreto del bosco vecchio* (1935; 'The Secret of the Ancient Wood'), introduced the Kafkaesque surrealism, symbolism and absurdity that suffused all of his writing.

The novel generally considered Buzzati's finest, *Il deserto dei Tartari* (1940; 'The Tartar Steppe'), is a powerful and ironic tale of garrison troops at a frontier military post, poised in expectancy for an enemy who never comes and unable to go forward or retreat.

Of Buzzati's extremely popular plays (some of which were taken from his short stories), the most important is *Un caso clinico* (performed and published 1953; 'A Clinical Case'), a modern Kafkaesque horror story in which medical specialists and machinery destroy a perfectly healthy man.

The Opposition

In the years between 1930 and 1945, there emerged some writers who were very different from one another, but who can still be brought together with common denominators. Some define them as the Realists of the 30s, and others as The Opposition because they were known mainly for their opposition to fascism. Theirs was almost an unconscious anti-fascism, present almost unbeknownst to the author in their books. Among these Oppositionists were Alberto Moravia and Elio Vittorini.

From World War II to Present

In the second half of the twentieth century, we see a return to Marxism on the cultural scene. This ideology underwent several revisions leading up to the 1980s, whilst from a strictly philosophical point of view, existentialism was receiving a great response all over Europe. The 1960s saw the formation of structuralism, which encouraged the spread of new disciplines such as sociology, linguistics, psychoanalysis and cultural anthropology, while the political debate of the 70s was dominated by the consequences of the dispute of 1968. At the closing of the century, renewed attention was given to the interpretation of the subject under the sign of hermeneutics.

In the 80s developed post-modernism, which saw the contemporary era as characterized by the general wreck of each theoretical perspective. As for literary production, after the war, the dominant trend is neorealism, which in the face of the concrete problems of contemporary society, tells the story of things, people, in all their naked truth. This orientation is shared by cinema which made Italian film directors known all over the world.

The neorealist movement is exhausted over the course of fifty years, but the real rupture occurs with the birth of the so-called 'neoavanguardia', a movement developed by the Group 63, so called because the group of novelists, poets and critics were formed after attending a conference in Palmero that year to pursue it on a political level. After the dispute of 1968, the differences were exacerbated to the extent that the group was forced to dissolve.

The movement was born out of a shared intellectual reaction to the alienating processes of modernization, the experiences of the bourgeois-capitalist society during recent years, the commodification of cultural products, and the triumph of singular language. The group is divided into two different positions: one which follows the vision on a purely literary level, and another that wishes.

The Neorealist Novel

The postwar literary scene was characterized by the resumption of the novel modelled on nineteenth-century realism (Zola and Verga) and on the works of the European and American narrators of the 30s (e.g., Moravia and Hemingway).

The neorealist style aims to reproduce forms of realist speech, such as slang, dialect. The best representatives are writers like Vittorini, Pavese and Calvino, as well as Pier Paolo Pasolini. Primo Levi described his tragic first-hand experiences in Auschwitz in the story diary *If This is a Man* (1947) followed by *Respite* (1963).

A Bit of History

After the War and the fall of the Fascist regime, Italy returned to democracy. On 2 June 1946, the Italian people were called to choose by referendum between the old institutional form of the state (the monarchy), or to move to a republican system. Victor Emmanuel III abdicated in favour of his son Umberto in an attempt to make people forget the involvement of the royal house with fascism, but Italy chose to become a republic, with 54.2 per cent of votes in its favour.

At the same time, Italians voted to elect a constituent assembly, which would have the task of drawing up the constitution of the republic. The vote was universal: for the first time the right to vote was extended to women. The constitution came into force on 1 January 1948. It contained a series of very advanced items. However, the efforts of the assembly were thwarted by a judgement of the Supreme Court, which led to a differentiation between the parts of the constitution which would be immediately established, and those that would be established in an unknown future. As a result, some fascist rules such as 'the consolidated text of public safety' remained, and other relevant institutions were introduced only after many years. The constitutional court comes into operation in 1956, only two years after the state judicial council. Some rules which distinguished Italy as a civilized country, such as gender equality and the political and civil rights of women, were applied only after long delays.

On 10 July 1943, Allied forces landed in Sicily and began to liberate an Italy occupied by German troops. At the end of that year, Italy was a country cut in two: south of Naples was under control of the Allies, whilst the north was run by the Germans who had liberated Mussolini and put him in charge of the so-called Republic of Salò, the name of the location on the lake Garda where he was located. The north became the main site for the development of the armed resistance, the partisan struggle against the anti-fascists. Italy was not only the scene of fighting between the Allied and Nazi forces, it was also the site of a civil war. The economic situation was seriously compromised. Industrial production in 1945 dropped to less than a third of that in 1938, and the unemployment rate was high. The investigation into the misery of the early 50s reveals that almost a third of Italian families never ate meat.

There was a problem with overcrowded housing (an average of four people per room in makeshift places such as warehouses, caves and even shacks). 85 per cent of poor households were concentrated in the south, where poverty reached much higher percentages. At the beginning of the 50s, only 8 per cent of Italian households had (simultaneously) water, electricity, and a toilet. On this rubble, Italy began a period of reconstruction, not only economic, but also moral and civil. There was a growing need for different identities and new values. At this time, we see a new current of Italian literary and artistic life; for example, the creation of the neorealist cinema and literary genre.

Neorealism

The experience of the conflict, the resistance, the return to democracy, and the birth of a new society profoundly changed the relationship between society and culture. It imposed the need for a new literature which would break away from profoundly literary rhetoric of the last two decades. This was a conscious literature, attentive to the social reality and the ways of life of the individual and the community.

Literature became not only comforting in the face of tragedies of humanity, but on the front line against the horrors of the world. Neorealism leaves in its wake a strong civil passion which becomes a testimony to Italy's conditions of backwardness and misery, but also a sign of confidence in the strength of the recovery and renewal.

In the 40s, it affirms literature as a commitment, as demonstrated by the ongoing debates about politics, culture, and the role of the intellectual in society. Such debates feature in numerous magazines which see the light of the new democratic context: for example, the newspaper *Polytechnic*, produced by Elio Vittorini. Neorealism is expressed in literature and in cinema. A major turning point is the publication of *The Leopard* in 1958 by Tomasi di Lampedusa, in the story of the prince of Saline and of his family.
Set in Sicily, the author proposes a vision of historical development steeped in fatalism and resignation, reminding the world of Verga and pushing away the romance of the neorealist models of committed literature by wrapping it in an almost decadent aura.

Another novel which marks the overcoming of neorealism is *The Garden of the Finzi Continis* (1962), which tells the story of a family of Jewish origin in Ferrara wartime. The author is Giorgio Bassani, and in the novel, the inner conflicts of men are examined, presenting a melancholic view of the world and the frailty of men.

Carlo Emilio Gadda (1915–1973)

His work is distinguished by a great deal of original personal linguistic research, which led him to mix elements from different dialects in his description of a chaotic reality, using an ambiguous narrative technique which neorealists were not able to grasp. His work included *The Mess on the Via Merulana*, 1959.

In the decade after the end of the war, Italian society experienced deep economic and social transformations. Facing the new industrial realities and the economic miracle, the neorealist models seemed insufficient in both ideological assumptions and formal style. The search for a new literary language was concentrated on the debates found within magazines such as *Workshop* and *Statements* (to which Pasolini, Vittorinim and Calvin contributed).

In break with the traditional models, but strongly at odds even with the contemporary writers, the neoavanguardisti rejected the ideology behind the mere literary, placing language at the centre of their poetics. For them, the language of contemporary society was false and alienated. All that remained was its syntactic and semantic disruption as a symbol of the impossibility of communicating. This was the perspective of Umberto Eco and other representatives of the new avant-garde who founded the Group 63.

More History

The face of Italian society was quickly changing as the country transitioned from a predominantly agricultural society to a highly industrialized and capitalist one. In the late 1950s, the number of Italian employees in the industrial sector exceeded those in the rural sector. Italy was experiencing a so-called economic miracle. Following the unification of Italy in 1861, d'Azeglio uttered the famous phrase 'made in Italy must make Italians'.

Large numbers of Italian people migrated from the south to the north, changing the face of many large urban areas (especially Milan, Turin and Genoa, but also Rome and Bologna). At the same time, the symbols of the new wealthy, industrialized Italy were being constructed: for example, the 'Velasca' tower and the 'Pirelli' skyscraper in Milan. Huge residential suburbs and dormitories sprung up to accomodate the newly arrived anonymous mass of cheap labour.

The Velasca Tower and the Pirelli skyscraper are prominent symbols of the first generation of Italian modern architecture and represent the economic recovery of Italy after the devastation of World War II. Both were completed in the year 1958.

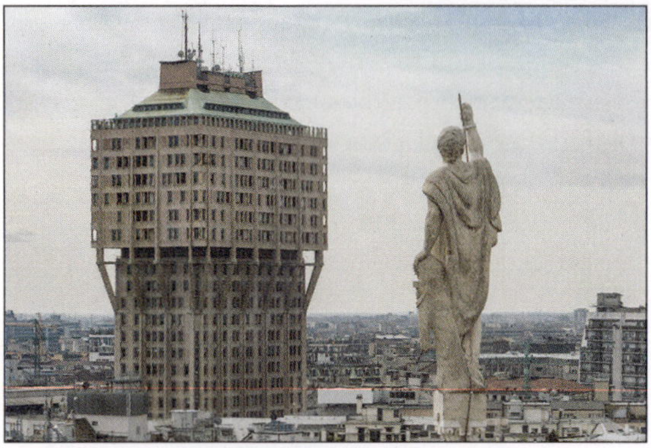

The Velasca Tower

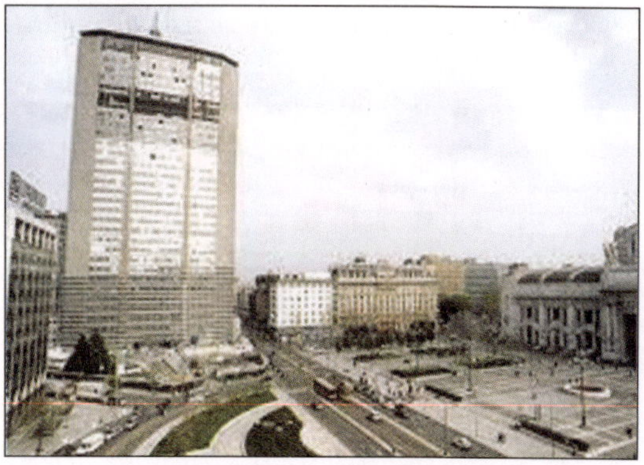

Pirelli Skyscraper

'This book will appear to the reader in stark contrast to the pictorial image of southern Italy which is frequently found in the literature…; writes Ignazio Silone in the preface of *Fontamara*, his novel which came out in Switzerland in 1933. It tells the story of a small town in Abruzzo, Fontamara, which becomes a symbol of a rural world within which exists the marginalized as well as the bourgeois. The realist narrative is very distinct from the formalist style which was dominant at the time. In 1929, Alberto Moravia published *Indifferent*, a novel which offered a raw portrait of the Roman bourgeois society of the 1920s.

Although neorealism flourished between 1943 and 1949 and its ideological political awareness was expressed in 1947-48, it must be remembered that the origins of the movement date back to the late 20s, before the war and resistance, to the intellectual reactions to the culture of the ruling regime in those years. Realism does not have a properly devised poetic. As Calvin wrote, neorealism was not a school; it was a set of entries, of devices, consisting of multiple discoveries of different sizes, most unusual for Italian literature. However, through the works of this set, it is possible to recognize some fundamental aspects.

Firstly, neorealism arises in connection with current events, with the daily realities and the problems of contemporary society. It distances itself from naturalism. Realism in literature does not pursue a description of the real, which is never possible, but it resorts to a narrative technique and descriptive style which convolutes reality and derives from it a starting point for a narrative in which reality becomes a paradigm, and in doing so, reveals and documents the contradictions. In this way, the issues of neorealism include the crisis of the bourgeoisie during the Fascist period (which was expressed in the so-called 'white telephone films'), the miserable living conditions during and immediately after the war, the condition and strength of the labourers of the south, and the tough recovery of daily life amongst the rubble of moral conflict.

Elio Vittorini (1908–1966)

He was one of the fathers of neorealism, and one of the most original voices of the cultural debate after the war. His native land, Sicily, was the backdrop to one of his most famous novels, *Conversations in Sicily* (1941), which tells the story of the return of the hero, Sylvester, to the island, employing a realistic language full of symbolism. *Men and Not Men* (1945) is based on his experience of the partisan in Milan.

Alberto Moravia

This was the pen name of Alberto Pincherle, whose novel *The Indifferent* was censored by the Fascist government, forcing the author into a period of hiding. In *The Two Women* (1957), he retraces his harsh experience of the war. In *Roman Tales*, 1954, he uses a neorealist language, and these works have often been used as film scripts. In 1960, he published *Boredom*, and around this time Moravia too, sensitive to the needs of the new avant-garde approaches to the experimental novel, explored themes related to psychoanalysis. He died in Rome in 1990.

History Continued

As Italy was recovering from the wounds left by the war, the communication network was still very rough and did not allow for rapid development of the automotive market. However, the need for individual mobility pushed an aeronautical engineer, Corradino D'Ascanio, to design the Vespa (a famous scooter) in 1966. After 10 years, 1 million units had been produced. The Vespa soon became not only a commercial success, but a symbol of various generations. It became an icon, present in advertising campaigns and in many movies. It was a symbol of the economic boom and the rising winds of 1968. As of 1955, Fiat produced a car that would become another symbol of the 60s: the Fiat 600. This represents the average Italian car in the era of mass motorization, which was now possible thanks a renewed road network.

Primo Levi

Levi was born in Turin in 1919 to a Jewish family. He became a partisan after the fall of fascism, and was taken prisoner and deported to the concentration camp of Auschwitz, where he remained for nearly a year between 1944 and 45. This traumatic experience was the centre of his narrative production; in *If This Is A Man* (1947), he tries to understand the universal underlying reasons that can push a human being to generate so much violence. In the *Submerged and Saved* (1985) and *Truce* (1966), he records his return to real life after his experience in the concentration camp (even though nothing can bring back the life he had before). He died in Turin in 1887.

Se questo è un uomo.

Voi che vivete sicuri
nelle vostre tiepide case,
voi che trovate tornando a sera
il cibo caldo e visi amici:
Considerate se questo è un uomo
che lavora nel fango
che non conosce pace
che lotta per mezzo pane
che muore per un si o per un no.
Considerate se questa è una donna,
senza capelli e senza nome
senza più forza di ricordare
vuoti gli occhi e freddo il grembo
come una rana d'inverno.
Meditate che questo è stato:
vi comando queste parole.
Scolpitele nel vostro cuore
stando in casa andando per via,

If this is a man.

You who live safe in your warm houses, you find coming back in the evening hot food and friends faces: Consider if this is a man who works in the mud That knows no peace through fighting bread who dies for a yes or a no. Consider if this is a woman, without hair and without name without more strength to remember the empty eyes and cold the womb like a frog in winter. Meditate That was this: I command you these words. Carve them in your heart staying at home by going way, lying down, getting up. Repeat them to your children. Or you get the house out of your face, the disease Prevents you, your births twist your face from you.

coricandovi, alzandovi.
Ripetetele ai vostri figli.
O vi si sfaccia la casa,
la malattia vi impedisca,
i vostri nati torcano il viso da voi.

Cesare Pavese

Pavese was a poet, a storyteller, and one of the greatest voices of Italian literature in the twentieth century. He set many of his scenes against the backdrop of the Langhe. After the release of *Your Country*, written in 1939 and published in 1941, he was counted by critics among the neorealist writers. Pavese's work featured a complex interplay between life and literature which gave rise to original poetic research, such as in the collection of poems *Work Tired* (1936), in which the poetry-story was detached from hermetic models. In his prose, he united his political commitment, the symbolic return of realism, myth, and the recovery of childhood purity.

His *Moral Works* is counted amongst the canons of neorealist literature. In later works, after the war, he approaches a deep inner loneliness and disillusionment. One important work of his is *The House in the Hills*, a novel that talks about a character named Corrado, who talks about the fall of Fascism. He takes refuge in places of childhood, in the hills of the Langhe, while his friends participate in the partisan struggle. He will escape the horrors of war, struggle and death. The myth of childhood is shattered in front of the historical reality. He will meditate on his life lived in long isolation.

More History

In the early 60s, Italy experiences its economic miracle and rapid and profound changes. Society is transformed and a new subject appears—young people—who will have a key role in the season of revolutions. Italy is a country with a new face, but this is in contrast with its conservative political aspect, its often perverse myopic cultural closures, and its inability to deal with the necessary renewal in the social sphere and the field of labour world. 1962, which sees the resignation of the government headed by Democrat Tambroni, is characterized by a repressive policy which creates the possibility of a rapprochement between the Christian Democrats and Socialists.

The latter had already made themselves autonomous from the Communist party. The ministry, chaired by the democratic Fanfani, inaugurated the new political center-left, which aimed to reduce the profound social imbalances (which had resulted from the unplanned economic growth) through a series of reforms and greater government intervention. In addition to school reform, an important step was the nationalization of the electrical industry and the birth of Enel, the national body for energy.

In 1963, Aldo Moro formed the first center-left government with the participation of the Socialists, but he did not launch reforms. This was because of the obstructionism of those politicians who were disinclined to real reform policy, and also due to an economic recession which marked the end of Italy's economic miracle.

Italy had a one-party government under the leadership of Christian Democrats, who had to face the great renewal of 1968, as well as the neo-fascist bomb in the Piazza Fontana in Milan, which ushered in the so-called 'strategy of tension'.

Italo Calvino

He was born in Cuba in 1923, but his family returned to Italy when Calvino was two years old. He moved to San Remo, and Calvino took part in the partisan struggle. In 1967, he moved to Paris, and died in Siena after suffering a stroke in September 1985. Calvino's debut came in 1947 with *The Path to the Nest of Spiders*, in which the experience of the partisan struggle, as seen through the eyes of a child, assumes the style of a fable (which will become central features of his poetry). In 1952, he published *The Cloven Viscount*, which tells the story of the Vicomte de Terralba, who returns from the war after being split in half by a cannonball. One half of the Viscount does good deeds, and the other half does bad.

This story, along with *The Baron in the Trees*, and the *The Nonexistent Knight*, form a trilogy through which Calvino expressed his denunciation of the human condition and of modern society. In 1956, he produced *Italian Fairy Tales*, a collection of tales from different dialects. *I*, Calvin's short story collection, was published in 1958. Through the fantastic transfiguration tinged with humour, a bitter view of life emerges. He transposes through the melancholy fairy tales a clear awareness of the contradictions which dominate real life and modern society. Emblematic are the adventures of *Marcovaldo*, in which the protagonist, a factory worker, looks for contact with nature to overcome the loneliness and frustration with which the great city has forced him to live.

Italo Calvine—The Path to the Nest of Spiders (1947)

This is a coming-of-age novel about a child called Pin, set against the backdrop of World War II. Pin searches for an identity within a partisan group, but the people mock him. However, he knows a secret place, a nook where spiders make their nests and where the imagination of children can run freely. He will reveal its secret only to the people who earn his trust. By describing the resistance through the eyes of a child, Calvino's story is in an original position in relation to the literature on partisan warfare.

Pier Paolo Pasolini

Born in Bologna in 1922, he died in 1979 in mysterious circumstances. Pasolini established himself as a novelist with *Hustlers* (1955) and *A Violent Life* (1959). The two novels are both set in villages, disadvantaged neighbourhoods on the far outskirts of Rome. They focus on the underclass of the capital, whose life consists of misery, violence, and a struggle for survival. Their life is described through a large, realistic fresco, departing from neo-realistic style and activism. The optimistic outlook and confidence in the future which pervades most neorealist literature here takes on the flavour of complaint about the brutal human context. The mood is miserable, cynical, yet innocent and pure, with a primitive essence of childhood. It is humanity described without populist filters and devoid of a progressive historical function. Pasolini emphasized a linguistic research which fused the vernacular and jargon of the Roman suburbs (mostly in direct speech) with an interweaving of language and dialect in the narrative parts.

His poems include the collection *The Best of Youth* (1949). In 1959, he published *The Ashes of Gramsci*, eleven triplet poems reflecting the contradictions of Pasolini's thoughts: between the decadent feeling of returning to the past, the aesthetic passions of the people, and the ideological principles of progressive civil commitment.

The Neoavanguardia

The 60s are dominated by the diffusion of the neoavanguardia movement, according to which, art's primary purpose is to expose the total lack of sense in contemporary society invaded by alienation. On the formal and stylistic level, this translates into the 'anti-novel', a true negation of the traditionally understood novel with its logical sequence of events. The neoavanguardia takes over the 1970s, during which the economy returns to normal. The popular novels include: Umberto Eco's *The Name of the Rose* (1980), Alessandro Baricco's *Anger Castles* (1991), and the work of Andrea Camilleri, inventor of Montalbano.

The Poetry of the Late Twentieth Century

The post-war commitment to civilian reconstruction also reflected on the level of opera production, which was dominated by ethical and political themes, as well as by the aesthetic of neorealism. Salvatore Quasimodo translated a hermeneutic experience to more open poetic forms. The influence of the neo-avantgarde determined the poetic output of the 1970s and 80s, when the links between political commitment and linguistic experimentalism melted again, and when formal research led to the discovery of unusual associations between words and images. A prime example can be found in the work of Andrea Zanotto. Another strand of the latest style of poem is the so-called, 'Line of Lombardy', in which the main themes are ethics and the problematic reality.

The Theatre after Pirandello

After the war, the theatre of Eduardo de Filippo, who brought to the stage the most authentic aspects of the Neapolitan tradition, received critical acclaim around the world. The 1960s were characterized by an intense literal renewal, after Pier Paolo Pasolini ushered in the so-called Theatre of Words, aimed at provoking debate, the exchange of ideas, and invoking literary and political struggle. It was directed to an upper middle-class audience. The same processes affected the theatrical renewal instigated by Mario Luzzi, whose texts were located on the border between the theatrical genre and the dramatic poem. Between the years 1960 and 1970, the most significant theatrical trend was the experimentalism of the new avant-garde. Carmelo Bene, an actor, poet, director and screenwriter, was an important avant-garde exponent, who rewrote a number of texts from the classical repertoire, including Shakespeare's *Hamlet, Pinocchio* (1961), *Our Lady of the Turks* (1966), and *Romeo and Juliet* (1976).

Dario Fo, who received the Nobel Prize for Literature in 1997, was inspired by the jesters of the Middle Ages to write material aimed at scourging authority (the neo-capitalist and bourgeois society) and upholding the dignity of the downtrodden. He instigates a recovery of the commedia dell'arte. The author considers his texts as a simple framework, which he interprets using improvisation with outstanding ironic qualities. He also makes use of the 'grammelot': consisting of gimmicks in speech from an invented language, whose words mean nothing, but imitate the sound or cadence of a certain language or dialect. Works include *Isabella, Three Ships and a Cacciaballe* (1963), and *The Pope and the Witch* (1989).

The Second Republic

In 1992, a group of judges in Milan (of which Antonio Di Pietro became a symbol) uncovered the Tangentopoli: a corrupt system involving bribery, government contracts and hundreds of politicans. This led to the demise of the First Republic, a system which had lasted for half a century. The Italian Socialist Party, along with a number of other smaller parties, was dissolved, and this event marked the beginning of a century of profound change. Soon after came the entry into politics of politicians like Silvio Berlusconi, Carlo Azeglio Ciampi and Romano Prodi, who led Italy in the area of the Euro, various attempts to change the constitution, the second Republic, and the increasing flexibility of the old system of government.

Literature in the 1980s

The protagonists of the Italian literature of the 80s were a few young artists, all born between the years 1940 and 1950, and were thus defined as the 'forties' generation. They did not have a firm tradition to draw reference from: on one side there was the so-called crisis of literature (referring to the lack of energy of new authors in theoretical discussions and debates), and on the other side there was certain structural linguistic experimentation (like the work of Umberto Eco), which could not be a reference or an indication of a school of style. The value of those works had to be closed within the limits of their own narrative and poetic experiment. Meanwhile, the big names had left the literary scene because they had exhausted their artistic talent (as was the case with Moravia), or because they were dead (such as Italo Calvino).

As a result, the generation of the forties had to invent a new Italian literature for the twenty-first century. In truth, some of the general characteristics of twenty-first century literature had already been suggested by Italo Calvino in his book *American Lesson*. Calvino pointed to three important points for the study of the literature of the millennium: a) The predominance of poetry in verse as a bearer of values (which even prose writers and storytellers pursued by different means but with common goals) b) The story predominates c) The representative figures are irregular, eccentric and atypical. You could say that Calvino has indicated the three most important points which summarize the landscape of Italian literature at the start of the 2000s. It is true that like all theoretical schemes, Calvino does not include all the phenomena of recent literature. Italian literature up to the year 2000 is full of exceptions and circumstances. But it is also true that he only gives general guidelines and summary points by which each person can arrange their knowledge.

Italian fiction since the year 2000 does indeed seem to prefer the story to the novel, and this also applies to those writers who clearly adhere to the romantic tradition of the classics. To give a definition for existing literature is impossible, but you can describe an overall picture within which you can place, more or less exactly, new authors. In this way, under the label 'traditional' we can place those authors who have an elegant style—linear and light. In addition to these authors, we can include the young people who have chosen to place themselves in a dialectical relationship with respect to the Italian literary language tradition, rather than, looking at the experience of American writing, which boasts the beat generation and minimalism. Pier Vittorio gained a following with his novels, and became the emblematic writer for a generation. Tondelli announces the death of the novel: proposing the story, as the only possible future of Italian fiction. Within the genre of the story, we find the narrative writings of the most promising young authors belonging to the new pulp currents. There is a whole team of atypical investigators who continue to work on the story, putting together a language which is a mixture of languages: dialects, standard languages, special languages, slang languages, or the current language of the traditional language. An example is Andrea Camilleri. In the intellectual landscape of poetry, we see a clear trend towards the intimate, the private: the revenge of the small against the big linguistic experiments.

All experimentalism invested in the 1900s seems permanently exhausted. Even today, after the excesses of the neo avant/post-avant garde, the key feature of the latest poetry seems to be that of a retreat towards one's own identity and one's own experience alone. But this is only one similarity: this era is very different from the beginning of the twentieth century. There is no possibility of returning, as there was in the early nineteenth century, to the traditional expressive and technical metrics and style. Since the 60s and 70s, no one has thought of writing poetry in the form of the sonnet and song of Petrarch. Also, with regard to the themes of poetry, traditional themes such as the esoteric myth are outdated.

On the contrary, poetic research today focuses on language, the language that crystalizes in everyday speech habits: even without resorting to the language of the Italian poetic tradition, the language of the current poetry can be original, new, and recount the intimate experience of each poet. In the 80s and 90s, the most significant poems were created by authors who had almost evenly split their literary engagement with the criticism. Their poetic writing over the last two decades was fuelled by and confronted with their critical writing. Alongside these intellectuals can be seen poetic voices which could be called extravagant or eccentric, like that of Alda Merino.

Art

The twentieth century is characterized by constant and rapid evolution of figurative language and the artistic experiences, both because of scientific and technical developments, and the equally rapid political and social changes. In this century, the planet, always becoming smaller and increasingly globalized, was crossed by two world wars, the emergence of the Communist model, and the technological revolution linked to the Internet and digitalization. New challenges are launched in these first years of the third millennium: including the global economic crisis and Islamic terrorism.

Liberty in Italy

In the early years of the new century, Italy experienced an intense economic development, and art was influenced by modernism (which was called Liberty or floral style). The Liberty style was expressed in architecture. Even today you can see Liberty palace built in many Italian cities: especially Turin, but also in Milan, Venice, Genoa, La Spezia, Rome, Naples and Palermo. The Piedmont capital saw one of the first examples of this type of architecture: 'Pavilions for the Turin Exhibition' built in 1902 and designed by Raimondo d'aronco (1857–1932), a native of Udine who was very informed about foreign cultural and artistic trends (in particular, the Austrian ones). The pavilions appear to be manufactured in a fanciful style, and are characterized by a flowing rhythm and floral motifs, rich but elegant, and never overloaded.

The Art Nouveau style was quite a modest development in painting and sculpture, and became the most original and most durable style in the field of decorative arts. The look was achieved through the highest quality in the processing of the ceramics, in graphics (especially in Cartellonistica), and in the art of wrought iron. On the other hand, we must not forget that modernist art tried to break down the differences between major and minor arts.

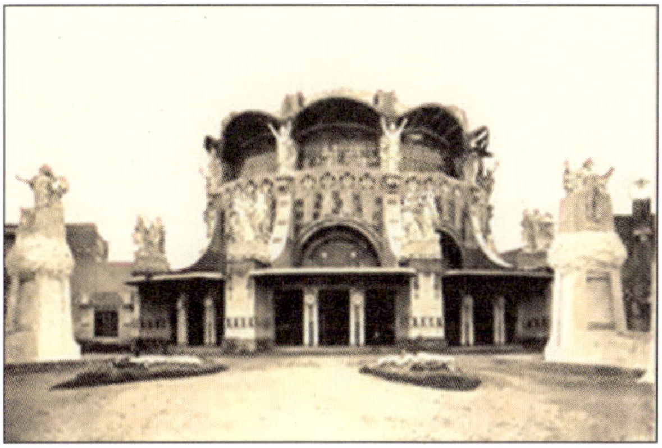

The First International Exposition of Modern Decorative Arts, held in Turin in 1902, was integral in spreading the popularity of Art Nouveau design, like this pavilion

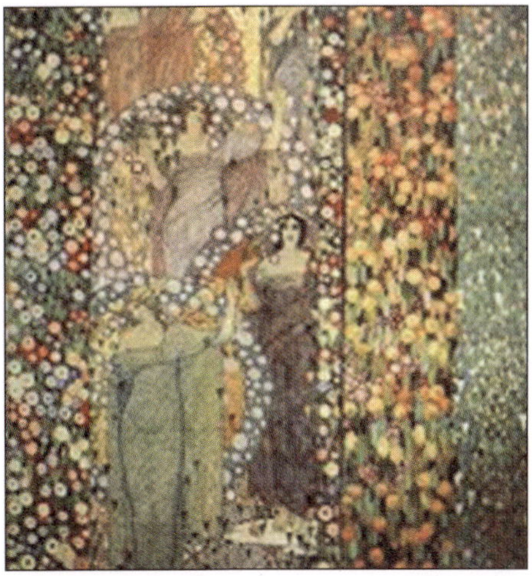

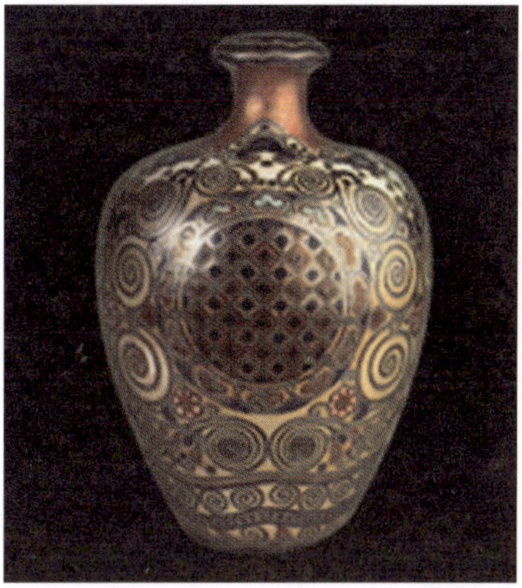

Art Nouveau, also called New Art, is an international style of architecture and art which is inspired by natural forms and structures, like flowers and plants.

The Vanguards

The profound transformations in art and culture during this era stem from the rediscovery of the art's practical function (in which it must respond to precise requirements of rationality and usability), and on the other hand, the tendency to allow the deep expression of the artist, without any objective or rational logic. This assumption underlies the 'vanguard' movement, begun by a group of intellectuals and artists who wanted to give their work an ideological motivation, and give a message (often breaking with the past) of denunciation and renewal.

Among the major artistic movements of the first two decades are: Fauvism in France in (1905), Expressionism in Germany, Cubism in France (1907), Futurism in Italy (1907), Abstractionism (1910), Suprematism and Constructivism in Russia (1913–1915), Neo-plasticism in the Netherlands (1917), Dadasim (1915), Italian metaphysical painting (1917), and Surrealism in 1920.

Fauvism

This was the French art movement which developed between 1898 and 1908. The 'Fauves' (the term literally means 'beasts') was used in a derogatory sense to indicate the use of colour which painters (from 1905) exhibited in their works in Paris for the first time. They abandoned the soft tones and hazy Impressionist style, preferring the bold and violent colours used by Dali and post-impressionists such as Vincent Van Gogh. A representative of Fauvism was Henri Matisse. The definition of the Fauves was never accepted by these artists, who felt that it did not reflect their lyrical and solar language. The strict contours and the simplified design matched with an intensely dramatic and casual use of colours, exploiting the expressive potential of the image rather than its resemblance to reality.

Henri Matisse (1869–1954)

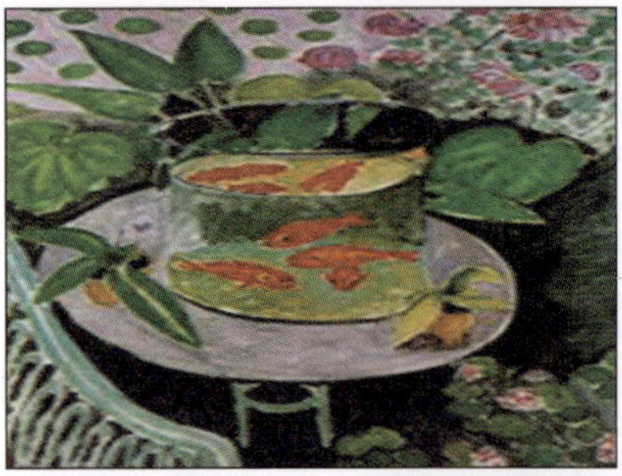

The Goldfish, Henri Matisse, 1912

His work represented the final break with the use of light and colour, so that, for example, a woman's nose could be green if it contributed to the composition and expression of a painting. He said: 'I do not paint women; I paint pictures.' He saw colour as a personal expressive element—subjective, and totally independent. Amongst his works we remember: 'Poisons les Rouges', 'La Dance' and the 'Icarus' collage—seven paintings in the Pinacoteca Giovanni e Marella Agnelli in Turin. Also important are 'Femme et Anenomes' and 'Meditation apres le Bain' (1920). (Matisse paints goldfish in many of his works, and this could be due to a visit by him to Morocco, where he observed how the local population of the town of Tangier would daydream for hours and gaze into goldfish bowls.

Expressionism

Expressionism was a cultural current which arose in Germany at the beginning of the twentieth century as a reaction to impressionism and naturalism. It originally established itself in the field of fine arts, then spread to literature, music and film. Expressionism proposed a revolution in language. It found its first real historical example when, in Dresden, in June 1905, some young architecture students formed a group called die Bruke (the bridge).

A key element in their work was the emotional experience of life, a portrait of reality according to the emotions which it arouses in us; thus there was an aversion towards realist focus on objects and an abolition of three-dimensionality. The philosophy of the group was based on the spontaneity and the immediacy of the expressive form, in opposition to the bourgeois conventionalism. The formal features of the artistic production included: deformed and exasperated expressive images, irony and caricatures of reality, use of marked contours, broken lines, inspiration from primitive art, graphic works based on the contrast of wide black and white tonal masses, and strident colour contrasts.

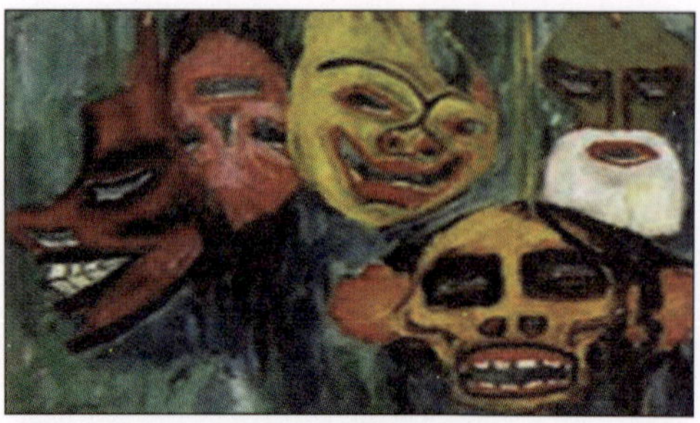

Masks (1911)

In Berlin, in 1913, on the eve of the outbreak of World War I, the group disbanded due to artistic differences. Masks, 1911 by Emil Nolde, is a noteworthy example of their work. Nolde, who was the oldest member of Die Bruke, often included masks in his art as a symbol of alienation and disconnect. This work is also inspired by his intense study of African and Pacific masks at the Ethnological Museum in Berlin.

Expressionism in Italy

Italy did not develop a group of artists who could explicitly be called expressionists. However, they were often found amongst the painters of the so-called 'Roman school' founded in 1938. The label of the Roman school, or 'school in Via Cavour', was given to artists including Scipio, Gino Bonichi and Marino Mazzacurati, but perhaps they cannot be described as members of a school, because you can not find a common agenda. Rather, it's possible to find a taste expressed each time in a very personal way. Some works of these artists are kept in the Modern Art Gallery in Rome, including 'The Cardinal Dean' (1929) and 'Scipio'.

The members of the group were active from 1938 to 1943, and seemed to refer in particular to an expressionist experience of the new objectivity, rejecting both classicism and abstract art intellectualism, and instead affirming the need for a realistic representation with strong colours. Artists include the Sicilian Renato Gattuso (1911–1987) who was an intellectual and was highly influential in Italian culture post-World War II. The modern and contemporary national art gallery in Rome holds many of his works, among which are 'Shooting in the Countryside', 'Escape from Etna', 'Portrait of Mother' and 'La Vucciria'.

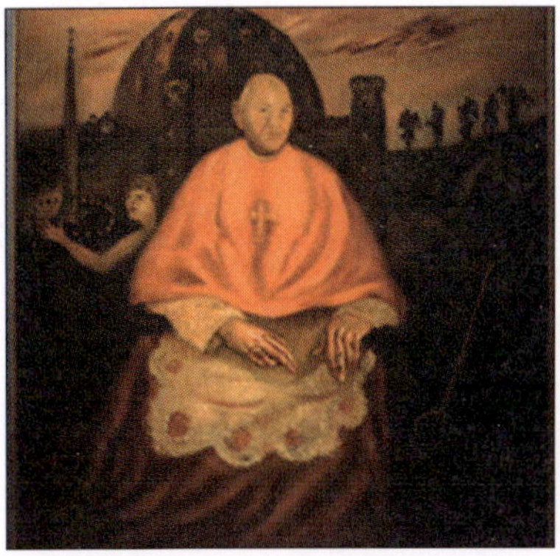
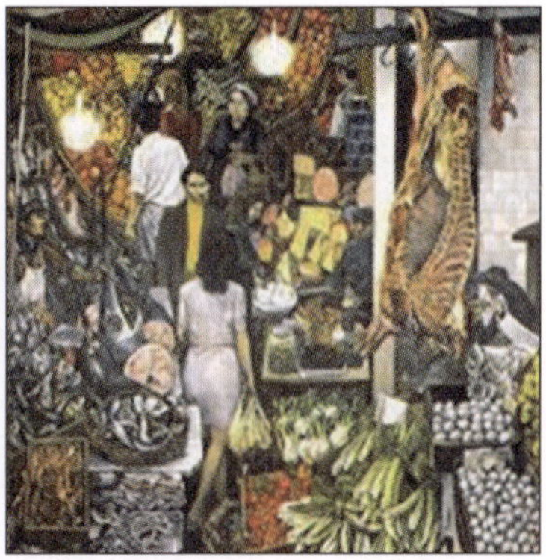

The Cardinal Dean-Portrait of Cardinal Vannuttelli, by Gino Bonichi, also known as Scipione, Rome, 1930 (left). La Vucciria by Rennato Gattuso (right)

Cubism

The term Cubism was used for the first time by the critic Louis Vauxcelles, who, on reviewing some works of Braque in 1908, commented that were formed from cubes. It now refers to a twentiethcentury painting movement started by Pablo Picasso and Georges Braque, which revolutionized the way of representing subjects in paintings. Instead of faithfully describing the world around them, the Cubist painters used basic geometric shapes to synthesize a single composition from different points of view (which in reality could not be adopted simultaneously).

We can distinguish two phases of Cubism: the first being Analytic Cubism (1909–1910), characterized by accentuated fragmentation of plans and geometric shapes, which are almost dissolved, and the use of dull colours and monochromatic compositions. Secondly came synthetic Cubism, developed from 1912, which implemented a partial recovery of the colour of the shapes, which were now completely released from the traditional conception of space.

The basic principles of Cubist painting were: the negation of perspective vision and the realistic definition of volumes, the breakdown of volumes in faceted planes, the possibility of multiple views, the decomposition of figures into their constituent elements, and an identity between bodies, objects and surrounding space.

Pablo Picasso

Spanish artist Pablo Picasso (1881–1973) moved to Paris in 1904, and on entering into the environment of the poets and intellectuals, he soon became a promoter of radical change in artistic conceptions. In 1907, along with Broque, he outlined the principles of Cubism. In 1914, he moved to the South of France, and, after a trip to Italy, began a classicist recovery of figurative language. After the war, he devoted himself intensively to graphics and ceramics, yet he also devoted himself to politics through participation in the conference for peace (for which he produced the drawings of his famous 'Dove of Peace').

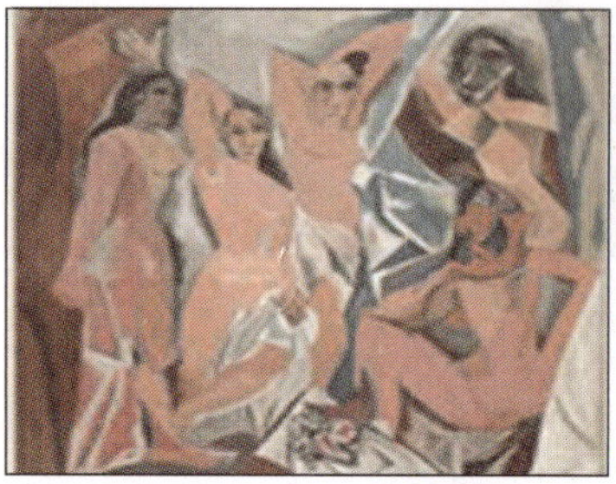

Les Demoiselles d'Avignon, or The Young Ladies of Avignon

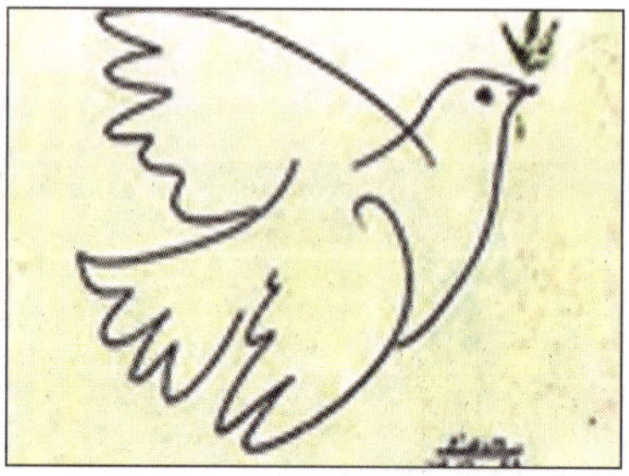

Peace Dove, Pablo Picasso, 1961

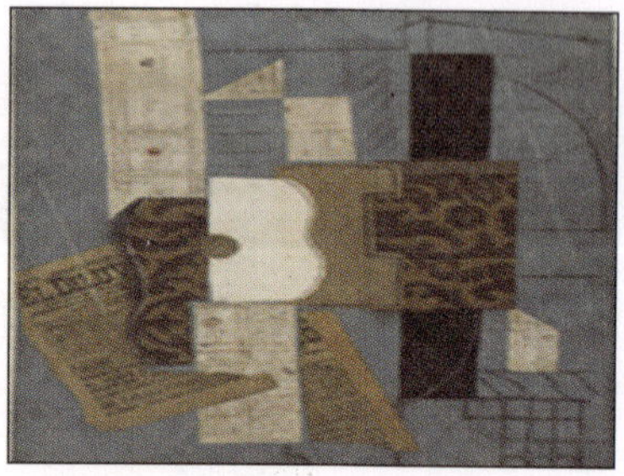

Guitar, Pablo Picasso, 1912

His so-called Blue Period lasted from 1900–1904, during which he produced various post-impressionist works in sombre tones. The Rose Period, marked by the use of oranges and pinks, lasted from 1904–1906. In 'Les Demoiselles d'Avignon' (1907), Picasso addresses the problems of volume, making this the work with which he equates the birth of Cubism.

'Guitar' (1912) is a painting featuring, broken, free images and is a radical leap from the sculptural tradition of modelling (carving or moulding) to a new technique of assemblage.

Guernica (1937) is a dramatic representation in white, black and gray of the massacre of Guernica. The work, which marked a fundamental stage in his artistic and political commitment, depicts a historical event whilst highlighting effective visual and essential emotional components. 'Head of a Woman', 'Naked Woman', and 'Still Life with Candle' are all preserved in Italy in Milan's Museum of the Twentieth Century.

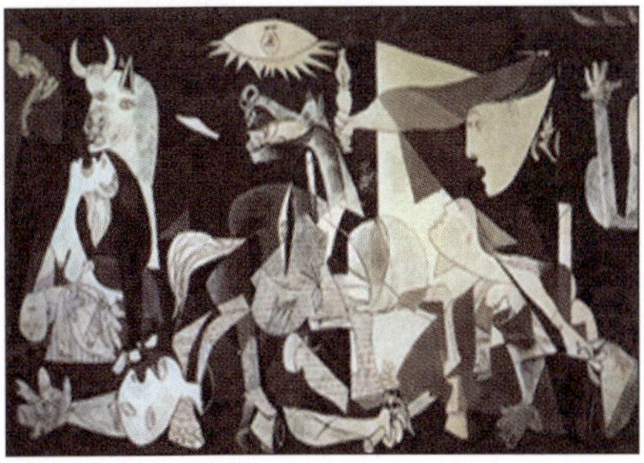

Guernica, Pablo Picasso, 1937

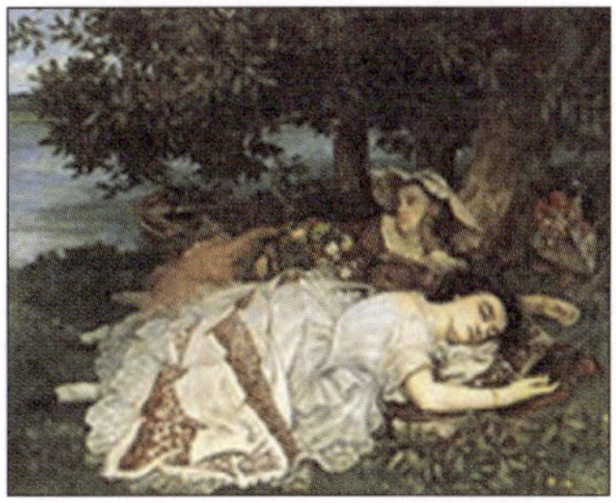

Young Ladies on the Banks of the Seine, Gustave Courbet, 1857

Georges Braque (1882–1963)

Greatly influenced by Cezanne, Braque became the founder of Cubism. Typical of his productions are still lifes featuring musical instruments, created in relation to the guidelines of analytical and synthetic cubism.

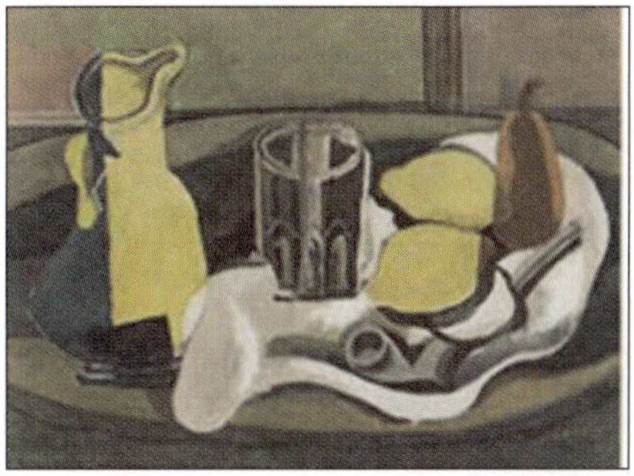

Lemons, Georges Braque, 1929

Futurism

Futurism was an artistic cultural movement founded by Filippo Tommaso Marinetti in 1909. Those who took part included musicians, writers, photographs, sculptors and designers. The futurists proclaimed a break with the past and adherence, through expressive forms, anti-traditionalist controversy, to the dynamism of modern life, with a positive attitude towards new technological achievements.

The first Futurist manifesto appeared in 'Figaro' on 20 February 1909, and advocated the destruction of the syntax and the use of free speech in poetry and prose. In subsequent years, further posters were released, each relative to the individual arts. In February 1910, the Manifesto of Futurist Painters was published, which was followed by the Technical Manifesto of Futurist Painting, and the Architectural Manifesto in 1914. The Futurists give geometric shape and colour to that which is invisible and not measurable physically: the forces, movement, speed, sound, noise, light and smell. In an era of transition, futuristic art manifested itself with the exaltation of the means of locomotion and the speed of the machine.

Giacomo Balla (1871–1958)

Balla's artwork marks the transition to futurism. His focus on dynamic movement is evidenced in 'Girl Running on a Balcony' (1912), which is preserved at the Museo de Novecento in Milan.

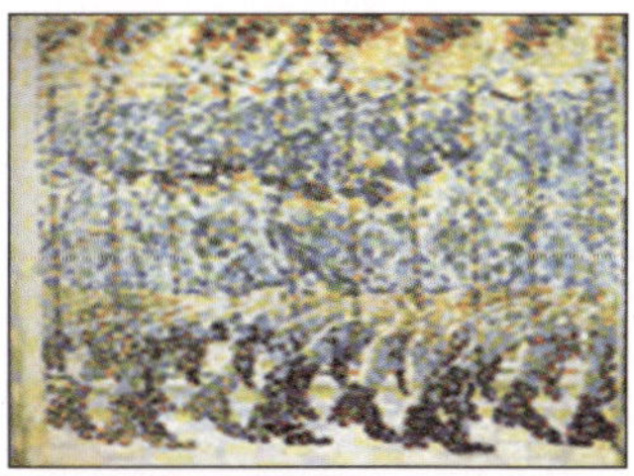

Girl Running on a Balcony, Giacomo Balla, 1912

Umberto Boccioni (1882–1916)

Born in Calabria, Boccioni was one of the signatories of the Manifesto of Futurist Painters. He strongly affirms the need to destroy the worship of the ancient past of academic formalism, the need to eliminate the artistic representation of the reasons and subjects already exploited, and the need to exalt every form of originality, however daring or violent. 'Elasticity', a painting depicting the pure energy of a horse, is preserved in the National Gallery of Modern and Contemporary Art in Rome. It fully expresses the artist's reflection on the theme of movement and the environment; the shape is completely replaced by the representation of action.

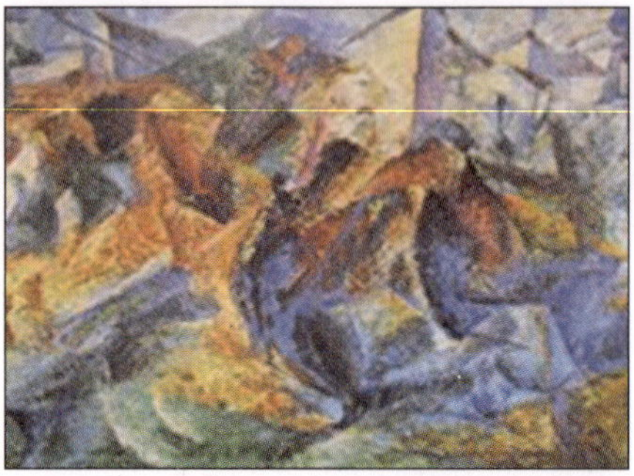

Elasticity, Umberto Boccioni, 1912

Abstraction

Abstract art was born in Monaco in 1910. Abstract art deliberately abandoned the representation of the 'reality' of things, instead pursuing the expression of particular visions of structure and forms in a free and fantastic creation of decorative and symbolic value. The creation of the abstract image, which had already been created with impressionism (which had given colour to narrative value and sensation) and the cubist manifesto (which stated a four-dimensional geometric representation of the world) was finally brought to completion. Great exponents of the style were the Swiss artist Paul Klee and Kandinsky, the Russian Vaslij, who in 1912 declared the absolute independence of artistic creation from the world of objects. The works of Paul Klee are preserved in the civic gallery of modern art and contemporary art in Turin, at the Museo de Novecento in Milan, and the International Gallery of Modern Art in Venice.

Piet Mondrian (1872–1944)

Mondrian, a Dutch painter and theorist, approached Cubism by creating a series of paintings on the theme of the tree. His work was based on the simplification and decomposition of the organic form. His abstractism became increasingly stringent in his later works, which were centred on the progressive subdivision of the plane in space and entrusted solely to lines and colours.

The works 'Composition' and 'Composition with Black, Red, Gray, Yellow and Blue' are preserved in the National Gallery of Modern and Contemporary Art in Rome.

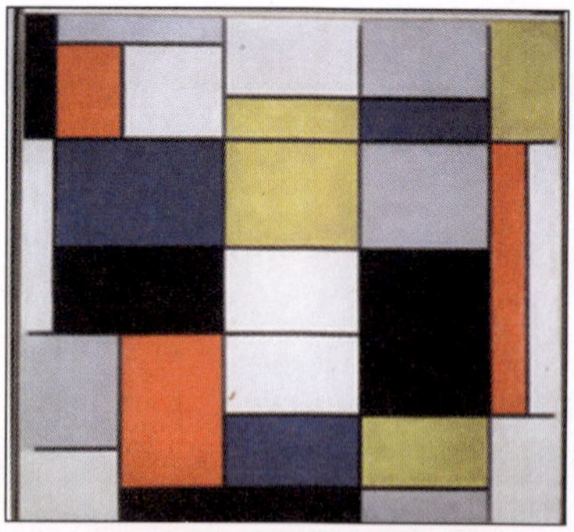

Composition with Black, Red, Gray, Yellow and Blue, Piet Mondran, 1921

Dadaism

This was a literary and artistic movement that was born simultaneously in Switzerland and America around the year 1916. Its aim was to demystify all the values created by culture using actions inspired by the ideas of primitivism, that is, rational creative spontaneity. The name 'Dadaism' came from Tristan Tzara, who found the word, which means nothing, by randomly flipping a dictionary. The philosophy of the movement was to refuse all rationality and rational motivation, and instead identify the madness and the show in artistic act.

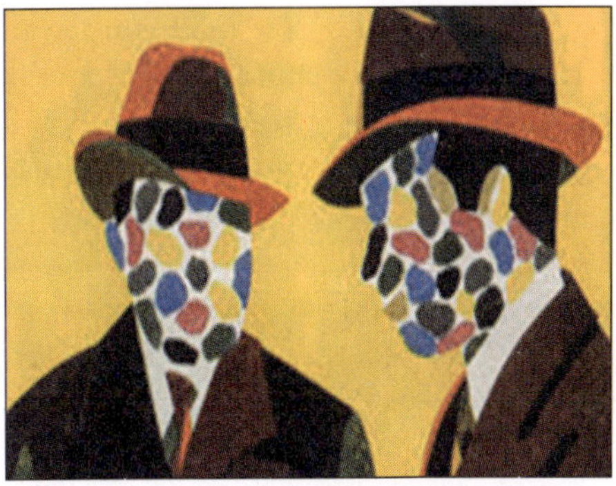

A painting from the Dadaism Era

The paintings, sculptures, collages (the French term for a technique based on the re-composition of fragments of dif erent materials on canvas using glue), and the photographic processes of Dadaism highlight the great importance attached to language as a source of creativity.

Metaphysical painting

Metaphysical painting refers to an artistic trend of the Italian twentieth century, which emerged in 1910 as a result of the production of paintings by Giorgio De Chirico. This trend would leverage the effect of surprise and suggestions raised by the immediate context, through the use of unreal and fantastic images. The setting was hugely important—a razor sharp scene without anything deformed and unrecognizable, with cool colours and tones and highly contrasting light and shade. The setting announced solitary presences: squares, towers, statues, buildings, still lifes, and small figures of men who appeared to be under a spell. Metaphysics was never a movement, but a pictorial intellectual experience.

Giorgio de Chirico (1888–1978)

Giorgio de Chirico was the author of compositions of classical taste set in large, deserted, twilight scenes made even more disturbing by the insertion of external elements—puppets and dummies. In the National Modern and Contemporary Art gallery in Rome one can admire 'Hector and Andromache' (1917) and 'The Disturbing Muses' (1925), and in the Museo de Novecento in Milan, you can admire the beautiful portrait of 'The Prodigal Son' (1922).

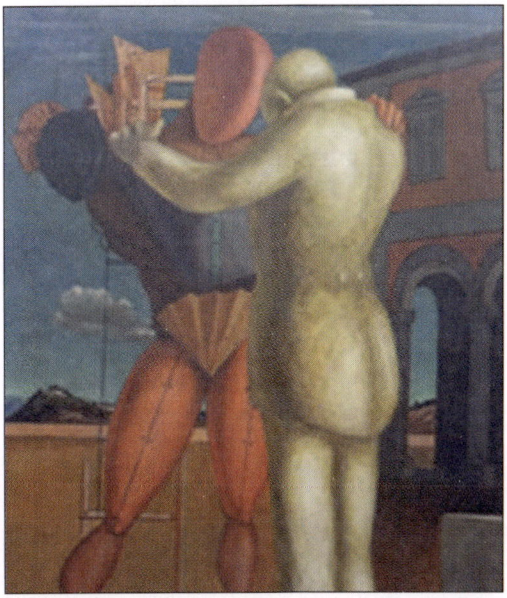

The Prodigal Son, Giorgio de Chirico, 1922

'Red Tower' and 'Piazza of Italy' are the amongst the first of de Chirico's paintings: striking because of their simplicity. Many of his paintings show architectural vision: buildings with porches, streets lonely and deserted. But his visions of reality are different to the reality which the observer understands in the paintings. The light is the actual colour of objects, the sky features unnatural colours, the shadows which contrast with the bright areas are excessively long. The perspective is almost always deliberately deformed, thus the space has an unusual appearance.

His scenes are dominated by the absence of life, the absolute silence. The atmosphere of these paintings is similar to that of a dream or a vision. 'In the Square of Italy', we see two tiny human figures in the background, and a steam train passing. At the centre, on a low pedestal, sits a statue: a statue in a square is a great thing, says de Chirico, because it represents the human form and yet is still, marble, and permanent.

'Red Tower' was the first painting sold by de Chirico. In this painting, behind a wall on the right you see an equestrian statue which is similar to those often found in Italian markets, especially in Turin. We can say that representations of de Chirico exceed the reality in the sense that they go beyond reality. The spaces and objects which come from our experience are shown to us with new aspects which surprise us, and confuse the things we know with mysteries and secrets.

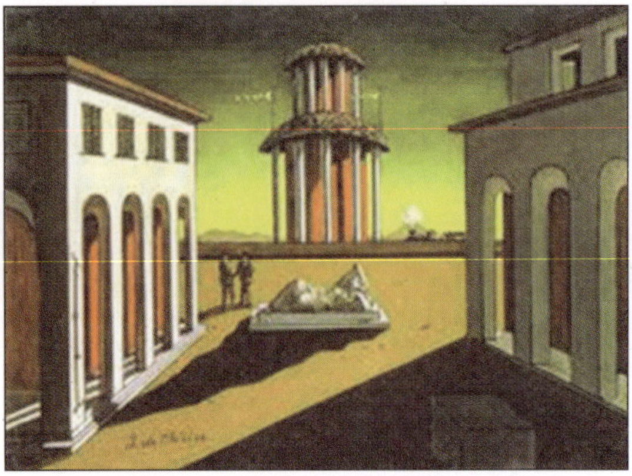

Italian Piazza, Giorgio de Chirico, 1913

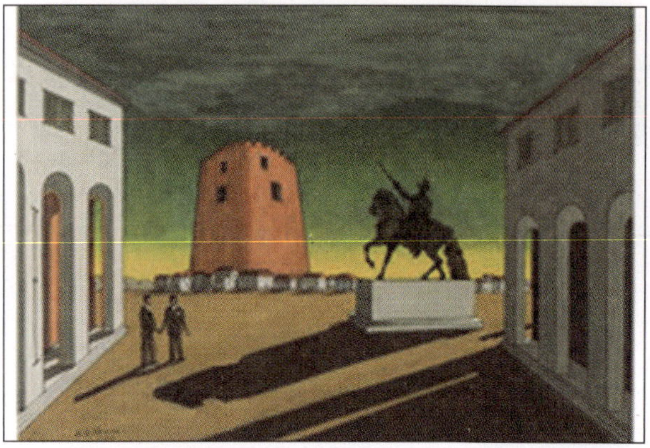

The Red Tower, Giorgio de Chirico, 1913

Surrealism

Surrealism established itself in Paris as a cultural and artistic movement with the first Surrealist Manifesto written by the poet André Breton in 1924. The term 'Surrealism' is created by Apollinaire and taken up by Breton, meaning a dream dimension beyond the real. Inspired by the principles of metaphysical painting, but mostly by the theories of Freudian psychoanalysis, the surrealists affirmed the need to express, even in the waking state, the unconscious forces of man. In the field of visual arts, the primary artists are: the Italian painter Paolo Uccello and the British artist and poet William Blake. In the mid-1920s, many painters begin to adhere to Surrealism, including Salvador Dali, who approaches the movement in 1930, but was chased, accused of pursuing private business interests. Paul Klee and Pablo Picasso both showed strong adherence to surrealist principles. Two authentic surrealist masterpieces are 'The Birth of Liquid Desires' by Salvador Dali and 'The Empire of Light' by René Magritte.

The 1800s and 1900s

L'École de Paris

This generic definition includes the names of those French artists who, without adhering to the avant-garde movement, seek inspiration in the same Parisian cultural climate from which it developed.

Amedeo Modigliani (1884–1920)

A painter and sculptor from Livorno, Modigliani had a restless character and a poetic sensibility. He settled in Paris from 1909. After creating some Cubist-inspired sculptures between 1915 and 1920, he produced a large number of paintings, mainly portraits and female nudes characterized by an extreme simplification of design and an elegant, sinuous stretching of the forms. Modigliani never retouched his paintings. Many of Modigliani's works are still in private collections, and the rest are scattered in museums around the world.

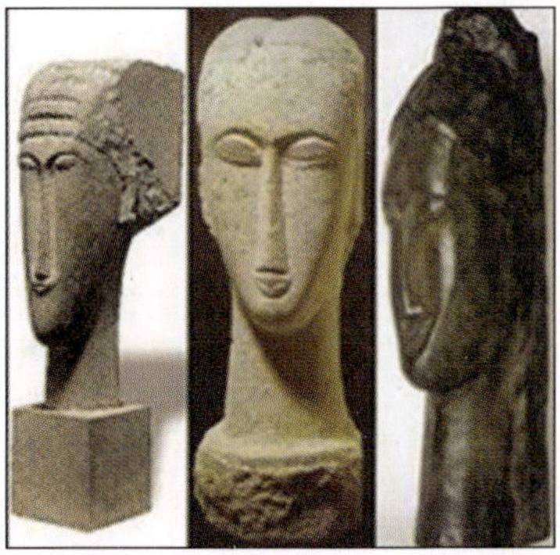

Tete, Amedeo Modigliani, 1911

According to a legend in Livorno, Modigliani threw some of his statues into a canal in the city because he was unsatisfied with the results, or perhaps in reaction to the criticism of other artists. In the summer of 1984, in a canal which crosses Livorno, three sculptures were found, depicting three heads. Famous art critics, after carrying out analysis and comparison, confidently attributed the sculptures to Modigliani. But a twist revealed that the creators of the head sculptures were in fact three students from Livorno.

As a joke, with simple masonry tools, they had made the sculptures, and at night, had thrown them into the canal. On television they showed how they had created one of the sculptures in a few minutes. The art critic Federico Zeri, on a TV show, asked the creator of the other sculptures to emerge from anonymity. A worker from the port of Livorno came forward, a passionate sculptor, who declared that his work was not a joke, but it was an artistic aesthetic to check to what extent people believed in the myths.

The echoes from this sensational story are still present; in 2004, the critic Giovanni Morandi published the essay 'Modigliani Insult', in which he raised questions about the parameters by which one defines an object as 'art'. According to Morandi, the episode reveals deception, because during the period of the discovery of the statues, Modigliani's daughter received an anonymous letter in which it was revealed that the heads were false.

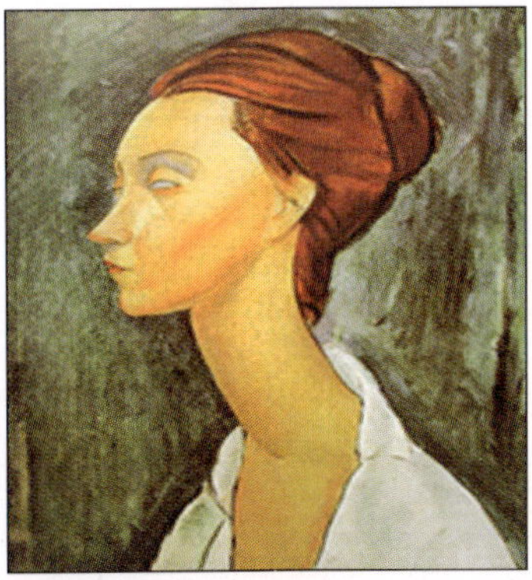

Portrait of Luna Czechovska, Amedeo Modigliani, 1919

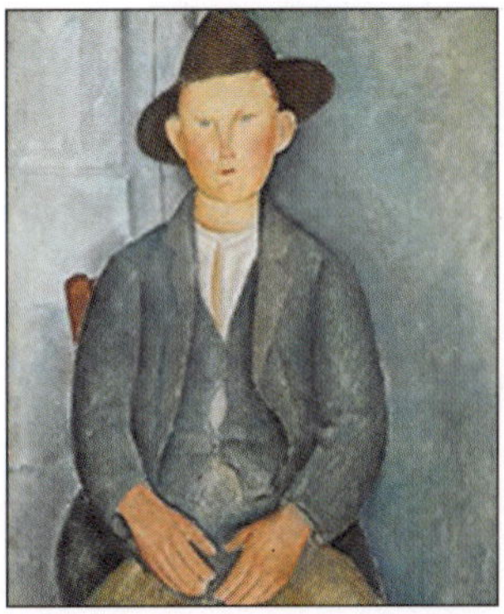

The Little Peasant, Amedeo Modigliani, 1918

Architecture in the 1900s

The industrialization of society was a driver of the mass-production and commercialization of everyday objects. This resulted in a gradual loss of a wealth of traditional skills used within the handicraft industry. For this reason, art came to be seen as something which ought to help man achieve his daily needs. On one side, the artist regained the role of craftsman, but on the other, market forces and the increasing complexity of products determined the birth of requirements for new applications of artistic fields, with particular reference to design, planning and advertising. New materials and new technologies meant that artists and designers were faced with new expressive possibilities. The foundations of modern architecture were considered to be: the technology of iron structures already adopted in the previous century, the theories of Morris and the Arts and Craft movement, and the architectural solutions of the Chicago school.

One of the most important architects during this period was Charles Eduard Jeanneret le Corbusier (1887–1965). A French town planner, architect and theorist, le Corbusier is considered the father of rationalism and one of the major architects of the modern architectural language. He was responsible for the definition of the house and the city as 'machines for living', and he also devised the Modular anthropometric scale of proportions: a design model based on average man's height. Equipped with classic sensitivity, his work delivers a crisp, volumetric architectural design based on the use of exposed concrete (but not without imaginative solutions), as in the famous 'Chapel at Ronchamp'. He was also responsible for the design of the city of Chandigarh (capital of Punjab) in India.

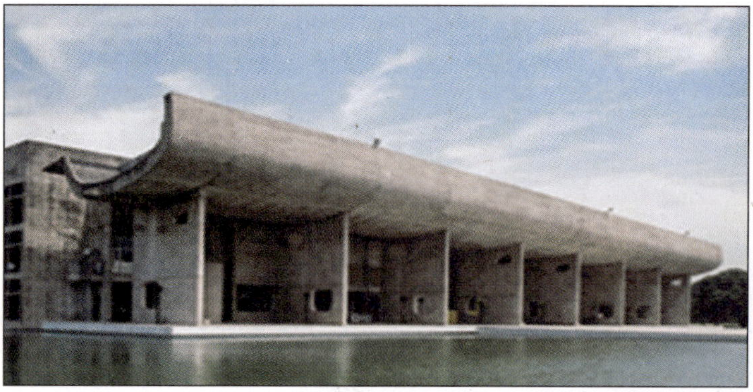

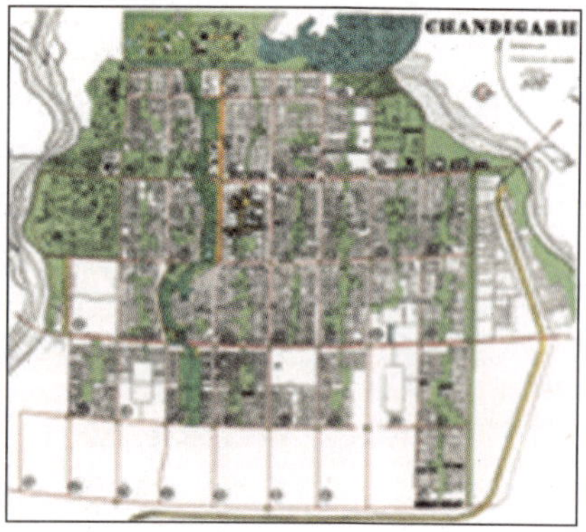

The Palace of Assembly, or The Assembly Building, is a part of the Capitol Complex, in Chandigarh, built by the Swiss-French architect Le Corbusier in the 1950s

Bauhaus

The Bauhaus school of art and crafts was founded by the architect Walter Gropius in 1919, and it became the centre of design in Germany. Taking up some of the themes of socialism, the philosophy of the Bauhaus was to bring art and design within the scope of everyday life. Gropius regarded artists and architects as craftsmen, and argued that their creations should be practical and affordable. The institute's students were painters, architects, weavers, potters, sculptors and designers, who all engaged in group activities just like the artisans of the Renaissance.

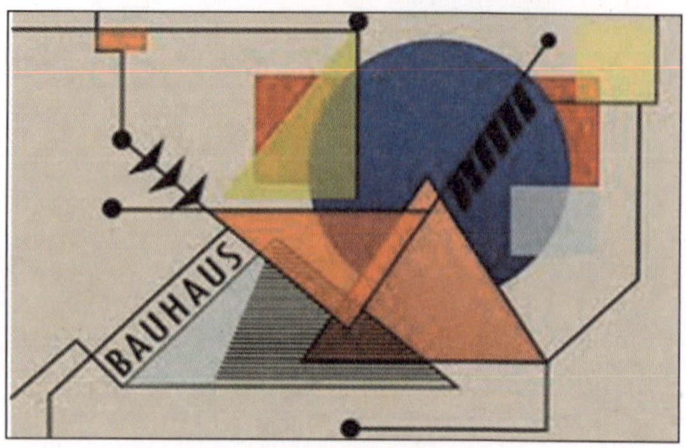

Bauhaus design

The characteristics of the Bauhaus style were:

simplicity, geometry and accuracy. In 1933, the school was closed by the Nazis under the pretence of it being a communist intellectual centre. Despite the abolition of the institute, Bauhaus spread to the rest of the world on account of the migration of many of the school's members. The Bahaus school of art was founded with the idea of creating a 'total' work of art which would include all art forms, including architecture, and these would ultimately be brought together.

Italian Landscape Painting

In the twentieth century, Italy was no longer at the centre of the cultural life of Europe. Instead, the driving forces were mainly Paris and Germany. However, in the 1950s, different Italian artists attempted to create an art fundamentally new and different, an art free from figurative constraints and based on the value of the creative act itself.

Renato Guttuso (1902–1987)

Guttuso was a Sicilian painter who moved away from informal trends and thus became the founder of social realism in Italy.

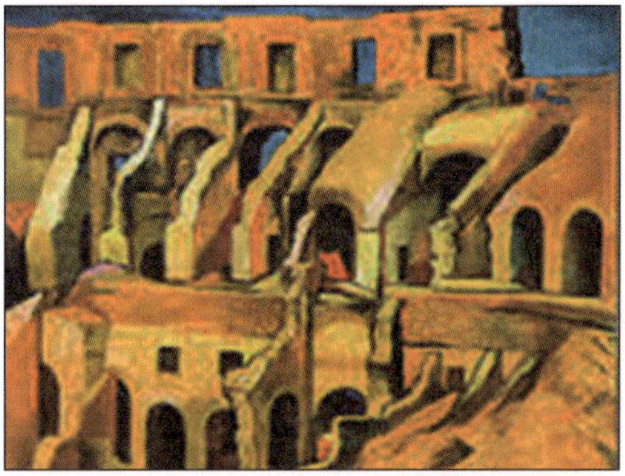

Colosseum, Renato Guttuso

Trends in Contemporary Art

'Informal' art, defined as abstract impressionism, is placed alongside Expressionism, Dadaism, and Surrealism in claiming that art is only the creative act which enhances the inherent expressive possibilities of the materials used. Moreover, by refusing the rational composition of images and considering artistic expression to be a result of chance and unconscious spontaneity, the artist must create art with a continuous attitude of experimentation. Examples can be found in the work of Piero Dorazio and writer Arnaldo: 'The Spear of Light' in Terni, 'The Traveller Column' in Spoleto, and 'Bronze Sculpture' by the seaside in Pesaro.

Art Neoconcreta

This definition refers to a current of non-figurative art, which aimed at making abstract ideas 'concrete' realities. The ideas were first theorized in 1930 by Van Doesburg, who aimed at integrating architecture, sculpture and painting using mainly geometric composition.

Neo-figurative currents

Neo-figuratism was an expressionist revival in the domain of figurative art. Painters like Francis Bacon and Henry Moore interpreted figurative elements in a modern style.

Action Painting (Gesturalism)

This term indicates a movement born in New York, characterized by the expressive, energetic brush strokes which clearly emphasize the movements of the artist. The gesture of creating the art is considered important. The term was originally used to describe the painting of the abstract expression artists, including Jackson Pollock, who was known for the technique of 'dripping' (a particular painting technique which consists of pouring colour drops on the canvas directly from a tube or jar without a brush).

New Dada

This was an American movement presented in New York in 1959 by Rauschenberg and Jhons. It marked the point of transition between abstract expressionism and pop art.

Pop-Art

Pop-art was a major Anglo-American artistic movement of the 1950s. In relation to the subjectivism of abstract expressionism (a movement which ran parallel to the war), Pop-art directed its interest to the images of popular culture drawn from everyday urban life, the mass media, comics, advertising, and industrial objects. The technique took its cue from the neutrality of objects used and consumed daily. The trival was magnified; toothpaste tubes and clothes pegs turned into sculptures, light switches and typewriters were created in soft material.

Andy Warhol (1928–1987)

Warhol painted celebrities like Elvis Presley and Marilyn Monroe, always basing his work in contemporary society. It was 1975 when the artist arrived in Naples for the first time, at the invitation of gallery owner Lucio Amelio. In the aftermath of the 1980 earthquake in Irpinia, he created a monument entitled 'Hurry', a reproduction of the front page of the morning's newspaper. The work forms part of the collection in the Caserta Royal Palace, which contains the works of many contemporary artists.

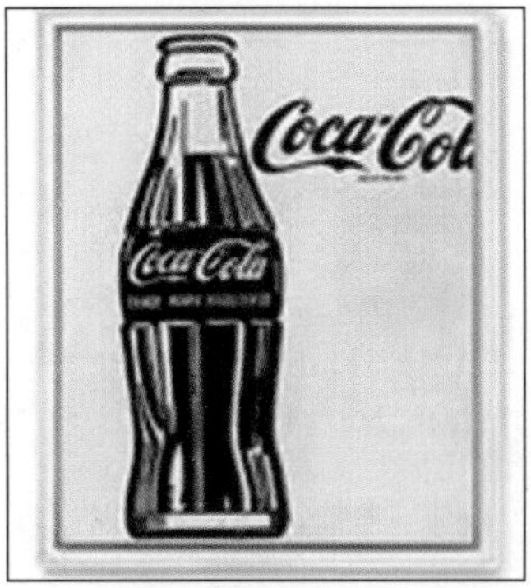

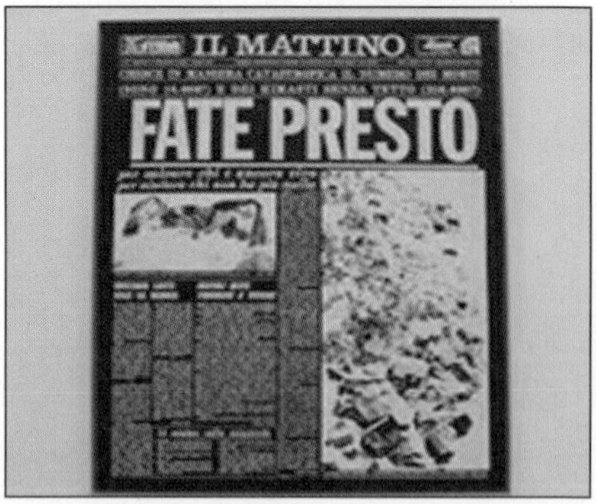
IL MATTINO

FATE PRESTO

Coca Cola, Andy Warhol, 1962. Warhol was known for work which explored artistic expression, celebrity culture, and advertising, which existed in the 1960s

Op-art

This was a movement which became established in the late 1950s, based on visual research by Moholy-Nagy. Op-art (Optical art) analysed and used various optical effects within geometric designs.

Conceptual Art

This term refers to an artistic movement developed during the 1960s and 1970s, in which the concept behind the artwork takes precedence over the finished article. Conceptual artworks could be anything from performances to film to photography. A key figure in the movement was Joseph Kosuth.

Post-Modernism

This was a graphic architectural style developed in the 1980s, used to indicate a move away from modernism and a recovery of traditional styles and elements.

The Photograph, Primoli and the Belle Epoque

In this period, the Italian nobility, just like the French, are still intrigued by photography. In Rome, the prince Giulio Cesare Rospigliosi starts the trend which becomes rampant amongst the leading families. Count Giuseppe Primoli, who was friends with much of the Italian and French aristocracy, produced an extensive photographic collection which documented the refined world of European nobility during the belle epoque. The Count, with his extremely dynamic personality, travelled across Europe to portray Italian rulers during receptions, ceremonies, horseback rides and carriage rides. Primoli was not an amateur.

His taste was refined, and his technique similar to that of a modern photojournalist. He was not satisfied until he had accurately portrayed his subject: photographing it from different angles, revealing every detail, trying to render the spirit of a situation by capturing the reactions of those present. Often he was accompanied by his brother Luigi, and by a row of servants who carried his collection of cameras, his dark-room equipment, and many glass sheets. Between 1888 and 1894, he produced more than 13,000 photos. He was deeply sensitive to the reality of life, and he was interested in everything and everyone. When Buffalo Bill arrived in Rome, Primoli was there waiting for him. He also placed the curtain of the dark room next to a group of American Indians, convincing them to let themselves be photographed. His best pictures are those less known, those which represent the material poverty of the common people of Rome: peasants, shepherds and shoemakers.

In the late nineteenth century, a photographic revolution takes place (slightly delayed compared to that in other countries). At least five magazines are dedicated to photography, and more than fifteen companies are engaged in the production of cameras and photographic material. Taking photos is no longer a privilege of the nobility: clubs of amateurs become numerous, while professionals are beginning to leave the confines of their studios. The photograph is applied to medicine, psychiatry and the social survey, and Giuseppe Vittorio photographs the Alps.

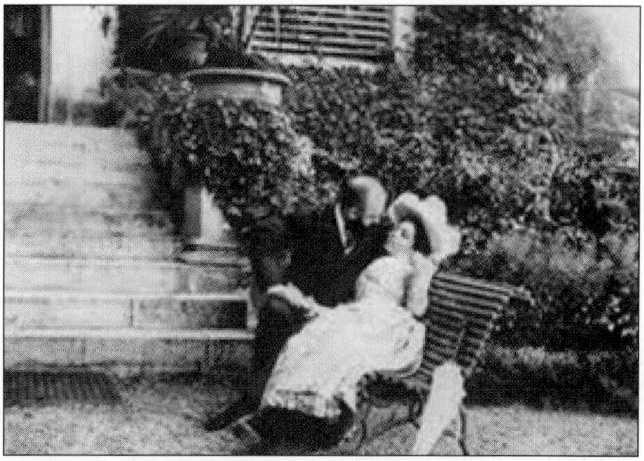

Guiseppe Primoli was an Italian nobleman and photographer, who produced over 10,000 photographs

The first congress of the Italian

photographers is convened in Turin in 1898, for first time photography is officially discussed in Italy. The second congress was held in Florence: technical photographers, scientists and scholars from all over Italy met to discuss important issues such as the possible applications of the new medium. Among the participants were Anderson from Rome and Philotheus (inventor of the kinetograph: equipment for the recovery, development and projection of film, patented in November 1895).

At the turn of the century in Italy, the tendency to realism dominated, seen in precise parallels between literature and photography. The writer Giovanni Verga, the main representative of literary realism, learned the basics of photography from Luigi Capuano and began to take pictures in Sicily. Many of Verga's images are loaded with meanings which reflect a literary atmosphere. They are technically wrong: blurred and confused, yet they convey the desire to portray the people and to represent their mood. Verga's pictures establish a strong link with French literary naturalism, whose maximum exponent is Emily Zola. Another important figure was Francesco Paolo Michetti, an Abruzzo artist of Neapolitan education, who portrayed the young peasants of his homeland in a markedly realist style. He used his photographs to create great paintings, and was influenced by the language of Gabriele D'Annunzio.

The Futurist Photodynamic

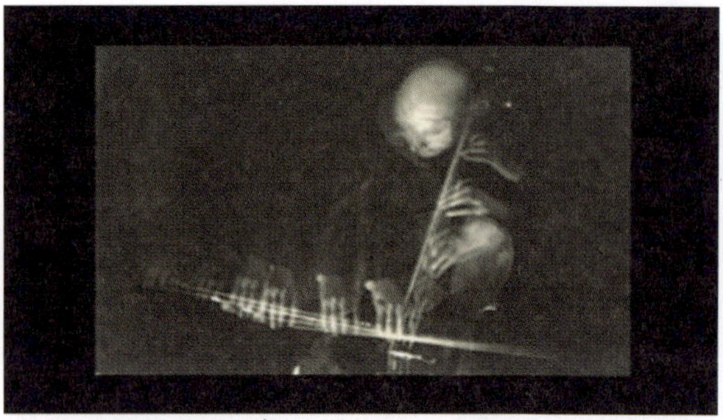

Man playing the double bass, Anton Giulio Bragaglia, 1911

In Italy, avante-guarde experimentation preceded the European avante-garde by some years, thanks to Anton Giulio Bragalia, Arturo Bragalia and Carlo Ludovico Bragaglia. The brothers, mesmerized by Futurist cinema, proposed in 1911 a hypothesis for futurist photography: photodynamism. Between 1911 and 1913, they created a series of images aimed ar representing the inner essence of things. For the first time in the history of photography, there is an interest in capturing concepts and ideals rather than portraits of figures. Physical movement is expressed by manipulating exposure times and using experimental techniques: the transition from one image to another is not shown via a series of discrete intervals, but by a trail made by the superimposition of several figures. The results of these experiments were published by Anton Giulio Bragaglia in a volume titled 'Futuristic Fotodinamismo' in 1913. Futurist photodynamism was also interesting because it represented a break from academic photography. But not all futurists appreciated the photodynamic style. This difference of opinion led to setbacks in Futurist photographic research. It was not until 11 April 1930, in the journal *Futurism*, that Marinetti released the Manifesto of Futurist photography.

Photography and the Regime

During the period of fascist rule in Italy, the photographic medium was exploited for purposes of political propaganda, war and territotial expansion. The regime relies heavily on the image: photos in all newspapers and magazines were subjected to the scrutiny of the press office of the prefectures. The Italian photographers followed a self-censoring mechanism: not because they adhered to the regime or feared retaliation, but rather to meet the demands of the newspapers which commissioned and released the images.

Key ingredients in fascist iconography were the crowds and the political authorities, photographed using standardized homogeneous techniques. The crowds which gathered to hear speeches could be recorded in two ways (depending on the effect desired). To highlight the number of people present, photographs were taken from above and from frontal and lateral locations, so that the human mass received a multiplication effect. In order to create the impression of a crowded event, it was also possible to shoot the event from the centre of the crowd, so that the viewer received the impression of being surrounded by the crowd. If the political leaders were photographed in groups, then overhead shots were used; if the leaders were photographed individually, then they were shot from below, giving the subject a heroic stature. The photograph in the fascist age was subservient to the communication needs of the regime.

In 1942, a year in which the living conditions of the Italian people was deteriorating significantly, there was a reduction in the space allowed in newspapers for photographs (a result of the war-time paper shortage). Additionally, the vetoes imposed by censorship prevented the publication of photographs of areas bombed by enemy planes without specific authorization.

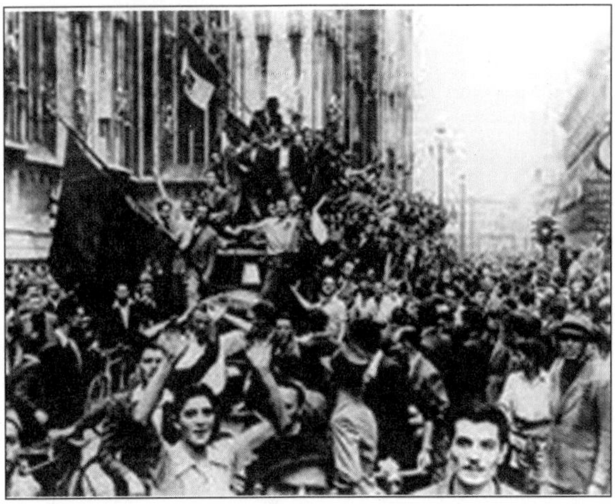

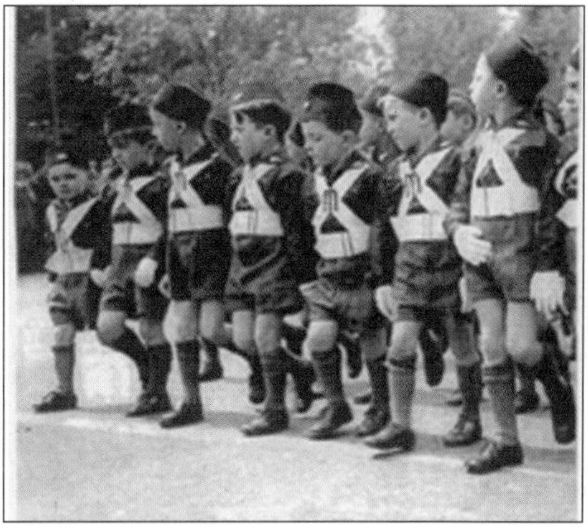

Photography was heavily used by the Fascist regime of Italy to push forward their propaganda

The Picture Story

The picture story, or tale of images, unfolds through a chronological sequence of pictures, accompanied by text in captions enclosed in clouds or square boxes. Many magazines published weekly stories of this kind. Besides romantic fiction and cartoons, the picture story took its contents from the cinema (and was distinctly melodramatic). Originally called 'cineromanzo', the frames provided didactic summaries of the plot of a film already shown in cinemas. The cineromanzo catered to a predominantly female audience which, in the absence of television, wanted to relive the movies.

In the 1930s, 'The Two Orphans' and 'Fedora' were released, and the series ended in 1974 with 'Last Tango in Paris' by Bernardo Bertolucci. The first issue of 'Grand Hotel', the title borrowed from the 1932 Hollywood film starring Greta Garbot, was released on 29 June 1946, with a story taken from the novel *Souls Chained*. 'Grand Hotel' makes use of illustrations by Walter Molino and screenplays by Julius Bertoletti. Given the success of the publication, Luciano Pedrocchi, who is active in the field of publications for children, replaces drawings with photos. Pedrocchi submits his idea to the publisher Arnoldo Mondadori, and thus 'Bolero film' was born. The success of the Bolero films and *Dream* (the new weekly magazine published by Rizzoli) also obliges Grand Hotel to replace, in 1950, drawings with photography. The photo stories always tell of thwarted love: a man or woman must overcome all sorts of obstacles before the happy ending. In a semi-literate country like Italy in the post-war period, the picture story is able to bring many people to literature.

The high revenue from the sale of soap operas is used to support cultural production of a high quality. Thanks to fotoromanzi, actors like Sofia Lazzaro (Sophia Loren) and Gina Loris (Gina Lollobrigida) make their debut, as do film and television directors like Federico Fellini. The transition from the pages of the soap operas is also made by TV presenters like Mike Bongiorno, Raffaella Carra and Pippo Baudo, and singers like Orietta Berti, Gianni Morandi, Albano and Romina Power. Fotoromanzano hagiographies of saints are also produced, alongside 'Christian Family' of 1959, and many classic Bible sories. In the 70s, the Roman publishing house Launch monopolizes the market with the most incredible stories, featuring themes such as abortion and divorce.

When televisions became widely popular, the photo series genre fell into crisis, yet the fiction offering remained large. At the end of the 1990s, monthly sales of titles from Launch were around half million; the year 2000 opens with the free distribution of a few pages of 'An Enemy to Win', starring television presenters Tiberius Timperi and Roberta Capua, a former Miss Italy. The story was created by the Minister of Health (in collaboration with some grand hotels) to help fight AIDS. It was distributed on newsstands on 29 October 1999, and published as a brochure at clinics and hospitals. Meanwhile, the soap operas were prepared for launch on the Internet.

Recent Trends

After the Second World War in Italy, some photographers joined forces to do research on the role and characteristics of the photographic language. Two opposing circles were born in Venice in 1947. 'The Compass' interprets the art of photography as an end in itself, distinct from practical implication. In the group's manifesto, published in the journal *Serrania*, the authors write of their intention to remove the photograph that has pretensions of art from the dead end of the documentary record. In contrast, the group 'La Gondola', led by Paolo Monti, follows an avante-guarde style in line with neorealist conceptions.

Music

For years, official culture had nurtured a strong prejudice against the song, which had wrongly been considered a minor genre. This was due to the narrowness of views found in academic circles, which still persist in identifying the subaltern culture with a kind of inferior culture. It was not that the song is strictly identified with having popular roots. In the sixteenth and seventeenth centuries, songs were written by some of the most authoritative representatives of the official culture. However, it was the profane compositions, predominantly concerning amorous themes, which were not valued in the culture of the time.

Although the song was not lacking famous authors and different styles of music, in Italy it always lacked a capillary diffusion circuit as happened in France and in the Latin American countries. As for the supposed 'poverty' of the musical song, it was necessary to clear up certain misunderstandings; the bare essence of music in a song is the result of a synthesis, a skimming off of all those elements which overly complicate the shape. The music in a song serves to enhance the text and its inherent musicality.

History of Music

Inspired by the events in Berkeley (California) in May of 1968, France became the high point of the student revolt. Even in Italy, the phenomenon of student protest was widespread. Alongside these student movements, there was a growing armed rebellion in Germany (the rote armee), and in Italy (with the Red Brigades), the rebellion assumed violent forms. This changed the lives of hundreds of people who became engaged in leftist parties. The most famous victim of the attacks was Aldo Moro, the leader of the Christian Democrats who had proposed a government also supported by the Communist party. The day the government was sworn in, in 1978, Moro was kidnapped, and fifty-five days later, his body was found in a car parked a few metres from the offices of the DC and the PCI.

Italian popular music experienced huge commercial success in the late 50s and early 60s, and even today it continues to enjoy considerable popularity. The main features of this movement are: the stylistic refinement of the text, which becomes the true strength of the song, the use of minimalist music to emphasize the feelings and emotions conveyed by the words, and the importance of the interpretation of the singer.

The songwriters are able to express very different stylistic experiences between them, but all are attentive to the values of the text. The works served to counter and correct the tradition of Italian song as being based on common places, on the longing of a person for a country far away, or on conventional figures such as the beloved mother and the cruel mistress. The first official fracture, so to speak, with the ways and traditional content of the Italian song came in 1958, when Cantatore Domenico Modugno won the Sanremo festival with the famous song 'In the Blue Painted Blue', commonly known by the title of ' To Fly'. The success of this song was due to the unusual and evocative text, and the music which was totally new compared to melodic clichés of traditional Italian song.

Modugno's success clearly showed that tastes had changed. No more trivial texts and sentimental melodies, but instead the words made reference to the new reality, the singers were freer and more attentive to the suggestions of the music, and the rhythms were inspired by jazz and American rock. During the 60s, the songwriters, following the path laid by Modugno, offered the public songs which spoke of a reality full of contradictions, imaginative situations, often surreal. With the change of the contents also came a change of form. This meant that the different songs had a blending of linguistic registers, ranging from the high to the vulgar.

Important figures included the members of the so-called Genoese school: Gino Paoli and Fabrizio de Andrè, and the French singers Brassens, Trenet and Ferre. The shared model did not prevent the members of this school to speak with their own originality. For example, the songs of Francesco de Andrè mostly condemned the war, denounced the bourgeois hypocrisy, and enacted stories of passion in which the theme of love was intertwined with social themes. Alongside the Genoese, we must also mention the Milanese (like Giorgio Gaber), who in their songs often resorted to irony and an acting style which made them more like artistic cabaret performers than singers.

What was remarkable was their civic stance, which saw them fighting for human rights alongside the Nobel laureate Dario Fo and the famous theatre director Giorgio Strehler. In the late 60s and early 70s, in the midst of a general climate of student protest, the songwriters assumed even more evident tones of civil and political protest. In those same years, a young musician called Lucio Battisti, emerged on the scene. His music returned to more familiar themes such as love. Other key figures include: Roberto Vecchioni, Francesco de gregori, Lucio, Claudio Baglioni, Antonello Venditti, Cocciante, and those who are considered the stars of Italian rock: Francesco Battiato and Edward Jackson. In the 1980s and 1990s, singers like Paolo Conte combined lyrics with music arising from jazz and South American rhythms, Pino Daniele created songs in which he united his passion for the blues and his great love for the Neapolitan debate, and the new Rock is produced by Vasco Rossi and Luciano Ligabue.

Francesco de Andrè: via del campo

Via del Campo c'è una graziosa
gli occhi grandi color di foglia
tutta notte sta sulla soglia
vende a tutti la stessa rosa.

Via del Campo c'è una bambina
con le labbra color rugiada
gli occhi grigi come la strada
nascon fiori dove cammina.

Via del Campo c'è una puttana
gli occhi grandi color di foglia
se di amarla ti vien la voglia
basta prenderla per la mano

e ti sembra di andar lontano
lei ti guarda con un sorriso
non credevi che il paradiso
fosse solo lì al primo piano.

Via del Campo ci va un illuso
a pregarla di maritare
a vederla salir le scale
fino a quando il balcone ha chiuso.

Ama e ridi se amor risponde
piangi forte se non ti sente
dai diamanti non nasce niente
dal letame nascono i fior
dai diamanti non nasce niente
dal letame nascono i fior.

Via del Campo there is a pretty one
big leaf-coloured eyes
all night stands on the threshold
sells the same roses to everyone.

Via del Campo there is a girl
with dew-coloured lips
gray eyes like the road
flowers hide where she walks.

Via del Campo there is a whore
big leaf-coloured eyes
if you want to love it
just take it by the hand

and you Seem to go to
she looks at you with a smile
you did not believe That paradise
it was only there on the first floor.

Via del Campo there is an illusion
to beg her to marry
see her climbing the stairs
until the balcony has closed.

Love and laugh if love answers
cry out loud if you do not hear
Nothing is born from diamonds

The flowers are born from the manure
Nothing is born from diamonds
The flowers are born from the manure

The Genoese School

The style of the French song certainly influenced the school of authors defined as the Genoese school (created by Gino Paoli). The element which bound all these authors to the French songs was two-fold: on the one hand they favoured the dissemination of their works in circuits unrelated to the mainstream media, and on the other they selected themes which ranged from daily life to political commitment to reflections on love, freedom, and the hopes and frustrations of the time. Sounds from across the Mediterranean were combined in suggestive and expressive models.

However, the French atmosphere was not the only source of inspiration for the Italian song. The work of American songwriters like Bob Dylan were used as the starting point for sensitive and refined authors such as Francesco Guccini and Francesco de Gregori. Even in the work of American jazz born artists (such as Paolo Conte), one could find all the nuances of the sweet melancholy of certain Italian provinces, a representation of nostalgia for a lost world.

The Return of the Minstrel

A character who was 'typical' in the panorama of Italian song was Angel Branduardi, whose music was inspired largely by the compositions and expressive forms of the Renaissance and early Baroque periods. The themes he chose had the character of timelessness, and his music was strengthened by the poetry of the lyrics which evoked a refined, fairy-tale atmosphere. The songs of Branduardi were not tied to current events, but referred to tradition and the spirit of minstrels: telling of love, death and disenchantment.

Neapolitan Music

Featuring traditional folk percussion musical instruments such as the putipu, this form is often combined with dance, music and drama. Popular musical instruments used in this kind of music include the tambourine, triccaballacca and the mandolin.

History of Italian Cinema

After the artistic repression of the fascist period, Italian art took two paths. One aimed to revive the logic of socialist realism in Italy, basing it it cinematic neorealism, whereas the other tended towards abstract art. Some artists of the 50s and 60s were original, as in the case of spatialism, but others moved closer to American art, for example, using the dripping techniques popularized by Pollock. The main place for the modern Italian art exhibition was the Venice Biennale, which held a world exhibition of art, as well as performances of modern theatre and dance, architectural displays, and also films (the famous Venice film Festival in September was perhaps the most famous international festival of quality cinema).

The film is rightly a key part of twentieth-century culture. According to some, the film was as important in the twentieth century as the narrative was in the nineteenth century. There is no denying that the standards of the film (the editing, narrative techniques, framing, soundtrack, etc.) were established by US cinema. The main differences between Italian cinema and American cinema is definitely the fact that Italian cinema is spoken in Italian, and so is barely understandable by foreigners in the original version, yet rarely dubbed in a foreign language. This has meant that few Italian films left the screens of the country. If they were to become famous abroad, the viewer was required to read the subtitles, and therefore would get distracted and not fully enjoy the acting.

Only one among the great Italian directors, Sergio Leone, used English in his movies. This was in a series of 'spaghetti westerns' produced in the 60s. His masterpiece was *Once upon a Time in America.* The second characteristic of Italian cinema was a tendency to favour the director-artist, who wants to express his vision of the world or play with the shape of the film, rather than the craftsman-director, a good professional who is attentive to the collections as well as to what he has to say. Aware of this peculiarity, the state intervened to support Italian cinema with 'film quality contributions', where quality was determined on the basis of reading the script. This led the filmmakers to feel less and less dependent on the public and more and more intent on pursuing their ideas, almost writing poems instead of thinking about entertaining the people who pay to go see a movie. This caused the death of Italian cinema (except for a few happy cases) and a widespread lack of interest amongst the spectators, who now only go to see American films.

The films of the early decades of the century are not worth mentioning, because during this period artistic pursuits such as cinema were severely restricted by the fascist regime. However, during the war and in the following fifteen years, the great lessons of Italian realism resulted in the production of many good-quality films. These included: the first films of Luchino Visconti (*Obsession* in 1943 and *The Ground Shakes* in 1948), Di Federico Fellini's *The Bulls* in 1953 (which launched one of the greatest Italian actors, Alberto Sordi), Roberto Rossellini's *Open City* in 1945, Vittorio De Sica's *Bicycle Thieves* in 1949 and *Miracle in Milan* in 1951, and the great Pier Paolo Pasolini's *Beggar* in 1961 and *Mamma Roma* in 1962. The films are usually shot in black and white, and focus on the stories of the last moments of the war, the poor people, and the metropolises which are exploding.

In the 1960s, cinematic production began to take two opposite roads. The experimental trend was more prestigious, and had the greatest champions. Federico Fellini, after the famous neorealist *The Sweet Life* of 1960, began working on a film based on the dream, displaying a total disregard for the reality of the story and preferring to base the scenes on the visions of his characters (who were often played by Marcello Mastroianni). Example of such films are *8 1/2* (1963), *Rome* (1972), *Amarcord* (1974) and *The Voice of the Moon* (1990). Pier Paolo Pasolini often creates his movies through rewriting the stories of classic myths, such as *Oedipus Rex* (1967), and *Medea* (1970), or the great medieval narrative cycles drawn from an age when men had not yet been ruined by Borghese logic, and when life was natural and free, despite the miseries of those centuries.

Another trend was the combination of the comic and bitter; in Italy, this took the form of a denouncement of the evils of the economic boom, internal emigration, and the mechanization of society. An example of this trend include Dino Risi's *Overtaking* (1962), and all the films of Alberto Sordi. These movies often feature the typical Italian character of those times: the poor guy who tries to succeed using desperate cunning. These films have tenuous cinematic value and are made by talented amateurs, but they do not compare favourably with the pace of American films. International awards are won by the Giuseppe Tornatore film, *New Heaven* (1988), Roberto Benigni's *Life Is Beautiful* (1997). Many of the films of this era are wonderful, worthy of being remembered in film history, but they remain brilliant works of talented amateurs, who occasionally manage to put together their poetry and their complaints with their own cinematic language.

More Details

In 1911, Milano Films created the first Italian feature film: 250 metres of film for a great and accurate historical reconstruction of the capture of Rome. Around 1906, film production began to be organized industrially, and by 1907, Cines and Ambrosio had produced several feature films. The historical genre was designed to impress the audience, with lavish costumes and reconstructions of cities, and it dominated the international market. In the spring of 1914, *Cabiria* was shown in the theatres of Turin, Rome and Milan. It was produced by 'Itala' films of John Pastrone, who wrote and directed by under the pseudonym Piero Fosco; although the film was credited to the great poet Gabriele D'Annunzio, D'Annunzio merely reviewed the captions and changed the names of some characters. Alongside the historical genre, many films were produced based on bourgeois novels, featuring new stars like Francesca Bertini and Leda Gys. With these actresses came the idea of 'stardom', a phenomenon whereby the public is not interested in the film itself, but in the physical presence of its protagonist. Stardom is one of the new features of cinematic art: the film actor becomes important not only as an interpreter, but as the raw material through which the film is made. The advent of sound technology sends all cinemas and production houses into crisis, including the Italian. The facilities had to be radically changed, and the expense marked the end of many small factories based in Naples (which had already been harassed by the censorship regime). From 1928, all production activities came to be focused in Rome.

The Cinema of the Fascist Period

The arrival of the Fascist regime gave greater impetus to the recovery of national cinema. Laws prohibited the circulation of films in foreign languages. The regime realized that cinema could be a powerful weapon. In Italy, over a span of thirty years, a regime style of cinema developed. The censors paid attention to stories that were brought to the screen, requiring actors and authors, but mainly the regime exploited the medium of film to aid their expansionist policy and propaganda campaign. In 1924, for the purpose of 'syndicated film education', 'the Educational Union Film (Light)' is set up, which, in 1925, turns into 'National Institute of Light' and, in 1937, finds its permanent location in a new construction near Cinecittà in an experimental centre. In 1932, the Venice Film Festival is founded here, an international exhibition. Through this series of initiatives, and with the foundation of Cinecittà, Mussolini decreed the birth of a state cinematography. But, at the same time, the private film industry was developing with Sandro Pallavicini.

Toto

Antonio De Curtis, who often went by his stage name, Totò, was born in Naples in 1898 and died in Rome in 1967. He was an extremely popular comedian, as well as being a singer, actor and songwriter. Between 1920 and 1925, he performed as a disjointed puppet; between 1928 and 1932, he acted with several theatre companies, and from 1933, he acted in and managed his own theatre company. Between 1941 and 1949, he produced many succesful magazines, often collaborating with Anna Magnani. He won the favour of the cinema audiences, and in the late 40s, produced a series of farces with plenty of room to showcase his unparalleled ability to improvise in front of the camera. He was the protagonist of over 100 films. In 1952, he acts in *Toto in Colour*: the first Italian film in colour, produced by Dino de Laurentiis.

Hugely popular in the 1930s were the Telefoni Bianchi films ('white telephone', so called because the sets would usually feature expensive white art-deco phones). They were socially conservative, facist-regime-approved comedies about wealthy bourgeois families. The characters had cars, small appliances, modern furniture and fashionable clothes. But the 'ministry of popular culture' (the 'Minculpop') prefered movies which told of the glorious past of Italy, the military victories of Italian armed forces, the new colonialist effort, and the drama of immigration. They promote titles like *Black Shirt* by Joachim Force, *Squadron White* by Augusto Genina, or *Scipio Africanus* by Carmine gallon.

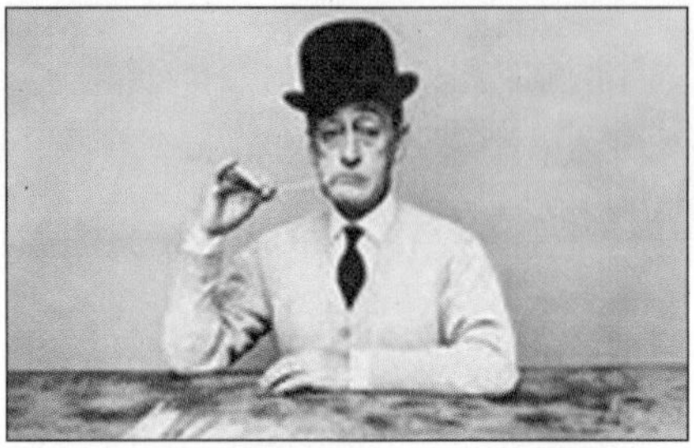

Antoni de Curtis, also known as Toto

The film exhibition in Venice, paused following the outbreak of World War II, is resumed in 1946. However, during this period, cinema does not stop. In the early 1940s, the formalistic trend is born; the films are distinguished by their formal refinement and expression, and are derived mostly from literary works. This period also marks the directorial debut of future masters of neo-realism: De Sica (1901–1974), who had already directed the Telefoni Bianchi film *Two Dozen Scarlet Roses* in 1940, and Roberto Rossellini (1906–1977), who produced *Man of Cross* in 1943.

The International Film Festival of Venice was set up in 1932, after an agreement between the International Biennale art exhibition in Venice and the International Institute for Educational Cinematography. The main aim was to show the real value of cinematography as a means of expression in the artistic field, alongside the promotion of knowledge and understanding amongst peoples. The first edition, called 'Film Biennale', took place between the 6 and 21 August 1932. In 1934, prizes were awarded for the first time, judged by a panel of experts and by popular referendum. Initially, it occured every two years, but in 1935, after a government decree, the event became annual. The international jury still mainly comprised Italians, and Italians are assigned four of the eleven prizes.

In 1936, the exhibition is given a new home in a specially built complex, the 'lido of Venice'. The French, British and American delegates protest, following the distribution of the Mussolini Cup prizes to the documentary *Olympia* (German) and to a movie made by Vittorio Mussolini (son of Benito). The most vigorous protest came from the French, who present their government with a petition for the establishment of an alternative film festival to counteract the Venice exhibition, which they saw to be a clear expression of Italy's fascist regime. This came to be in 1939: The Cannes International Festival of Film.

Cinecittà, a large film studio in Rome, was created by the fascist regime as part of a mission to limit the Hollywood movie industry and take control of all activities of the national cinema. On 9 January 1936, Benito Mussolini laid the first stone of the complex, which is located about 7 kilometres from the centre of the capital. Cinecittà was built in just 475 days by Charles Roncoroni, and designed by the architect Gino Peressutti. Mussolini inaugurated the completed construction on 27 April 1937. It housed 16 studios, 14 of which were used for normal production, and two for special processing. It offered technical services, a swimming pool with an aquatic dinner, three restaurants, and executive and administrative offices. Not only the workers, but also all technicians and operators were on fixed salaries: a total of 900 people.

In January 1944, the Cinecittà Studios suffered damaging bombing, and then the studios were occupied by German troops before being abandoned when the Allies entered Rome on 4 June of that year. The Allied command took possession of Cinecitta and used it as a refugee camp. In 1947, it was finally restored. After the war, the building rules change, at the expense of the film industry. The city of Rome expands into the suburbs, and in 1949, a new law designates 150 hectares of the Cinecittà grounds for the construction of new buildings to use as civilian homes.

Neorealism

In the summer of 1943, the Cinecittà plants were emptied of technical equipment and furniture during the German occupation. Italian cinema, now devoid of technical and financial resources, turned to a neorealist, documentary style. However, unlike the documentary genre, which simply records reality, the neorealist documentary alters reality through fiction. The neo-realist film does not want to simply tell a story, but it is intended as a document which leaves a testimony. The movement expresses naturalism and a strong social consciousness, choosing to represent reality not only in the simplest way but also in a critical way. Owing to pre-war censorship, it had previously been impossible for Italian cinema to criticize the conditions of life of the ordinary people.

In this period, it becomes possible to exploit the poverty of means and transform it into expressive capacity. Unable to use the soundstages and studios, producers turned to the streets. A theorist of the movement was Cesare Zavattini, former writer of realistic films for the two directors critics considered the forerunners of neorealism: Alessandro Blasetti and Carmine Gallone. Both the *1860* (Alessandro Blasetti, 1933) and the *Scipione l'Africano* (Carmine Gallone, 1937) using historical costume, promoted more or less openly the main arguments of the official propaganda. Both films are examples of how national identity was shaped in the country, which at the time was only seventy years old.

A prototype of the so-called Italian realism genre was *1860* by Alessandro Blasetti, a 1933 costume drama about the life of Garibaldi in Sicily, inspired by the literary realism of Giovanni Verga. Also significant was *Obsessed* by Luchino Visconti (1943), which marked a key step towards the formation of new Italian cinema. Realism was born with *Open City*, a film directed by Roberto Rossellini in 1945. The initial idea involved the creation of a documentary about Don Luigi Morosini, a Roman priest executed by the Nazis during the occupation; however, eventually it turned into a history of the Roman people under German occupation.

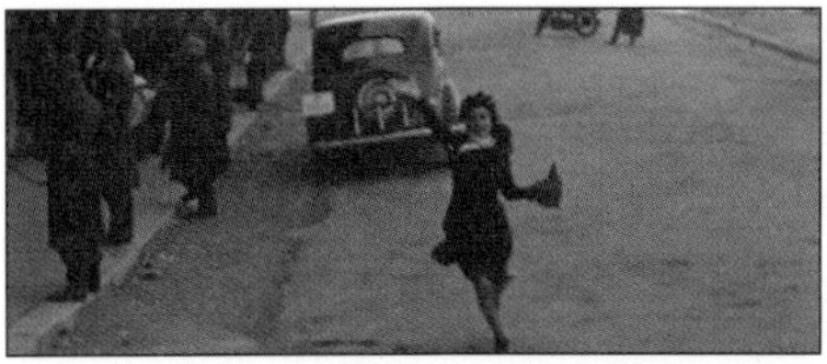

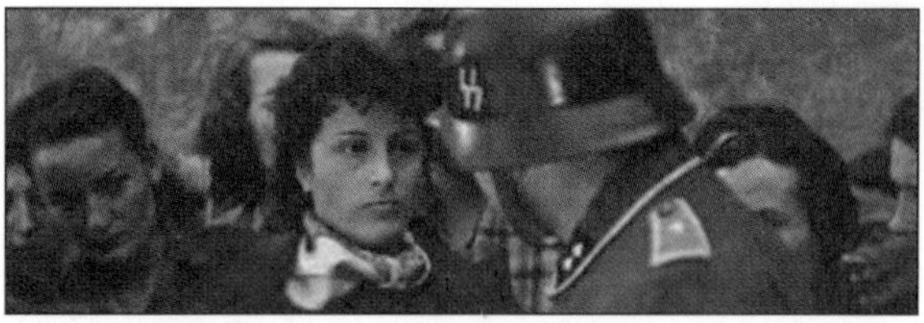

A shot from Roberto Rossellini's war trilogy Paisan made in 1946 (top-left), another shot from the same movie (top-right)

Paisan (1946), another Rossellini film, was based on the suffering endured by the Italians after the liberation. Vittorio De Sica established an artistic partnership with Zavattini, which led to the movies *The Children Are Watching Us* (1943), *Shoeshine* (1946) *Bicycle Thief* (1948) and *Miracle in Milan* (1951).

Despite its lack of means, Italian neorealist cinema reached international fame and exerted considerable influence abroad. However, the audiences preferred the melodramatic tones of 'popular neorealism', or the comedies of 'pink neorealism'. These years gave rise to a typical contrast in Italian cinema: on the one hand the internationally favoured neorealism, which included a long series of films telling realistic stories through the medium of film, whilst on the other hand the very minor strands, only popular domestically

Around 1904, the young Neapolitan Gustavo Lombardo (1885–1951) decided to found a film production company, Titanus.

Popular Melodrama

Until 1949, Titanus had to restrict itself in the distribution of its film production, blocked by the outbreak of World War II. After the resounding success of *Chains* (Raffaello Matarazzo, 1949) the productive activity of the company is increased, and this marked the advent of the melodramatic genre. Although the company tried to focus on the neorealist genre *Roma, 11.00*, produced by Giuseppe De Santis in 1951 was inspired by a true story), this resulted in commercial failure. So, the company returned to the melodramatic genre of so-called 'popular neorealism' with a series of films directed by Matarazzo. After popular neorealism came pink neorealism, which opened with the series *Bread, Love and Dreams* by Luigi Comencini in 1953, cashing in record numbers. Titanus also undertook the publishing of the musical scores of the films it produced.

In the mid-50s it tightened production agreements with foreign companies (particularly French and Spanish-Americans), than with other Italian film houses. In 1963, despite being the first Italian film distribution company with a list of important titles like the *Leopard* and *Monsters*, Titanus is forced to announce the suspension of production. The company had to focus only on the distribution of movies, and yield financial control to Edison, the main company in the Italian electricity sector. The gradual recovery of Titanus coincided, in the 70s, with a general crisis in the Italian television system. Titanus became the first film company to work with state television for the creation of fiction.

Hollywood on the Tiber

Until 1947, Cinecitta is a huge refugee camp. After 1948, the facilities were refurbished to enable the production of foreign films. Rome in the early 1950s became the Mecca of cinema: Cinecittà was dubbed the Hollywood on the Tiber. The Neapolitan producer Dino de Laurentiis produced films which demanded international attention. The films shot in the capital included *Roman Holiday* in 1953. The sets built for the American giants were recycled for Italian companies at low cost. Among them were a line of successful historical-mythological genre films with Hercules or strongman protagonists. The 50s saw the rise of Italian comedy, a direct descendant of pink neorealism, a pure entertainment genre which became a constant in the national film production. A major contribution to Italian comedy came from comic actors such as Alberto Sordi.

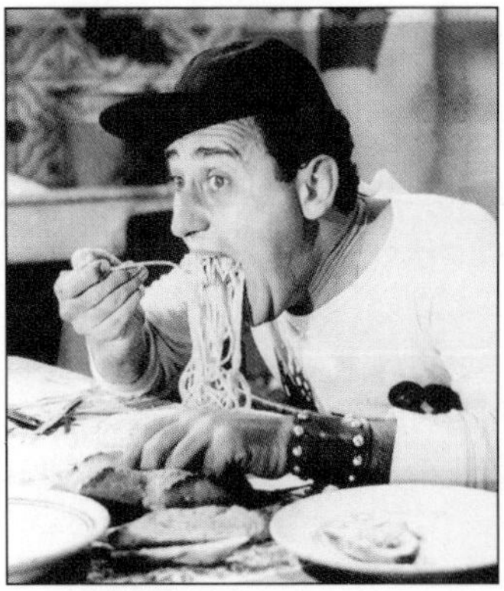

An American in Rome, Alberto Sordi

In the 60s, Rossellini dedicated himself to television production, whilst Fellini began to observe daily life from a very personal point of view and created films with surreal polemical hints (*8 1/2* in 1964, *Amarcord* in 1975, *Casanova* in 1976, and *Conductor* in 1979). Luchino Visconti's reputation precedes him, and it is slightly terrifying; his relatively small filmography spans divergent impulses that can seem so unbridgeable as to be self-contradictory. As an auteur, he rose to prominence as part of the Italian neorealist movement, alongside contemporaries Roberto Rossellini and Vittorio De Sica, but become most famous for wildly decadent, brocaded period melodramas, often so theatrical as to be operatic and sometimes so stately as to be stultifying. Vacconti made a series of period films, in which he managed to combine realism with the rigista opera experience, such as *Ocelot*. Bernardo Bertolucci was influenced by new trends of foreign cinema such as the French *Nouvelle Vague*. But Italian cinema was characterized by the presence of individual artistic personalities, including Pier Paolo Pasolini, who entered the domain of screen writing with *Matthew* in 1964.

In Italy, film production and distribution took refuge in the lucrative domestic comedy industry. Unlike the rest of Europe, in Italy, the relationship between cities and television relied solely on capital investment plans. Excluding some quality products made by Radio Audizioni Italiane (RAI) in the years 1960–70, the results are uneven because of the growing competition between public and private television broadcasting. A law of 1965 required the state to contribute public money to the production of quality films, giving funding grants or facilitating subsidized bank loans. In the 70s, the film industry survived on the proceeds of smaller productions, like the pornographic genre or spaghetti westerns.

In the 80s, the market became particularly sensitive to the needs of the cassette. This led to the inauguration of a line of Christmas movies, so-called cinepanettoni, acted by TV personalities and distributed in theatres during the holiday season. Most of Cinecittà was now home to the television studios of RAI and Mediaset. The only significant production comes from the latest works of Federico Fellini. Several Italian films received Oscars during these years: Bertolucci (Best Director and Best Foreign Film in 1988 for *The Last Emperor*), and Benigni (Best Foreign Film and Best Actor for *Life Is Beautiful* in 1999). Oscars for Best Foreign Film are also given to *New Heaven* by Tornatore (1990) and *The Great Beauty of Sorrento* in 2014.

During the 1960s, Italian musicals and westerns became very popular: so-called spaghetti westerns. Manufactured at low cost, musicals transformed singers into actors. Several Italian films are made in which actors recite and sing, taken from the popular San Remo Festival, giving rise to 'singing under the stars'. The directors and the actors from spaghetti westerns, in order not to jeopardize their careers, often adopt Anglo-Saxon pseudonyms. For example, Sergio Leone, with the pseudonym Bob Robertson, produced *For a Fistful of Dollars* (1964), *The Good, The Bad and The Ugly* (1966), and *Once upon a Time the West* (1968).

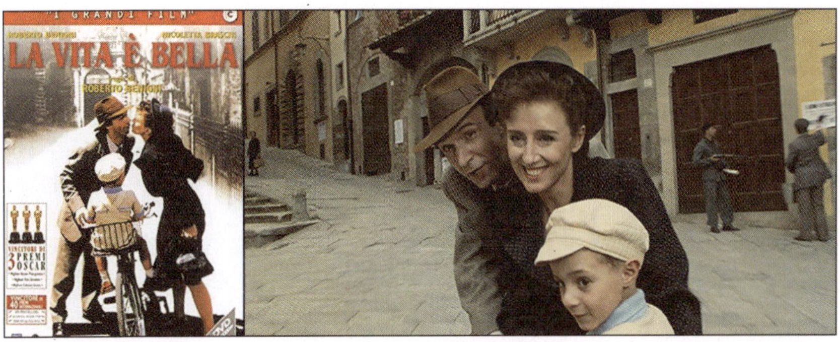

Poster of Roberto Benigni's awarded movie La Vita E Bella (Life Is Beautiful) for Best Foreign Film and Best Actor (left), a scene from the same movie (right)

Theatre

The theatre undergoes deep changes, mainly because of the emergence and spread of new forms of communication such as the cinema, radio and television. The style of realistic representation focusing on family dynamics and social issues of the bourgeois class falls apart because of the emergence of a new vision of the personality, disintegrated, subjective, and contentious. Already Pirandello shows the falsity and the absurdity of the situation of the individual, which he perceived as a universal existential condition not determined by particular social and economic factors. Man Pirandello, imprisoned in the mask of life, showed the boundaries between reality and madness, between truth and fiction. On another side was Brecht, who created an educational theatre which aimed not to emotionally engage the viewer but to make him an observer.

In World War II, great storytellers as Joyce and Kafka reveal the absurdity and the absence of logic in human life, in a society where there are no rational universal coordinates. One of the most significant expressions of this mood is the so-called theatre of the absurd. The nonsense of the human condition also emerges in the work of Beckett.

The Bourgeois Drama in Italy

Amongst the dramatic actors active in the late nineteenth century and the beginning of the new century, we remember Giuseppe Giacosa (1847–1906), Marco Praga (1862–1929), and Giacosa Roberto (1862–1943). Bracco was the famous librettist of Puccini's *La Boheme*, *Tosca* and *Madame Butterfly*. Giacosa performed analysis of bourgeois society with a preference for the elegiac and humble tones: in his work, he reveals his vocation to record the frustration of the middle-class world, the mediocrity of daily life which flattens the character and feelings. Among his works in Prague are *Closed the Door* (1913) and *Virgins* (1889), which feature scenic environments, typically bourgeois figures, and focus on the themes of marriage, adultery, and the relationships between spouses and their repercussions on the children. By bringing the bitter comedy of the bourgeois world to the stage, he reveals the hypocrisy, the fundamental lack of loyalty and love, and the corruption. His production was quite varied, ranging from realistic drama to comedy (such as *The Infidel* in 1894). He reveals an extraordinary force of representation, especially of unhappy humble characters immersed in an inner restlessness and pain.

The theatre of Gabriele D'Annunzio (1863–1938) was opposed to the realistic tone of the bourgeois dramas, preferring a combination of French symbolist theatre and English aestheticism. Initially, the author constructed an outdoor theatre for the actress Eleonora Duse. D'Annunzio's literary creations were strongly influenced by the French Symbolist school, and contain episodes of striking violence and depictions of abnormal mental states interspersed with gorgeously imagined scenes. One of D'Annunzio's most significant novels, scandalous in its day, is *Il Fuoco* (The Flame of Life) of 1900, in which he portrays himself as the Nietzschean Superman Stelio Effrena, in a fictionalized account of his love affair with Eleonora Duse. D'Annunzio was associated with the Decadent movement in his literary works, which interplayed closely with French symbolism and British aestheticism.

Such works represented a turn against the naturalism of the preceding romantics and was both sensuous and mystical. He came under the influence of Friedrich Nietzsche, which would find outlets in his literary and later political contributions. De Ambris who was the leader of a group of Italian seamen and provided the legal and political framework, to which D'Annunzio added his skills as a poet. The constitution established a corporatist state, with nine corporations to represent the different sectors of the economy (workers, employers, professionals), and a tenth (D'Annunzio's invention) to represent the 'superior' human beings (heroes, poets, prophets, supermen). D'Annunzio refused bourgeois theatre that staged the events of daily life, especially in their private spheres, in the name of poetic theatre that transfigured reality representing characters and passionate psychological conflicts out of the ordinary. He would use a complete symbolic plot, for example, a place where the drama of D'Annunzio occupies 'the daughter of Iorio' pastoral tragedy. D'Annunzio's greatest play was *La Figlia di Iorio* (performed 1904; The Daughter of Jorio), a powerful poetic drama about the fears and superstitions of Abruzzi peasants. Unlike the typical decadent taste for the barbaric, primitive expressions by the rural world was seen as a symbol of the irrational.

The Theatre of the Grotesque

During World War I began the Theatre of the Grotesque, based on the appearance of reality, the masks which each of us wears in public life, and how these inevitably collide with our private feelings.

Luigi Pirandello

An important figure in the Italian theatre of the early twentieth century was Luigi Pirandello (1867–1936). The author, born in Agrigento, dedicated himself as a playwright during the years of the First World War. The basic theme of Pirandello's theatre matched the view expressed by the writer in the narrative works: that everyone builds his personality according to the roles he must take on in society. It is a question of socially-imposed masks that the individual must wear.

As a result, an inner conflict is born in man, one which exists between his needs and the external contingencies which hinder him. The work which best expresses this vision is *Right You Are (If You Think)* (1917), in which the protagonists are Mr and Mrs Flora Ponza and her mother-in-law. The truth is expressed as 'different', symbolizing that the reality depends on one's subjective point of view. This interest in a multiform reality, complex and layered, is clearly expressed in the trilogy *Theatre within the Theatre*, which includes *Six Characters in Search of an Author* (1921), *Each in His Own Way* (1924) and *Tonight We Improvise* (1930). In these works, Pirandello finally breaks with the scheme of the fourth wall, the imaginary wall which separates the actor from the viewer, to explore different levels of stage illusion involving the same audience.

In *Six Characters in Search of an Author*, characters in a drama interrupt a rehearsal, requesting that their own story be staged. In *Each in His Own Way*, some scenes are all set in the corridors of the theatre, where viewers discuss the drama. Finally, in *Tonight We Improvise*, a director wants his actors to improvise on stage. In all three cases, the stage actually ends up confused with the reality of life. In 1924, Pirandello founded the company Art Theater, in which Marta Abba (1900–1988), became the first actress. In the following years, the company performed on tours around the world. A step forward in the direction of an improvement in Italian theatre production was brought about by the creation of the foundation, in 1936, of the 'Academy of Dramatic Art', directed by Silvio D'Amico (1887–1955).

The Magic Realism of Bontempelli

In the Italian theatre scene of the first half of the twentieth century, a place must be given to Bontempelli (1878–1960), a novelist, critic and playwright from Turin. With *Minnie Candida* (1927), the playwright came to realize his most striking idea of theatre: magic realism. He had already pursued this idea in his novels, and was also spreading it from the pages of *900*, the magazine he founded and directed. The project consisted of a desire to foster the emergence of the art of theatre amongst a mass audience. The writer's purpose was to get in tune with the present and to rework the myths of modern society. In order to do this, the author created events that, focusing on invention and imagination without neglecting the plot, mingled 'realism' with 'magic'.

Italian Theatre after the Second World War

In the post-war years, the figure of the great actor disappeared, while state companies determined the quality of theatrical productions. A figure in his own right on the theatrical scene between 1945 and 1968 was Vittorio Gassman (1922–2000), who led several companies in which actors took to the stage to perform high-level works. The most important event of his theatrical career was the foundation of the Italian folk theatre, which opened in 1960. It was a monumental structure which was supposed to be travelling like a circus tent, but designed with new criteria so as to allow a very wide stage and 3,000 seats for spectators.

The National Theatre was intended essentially to offer a permanent theatre to the touring companies, to offer significant events from the perspective of content, and to offer accessible economic conditions and no discrimination to the public. The experience created by Gassman, however, was short-lived, although the theatre-circus company had set up, among other works, an Italian play which was very successful: *A Martian in Rome* by Ennio Flaiano (1910–1972). In later years, the first permanent theatres were subsidized by the state. The first was the Little Milan, founded in 1947 by Giorgio Strehler (1921–1997) and Paolo Grassi (1919–1981).

The Playwrights of the Sixties

The transition from the literary scene to the theatre scene was not a new phenomenon for writers in the early sixties, as previous attempts had been made by authors such as Dino Buzzati (1906–1972). In recent years, the conversion to the stage amongst the literati increased with quite interesting results, thanks to the work of a group of writers who worked to slow the huge success of foreign scripts in the country. Moravia (1907–1990) wrote, in 1966, *The World Is What It Is*: a comedy with a critical discourse on language. Cosimo, an young industrialist, and Milone, an unemployed professor of philosophy, spend their time talking of 'speech therapy': given that all languages are more or less sick, the cure is to identify and eliminate infected words.

The discussion hides a serious issue: must we change the world or not? And, if so, must it be done by changing the order of things? The play does not give an answer to these questions. The theme of the language returns in *Interview*, in which the author brings to the theatre the problems raised by the new philosophies of communication and language. Moravia believes in the power of a theatre of ideas: the opera *The God Kurt* (1968) argues, using the metaphor of the theatre in the theatre, the thesis of the end of Christian civilization and the return of Jewish morality, disregarding the taboos related to sex and incest.

Leonardo Sciascia (1921–1989) was a playwright from the world of literature, the author of the *Day of the Owl*. Together with Giancarlo Sbragia, he staged this work in 1963. The story revolves around a number of crimes committed by the Mafia, and the futile efforts of a police officer to shed light on the events and punish the culprits.

Pierpaolo Pasolini (1922–1975) was a writer, poet and filmmaker who also tried his hand as a playwright. Critical to understanding his foray into the theatrical world is his essay, which appeared in the magazine *New Topics*. He called the essay 'Manifesto for a New Theatre', and in it he theorized the so-called Theatre of Words. He wrote the very original *Il Vantone* (1963), a translation of *Miles Gloriosus* by Plautus. This text of Pasolini was unique because his characters used the language of the Roman slums. Starting with the title, Pasolini invented a word of his own, a synonym of the most common adjective that had always accompanied the famous Miles Gloriosus. 'Vantone' is in fact a word from the Roman dialect, whose contribution to the text's vitality and dynamism is the main element of the success of the show. The show 'In '46' (written in 1946 but only released in 1965), was described as 'a strange composition that represents the images of a dream and the disturbances of consciousness of a young teacher in a Catholic school.'

Avant-garde and Experimentation

An exponent of the Italian theatrical avant-garde was Carmelo (1937–2002), a playwrite, actor and director from Salento. During the rejuvenation and radical transformation in experimental theatre, Carmelo was the first to move towards the final settlement of style and technical direction, which was a process of interpretative mediation of the dichotomy between text and staging. According to Carmelo, the figure of the director had no reason to exist; since he had not designed the text, the score, the lights, the sets or costumes, he could not direct the show. Indeed, Shakespeare often covered minor roles in the performances of his texts in order to be able to control the chaos on stage. For Carmelo, the most important aspect of theatre was precisely the disappearance of structure and superstructure in the name of the total performance. In fact, the theatre became a laboratory for the disassembly of the dramatic traditions. Among the works of Carmelo were *Our Lady of the Turks* (1965), *Pink and Black* (1966) and *Pinocchio*: these works highlighted the technical language of the scene, and constituted the backbone of the author's theatrical proposal.

The Feminist Theatre of the Seventies

In the seventies, a trend for female participation in theatre began to be established. Women became authors, directors and actresses in order to assert their presence in society and in contemporary culture, not oblivious to the struggles undertaken by the feminist movement at the end of the previous decade. The female voice in theatre was represented by La Maddalena, an acting group of women from the capital. With a magazine, a library and a theatre group, they tried to address the problems faced by women in Italian society. The theatrical journey of these authors and actresses starts began with *Mara Maria Marianna*, a text written in 1973 by Marie Claire Boggio, Edit Bruck and Dacia Maraini. In the play, the authors tell stories of seven women whose poverty, ignorance and prejudice deny them human dignity.

Dario Fo (1926–2016), who was awarded the Nobel Prize for Literature in 1997, began working on stage in the 50s, staging political satires. In the late 60s, Fo began to turn to the proletarian public, putting on shows closely related to current affairs. Amongst his later works was *Comic Mystery* (1969), a text which was a mix of elements from medieval farce, mime, and contemporary society. *The Two-Headed Anomaly* was his last work, which is at one level a farcical romp, but on a closer look reveals an intricate metatheatrical structure that allows Dario Fo and his fellow-performer Franca Rame to deliver their political satire. It had great success in the Italian theatres in the 2003-2004 season. It was a satire on the figure of the Italian prime minister, Silvio Berlusconi.

The recurring themes—nonconformity and strong satire—aim to hit the political powers, the church, and the bureaucratic machine. They are recurring irreverent barbs directed at the hypocritical morality of the society in which the author lives, which is full of the rhetoric of official discourse, business, and greedy self-interest. Weird, crazy figures emerge out of the more reasonable heads of the 'normal' prostitutes, crooks and imaginative poor people of all sorts. Fo is recognized as having invented an original language, uniquely suited to expressing his favourite themes.

Fashion

In 1900, the first world exposition in Paris devoted ample space to the fashion industry. The industry continued to grow and develop in Paris, whilst in Italy, Elsa Schiaparelli began years of competition with France's Coco Chanel. Overseas, the menswear industry was developing in America. Essential to this was the invention and development of the sewing machine, and the huge labour supply guaranteed by European emigrants. The most significant fashion item of this period was the blue jeans, which was first promoted in 1853 in San Francisco by a Bavarian immigrant called Levy Strauss. The new Italian fashions, more current than the French, were most appreciated by American customers, and thus the United States become a huge growth market for Italian fashion brands, who exported huge quantities of garments.

The origins of Italian fashion can be traced back to the early twentieth century, but the Italian textile industry was initially prevented from spreading to an international level due to fabric production shortages. The objective to affirm Italian fashion was taken up with vigour by the fascist regime: Mussolini wanted to build a national style both in clothing and in decor. For this purpose, exhibitions and parades were held in Turin. In the fashion magazine *Lidel*, a new ideal of the slim Italian woman was promoted. In 1935, a national fashion organization was founded which promoted clothing of Italian origin, i.e., those using Italian fabrics and Italian design. After World War II, favourable conditions were created for the development of this national fashion system. This was on account of two main factors: reduced labour costs (which enabled low prices of clothing), and an open trade with the United States. Americans were attracted by the beauty of Italy, and when they visited on vacation, they became the best clients of the fashion industry.

The cultural, social and economic dimensions of the fashion industry were not uniform across the country. In Rome, the clientele were made up of Italian and Hollywood actresses, whereas in Milan, the clients came from the city aristocracy and the industrial bourgeoisie. The Roman tailors (from Schubert to the Fontana Sisters) collaborated with Hollywood film producers to design costumes, whilst in the north, the textile sector subsidizes the clothing sector. The re-launch of Made in Italy was not without limitations. Although the elegance of the designs could be reproduced by hand, it was more difficult when it came to producing the patterns en masse for sale (introduced by the Fontana Sisters in 1955). Zoe (1911–1979), Micol (b. 1913), and Giovanna (b. 1915) Fontana were born in Traversetolo, near Parma, Italy.

Based on their experiences in Milan and Paris, the sisters felt they were ready to go into business for themselves. Although French fashions were still dominant in the world of haute couture, the sisters opened their own workshop in Rome in 1943, changing the name from 'Fontana' to 'Sorelle Fontana' and leading members of the Italian aristocracy soon began patronizing it. What the consumers needed was a mass-produced product which was of good quality, and resembled the styles seen in magazines as much as possible. The solution came in two stages: first research was carried out and new workshops were opened, and then schools were opened for tailors and new fashion professionals.

Entrepreneur Giovan Baptist Giorgini, in order to attract buyers from US department stores, called on the Italian designers to perfect the new national product and then planned several initiatives to promote Italian fashion. He organized the First Italian High Fashion Show in 1951 at his home, Villa Torrigiani; this successful event was reproduced the following year in Florence's Grand Hotel, and then in 1952, in the Sala Bianca of the Pitti Palace (which became its official location).

Factory made, ready-to-wear fashion was still far from being a successful industry in Rome in the 1960s. This only happened when the Roman fashion brands replicated the Milanese industrial culture, leading to the professional management of design and creation. From that moment, the spread of a modern culture of fashion began in Italy. During this period, the youth emerged not only as a social class but also as a market segment. They became the protagonists of a fashion revolution of international dimensions. With shared political ideals and musical interests, the young searched for a style of clothing through which they could build a self-identity distinct from that of the adult generation. Amongst them spread a sort of anti-fashion, contrary to the rules that were spreading amongst older consumers- starting in flea markets but then to trendy boutiques in London and Paris.

The textile sector which best realized the demands of the new generation was knitwear, the colorful stores of Max Mara, Benetton and Fiorucci produced a highly innovative range of clothing which was quite cheap compared to the high fashion favoured by adults. Also during this period, Valentino opened his own fashion house, setting the stage for ready-to-wear Italian fashion. The modern fashion industry combined sartorial quality with the convenience of mass production. The change also affects the profession of the fashion designer, who now lent his work for the creation of various collections. In 1967, the ready-to-wear collections were shown at the Pitti Palace exhibition, whilst the sartorial creations were presented in the workshop. The most succesful and powerful players in the new fashion system were no longer the creator of clothes, but the brands which produced and distributed them. Loss of customization was one of the distinctive features introduced by the ready-to-wear fashion revolution, and the industrial logic was finalized with the standardization of sizes.

In the 1970s, Milan became the centre of Italian fashion in Europe. The textile industrial area was home to major publishing companies as well as all the newest clothing brands. On account of the rise of the middle income groups and the economic boom in the 60s, the fashion market grew. At the same time, the luxury fashion market was becoming more exclusive, and this prompted a major restructuring of the industry's geography. In each district, a different stage of production, textile type or commodity type was located (knitwear in Capri and in Venice, sportswear in Perugia, wedding dresses in Puglia). The driving force behind the development of these specialized areas is precisely the physical proximity of the various bodies, which facilitates the exchange of knowledge and the containment of logistical costs.

Emerging fashion designers and brands included Versace, Ferre and Armani. During the same period, there was a change in models of distribution: early forms of franchises developed, for example, Benetton. The 1980s were the years during which Italian fashion was affirmed across the world. They were the years of transformation: the previous ideologies no longer existed, and people now preferred the lightness, appearance and culture of Italian design. The new rich wanted to show their social status, and they did it through conspicuous consumption. The communication of their social status demanded an apparatus constructed of materials capable of transmitting a highly symbolic message. The designer must be able to impose a certain style, through which the consumer can advertise their own taste and status. Gianfranco Ferre creates an impressive line, decisive and without excess; Valentino produces a stable and elegant feminine silhouette; Versace is characterized by an extravagant yet refined language. The brand has a signalling function; it is a certificate of the buyer's economic and social being. In this period of yuppies, any possession, from clothing to accessories to household itemsm, must be branded.

At the end of the 1980s, the American market (which is still the greatest importer of fashion (Made in Italy) goes into crisis and start to favour Japanese designers. This also sends Italian exports into crisis.

The companies which produce clothing can be classified into five categories:

Firstly, the industrial groups, who were sometimes linked to textile groups, and created a variety of products targeted at various market segments (especially knitwear, jeans and jackets). They had international distribution based on the image of its brand (for example Diesel, Max Mara, Zegna). Secondly, there were firms which produced items for a brand, a household name of great prestige like Valentino, Armani, Versace, or Dolce and Gabbana. There was also the average enterprise, characterized by a more limited sector of production such as The Pearl. There were the small companies who specialized in certain industries, such as knitwear or children's accessories. Finally were the production plants which made finished products as a subcontractor.

Italian Fashion Today

The Italian fashion industry (as well as the manufacturing industry as a whole) has enjoyed a profound change in recent years. Today, the Italian industrial sector is supported by small businesses, and gains its strength and ability to establish itself as a world leader in particular areas through the exploitation of niches which cannot be filled by international competition. Even the famous French brands Dior and Chanel still carry out part of their production in Italy. However, since the 1951–53 fashion soirées held by Giovanni Battista Giorgini in Florence, the Italian school started to compete with the French haute couture, and labels such as Ferragamo and Gucci began to contend with Chanel and Dior. In 2009, according to the Global Language Monitor, Milan, Italy's centre of design, was ranked the top fashion capital of the world, and Rome was ranked fourth. Italian fashion became prominent during the eleventh to the sixteenth centuries, when artistic development in Italy was at its peak. Cities such as Palermo, Venice, Milan, Naples, Florence and Vicenza started to produce luxury goods, hats, cosmetics, jewellery and rich fabrics. Italian fashion can be also connected to the most generalized concept of Made in Italy, a sort of merchandise brand expressing excellence of creativity and craftsmanship. Italian luxury goods are renowned for the high quality of their own textiles and the elegance and refinement that goes into making them, as well as for the guarantee of quality materials. Many French, British and American top luxury brands (such as Chanel, Dior, Balmain, the main line of Ralph Lauren, to name a few) also refer to Italian craft factories, located in highly specialized areas, especially in the metropolitan area of Naples and in the Centre-North of Italy, to produce either part or all of their apparel and accessories.

In terms of employment, fashion is one of the most important sectors in the Italian economy. It includes about 60,000 companies and employs more than 8,00,000 people. The sector suffers somewhat from the spread and success of low cost brands (such as Zara), but it can still rely on the strength of the brand names and the international market for luxury Italian goods.

Design

Until the mid-nineteenth century, Italy had an essentially agrarian character, with little industrial development. Due to a fragmented policy framework, the wide economic gap between the north and the south resulted in a marked delay in the economic development of the country: after the unification, industry was essentially limited to textile crafts. In the early twentieth century, the Italian 'Liberty' style, inspired by French Art Nouveau, directed the artistic productions, craft and emerging architecture. In 1902, Turin held an international exhibition centred on the modern decorative arts. At the beginning of the twentieth century, it is the automobile sector which becomes dominant.

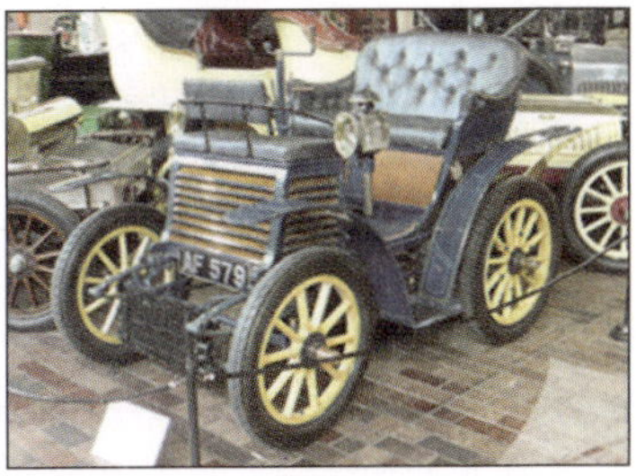

FIAT 4 HP

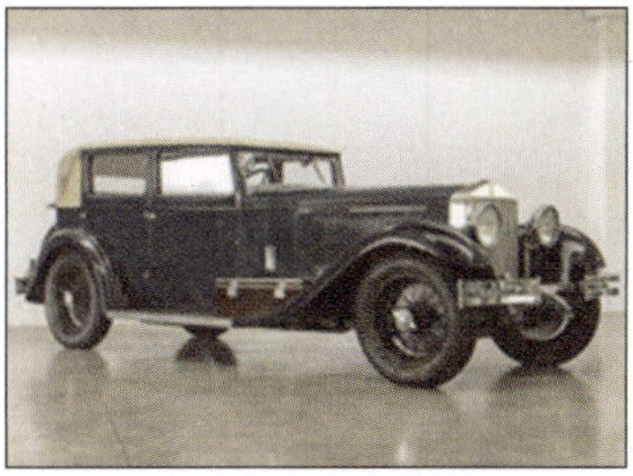

Isotta Fraschini Tipo 8A

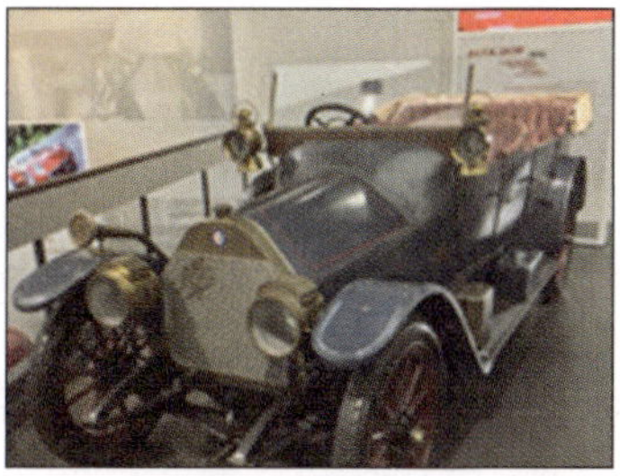

ALFA 24 HP

A primary role is played by Fiat (Italian Automobile Factory Turin), founded by a group of entrepreneurs from Piedmont in 1899 with the aim of producing and selling cars on a large scale. The Fiat plant in Turin (known as Bullion, the name of the neighbourhood where it is located) becomes famous. Also in Turin, Spear was founded in 1906, specializing in luxury sports car production. Some models are identified by letters of the Greek alphabet.

Futurism

In the first two decades of the twentieth century, the spread of Futurism began, an artistic movement geared towards modernity and innovation. The Futurists were inspired by the innovations produced by recent technological and scientific discoveries. The house became a place of interest for designers, and the industry began to address the production of items of furniture. In 1915, the two artists Giacomo Balla and Fortunato Depero drafted the futurist manifesto 'The Futurist Reconstruction of the Universe', in which they launched an art form which had a strong impact on fashion, music, the visual arts, furnishings, and on everything related to the living environment. Household objects were placed at the centre of the design.

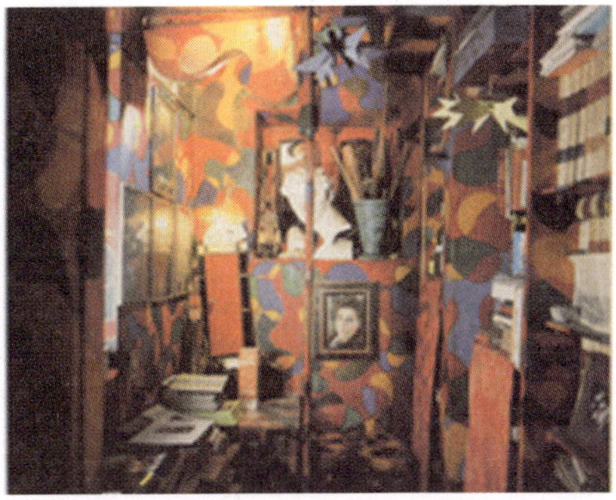

An example of Futurist art

In 1915, Giacomo Balla and Fortunato Depero signed the Ricostruzione Futurista dell'Universo (Futurist Reconstruction of the Universe) manifesto; the Futurist movement was moving towards a second phase in which the need for total art aspired to influence many aspects of life through a radical transformation of the environment: from furniture to fashion, from cinema to theatre, music to dance, and from billboard design to designing everyday items. With his art house, Balla had designed and built all the furnishings for a home while Depero instead, with a production of tapestries and cushions, created a space in which to create art objects, furniture, toys, models marked by a basic structure and dynamic lines). In the text of the manifesto text is written: 'We Futurists, Balla and Depero, want to realize a total fusion, to reconstruct the universe and recreate it in full. The skeleton embodies the invisible and impalpable.' With this, Futurism determined its style, which would dominate for a long time. In architecture, the chief proponent was Antonio Sant'Elia, author of the manifesto Futurist Painting in 1914, who created the new city: a housing model centred on the combination 'feature-beauty', with buildings with dynamic lines. Architecture is seen as the endeavour to harmonize, with freedom and great audacity, the environment and man, to align the world of things with the world of the spirit.

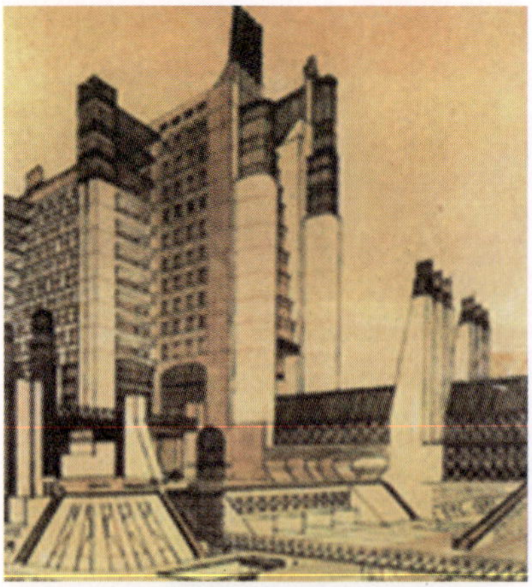

La Città Nuova, The New City, 1914 by Antonio Sant'Elia

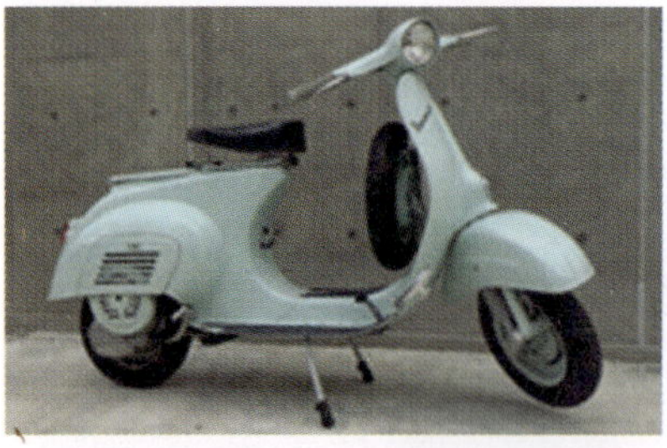

The iconic Vespa

The Futurist momentum comes to a halt during World War I, as all production sectors are at full capacity due to military commissions. Immediately after the war, there was a return to order in the arts, with a Renaissance style recovery promoted by the 900 Group formed in Milan. In 1926, the first exhibition is held inside the Royal Palace of Milan, but the artistic experience runs out a decade later, owing to the rise of fascism. After World War II emerges the need to focus on lightness, optimism and momentum towards a future of economic recovery.

People started travelling by the Vespa manufactured by Piaggio, also commonly known as a scooter, and there is a move towards mass motorization amongst the middle class.

From the 1950s and towards the end of the twentieth century, the first mass-produced goods entered the home: refrigerators with rounded lines, low-cost lamps and coffee makers.

Refrigerators had a profound impact on twentieth-century society, according to a new Université de Montréal study. Plug-in conveniences transformed women's lives and enabled them to enter the workforce.

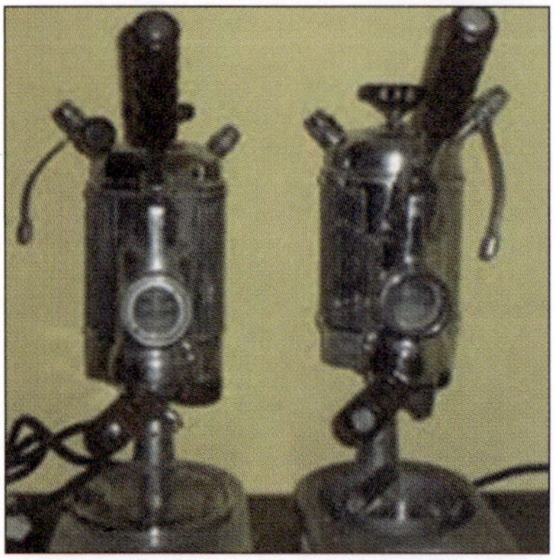

Steam pressurized coffee machine

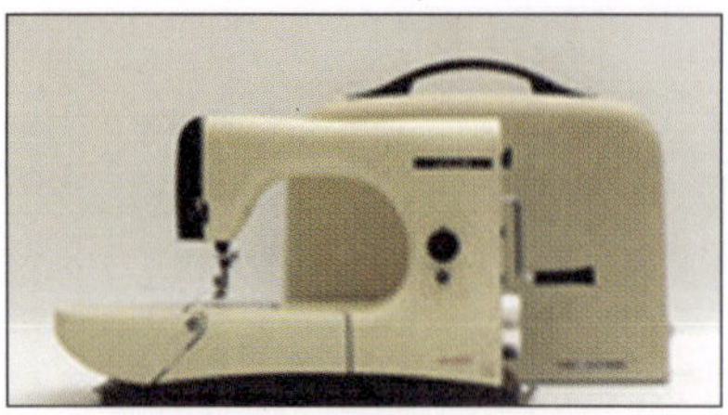

Mirella sewing machine commissioned by Necchi

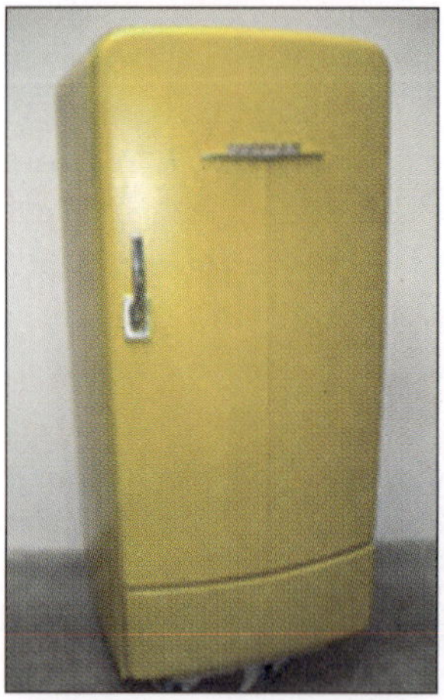

Refrigerators in the 1950s

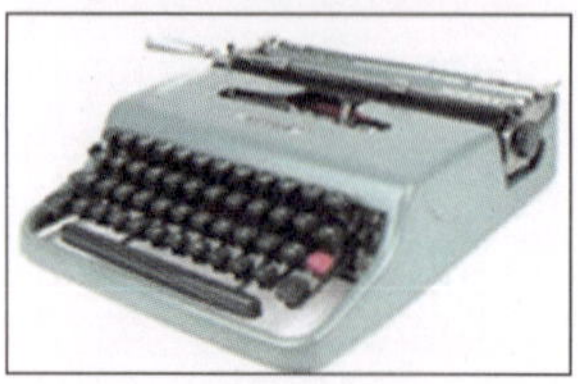

Typewriter 'Letter 22' for Olivetti created by Marcello

The 60s were characterized by the use of plastic and radiant colours.

The value of Italian design was also recognized internationally, and in 1972, it was celebrated as part of an exhibition at the MoMA (Museum of Modern Art in New York) entitled: 'Italy: The New Domestic Landscape". Showcased were all the objects of significance produced by Italian designers up to that point.

A famous chair that was designed for the Italian design company Zanotta called the 'Bean Bag' was created by Piero Gatti, Cesare Paolini and Franco Teodoro. A bean bag was a plastic seat stuffed with expanded polystyrene balls. Another plastic invention called the 'Inflatable Armchair' was created in 1967 by Jonathan De Pas, Donato d'Urbino and Paolo Lomazzi. The inflatable armchair was light and easy to carry.

By the end of the twentieth century, many Italian companies had specialized in the production of items of furniture, such as the Alessi company, Achille Castiglioni founded Adi Milan (Association for Industrial Design), and Ettore Sottsass formed the Memphis Group (consisting of architects and designers who are among the best known exponents of post-modernism between the years 1980 and 1990). (Richard Sapper created the famous coffee machine 'Espresso 9090')

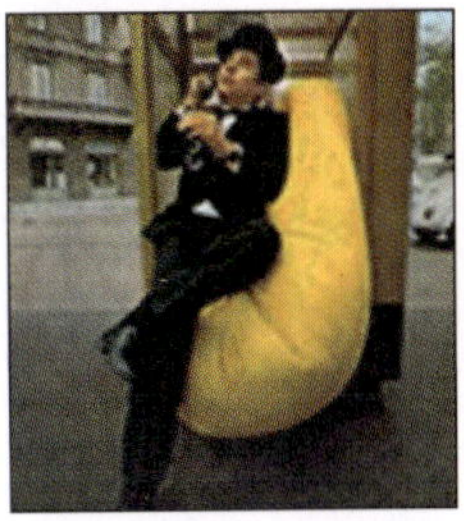

Bean bag

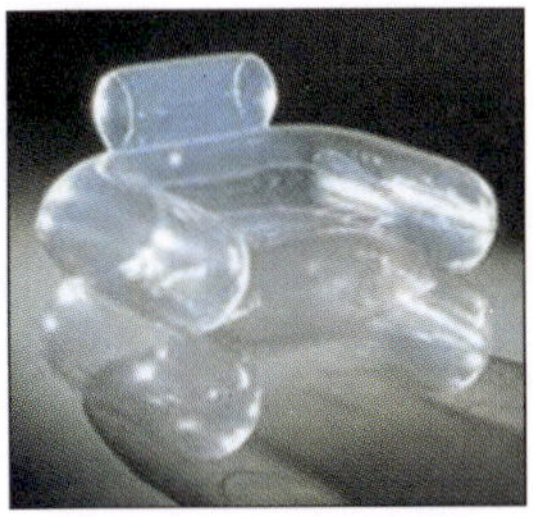

Inflatable armchair

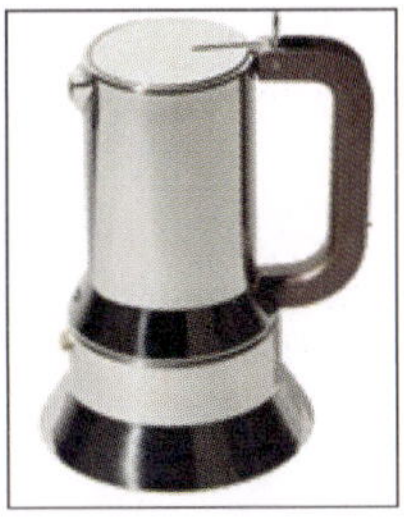

Espresso 9090

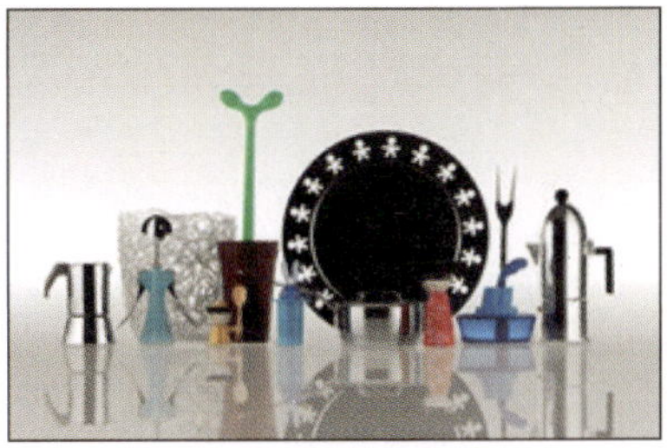

Italian products

The Genoese architect Renzo Piano builds the 'Paganini' auditorium in Rome, the 'Pinacoteca Agnelli' in Turin, the 'Auditorium Paganini' in Parma, and the 'Auditorium Parco della Musica' in Rome. Numerous small and medium enterprises are very active in Venice and in the regions of central Italy; they are operating in the fields related to furnishings and accessories.

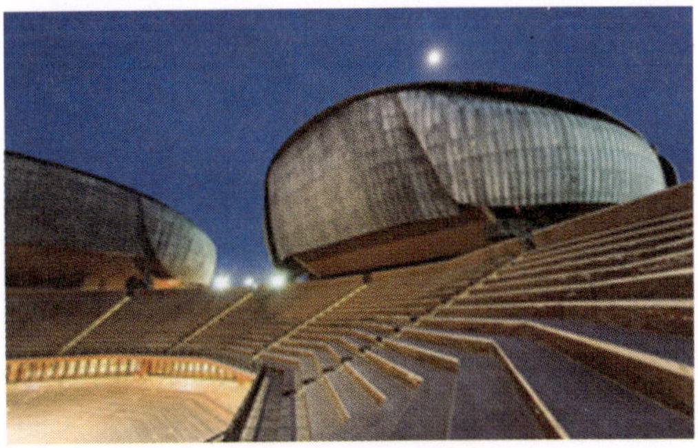

Auditorium Parco della Musica

(Auditorium Parco della Musica is a large public music complex in Rome, Italy, with three indoor concert halls and an outdoor theatre in a park setting. The Paganini Auditorium is named after a great musician from Genoa (1782–1840) who had a home in Parma and is buried in Parma's Viletta cemetery. The auditorium was built, based on the design of famed architect Renzo Piano, inside a historic sugar factory, Zuccherificio Eridania).

The term 'industrial design' is an abbreviation indicating the creation of industrially reproducible objects which combine advanced technical skill with aesthetic quality. The final statement of the Italian design movement comes in the 80s, when 'Made in Italy' becomes a driving force for the economic development of the country. The Italian companies which remain (dimensionally) small are able to make research and innovation their corporate assets, including Poltrona Frau, Artemide and Alessi.

Specialized production of furniture began by companies like Alessi. The Italian design industry is focused now on the field of furniture and furnishings, including lamps, kitchens and bathrooms.

The companies in the industrial triangle of Milan-Turin-Genova join the established Tuscan brands. The world's leading trade fair in the furniture industry is the 'Salone del Mobile', now held every year in Milan. The reference models for production systems could now be classified into: artisanal production, mass pro-

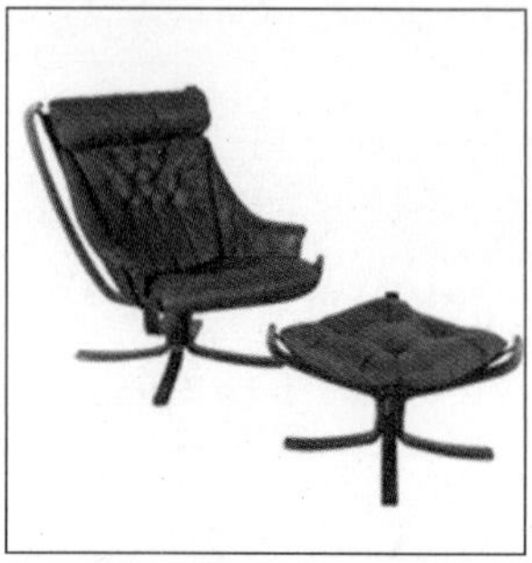

Industrial design

duction, and flexible production networks. The predominant model of production had been artisan, until the first industrial revolution marked the beginning of mass production (thanks to the technological innovations which accompanied the invention of the steam engine). The artisan production units (the craft shops) produced a limited range of artifacts, and handicraft production is a term which is today applied to fields which specifically require the intervention of man, such as completion of measurement, the creation of luxury cars, and customizations. Between the eleventh and the fourteenth centuries, the intensification of trade and the consequent increase in disposable income meant that there was an increased demand for products. This led to the first transformation of the production processes, and craft work became semi-industrial. Soon after, with the founding of the first factories, the era of mass production began. Subsequently, in the second half of the eighteenth century, new technologies (such as the steam engine) again changed the production system, enabling even greater quantities of goods to be manufactured.

In the second half of the nineteenth century, further technological innovations (the production of acid, electricity, the internal combustion engine, chemistry), enabled the second phase of the industrial revolution. However, there was not an accompanying increase in the living standards of consumers. The technical modes of production were used in all stages of manufacturing, except in the final quality check. This solution allowed the manufacturer to achieve an equal quality across their products, but with considerable saving of time and materials.

Another innovation in production was the introduction of the assembly line system in car factories pioneered by Henry Ford. This allowed the creation of highly advanced products at lower prices, and ensured that the network was flexible to changes in demand. The focus is on innovation and the search for ever more sophisticated and environmentally friendly materials. The design and construction phases are numerous and complex. The starting point is the initial idea of the designers (the concept), which is then transformed into a graphic sketch, and then a three-dimensional model. During this stage, the functionality of the project is assessed, and the techniques of production and the materials are selected and costed. After all of this, the design is transformed into technical scale drawings, then realized through CAD, and finally it is produced, distributed, and sold.

Conclusion

Globalization has hastened processes of cultural exchanges around the world. However, ideas, since the beginning of human civilization, have always circulated, especially those related to military scope, trade opportunities and aspirational values.

There are cultures which have been 'stronger', and have spread and influenced in a much more consistent way than others, especially in the domains of the arts, architecture, literature and innovation.
Italy is one of those cultures which has been particularly strong, and, from the era of Romans to the contemporary Made in Italy campaign, its ideas and historical innovations have been exported and adopted all over the world. Italy is a very tiny country, yet it has had a profound impact on world history and culture.

I believe that this has not happened because of some fortuitous coincidence; Italy has developed a very effective cultural model out of very specific and unique processes. Such processes can be examined, learnt, and used in the development of innovative and special designs.

What is language? What is art? Poetry? Philosophy? Architecture? They are all expressions. Expressions of a mindset, of either a person or a society. Language shows which path a person will follow to reach a certain point; if we focus on the creation of a single man, in terms of art, we can draw the main line of his spirit, of his inner philosophy, of his thoughts. If we observe, on the other hand, what a society creates—the shapes used, the materials used, the religion they follow—most likely we will be able to draw the main line of the foundation that the society is constructed on.

Let's start from the Romans: a civilization which spanned over 1200 years. Without going too far into the specifics, we can consider the Roman period as a macroblock (without going into the various phases which characterized this era) and thus quickly analyse its outcomes. Let's start by looking horizontally at the Roman city map. We find ourselves in front of a network of parallel lines that intersect perpendicularly with others, forming a structure of order, rigour and discipline. Looking vertically up at the buildings, we notice that they are built with large blocks of stone, which conveys the idea and intent of stability, strength and desire for eternity.

The religion. One of the key aspects in studying a group of people is to consider their God, their idea of perfection and their aspiration. The Romans had an anthropomorphic, polytheistic religion that painted the gods as a representation of human passion, with features and human behaviour.

Here the observation of a few outcomes allows us to create an outline of the society we are facing. A military society, with man as the centre of attention. What kind of man? A military man, who founds himself on order, discipline and strength. A citizen, who is a public man and interested in public affairs. How do we notice this? From the mapping of the spaces in which the city is formed; in this case, a city that prefers and gives importance to common areas. Examples include the Colosseum, an amphitheatre where games for the population were organized (note the difference compared with Greece, where the amphitheatre was intended for the theatre, now it is destined for gladiators who conquer life, proper to military society), the pantheon, and the thermal baths.

But if the individual is the microcosm of society, this proposition can be seen in the macrocosm of the city and of the house.

The rooms of the Roman house all adjoined the atrium (the living room), where people met. In accordance with the ideas of the perfect military, practical society, furnishings were kept simple and practical, while all that was useful (including hot water) was engineered to sophisticated levels.

Following this scheme, we could retrace the whole of history by simply observing the various disciplines, building a skeleton of each society and seeing how the ideas which ran through each historical period were common to all the arts, simply communicated in different languages.

I could continue in this analysis approaching the year zero, the birth year of Jesus Christ, and point out to you how the religion preached in the Middle East was one of the causes of the fall of an empire founded on gerachia (remember that the only citizens with rights were the Romans themselves, not the other people from the provinces). Christianity, on the other hand, is a religion based on the idea that we are all children of God, an idea that levelled the population and created an ideological conflict that pushed to the south-east of the empire, just as in the north-east there was a real danger: the barbarians.

But what happens when an empire falls? To answer this, you have to take a piece of paper and fold it to the left for a long period of time, applying considerable force. In order to have the same sheet stretched out again, you must bend it in the opposite direction for an equally long period of time, applying the same power (or greater power if you want to speed up the operation).

Here's what it is, what I have decided to define as a historical knot. The period in which the sheet must be folded in the opposite direction. That period which is also the transition between the Roman era and the Middle Ages: where the centre of attention is completely distorted, passing from man to God, without intermediate phases.

The moment that sees passing from one extremity to another: from complete pride in human forms (as represented in a Roman fresco of naked women) to a pious and almost nonexistent art (the high medieval era). I refer to the appearance of art which shows human skill; I beg you not to misunderstand my words by thinking that in the early Middle Ages, there is no art. Personally, I do not agree with using the term 'Dark Ages' to define this era; on the contrary, I have always supported the beauty of the work of the amanuensis monks, not to mention the love I have felt reading Dionigi Aeropagita or San Agostino, with *The City of God.*

We see an attempt to share these two extremes, man and God, with St Francis of Assisi, who praises God through his creatures, and what is the creature par excellence if not that in his image and likeness? This attempt is developed first by the poets of the Sicilian school and then by the Dolce Stil Novo movement, which raises the woman to the position of an intermediary between God and man, an angel, until eventually that characteristic common to both, love, is found, which brings them together and gives again dignity to the human being. We see the circle returning almost to the point of its departure, but this is a richer starting point containing the beginning, the end and the path (in the Renaissance) where man, in his genius, returns to the scene.

A historical knot which lasts for centuries, and that marks, in all the arts, the various steps of an incredible journey of emotions.

There are many historical nodes in this history, and the reader, I am certain, through the exposure to all of the outcomes in the various disciplines which are collected in chapters spanning the centuries- will be able to catch them only by reading.

If I may give a suggestion:
Baroque? When someone opposes you, isn't your first reaction to defend yourself?
The macrocosm is a mirror of the microcosm, so generally, when we have difficulties in understanding, we should just stop a moment and think about the reaction we would have had if the situation had involved us. Isn't Baroque the period directly after the spread of the new religion of Martin Luther? And didn't it spread so fast thanks to the invention of the printing press? Could we see the Baroque as a reaction to an opposing ideology and the attempt to remake our beliefs?

Or... Why does the 1700s chapter not have many pictures? Why is there only figurative art and plain views of the city? Wasn't this the century where the mind is at the centre and logical thinking takes place? But art, in all its forms, comes from emotion, so maybe it shouldn't surprise us that in this the age of the mind, the treatises abound while the paintings and the poetry are blurred. If one extreme requires another before equilibrium can be reached, is not it obvious to see why Romanticism follows the Age of Enlightenment?

I would also advise you to dwell on the figurative arts before and after the invention of photography. You have certainly noticed that until then, the aim of art was to capture reality at its best. But if this goal is achieved by a machine, what will be the destiny of an art which no longer has a purpose? It must surely fail to compare the perfection of a photograph, and so we see how the arts are directed towards an object that a machine can not grasp: the unconscious and the internal movements. This new kingdom explored by Dadaism and by Futurism, which captures what photography cannot: movement. I could go on and on into the details of each historical period, examining with you the beauty of Expressionism in all its forms; I would do it but I do not want to distract you from your journey and your reflections.

I believe that all people gravely need to gain an understanding of art, its harmony, balance, creativity and fantasy, through a study of all the concepts of every field of art. Unfortunately, many syllabi throw the reader deep into the throes of one particular form of art, without lingering, even briefly, on the genesis of the creative process, or how the same ideas are carried out across art forms during a particular period of time.

A study of all the arts together, across the different periods of history, will enhance our natural ability to perceive beauty (despite the fact that this is a subjective evaluation). Being educated about the different concepts of beauty and harmony shall enable the reader to raise their awareness from the mundane.

Interestingly, 'art' is a well-defined process which can broken down into easily graspable cognitive steps:

Step One, Poiesis: This describes the fundamental inspiration of the artist in the artistic process;
Step Two, Mimesi: This is the expression of the masterpiece itself;
Step Three, Katharsis: This creates the link with the final effect, or, how the final product is or will be perceived by the public.

These three steps takes us to an aesthetical judgement, which is essentially a judgement of taste, and like all judgements, it is an evaluation of quality, quantity, relation and modality. But the aesthetic judgement differs from others: it is neither private nor shared. It is subjective, common sense, it does not claim that everyone should agree to a certain concept, but it also allows others' opinions to co-exist. So while Aesthetics cannot be imposed through dictation, it can be cultured through appropriate training.

This book focuses on Italy and its major historical nodes, those particular relevant peaks of Italian history when the most significant innovations and ideas were produced and spread.
Through history, we investigate these Italian historical nodes, and use them to develop new ideas for the future. The book will use the strategy of looking backwards at classic immortal models in order to consciously look forward.

The aim is to allow the reader to develop his own ideas and emotions in the present, with reference to their understanding and study of the Italian historical nodes and their most important principles. The objective is to teach the reader how to create a sense of purpose and feeling in a specific context.

The book will span various fields of the arts; will introduce the students to the concept of the culture of Italy: its beauty, harmony, aesthetic balance, and historical and ideological perspective. It will also provide an understanding of the basic concepts of Italian art, architecture and design.
How powerfully and concretely do ideas influence modern life?
How does learning to observe and to share a piece of our soul in our creation (whatever that is) influence our outcomes?
How powerful will our outcome be if we place our soul into it?

I bet on celebrating Italy.
I bet on whoever will honour the beauties of Italy.
I bet on whoever celebrates Italy.
I bet that unifying the Italian cultural model with our nature will create wonders.